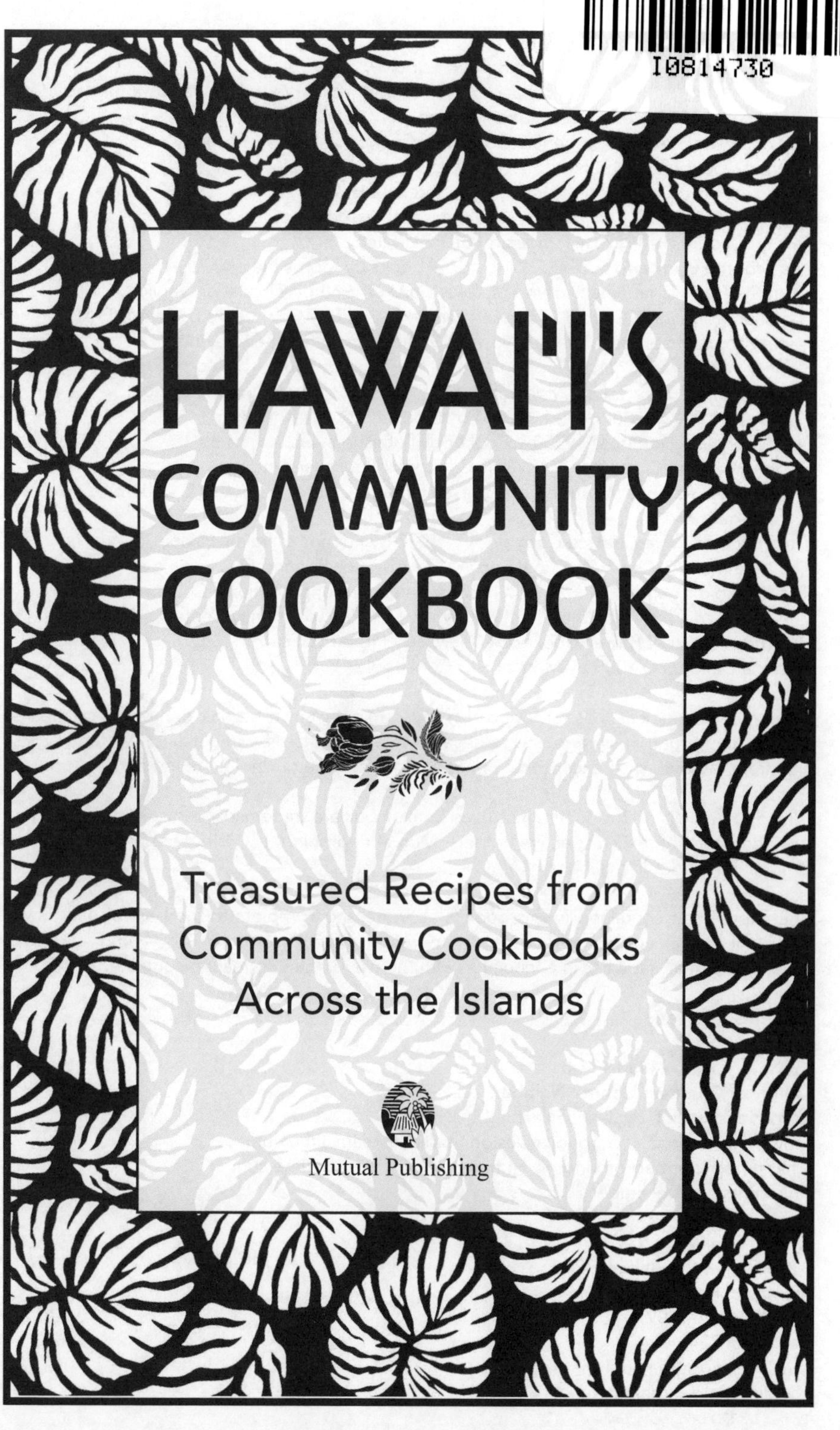
HAWAI'I'S
COMMUNITY
COOKBOOK
Treasured Recipes from
Community Cookbooks
Across the Islands
Mutual Publishing

ISBN-13: 978-1-949307-31-3
Library of Congress Control Number: 2022938083
Layout and design by Jane Gillespie
Flower illustrations © Corpholia Design Studio | Dreamstime.com
Chapter opener backgrounds © Farhan Sudibya | Dreamstime.com
Third Printing, December 2025

Mutual Publishing, LLC
1215 Center Street, Suite 210
Honolulu, Hawai'i 96816
Ph: (808) 732-1709
Fax: (808) 734-4094
email: info@mutualpublishing.com
www.mutualpublishing.com
Printed by RRD Dongguan, China

TABLE OF CONTENTS

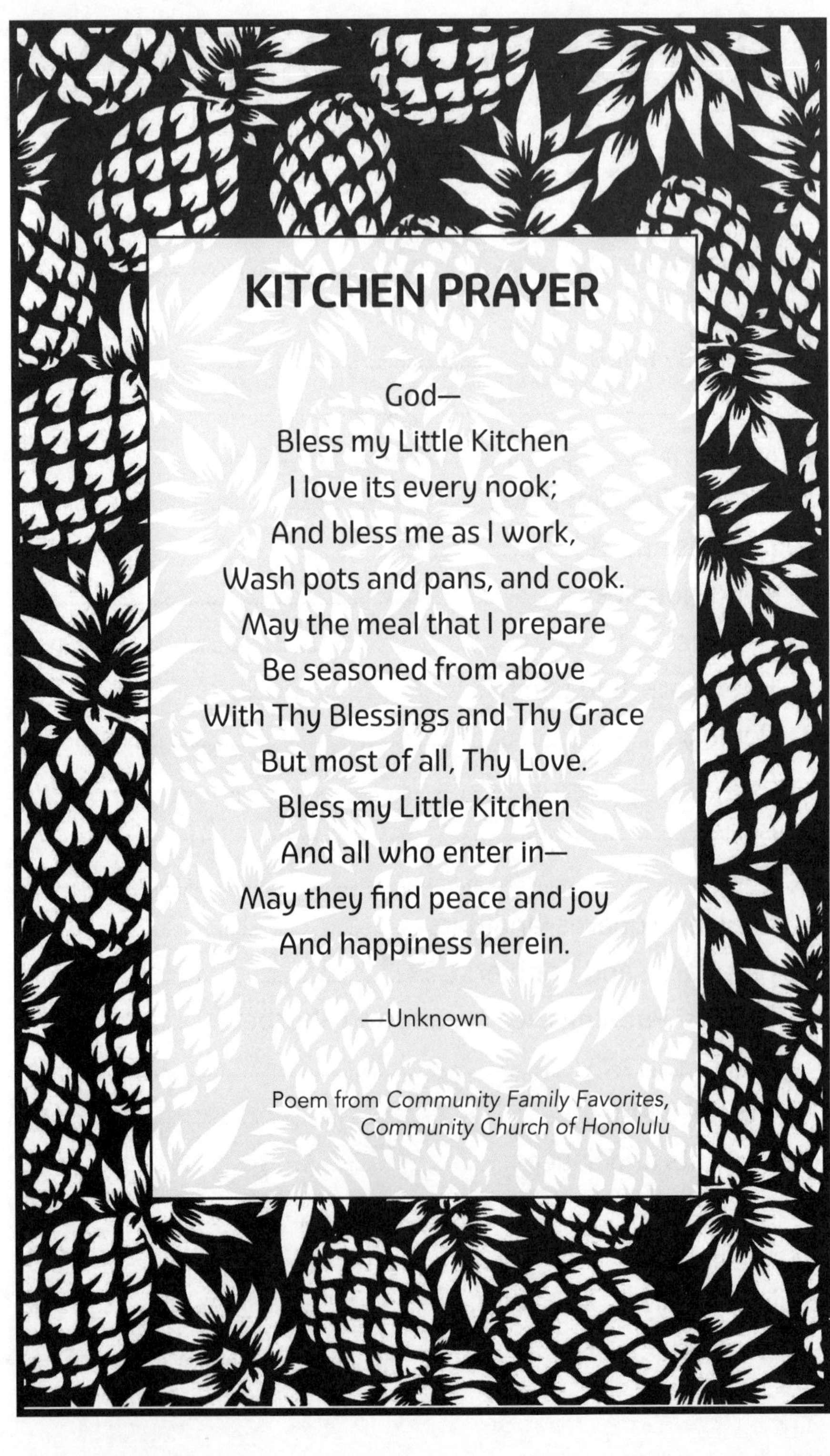

KITCHEN PRAYER

God—
Bless my Little Kitchen
I love its every nook;
And bless me as I work,
Wash pots and pans, and cook.
May the meal that I prepare
Be seasoned from above
With Thy Blessings and Thy Grace
But most of all, Thy Love.
Bless my Little Kitchen
And all who enter in—
May they find peace and joy
And happiness herein.

—Unknown

Poem from *Community Family Favorites, Community Church of Honolulu*

INTRODUCTION

"In our homes, life is centered around the kitchen."

In 1987, this phrase introduced the East, South and West O'ahu Extension Homemakers Council cookbook *Family Favorites.* It continued—"It is our fondest hope that sharing a good recipe with others will bring you as much pleasure and enjoyment as the committee has experienced in the compiling of this book."

Family Favorites is one of the fifty cookbooks included in *Hawai'i's Community Cookbook,* a long-needed anthology of community cooking that includes over 600 recipes from Hilo to Hāna to Hanalei.

Cookbooks fulfilled a valuable need in days ago. Many cooks did not keep written recipes, so culinary traditions were kept alive from generation to generation through from-the-heart community efforts.

HonFed Savings and Loan 1983's *Grandma & Grandpa's Hawaiian Island Cookbook* puts it best, "When people emigrated from their homelands around the world to settle in Hawaii, they refused to give up their native foods, customs and cooking styles," As neighbors, they generously shared food with each other. Community cookbooks reflected Hawai'i's diverse communities and how different cuisines were melded.

Cooks were proud. The Portuguese Heritage Club of Hamakua from the Big Island encouraged us to, "Cook, eat, and share these dishes so that future generations can keep alive the spirit of our heritage."

Community cookbooks remind us that throughout Hawai'i, organizations were started based on neighbors being from the same background. For example, the Hilo Chinese Christian Church, which became the United Community Church, issued *100 Years Sharing God's Love.* The Lionesses of the Moloka'i Lions Club compiled recipes in *From the Hawaiian Kitchens of the Molokai Lions,* and recipes from *North Kohala Favorites,* started by Mrs.

Clara Takata of Takata Store, reflected eleven different area sugar plantation camps which housed many ethnicities on the Island of Hawai'i.

One of the best-selling series of cookbooks was produced by the Honpa Hongwanji Betsuin in Honolulu. Their six volumes of *Favorite Island Cookery* celebrated the culinary culture of Japanese contract laborers.

Cookbooks were a means to spread the mission for organizations of every type—business groups such as Rotarians of District 5000, Puuloa Hawaiian Civic Club, Mō'ili'ili Community Center, and the Wahiawa General Hospital Auxiliary. Almost every affinity group is included from *Cooking with Honolulu Gardeners* by the Community Recreational Garden Program, to *Food for the Body and Soul* by West Kaua'i United Methodist Church, to *1988 4-H Local & Ethnic Food Show* by 4-H Clubs, to *The Hawai'i National Guard Auxiliary Cookbook* by the Hawai'i National Guard Auxiliary, to *The Kahikolu Country Cookbook* by Kahikolu Congregational Church, to *Nā Mea 'Ai Punahele* by the Hawai'i Youth Opera Chorus.

Back in the day, cookbooks were a way for women to raise funds for worthy causes. The Japanese Women's Society of Honolulu continues to exist long after it published *Hawaii's Aloha Recipes* that benefited seniors being cared for in Hale Palama Mau.

Who can resist trying the long list of delicious recipes here? You can cook soup-to-nuts from 'Ulu Chips, to Molokai Limu Salsa, to Fish Sinigang, to Hot Pepper Jelly, to Fresh Ginger Cake. Moa Ma Pua Kala is a fun recipe written in pidgin English. This anthology doesn't lack personality.

As *Family Favorites* mentions, "Many of our recipes are treasured family keepsakes, some are new: but all reflect the members' love of good cooking." You will enjoy these treasures.

—Lynette Lo Tom

Lynette is the author of Mutual Publishing's *A Chinese Kitchen: Traditional Recipes with an Island Twist; Back in the Day: Enjoy Hawai'i's Comfort Foods from Family and Friends;* and co-author *of Yum Yum Cha: Let's Eat Dim Sum in Hawai'i.* She is a food writer for several Hawai'i publications including the *Honolulu Star-Advertiser.*

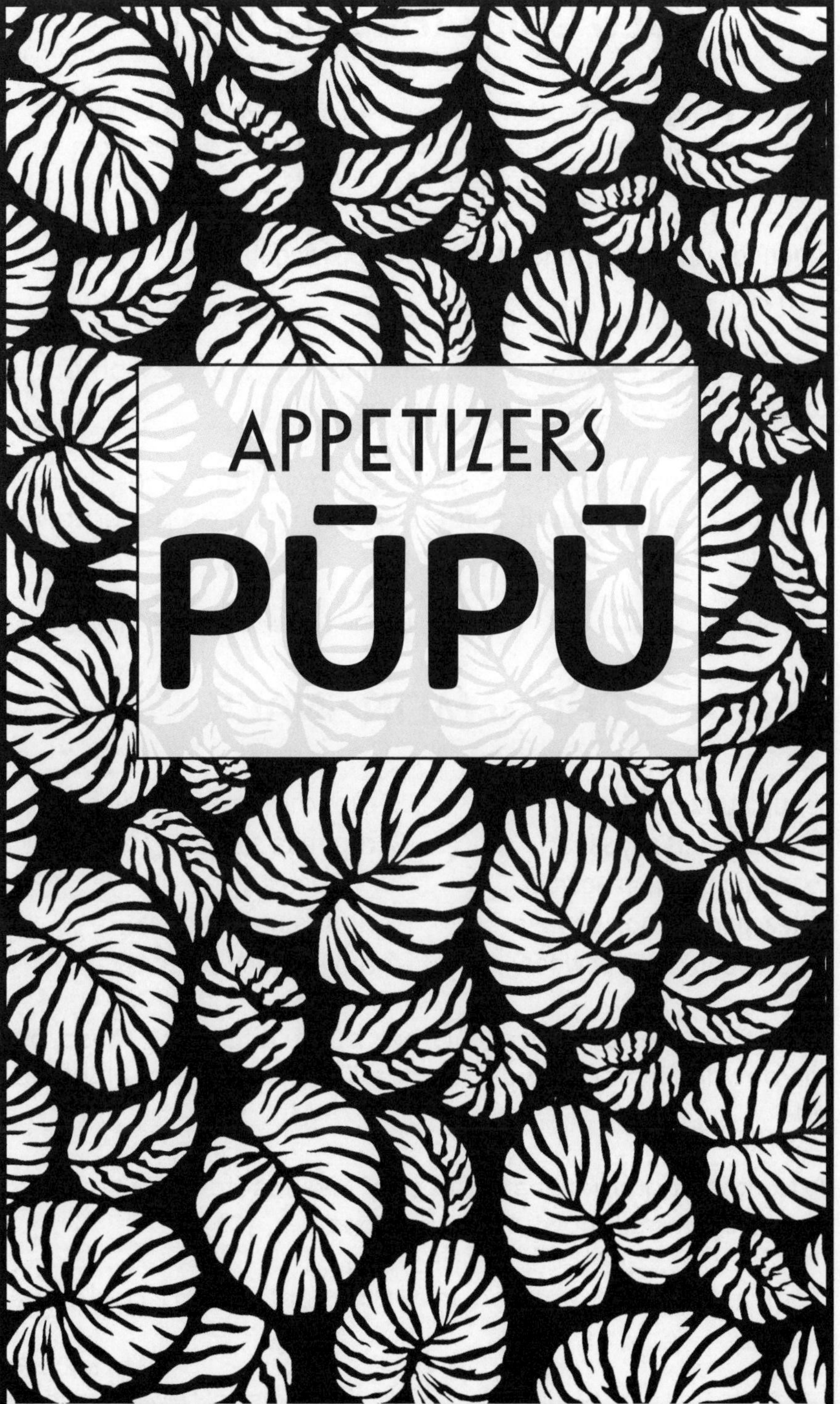
APPETIZERS
PŪPŪ

'ULU CHIPS (BREADFRUIT)

The largest collection of breadfruit in the world is located in Hāna, Maui. Here it is used in a variety of dishes, from appetizers to desserts.

3 pounds ripe breadfruit salt to taste
3 cups vegetable oil

Peel breadfruit and wash under running water. Dry on paper towel. Remove, core and slice paper-thin.

Heat oil in a deep pot to 350°F. Fry breadfruit slices, a small amount at a time, until golden brown. Drain on paper towel. Salt and store in airtight container.

Hana Maui Recipes from Then to Now

CHOW MEIN SNACK

½ cup butter or oleo
2 tablespoons soy sauce
½ teaspoon onion powder
½ teaspoon lemon pepper
¼ teaspoon garlic powder
2 cups chow mein noodles
2 cups bite-size crispy corn cereal squares
2 cups round oat cereal
1 cup unsalted peanuts

In a large skillet over low heat, melt butter. Stir in soy sauce, onion powder, lemon powder, and garlic powder until well-blended.

Add other ingredients and stir over low heat for another 2 to 3 minutes, or until moisture is absorbed.

Cool on paper towels. Store in airtight container in a cool place.

IRMA MEYERS
We, the Women of Hawaii Cookbook

JAPANESE RICE CRACKERS

Makes about 100 rice crackers

¾ cup flour
¾ cup mochiko
1½ tablespoons sugar
1 tablespoon black sesame seeds
1 teaspoon baking powder
½ cup water

Vegetable oil for frying

Glaze
¼ cup corn syrup
¼ cup sugar
¼ cup soy sauce

Combine flour, mochiko, sugar, sesame seeds, baking powder, and water to make a smooth dough. Add a little more water if dough is too dry.

Flour work surface lightly with mochiko. Roll out dough in small batches. Dough must be very thin, almost paper-thin. Use a knife to cut into ½-inch squares.

Heat oil to 375°F. Fry until light golden brown. Place cooled rice crackers on a cookie sheet.

To make Glaze: Combine corn syrup, sugar, and soy sauce in a pan and bring to boil over medium heat. Cook until sugar dissolves and mixture begins to thicken, about a minute. Do not overcook or the glaze will be difficult to spread.

Pour glaze over rice crackers and mix to coat evenly. Work quickly, as glaze will harden as it cools. Spread crackers into a single layer and separate pieces.

Bake 15 to 20 minutes, until glaze is set and crackers are dry but not quite crisp. They will harden and get crispy as they cool. Do not overbake or glaze will burn.

Wisteria Delights, A Collection of Recipes
by Pearl City Hongwanji Mission

PARMESAN ROUNDS

¾ cup grated Parmesan cheese
½ cup flour
⅛ teaspoon cayenne pepper
¼ cup butter or margarine
2 tablespoons cold water
2 tablespoons sesame seeds
1 tablespoon parsley flakes (crumbled)

Stir together cheese, flour, and cayenne. Cut in butter. Sprinkle with water. Shape into a 1½-inch wide roll. Roll in sesame seeds and parsley. Refrigerate slightly.

Slice into ¼-inch thick rounds. Place on ungreased cookie sheet. Bake at 375°F for 12 to 15 minutes.

INGRID NELSON
We, the Women of Hawaii Cookbook

SPINACH DIP

1 (10-ounce) package frozen, chopped spinach, drained and well-dried with paper towels
1 cup sour cream
1 cup mayonnaise
½ cup fresh chopped parsley
½ cup chopped green onions
½ teaspoon dill seed
Juice of 1 lemon
Salt to taste

Mix well. May be made the day before.

To serve, hollow out a round loaf of sourdough or French bread. Slice and toast these soft pieces to serve with potato chips for dipping. Fill hollow loaf with spinach dip and enjoy.

LOIS ADAIR BIRNBAUM
Cook 'Em Up Kauai, The Kauai Historical Society Cookbook

ARTICHOKE DIP

1 (14-ounce) can artichoke hearts
1 cup mayonnaise
1 cup fresh grated Parmesan cheese
1 clove garlic, minced or chopped
⅛ teaspoon mustard
⅛ teaspoon salt
1 tablespoon lemon juice

Drain artichokes well. Put artichokes, mayonnaise, cheese, garlic, and mustard into a bowl (actually food processor). Mix until well-chopped. Add salt and lemon juice. Mix well.

Place in lightly buttered shallow baking dish. Bake at 350°F for 20 minutes. Serve hot.

ELAINE TORIGOE
Cooking with Honolulu Gardeners, Honolulu Community Recreational Garden Program

KAMABOKO DIP

Makes 2 cups

1 kamaboko, pink and finely grated
¾ cup mayonnaise
2 tablespoons finely minced garlic
½ teaspoon garlic salt
1 teaspoon grated onion

Combine ingredients and mix well. Chill several hours.

Serve with assorted vegetables, crackers, or chips.

HAWEA WAIAU
Haili Congregational Church, 175th Anniversary

HOT CRAB DIP

2 cans crabmeat, may use imitation crab
2 cups shredded cheddar cheese, about ½ pound
1 medium round onion, coarsely chopped
¼ cup coarsely chopped parsley
¼ to ½ cup mayonnaise

Combine everything. Add enough mayonnaise to moisten and help to hold mixture together.

Spray baking dish with Pam. Pour mixture into baking dish. Bake at 350°F for 20 to 25 minutes. Delicious with warm French bread or crackers.

KATHY BOW
The Hawai'i Youth Opera Chorus, Nā Mea 'Ai Punahele

CURRY DIP FOR VEGETABLES

2 cups mayonnaise
6 stalks of green onion, finely chopped
1 teaspoon curry powder
Dash of salt
2 hard-boiled eggs, chopped fine
4 teaspoons lemon juice
½ teaspoon ginger root

Combine all ingredients. Mix well and refrigerate. Serve with assorted fresh vegetables.

Hawaiian Hospitality,
American Business Women's Association Eleu Chapter

KIM CHEE DIP

1 cup chopped kim chee
1 tablespoon kim chee liquid
1 (8-ounce) package cream cheese

Place all ingredients into a blender for 1 minute. Chill. Serve with vegetables or chips.

North Kohala Favorites

POLYNESIAN GINGER DIP

1 cup mayonnaise
1 cup sour cream
¼ cup chopped onion
¼ cup minced parsley
¼ cup chopped water chestnuts
2 to 3 tablespoons chopped candied ginger
2 garlic cloves, minced
1 tablespoon shoyu

Mix all together and serve with raw vegetables or sesame wafers.

RUTH NELSON
We, the Women of Hawaii Cookbook

GUACAMOLE

Combine:

2 cups mashed avocado
2 tablespoons lemon juice
2 tablespoons grated onion
1 clove garlic, grated
1 teaspoon salt
Dash of pepper
Dash of cayenne
1 teaspoon Worcestershire sauce
2 tablespoons sugar
3 tablespoons mayonnaise

Serve with chips or vegetable slices. This can also be served layered in the following order in a square pan:

½ cup grated Jack cheese
1 can green diced chilies, drained
Guacamole
1 cup sour cream
Onions chopped and sprinkled on top
Parsley, sprinkled on top

A Lei of Recipes,
Kauai Association for Family and Community Education

A. S. CLEGHORN & CO.,

IMPORTERS, WHOLESALE AND RETAIL DEALERS IN

GENERAL MERCHANDISE

Corner of Queen and Kaahumanu Streets,

HONOLULU, : : HAWAIIAN ISLANDS.

☞ Particular attention paid to Island Orders of every description. ☜
Best Kona Coffee constantly on hand.

PINEAPPLE SALSA

Makes 4 cups

2 cups finely chopped fresh pineapple
1 cup seeded, diced, unpeeled tomato
½ cup peeled, seeded, diced cucumber
¼ cup finely chopped shallot
3 tablespoons chopped fresh cilantro
1 tablespoon finely chopped jalapeño pepper
1½ tablespoons red wine vinegar
1 teaspoon extra virgin olive oil
Salt (a sprinkling)
1 clove garlic, minced

Combine all of the Ingredients in a medium bowl and toss well. Let stand at room temperature for 1 hour. Serve salsa with chicken, pork, or shrimp.

100 Years Sharing God's Love, United Community Church

MOLOKAI LIMU SALSA

3 pounds whole tomatoes
6 ounces tomato paste
2 cups tomato sauce
1½ pounds round onions
1 large bell pepper
¼ cup parsley
½ cup green onions
1½ cups limu ogo (seaweed)
1 teaspoon black pepper
1 teaspoon salt
2 teaspoons chili flakes
¼ cup white vinegar

Take whole tomatoes, tomato paste, tomato sauce and half of the round onions, put into food processor until all is mixed and fine. Then cook down for about 30 minutes. Cool.

Cut remaining round onions, bell pepper, parsley, green onions, and ogo and mix all together with remaining ingredients.

Haili Congregational Church, 175th Anniversary

MANGO SALSA

Makes 3 cups

2 large ripe mangoes
½ medium cucumber, peeled, seeded, and cut into ¼-inch cubes
1 (4-ounce) jar roasted red peppers, drained and cut into ¼-inch cubes
½ medium red onion, cut into ¼-inch cubes
¼ cup chopped parsley
1½ tablespoons fresh lime juice
1½ tablespoons juice from pickled jalapeño peppers
Pinch of salt

Peel, slice, and cut mangoes into ¼-inch cubes.

In medium bowl, combine all ingredients. Toss gently but thoroughly. Let stand at room temperature 30 minutes to allow flavors to mellow.

Serve at room temperature with assorted grilled sausages or fish steaks.

LILLIAN MAEDA
Our Daily Bread Centennial Cookbook, Iao Congregational Church

TAHITI LEMONADE WORKS COMPANY.
D. T. BAILEY, Manager.
—MANUFACTURERS OF—
TAHITI : LEMONADE,
LEMON, : CREAM :-and-: PLAIN : SODA,
Sole Proprietors of BAILEY'S SARSAPARILLA & IRON WATER,
Ginger Ale, Hop Ale, Grenadine, Raspberryade, Sarsaparilla, Mineral Waters, Etc.
TELEPHONE 297.
All communications and orders should be addressed to
BENSON, SMITH & CO.,
Agents.
389 1m

LOMI SALMON

10 ripe tomatoes
2 tablespoons blended limu kohu
1 whole round onion
¼ bunch green leaf onion
1 pound raw salted salmon

Dunk 6 tomatoes into boiling water for 2 seconds. Soak in ice cold water 12 seconds. Peel and remove skin of tomatoes. Dice and put into blender with 2 tablespoons limu kohu. Liquify and place into a bowl. Place in freezer until ready to use. Defrost before use.

Dice 1 round onion. Place into bowl. Chop ¼ bunch green leaf onion into finely cut squares. Place in bowl. Dice 4 tomatoes into small squares. Place in bowl.

Slice 1 pound raw salted salmon into 4 parts and soak in fresh water. Rinse. Resoak 3 times. Let soak 20 minutes. Rinse. Dice into small fine squares. Place into huge bowl. Add all other ingredients. Serve cold with poi.

JUDY PARRISH
The Friends of ʻIolani Palace Cookbook

OGO KIM CHEE

1 cup shoyu
1⅓ cups vinegar
1 gallon parboiled ogo
Chili pepper to taste
2 rounds onions, sliced
1½ tablespoons grated ginger
½ clove garlic, grated

Combine all ingredients and let it soak for 1 day before eating.

DORA W. OTSUKA
From the Hawaiian Kitchens of the Molokai Lions

MISO CUCUMBER TSUKEMONO

1 cup shoyu
1 cup sugar
1 teaspoon ajinomoto
¼ cup vinegar
¼ cup salt
1 cup beer
1 cup miso
2 to 3 pounds cucumbers, cut in half and 2-inch lengths

Mix together and pour over cucumbers in a large gallon jar and soak for at least 1 day.

KAALA U.E. CLUB
Family Favorites, Oahu Extension Homemakers Council

WARABI APPETIZER

1 pound warabi (fern shoot)
1 cup boiling water
1 (4-ounce) package codfish, shredded
1 onion, thinly sliced
2 tomatoes, cubed
¼ cup soy sauce
⅔ cup lemon juice
⅔ cup sugar
¼ teaspoon ajinomoto
¼ teaspoon garlic salt

Wash warabi, removing hair. Cut into 1-inch length.

In a saucepan, cook warabi in boiling water for 3 minutes until tender. Drain.

Heat codfish in a saucepan on medium heat for 3 minutes. Combine warabi, codfish, onion, and tomatoes in mixing bowl.

Mix soy sauce, lemon juice, sugar, ajinomoto, and garlic salt together. Pour over warabi and toss gently.

AKIKO TSUBAKIHARA
Kalaheo Missionary Church Cookin' Book!

KOREAN-STYLE BEAN SPROUTS
Nak Doo Na Moal

Makes 5 to 6 servings

1 package bean sprouts
4 cups cold water

Sauce
1 teaspoon Wesson oil or sesame oil
1 teaspoon shoyu
½ teaspoon vinegar
2 stalks green onion, chopped fine
¼ teaspoon salt
Pinch black pepper

Cook bean sprouts in boiling water, uncovered, till the stems are clear, turning over gently often so they will not smash, about 10 minutes.

Take out and drain. Put in a big bowl and add the sauce.

Mix well with chopsticks and serve.

Parks & Recreation Family Favorites

PEKING CH'IAO TZE

Gau Gee

A big hit at one of our potluck dinners.

Filling

4 won bok leaves (without steams), chopped fine
¼ pound pork, chicken, or turkey, chopped
1 small clove garlic, chopped
3 slices ginger root, chopped
½ teaspoon salt
1 teaspoon soy sauce
1 teaspoon sugar
2½ teaspoons sesame seed oil
1 package round gau gee skin

Dipping Sauce

¼ cup vinegar
1 to 2 pieces ginger, finely sliced
Dash of salt

Wrap won bok in a clean dish towel and squeeze dry.

Combine ingredients, except gau gee skin. Place 1 heaping tablespoon of filling on gau gee skin, dampen edges of skin with water, and seal well. Pleat edges, if desired.

Bring a pot of salted water to a boil. Add 9 ch'iao tze in water; stir gently to prevent sticking. When water boils, add 1 cup of cold water and bring to a boil again. Do this procedure two more times. Remove with a strainer; place on a serving platter, separating them so they do not stick together. Cook remaining ch'iao tze.

Combine Dipping Sauce ingredients and mix well.

Serve plain or with the Dipping Sauce.

ROSE MAU
Community Family Favorites, Community Church of Honolulu

TOFU SPRING ROLLS

Makes 36 rolls

Marinade

1 tablespoon peanut butter
3 tablespoons soy sauce
1 tablespoon ginger root, grated
1 teaspoon wine vinegar
¼ teaspoon garlic powder

¾ pound tofu, cut into 1 x ½-inch strips

Filling

1½ cups Chinese cabbage, shredded fine
½ cup finely chopped celery
½ cup finely chopped water chestnuts
6 green onions, cut into ½-inch pieces
½ cup sliced fresh mushrooms
1 tablespoon soy sauce

Ready-made egg roll wrappers (sold in grocery stores)

Combine marinade ingredients and mix well. Put strips of tofu into bowl of marinade mixture for 2 hours.

Put 2 tablespoons oil in large skillet and stir-fry filling ingredients together until crisp-tender.

In a separate pan, heat 1 tablespoon oil; add tofu and fry until golden brown. Add any leftover marinade while browning. Gently mix tofu and vegetables together. If tofu mixture has too much liquid, thicken it with a mixture of 1 tablespoon cornstarch and 2 tablespoons of water.

To prepare each spring roll, place ¼ cup of filling in the center of each wrapper. Roll up, tucking in the sides. Dab a little water on top flap to secure. Deep-fry at 350°F, 3 or 4 pieces at a time, until golden brown. Drain on paper towel. Serve with sweet sour sauce or soy sauce.

Hana Maui Recipes from Then to Now

CRAB AND CREAM CHEESE WON TON

1 package imitation crab, minced
2 packages cream cheese, softened
1 can water chestnuts, diced
Green onions
Pepper, to taste
2 cloves garlic, minced
1 teaspoon Worcestershire sauce
Won ton wrappers
Oil for frying

Heat oil 300°F to 350°F. Mix all ingredients together. Place small spoonful on wrapper and seal edges with water. Deep fry until golden brown. Drain on paper towel. Serve hot.

AMBER HYDEN
Hugs & Kisses of Aloha, Aloha Airlines Flight Attendant Cookbook

HIDEO'S EASY GYOZA

Makes 24 to 36

1 pound lean ground pork or beef
Canola oil for frying
3 cloves fresh garlic, pressed
2 tablespoons grated fresh ginger
5 to 6 cups finely chopped cabbage
Salt to taste
1 (16-ounce) package mandoo wrappers

Dipping Sauce

¼ cup soy sauce
1 to 2 teaspoons sesame or chili oil

Brown meat in 1 tablespoon oil; add garlic and ginger and continue to cook. When meat is done, add cabbage; salt to taste and cook until cabbage is tender. Remove from heat and cool.

To make gyoza, place about 1 tablespoon meat mixture in center of mandoo wrapper. Moisten outer edge with water, then fold over; press edges firmly together to seal.

Pan-fry gyoza in hot oil over medium heat until golden brown on both sides. Combine ingredients for Dipping Sauce in a dish; serve with gyoza.

LUE ZIMMELMAN
The Tastes and Tales of Mōʻiliʻili,
A Collection of Recipes & Stories by Mōʻiliʻili Community Center

CHICKEN SIU MAI

Makes 24 pieces

Filling

1 pound ground chicken
6 pieces imitation shrimp, chopped fine
1¼ teaspoons cornstarch
4 pieces dried mushrooms, soaked in water to soften; chopped fine
1½ teaspoons sugar
½ teaspoon salt or to taste
1 tablespoon chung choy, chopped fine
1 tablespoon sesame oil
2 teaspoons light soy sauce
¼ teaspoon white pepper

1 egg (reserve for wrappers)
1 package siu mai wrappers

Mix Filling ingredients together except 1 egg for siu mai wrappers. Test for seasoning by frying a small amount and tasting it. Beat egg well. Brush lightly onto siu mai wrapper.

Place approximately 1½ to 2 tablespoons of filling in center of wrapper. Bring sides of wrapper up creating a pouch; gently squeeze until the filling reaches the top of wrapper. Gently tap siu mai on the table to flatten bottom. Repeat process until all filling is used.

Boil water in steamer; reduce to simmer and place siu mai on steamer rack and steam for 35 minutes. Turn off heat and let stand 5 minutes before serving.

LYNNE WAIHEE
The Hawaii National Guard Auxiliary Cookbook

BAKED TARO PUFFS

Taro root

Butter

Boil taro until soft in salted water. Peel and put through a ricer or mash well. Mix with a little water, using only enough to make a smooth dough. While hot, form into small cakes and place in a buttered pan. Make a dent in the top and add a dollop of butter.

Bake in a 375°F oven until browned.

Serve hot with butter.

50th Anniversary Best of Our Favorite Recipes,
Maui Association for Family and Community Education

NĀPŌʻOPOʻO FRITTERS

Grate equal parts of green Chinese bananas and fresh hard coconut meat. Mix together and add enough coconut milk to keep mixture moist. Shape into patties and fry until crispy. For pūpū, sprinkle with salt. For dessert, top with honey.

"BROTHER" HOSE
The Kahikolu Country Cookbook

CRISP FRIED TOFU

Makes 3 to 4 servings

½ pound tofu
¼ cup rice flour
2 tablespoons cornstarch
5 cups oil for deep-frying
Spring Roll Sauce

Cut tofu into strips, 2 x 1 x ¼-inches. Combine rice flour and cornstarch. Preheat oil for deep-frying on medium heat. Coat tofu with rice flour mixture. Deep-fry for 7 to 10 minutes, or until golden brown. Drain on absorbent paper towels. Serve with sauce.

Spring Roll Sauce

Makes 1 cup

¼ cup sugar
½ cup water
½ cup red wine vinegar
1 to 2 tablespoons fish sauce
2 to 3 teaspoons ground fresh red chili peppers
¼ cup coarsely chopped peanuts
½ carrot or daikon, shredded

In a small saucepan, combine sugar and water; bring to boil. Reduce heat and simmer for about 10 minutes, or until sugar is dissolved. Remove from heat. Stir in red wine vinegar, fish sauce, and red chili peppers. Pour sauce into serving bowl. Chill; top with carrots/daikon and sprinkle with peanuts before serving.

WENDI Y. MURASHIGE
1988 4-H Local & Ethnic Food Show

CRAB PUFFS

1 (6-ounce) can crabmeat
¼ cup chopped black olives
2 tablespoons minced onions
2 tablespoons minced green onions
2 tablespoons minced green pepper
2 tablespoons minced celery
3 drops of pepper sauce
¼ cup mayonnaise
24 miniature cream puff shells (halved)

Combine crab, olives, onions, green pepper, celery, and pepper sauce in mixing bowl. Blend in enough mayonnaise to moisten. Pile into bottom of puff shells and top with the lids.

Place on greased cookie sheet and bake in preheated oven 350°F for 20 minutes.

Serve hot. May be made in advance and frozen. To serve, heat as above.

NOTE: Shrimp or tuna can be substituted for crab.

ADELE DAVIS
We, the Women of Hawaii Cookbook

PIPIKAULA

Hawaiian Beef Jerky

Makes 8 to 10 servings

1 piece flank steak
2 tablespoons shoyu
1 tablespoon sugar
1 teaspoon fresh ginger juice or
¼ teaspoon powdered ginger
1 clove garlic, crushed

Pound steak on both sides with back of knife blade or mallet. Cut into 4 x 2 x ½-inch strips.

Combine the rest of the ingredients and marinate beef strips 1 to 2 hours. Place beef on rack in shallow roasting pan and sun-dry or place in 225°F oven for 5 to 7 hours. Slice and serve or it may be broiled or pan-fried and additional seasonings added to serve.

HAWEA WAIAU
Haili Congregational Church, 175th Anniversary

JIN-DU SPARERIBS

1⅓ pounds small spareribs
½ tablespoon soy sauce
½ teaspoon salt
1 teaspoon sugar
½ tablespoon rice wine
½ tablespoon chopped garlic
3 tablespoons cornstarch
6 cups oil for frying

Sauce
1 tablespoon Worcestershire sauce
1 tablespoon tomato ketchup
1½ teaspoons sugar
¼ teaspoon sesame oil
2 tablespoons water

Cut spareribs into 20 sections; mix with soy sauce, salt, sugar, rice wine, and garlic and let sit 20 minutes. Before deep-frying, mix with 3 tablespoons cornstarch. Heat oil for deep-frying; deep-fry spareribs for 4 minutes over medium heat; remove and heat oil until very hot. Re-fry spareribs for 1 minute over high heat; remove and drain.

Heat Worcestershire sauce, ketchup, sugar, sesame oil, and water to a boil; add spareribs and 1 tablespoon oil; toss lightly to coat spareribs with sauce. Remove and drain. Garnish with tomato slices.

FRANCES GOO
The Hawai'i Youth Opera Chorus, Nā Mea 'Ai Punahele

BOBBIE'S LUMPIA

1 box lumpia wrapper (Lorenzena brand)

Vinegar/Garlic Sauce
3 cloves garlic, peeled and crushed
1 cup vinegar

Filling
2 pounds ground pork
1 bunch chives (or ½ bunch green onions)
¼ pound bacon, 10 strips, chopped
½ small can black olives, chopped
1 tight fistful Kohala kim chee, minced
3 tablespoons Kohala kim chee sauce from bottle
2 tablespoons crushed & minced garlic
Salt to taste

Cornstarch Sealing Paste
½ cup water
½ cup cornstarch

Keep lumpia wrappers frozen until ready to use. An hour before wrapping, separate wrappers. Cover with damp paper towel and set aside.

To make Vinegar/Garlic Sauce, lightly sauté garlic and add to vinegar. Place in small bowl with teaspoon and set aside.

Combine Filling ingredients and mix well. There should be a strong garlic odor to the mixture. Add more garlic according to preference.

Mix ingredients for Cornstarch Sealing Paste and set aside. Add more of each, if needed, to make thin, watery paste.

Place wrapper on cutting board, starting at ½-inch of the lower end of the wrapper circle, place 1 heaping teaspoon of filling mixture and spread thinly and evenly in a horizontal line to the outer border. Mixture should not be thicker than ½-inch otherwise it will not cook well.

Roll wrapper tightly so it looks like a thin cigar, seal center end with Cornstarch Sealing Paste, but keep outer ends open so oil will sizzle through and cook mixture well. Use up wrappers, separating each layer with a damp paper towel or wax paper. Refrigerate if you are not going to deep-fry them right away.

Deep-fry at medium temperature, 5 or 6 at a time, depending how many can fit in without crowding them. Start at 325°F and turn heat up or down as needed. Cook until golden brown.

Be sure to give each one a light shake as you lift it from the fryer to get rid of excess oil before draining. Drain them upright with lots of paper towels at the bottom to absorb oil.

Serve lumpia warm with vinegar and garlic sauce. Guests should pour 1 teaspoon of mixture through top of lumpia.

VARIATIONS: Instead of pork, use shrimp, imitation crab, or oysters, finely chopped. Instead of kim chee, use water chestnuts chopped with seafood mixture.

BARBARA BULATAO-FRANKLIN
Food for the Body and Soul, West Kaua'i United Methodist Church

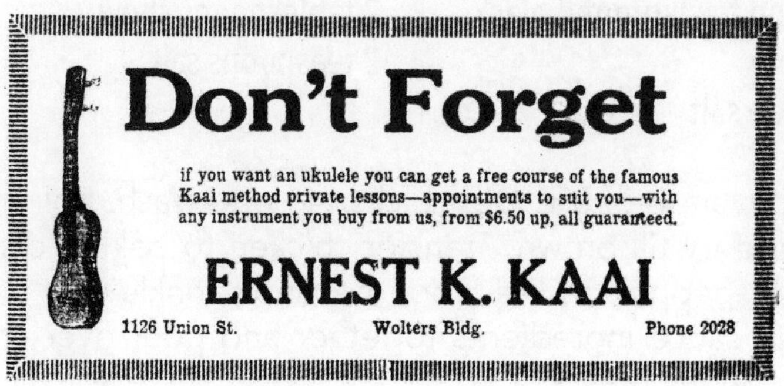

GOLDEN MARINADE CHICKEN ON STICKS

½ cup soy sauce
½ cup gin or sherry
¼ cup honey
½ teaspoon black pepper
1 teaspoon grated ginger root
1 clove garlic, grated
About a pound of boneless chicken
1 can large button mushrooms
Barbecue bamboo sticks

Combine first six ingredients and set aside. Cut chicken into small pieces that would hold on sticks then marinate in sauce for at least half an hour. Place on sticks with mushrooms in between. Broil.

KAY M. YAMADA
Cook 'Em Up Kaua'i, The Kaua'i Historical Society Cookbook

SWEET SOUR CHICKEN WINGS

Makes 10 to 12 servings

5 pounds chicken drumettes
4 eggs, beaten
2 cups cornstarch
½ cup vegetable oil
2 teaspoons garlic salt
1 teaspoon fresh ground black pepper
1 teaspoon salt

Sauce
½ cup chicken broth
1 cup sugar
1 cup cider vinegar
6 tablespoons ketchup
2 tablespoons shoyu
2 teaspoons salt

Preheat oven to 350°F. Dip chicken in egg wash. Roll in cornstarch and fry till brown. Transfer chicken to baking dish. Mix garlic salt, pepper, and salt together and sprinkle over chicken. Combine sauce ingredients together and pour over chicken. Bake for 30 minutes.

ALYNE KIKUKAWA
"Cooking with Lovely Hula Hands," Moana's Hula Halau, Kaunakaka

TERIYAKI STIX

2 pounds sirloin tip
3 cups shoyu
½ cup brown sugar
1 clove garlic, sliced thin
1 finger ginger, well-crushed
1 jigger gin or bourbon (optional)

Slice the sirloin tip in pieces 1½-inches wide by 1-inch long and ¼-inch thick. Marinate the sliced meat for an hour in the shoyu, brown sugar, garlic, ginger, and the gin or bourbon. Thread the marinated meat on bamboo sticks and cook quickly over a low charcoal fire. If you have a hibachi set up on the lanai, your guest can do their own.

TEONA POLOA
"Cooking with Lovely Hula Hands,"
Moana's Hula Halau, Kaunakakai

TAKO ONION POKE

2 tablespoons thinly sliced and boiled tako (octopus)
¼ cup shoyu
1 tablespoon sesame oil
Lemon juice from 1 lemon
½ cup chopped green onions
3 tablespoons grated ginger
Salt

Combine all ingredients and serve cold.

A Lei of Recipes,
Kauai Association for Family and Community Education

TOFU POKE

Makes 8 servings

1 block firm tofu
¼ cup ogo (add more as desired)
¼ cup shoyu
1 tablespoon sesame oil
2 teaspoons toasted sesame seeds
2 teaspoons chopped green onions
1 teaspoon grated ginger
½ large red chili pepper, chopped

Cut tofu into 1-inch cubes and drain well. Parboil ogo and chop coarsely. Mix shoyu and sesame oil and pour over rest of ingredients. Toss lightly and chill ½ hour before serving.

LILLIAN H. KOBAYASHI
50th Anniversary Best of Our Favorite Recipes, Maui Association for Family and Community Education

HAWAIIAN-STYLE AKU POKE

Makes 6 to 8 servings

1 fillet Hawaiian aku
½ small Maui onion (sweet onion), thinly sliced
2 tablespoons thinly sliced green onions
1 to 2 small Hawaiian chili peppers, seeded and chopped
2 teaspoons minced ginger
¼ cup soy sauce
2 teaspoons sesame oil
Salt to taste
1 teaspoon sesame seeds

Remove skin and bones from aku. Cut into ¼-inch cubes.

In a large bowl, combine aku, Maui onion, green onions, chili peppers, ginger, soy sauce, sesame oil, and salt; mix lightly. Chill for several hours.

Toast sesame seeds by heating in a heavy frying pan, stirring constantly until lightly browned. Sprinkle aku with toasted sesame seeds and serve.

NONA KAMAI
Puuloa Hawaiian Civic Club

WOOL AT AUCTION
AT ROBINSON'S WHARF,
On Thursday, January 22d
By Order of H. N. Greenwell, Esq., I will offer
77 Bales Wool,
Mark, "Keauhou Sheep Station,"
(Formerly the property of Dr. Trousseau.)
☞ TERMS AT SALE.
E. P. ADAMS, Auct'r.

COLD GINGER SASHIMI

2 to 3 pounds ʻahi
Wesson oil
Rock salt to taste
1 cup finely minced ginger
2 cups minced Chinese parsley
1 cup finely minced green onion
White pepper to taste
Shoyu (for dipping)

Cut ʻahi just like regular sashimi. Heat oil and salt and let cool. Mix together ginger, Chinese parsley, green onions, and white pepper. Pour over sliced sashimi. Serve shoyu on the side for dipping.

VARIATION: Place sashimi on a bed of sliced cabbage and garnish with slivered pickled ginger and radish sprouts.

Our Daily Bread Centennial Cookbook, Iao Congregational Church

ABALONE PŪPŪ

Sauce
¼ cup shoyu
½ of lemon (juice)
1 tablespoon sugar
Ajinomoto

2 tablespoons finely chopped Chinese parsley
2 tablespoons finely chopped green onion

1 can abalone, sliced thin

Mix and heat Sauce ingredients; add parsley and green onion.

Add abalone and soak overnight. Cooking abalone toughens it.

A Lei of Recipes,
Kauai Association for Family and Community Education

PŪPŪ TAKO IN SOY SAUCE

1 tako (approximately 2 pounds)
1 cup soy sauce
1 cup water
1 piece ginger, about 2 inches, grated
2 cloves garlic, crushed
2 jiggers whiskey
5 heaping tablespoons sugar
6 pieces anise
½ teaspoon five-spice powder
½ teaspoon sesame seed oil
3 to 4 stalks green onion, cut into 1-inch lengths

Sauce
3 tablespoons oil
¼ teaspoon Korean pepper sauce
2 cloves garlic
¾ teaspoon sugar
4 tablespoons soy sauce
¼ teaspoon sesame seed oil

Clean tako with Hawaiian salt and rinse well. Set aside.

Combine next nine ingredients and bring to a boil. Put in tako and simmer for about ½ hour. Poke with a fork to test for tenderness. Slice into chunks.

Cook green onion in microwave or steam for 2 minutes. Sprinkle cooked green onion over tako. Prepare Sauce and pour over tako and green onion.

Community Family Favorites, Community Church of Honolulu

SMOKED SALMON ROLLS

2 tablespoons finely chopped Maui onion
2 (8-ounce) packages cream cheese
2 teaspoons green capers
1 package soft taco size flour tortillas (10 pieces)
24 ounces sliced smoked salmon

In a medium mixing bowl, thoroughly mix onions and cream cheese. Add capers and stir until evenly distributed.

Spread a thin layer of cream cheese mix over the entire flour tortilla. Starting at one end, lay 1 to 2 slices of salmon, depending on the size of the slices, on the cream cheese side of the tortilla covering ½ to ⅔ of the tortilla surface. Lay a strip of cream cheese mix about a half-inch in diameter across the salmon about an inch from the salmon covered end of the tortilla. Roll the salmon covered end of the tortilla over the strip of cream cheese and continue to roll to the end. Wrap in plastic wrap and chill for at least 2 hours.

Cut into 6 to 8 slices and serve.

WAYNE ISHIZAKI
Lana'i Cooks, Lana'i High & Elementary School

MUSHROOMS STUFFED WITH CRABMEAT

3 tablespoons butter
2 cloves garlic, finely chopped
2 large shallots or 1 medium onion, chopped
1 pound large mushrooms, stems removed and chopped
¼ pound crabmeat, shredded
¼ cup chopped parsley
½ cup seasoned breadcrumbs
2 to 3 tablespoons dry sherry or brandy
1 cup grated Swiss or Parmesan cheese

Melt butter in frying pan; sauté garlic and shallots (or onion). Add chopped mushroom stems.

In a bowl, toss together with the rest of the filling ingredients.

Stuff mushrooms with the mixture and bake at 400°F for 10 to 12 minutes.

Community Family Favorites, Community Church of Honolulu

CRAB CAKES

1 egg
¼ cup milk
3 tablespoons mayonnaise
1 tablespoon all-purpose flour
1 tablespoon Worcestershire sauce
1 teaspoon prepared mustard
1 teaspoon salt
¼ teaspoon pepper
1 pound cooked crabmeat or 3 (6-ounce) cans crabmeat, drained, flaked, and cartilage removed
½ cup dry breadcrumbs
2 tablespoons butter or margarine

In a large bowl, whisk together the first eight ingredients. Fold in crab. Place the breadcrumbs in a shallow dish. Drop 1/3 cup crab mixture into crumbs. Shape into a ¾-inch thick patty. Carefully turn to coat. Repeat with remaining crab mixture.

In a skillet, cook patties in butter for 3 minutes on each side or until golden brown.

MABEL BUGADO
Our Favorite Recipes from the Portuguese Heritage Club of Hamakua

‘ONO FISHCAKE PŪPŪ

Makes 8 to 10 servings

1 pound raw fishcake
1 cup shredded crab (or imitation crab)
1 cup chopped water chestnuts
2 tablespoons sugar, or to taste
1 tablespoon cornstarch
1 egg
½ cup chopped green onions
1½ cup panko

Combine all ingredients; mix well. Coat 1 teaspoon fishcake mixture in flake crumbs and deep-fry till golden brown.

LEEANN NAKASONE
1988 4-H Local & Ethnic Food Show

SHRIMP ON TOAST

2 to 3 pounds shrimps, cleaned and deveined
1 can Spam®
Chinese parsley
2 eggs, beaten
1 loaf bread (day old preferred)
Oil for deep-frying

Chop shrimps, Spam®, and parsley very fine (or use blender). Add beaten eggs. Cut bread into 1½ x 1½-inch slices. Bread may be toasted before cutting, if desired.

Spread shrimp mixture on bread and fry in deep fat until brown. Serve hot.

The Hawaii National Guard Auxiliary Cookbook

GROGGY'S SHRIMPS IN BEER

2 to 3 pounds shrimp
2 bottles beer
2 tablespoons pickling spice
2 tablespoons salt
2 tablespoons sugar
½ cup vinegar
½ teaspoon celery salt
¼ teaspoon dry mustard
⅛ teaspoon cayenne
1 clove garlic
1 chopped carrot
2 stalks celery
Ground pepper

Boil shrimp in remaining ingredients for 10 minutes. Let sit until cool, then refrigerate.

PAT HODGINS
The Kahikolu Country Cookbook

SEVICHE HAWAIIAN-STYLE

1 pound fillet of mahimahi
Juice from a dozen limes (more if needed)
3 medium sized tomatoes (finely chopped)
3 Maui onions, chopped fine
2 hot peppers, remove part after 2 hours
1 green pepper, chopped fine
1 clove garlic, minced
1 tablespoon finely chopped parsley
Salt & pepper to taste

Clean mahimahi and let soak in salt water 10 minutes, then remove and pat dry. Place fish on ceramic platter.

Mix remaining ingredients and spread over fish, making sure you cover it completely. Let it set for a few minutes, then turn the fillet over so both sides of fish are well-covered. Cover platter and place in refrigerator. Turn fish several times. Let sit 8 hours.

Serve on bed of lettuce and eat with crackers.

JOHN AND MOLLIE GEYER
The Hele Mai, Ai (Come Eat) Cookbook, Flavors of Upcountry Maui

SALMON QUICHE

Crust
1 cup whole wheat flour
⅔ cup grated cheddar cheese
½ cup chopped macadamia nuts
½ teaspoon salt
¼ teaspoon paprika
6 tablespoons salad oil

Filling
1 (15-ounce) can salmon drained and flaked
3 eggs, beaten
1 cup sour cream
½ cup mayonnaise
3 dashes Tabasco sauce
½ cup salmon juice, add water if needed
¾ cup grated cheddar cheese
1 tablespoon grated onion
¼ teaspoon dill weed

Combine Crust ingredients and press into 10-inch quiche dish. Bake 10 minutes at 400°F. Cool.

Combine Filling ingredients and spoon into baked shell. Bake 45 minutes at 325°F.

RUTH HODGMAN
The Kahikolu Country Cookbook

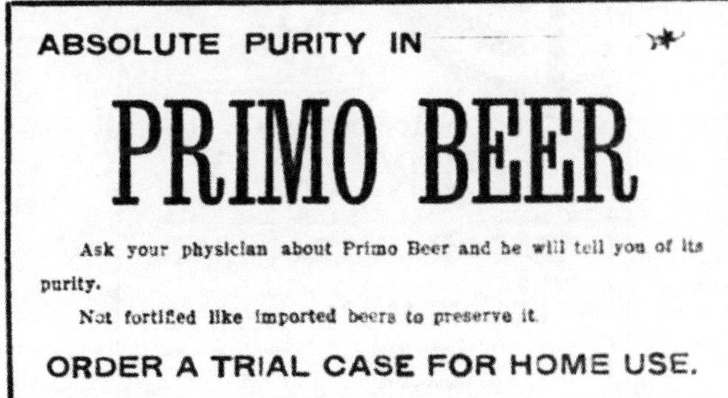

MACADAMIA NUT CHEESE BALL

2 (8-ounce) packages cream cheese, softened
1½ cups grated cheddar cheese
2 teaspoons minced onion
½ cup chopped sweet pickles
1 teaspoon salt
½ cup chopped macadamia nuts

Combine cream cheese, cheddar cheese, onion, sweet pickles, and salt; mix well. Shape into a ball; roll in chopped nuts. Cover and refrigerate several hours or until well-chilled. Serve with crackers.

Ka'u Hospital Auxiliary, One More Time

GOOEY MOZZARELLA STICKS

Makes 10 servings

2 cups all-purpose flour
1 teaspoon cayenne pepper
1 pound mozzarella string cheese sticks (½-inch diameter, sliced in 3-inch lengths)
3 eggs, beaten
1 (4-ounce) package panko
2 cups vegetable oil

Combine flour and cayenne pepper. Roll cheese sticks in flour mixture. Dip coated cheese sticks in beaten eggs and then roll in panko.

Heat oil to 375°F to fry cheese sticks. Sticks are fried until coating is golden brown. Remove with slotted spoon and drain on paper towels.

The cheese filling is very hot, so let the sticks cool down a little before serving. Real good with your favorite spaghetti or cocktail sauce.

LEONA M. PAGAY
Lana'i Cooks, Lana'i High & Elementary School

POI MAKING

Pounding Hawaiian Style

Pick: 6 to 12 mature ʻulu, brownish in color. Green fruits are not mature.

Slice: Knock off stem close to base of fruit with blunt side of knife. Cane knife is ideal. Slice downward in center of fruit.

Tub/Can: In 5 gallon can or medium tub, break and place little finger-sized twigs on bottom. Cover as much metal as possible, leaving little for fruit to contact. Place fruit in can, one on top of the other until full. Fill with water to cover edge of top layer, about 3 inches from top. Cover with clean, wet burlap bags.

Boil: Boil over outside fire for 1 hour, more or less.

Test for doneness: Check by pushing niau (coconut midrib) or wheat straw through fruit. If niau passes through easily and fruit appears to "crack," ʻulu is done.

Peel: Cut off skin until firm flesh is reached. Cut out center fibrous elongated core and remove from fruit. Butter knife or ʻopihi shells are used to remove skin.

Pound: On wooden poi board, pound ʻulu, breaking fruit into small pieces. Continue pounding until fruit is transformed into a smooth paste. Water is used sparingly to bring 'ulu to this stage. Wetting the bottom of the stone suffices.

NOTE: Poi from taro is made similar to this though the taro does not have to be sliced before cooking.

VIRGINIA AND JOE KELIIPAAKAUA
The Kahikolu Country Cookbook

CHAWAN MUSHI
Steamed Egg Dish

2 eggs
1 cup dashi (shrimp or fish stock) or chicken broth
Cooked chicken, sliced
Bamboo shoots, thinly sliced, as desired
Dried mushrooms, thinly sliced, as desired
Fishcake, thinly sliced, as desired

Beat eggs together with dashi. Add chicken and desired vegetables.

Pour mixture into 3 bowls. Place parsley sprig in each bowl. Place bowls in a steamer. Cover with a damp cloth; place lid on pot. Steam for 15 minutes.

ASANO YAMASHITA
Grandma & Grandpa's Hawaiian Island Cookbook, Honolulu Federal Savings and Loan Association

CHINESE SALT EGGS

9 cups water
1 cup salt
2 dozen island eggs, large
1 gallon mayonnaise jar
1 bag Lipton tea

Boil water. Add salt to dissolve. Cool.

Put eggs in gallon jar. Add salt water and tea bag. Let sit for one month under sink in the dark.

Boil eggs after one month on low heat so it won't crack.

Put eggs in refrigerator after they cool off. They will keep for one month.

Parks & Recreation Family Favorites

Just Arrived.

Household Sewing Machines

With latest improvements and attachments.

HAND SEWING MACHINES,
1 WASHING MACHINE, new ;

MUSICAL INSTRUMENTS:

Aristons, Accordeons, Guitars, Violins, Bigotphones, a new and comical instrument, can be played by anyone;

GUITAR and VIOLIN STRINGS,

VELVETEEN

Carpets & Rugs

ED. HOFFSCHLAEGER & CO.

VIETNAMESE SUMMER ROLL

Makes 20 rolls

1 ounce or 1 cup rice noodle
1 cup finely shredded lettuce
1 cup bean sprouts
¼ cup shredded mint
¼ cup shredded basil
1 package rice paper, pie-wedge shape
8 ounces imitation crabmeat
Water in a spray bottle

Dipping Sauce
¼ cup fish sauce
¾ cup water
3 tablespoons sugar
3 tablespoons vinegar
1 tablespoon shredded ginger
1 hot red pepper, shredded (optional)

Prepare rice noodles by soaking in hot water for about 10 minutes, drain and cut into 2-inch lengths; measure one cup of the noodles. Mix with lettuce, bean sprouts, mint, and basil.

Take one sheet of rice paper, handle gently, and spray both sides with water. Lay wet rice paper on work surface with point away from you. Meanwhile, it takes only a few seconds for the rice paper to soften and become pliable. About one inch from the near edge, place a heaping tablespoon of the mix, fold edge over. Then place one piece of crab leg on the folded rice paper and make one turn away from you. Fold the two sides toward the center and roll until the point is reached. Lay the point side down on the serving dish. The finished roll should be thumb-size and tightly rolled. Continue to roll the rest until finished.

Arrange the finished rolls with the crabmeat facing up and garnish with basil and mint. Serve with Dipping Sauce.

To make Dipping Sauce, cook first four ingredients together for 15 minutes. Add ginger and pepper. Serve with summer rolls.

Community Family Favorites, Community Church of Honolulu

BREADS

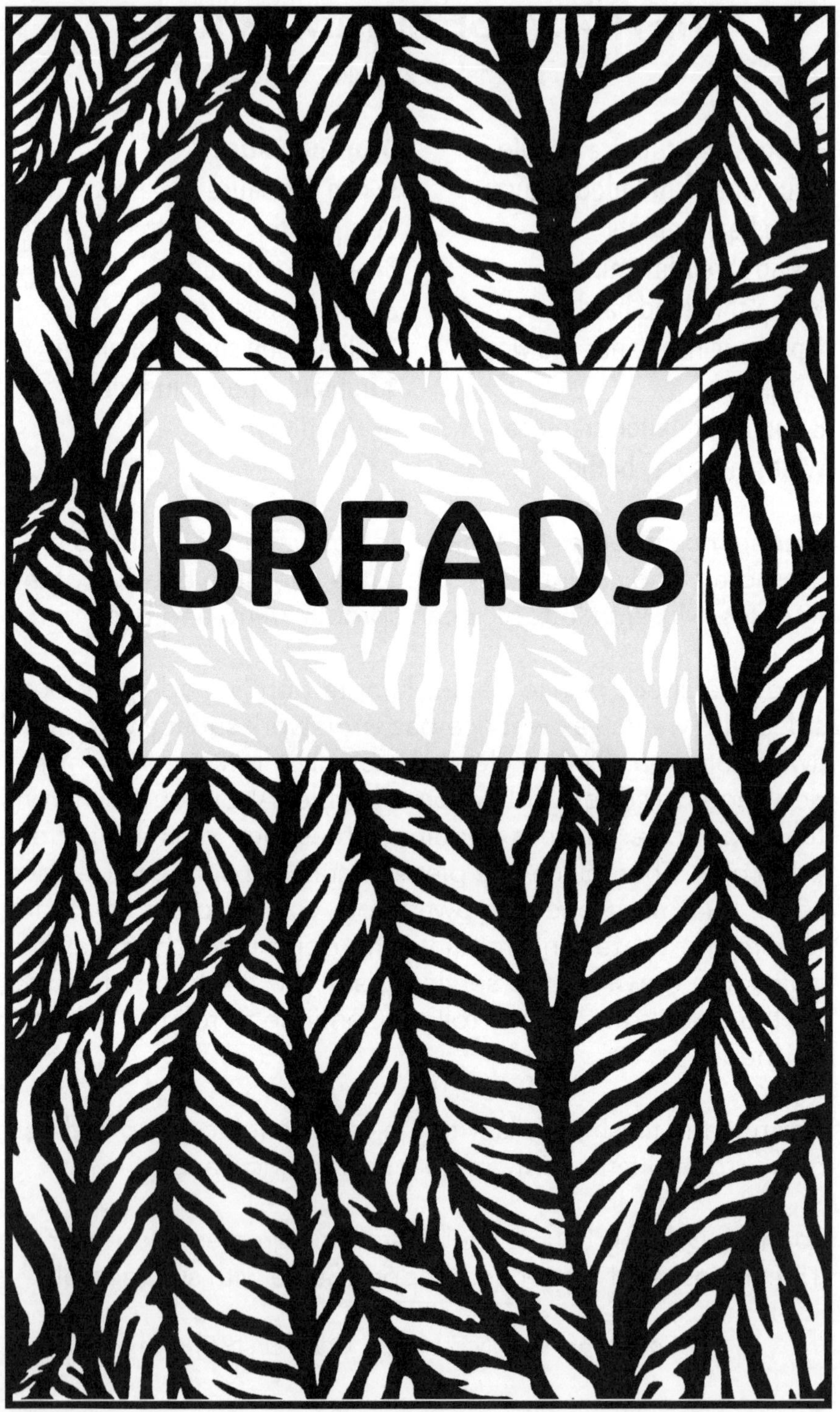

ORIGINAL KAUAI INN BANANA BREAD

Makes 2 (1¼ pound) loaves

Grease 2 loaf pans.

Cream:

2 cups sugar

1 cup shortening

Add:

6 ripe mashed bananas

4 well-beaten eggs

Sift 3 times:

2¼ cups cake flour

2 teaspoons baking soda

1 teaspoon salt

Blend wet and dry ingredients. Do not over-mix. Bake in 350°F oven for 45 to 50 minutes.

OPTIONAL: Add ¼ cup chopped walnuts.

Story:

The Kauai Inn is only a memory now, long gone the way of condominiums on the old property in Lihue. I usually used Chinese bananas when they began to get freckles on them, but haven't seen that type banana in the stores for a long time. Maybe they're a memory too. Anyway, before the days of mango, papaya, pumpkin, and whatever other kind of bread you can think of, banana bread was the big favorite, and Kauai Inn Banana Bread was famous.

This recipe brings back memories of a slower-paced era without television, FAX machines, cellular phones, fast foods, and accelerated lifestyles. Plantation life dominated the community and the biggest excitement around was a choice of the Immaculate Conception School carnival or the Little League baseball game. When McDonald's opened in Lihue, it was almost a county holiday. Traffic was held up for hours and it made headlines in the local newspaper. Wow! Are we getting old, or what?

JALNA KEALA
Puuloa Hawaiian Civic Club

CRANBERRY BREAD

2 cups flour, sifted
¾ cup sugar
1 teaspoon cinnamon
1 large egg
½ teaspoon baking soda
1 teaspoon salt
1 large can whole cranberry sauce
½ cup chopped walnuts (optional)

Grease and flour loaf pan. Sift dry ingredients into a large bowl. Drop in egg and sauce; mix thoroughly.

Bake at 350°F for 1½ hours or until done. This can be made in small muffin tins or small loaf pans for Christmas gifts.

A Lei of Recipes,
Kauai Association for Family and Community Education

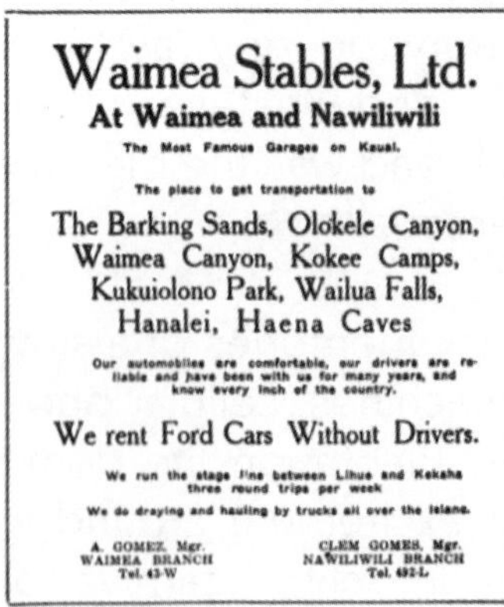

TROPICAL FRUIT TWIST BREAD

Makes 2 loaves, 20 servings per loaf

1 (16-ounce) loaf frozen white bread dough
1 (16-ounce) loaf frozen wheat bread dough
¼ cup sugar
1 teaspoon cinnamon
1 (6-ounce) package (⅔ cup) tropical fruit
1 egg, beaten
1 cup powdered sugar, sifted
1 teaspoon vanilla extract

Thaw doughs; halve lengthwise. On floured surface, roll each portion to form a 12 x 5½-inch rectangle. Brush with water.

Combine sugar and cinnamon; sprinkle over rectangles. Sprinkle with fruit. From long side, roll up jelly roll-style; seal.

On a greased cookie sheet, place a wheat and white rope, seam-side down. Twist together. Seal ends; tuck under. Repeat with remaining ropes. Cover; let rise till double.

Combine egg and 1 tablespoon water; brush loaves. Bake in 350°F oven 25 to 30 minutes. Cover with foil after 15 minutes. Cool.

Mix powdered sugar, vanilla, and 3 to 4 teaspoons water; drizzle over loaves.

SHEREEN NAKASONE
1988 4-H Local & Ethnic Food Show

GUAVA NUT BREAD

½ cup margarine
¾ cup sugar
½ cup sour cream
1 cup guava purée
1 tablespoon lemon juice
2 eggs
½ cup chopped nuts
2 cups flour
1 teaspoon baking powder
1 teaspoon baking soda
¼ teaspoon salt

Cream margarine and sugar. Mix rest of ingredients together. Add to creamed shortening and sugar. Mix well. Pour into loaf or oblong greased and floured 9 x 5-inch pan. Bake in 35O°F oven about an hour or until tester comes out clean.

Community Family Favorites, Community Church of Honolulu

MANGO BREAD

2 cups flour
1½ cups sugar
2 teaspoons cinnamon
2 teaspoons baking soda
½ teaspoon salt
3 eggs
½ cup Wesson oil
½ cup melted butter
1 teaspoon vanilla
2 cups chopped mango

Optional:
¼ cup chopped walnuts
½ cup raisins
½ cup coconut

Mix ingredients together. Pour into 9-inch square cake pan. Let stand in baking pan for 20 minutes. Bake for 1 hour in moderate oven, 350°F.

NOTE: For banana bread add 1 egg and substitute 2 cups mashed banana for mango.

KERITH POCOCK
A Chorus of Recipes, Kamehameha School Children's Chorus

ORANGE BREAD

Makes 1 loaf

Rinds of 3 oranges
3 teaspoons salt
1 cup sugar
⅓ cup water
3 cups flour
3 teaspoons baking powder
½ teaspoon salt
1 cup milk
1 egg

Cut orange rinds in small pieces. Cover with water and salt and boil ½ hour. Drain off water and add sugar and ⅓ cup water and boil 20 minutes. Add flour sifted with baking powder and ½ teaspoon salt, milk, and well-beaten egg. Let stand 10 minutes and bake 45 minutes at 375°F.

The Hilo Woman's Club Cookbook

PAPAYA BREAD

3 eggs
¾ cup oil
1 cup sugar
1 cup peeled and shredded carrots
1 cup puréed papaya
1½ cups applesauce
1 cup chopped walnuts
4 cups flour
1 teaspoon salt
1 tablespoon cinnamon
1 teaspoon nutmeg
1 tablespoon baking soda

Preheat oven to 325°F. Spray two loaf pans with nonstick cooking spray.

Mix eggs, oil, and sugar on slow speed for 1 to 2 minutes. Add carrots, papaya, applesauce, and nuts. Mix one to two minutes until well-mixed. Add flour, salt, cinnamon, nutmeg, and baking soda. Beat on medium speed 1 to 2 minutes. Do not over beat.

Pour into loaf pans; bake for 55 to 60 minutes.

Hilo Missionary Cooks

PINEAPPLE-ALMOND BREAD

Makes 1 loaf

2 cups crushed pineapple, well-drained
2 tablespoons butter
1 cup sugar
1 teaspoon salt
1¼ cups boiling water
1 egg, well-beaten
1 cup whole wheat flour
1¼ cups flour
1 teaspoon soda
1 cup ground almonds

Combine pineapple, butter, sugar, salt, and water. Let stand until cool. Add egg. Sift in flours and baking soda. Fold in almonds. Place in floured and greased loaf pan and bake at 350°F for approximately 1 hour.

Cook 'Em Up Kaua'i, The Kaua'i Historical Society Cookbook

PUMPKIN SPICE BREAD

1¾ cups flour
1½ cups sugar
1 teaspoon baking soda
1 teaspoon cinnamon
½ teaspoon salt
½ teaspoon nutmeg
⅛ teaspoon ground cloves
½ cup melted margarine
1 cup pumpkin
1 egg beaten
⅓ cup water

Sift dry ingredients together, make well in center. Add wet mixture (melted margarine, pumpkin, egg, and water). Mix until dry ingredients are moistened. Pour into greased and floured 9 x 5-inch loaf pan. Bake at 350°F for 1 hour and 10 minutes.

PATRICE PENDARVIS AND DAVID & DYLAN GOODDALE
Hanalei School Collective Cook Book

COCONUT LOAF

1¾ cups flour
3 teaspoons baking powder
¼ teaspoon salt
⅓ cup butter or margarine
1 cup white sugar
1 egg
¾ cup milk
¾ cup fresh shredded coconut

Sift flour and measure. Add baking powder and salt; sift 3 times.

Combine butter, sugar, egg, milk, and coconut; beat briskly. Add to sifted dry ingredients and beat 2 minutes.

Pour into greased loaf pan and bake at 350°F for 50 to 60 minutes or until done.

Remove from pan to cool.

LILA GARDNER
Cooking with Honolulu Gardeners, Honolulu Community Recreational Garden Program

BEER BREAD

3 cups self-rising flour
3 tablespoons sugar
1 (12-ounce) can beer

Mix well and place in greased bread pan. Bake 1 hour in preheated oven at 350°F.

LUCILLE GODERRE
We, the Women of Hawaii Cookbook

CHRISTMAS STOLLEN BREAD

Makes 2 stollen

1 package active dry yeast
¾ cup warm water (105 to 115°F)
½ cup sugar
½ teaspoon salt
3 eggs
1 egg yolk (set the white aside)
½ cup margarine
3½ cups unsifted flour, divided use
½ cup chopped nuts
¼ cup chopped citron
¼ cup chopped candied cherries
¼ cup raisins
1 tablespoon grated lemon peel
2 tablespoons margarine

Dissolve yeast in warm water. Add sugar, salt, eggs, egg yolk, softened margarine, and half the flour. Beat 10 minutes at medium speed on mixer or by hand. Scrape bottom and sides of bowl often. Blend in rest of flour, nuts, fruits, and lemon peel. Cover; let rise in warm draft-free place until doubled, about 1½ hours.

Stir down batter by beating 25 strokes. Cover tightly, refrigerate overnight.

On well-floured board, divide dough in half. Press each half into a 10 x 7-inch oval. Spread ovals with 2 tablespoons softened margarine. Fold each in half longways. Firmly press folded edges only. Place on greased baking sheets. Brush with slightly beaten egg white mixed with 1 tablespoon water. Let rise in warm draft-free place until doubled in bulk, about 1 hour. Bake at 375°F for 20 minutes or until done. When cool, frost and decorate with citron and candied cherries.

CAROLYN STEUER

A Book of Favorite Recipes, Compiled by United Methodist Women of Wahiawa, United Methodist Church

NAAN BREAD

Makes 8 pieces

4 cups all-purpose flour
1 tablespoon granulated sugar
1 tablespoon baking powder
¼ tablespoon baking soda
1½ teaspoons salt
2 eggs
¼ cup plain yogurt
¾ cup milk
2 tablespoons canola oil

In a deep bowl, combine dry ingredients and mix well. Make a well in center and add the remaining ingredients. Mix all ingredients until dough is somewhat sticky; add warm water, if necessary. Knead dough a little on a floured surface until dough is somewhat elastic. Pinch off golf ball-size pieces of dough and place on buttered pan to rest. Cover with damp cloth and let rise for about 1 hour. Dough may also be refrigerated for later use at this point. To cook, pat dough balls into thin circles, about 6 inches in diameter (they should look like tortillas when ready); place on sheet pan and bake at 450°F for 2 to 4 minutes or until dough puffs up and is slightly brown. Serve hot.

NOTE: These rolls burn easily, so keep a watchful eye on them while baking.

RAM ARORA, OWNER/CHEF, INDIA HOUSE RESTAURANT
The Tastes and Tales of Mōʻiliʻili,
A Collection of Recipes & Stories by Mōʻiliʻili Community Center

MONKEY BREAD

Dill weed, if desired
3 to 3½ cups flour
2 tablespoons sugar
1 teaspoon salt
1 package yeast
1 cup warm water
2 tablespoons margarine
1 egg
⅓ cup margarine

Grease 12-cup fluted tube pan. Sprinkle with ½ teaspoon dill weed.

In large bowl, blend 1½ cups flour, sugar, salt, yeast, water, margarine, and egg at low speed until moistened. Beat 3 minutes at medium speed. By hand, stir in remaining flour. Knead dough on floured surface until smooth, about 1 minute. Press or roll dough to 15 x 12-inch rectangle.

Using pastry wheel or sharp knife, cut dough into diamond-shaped pieces by cutting into 1½ to 2-inch strips diagonally across dough. In shallow pan melt ⅓ cup margarine. Dip each pan, overlapping pieces. Sprinkle each layer with about ½ teaspoon dill weed. Cover, let rise in warm place until double in size. Bake at 400°F for 20 to 25 minutes.

Cool 2 minutes. Then invert onto a plate.

Ono-Licious, Na Poe Humukuiki O Hawaii, Hawaii Quilt Guild

GREEN CHILI CORN BREAD

Makes 6 to 8 servings

Dry Mix
1 cup cornmeal
3 teaspoons baking powder
½ teaspoon salt

Wet Mix
3 eggs, beaten
1 cup buttermilk
1 (17-ounce) can cream style corn
½ cup oil

1 cup grated cheese
1 (4-ounce) can diced chilies

Add Dry Mix to Wet Mix. Pour a little of the batter mixture into an 8 x 8-inch flat Pyrex dish. Put half the cheese, add rest of batter, then add the chilies and top with the rest of the cheese.

Bake at 350°F for 45 minutes.

Let stand about 20 minutes before cutting.

BOBBIE MCCORD
Cook 'Em Up Kaua'i, The Kaua'i Historical Society Cookbook

ONION SHORTCAKE BREAD

1 medium sweet onion (Maui), chopped
¼ cup butter
1 box cornbread mix
1 (8-ounce) can cream corn
1 egg, beaten
⅓ cup milk
2 drops Tabasco (optional)
1 cup sour cream
Salt to taste
¼ teaspoon dill weed
1 cup sharp cheddar cheese

Brown onions in butter until tender.

Mix cornbread mix, corn, eggs, milk, and Tabasco in mixing bowl.

When onions are tender, mix with sour cream, salt, dill weed, and cheese in a small bowl. Pour cornbread mixture in greased baking pan. Square is best. Top with sour cream mixture and bake at 425°F for 25 to 30 minutes.

Let cool approximately 5 minutes before slicing.

JUDITH NOVIT
The Kahikolu Country Cookbook

POI NUT BREAD

- 1 pound poi (sold in supermarkets)
- ¾ cup water
- 2 cups flour
- 1 cup sugar
- 2 teaspoons cinnamon
- 1 teaspoon salt
- 2 teaspoons baking soda
- ½ cup chopped nuts
- ½ cup raisin
- ½ cup shredded coconut
- 3 eggs
- 1 cup salad oil
- 2 teaspoons vanilla

Mix poi and water together; set aside. Sift flour, sugar, cinnamon, salt, and soda. Mix together in a separate bowl 2 tablespoons of flour mixture, nuts, raisins, and shredded coconut.

Beat eggs; stir in oil and vanilla. Combine flour mixture, poi mixture, and egg mixture. Fold in nut-raisin mixture. Pour into 2 greased loaf pans. Bake in 350°F oven for 45 minutes.

JEANNIE PECHIN
Hana Maui Recipes from Then to Now

QUICK SOURDOUGH BREAD

2 cups sourdough starter
1 teaspoon dry yeast
3 tablespoons warm water (110°F, 43°C)
3 tablespoons sugar
1½ teaspoons salt
3 tablespoons powdered milk
2 tablespoons melted shortening (or cooking oil)
3 to 4 cups all-purpose flour

Measure out sourdough starter. In a small separate bowl dissolve yeast in warm water. Add to sourdough starter along with sugar, salt, powdered milk, and shortening or cooking oil. Mix well. Slowly add the flour until the dough pulls away from side of the bowl.

A Lei of Recipes,
Kauai Association for Family and Community Education

PORTUGUESE SWEET BREAD

¼ cup lukewarm water
2 packages dry yeast
1 cup sugar, divided use
1 teaspoon salt
5 to 6 cups flour, divided use
1 cup lukewarm milk
3 eggs
¼ pound butter or margarine, cut into small bits

1 egg, lightly beaten

In a small bowl pour in ¼ cup warm water. Sprinkle yeast on top. Add 1 teaspoon sugar. Let stand until yeast gets bubbly, about 3 to 4 minutes.

In a large bowl, combine sugar, salt and 4 cups flour. Pour in yeast mixture, milk, and eggs. Gently stir together until well-combined. Beat in butter; add 2 cups flour and beat vigorously.

Place dough on floured surface and knead it, adding more flour until dough becomes smooth and elastic. Shape into a ball and place in a buttered bowl and cover top with a towel. Set aside to rise until dough doubles in bulk, about 45 minutes.

Divide in two and shape into flattened round loaves. Place in 2 buttered 9-inch round cake pans.

Cover and let rise about 30 to 40 minutes. Brush top of loaves with beaten egg. Bake in a 350°F preheated oven for about 1 hour, or until golden brown and crusty. Cool on wire rack.

COILA EADE
Hana Maui Recipes from Then to Now

BIG PARKER HOUSE ROLL

1 package dry yeast
¼ cup warm water
1 tablespoon salad oil
1 egg
1 tablespoon sugar
1 cup flour

In a small bowl, mix yeast and water. Let stand for 5 minutes. Stir in oil, egg, and sugar (that have been lightly beaten with a fork). Add flour and mix.

Turn out onto a floured board and knead for 2 minutes. Roll into a 7-inch round and fold in half just off center. Place on greased pan or sheet and let rise for 25 minutes. (It will puff up.)

Bake at 350°F for 25 minutes. Easy and delicious.

JEAN KEYS
We, the Women of Hawaii Cookbook

TARO ROLLS

2 packages yeast
½ cup warm water
⅓ cup honey
⅔ cup butter
3 eggs, beaten
3 cups mashed taro (cooked)
¼ tablespoon salt
1 cup warm soy milk
8 cups flour
1 beaten egg (to brush on top of rolls)
Poppy seeds

Soak yeast in warm water. Cream honey and butter together. Add eggs, taro, salt, milk, and yeast. Add flour. Stir until dough is stiff. Place dough on lightly floured board and knead until smooth. Place dough in well-greased bowl and let rise until double in size. Make dough into rolls. Then brush tops with beaten egg and sprinkle with poppy seeds. Let dough rise again until it is double in size. Bake rolls in preheated oven at 375°F for 15 minutes.

TAYLOR, DESIREE, JAMIE, DAYNA, AND APRIL DEVORRE
Hanalei School Collective Cook Book

ORANGE ROLLS

1 cup milk
3 tablespoons butter
1 cake yeast
½ teaspoon salt
3 eggs, well-beaten
½ cup sugar
4 cups flour, divided use

Filling
½ cup softened butter
½ cup sugar
Grated rind of 1 large onion

Scald milk, add butter and cool. When lukewarm, add yeast and salt. Beat eggs well; add sugar and combine with the yeast mixture. Add 1 cup of the flour and mix well. Let rise for 2 hours. Then add the remaining 3 cups of flour and mix well with a spoon. Do not knead. Cover and let rise for 2 hours longer.

Divide the dough into 3 pieces. Roll each piece out and spread with the filling. Roll up like a jelly roll, cut into 1-inch slices and put into buttered muffin tins, cut side down. Let rise 2 hours and bake in 400°F oven for 20 minutes.

MRS. A.J. LAFFERTY
The Hilo Woman's Club Cookbook

PANIOLO BISCUITS

2 cups all-purpose flour
1 cup whole-wheat flour
4½ teaspoons baking powder
2 tablespoons sugar
½ teaspoon salt (optional)
¾ teaspoon cream of tartar
¼ cup butter or margarine
1 egg, beaten
1 cup milk

Preparation time is 15 minutes. Oven temperature is 450°F. Baking time is 12 to 15 minutes for 20 biscuits.

In a bowl combine the flours, baking powder, sugar, salt, and cream of tartar. Cut in butter until mixture resembles coarse cornmeal.

Add egg and milk, stirring quickly and briefly. Knead lightly on floured board.

Roll or pat gently to 1-inch thickness. Cut into 1 to 2-inch biscuits. Place in a greased 10-inch iron skillet or on a 9-inch square pan. For crusty biscuits separate on a cookie sheet.

LUCY ADAMS
"No Ka Oi" The Best of Hawaii,
Favorite Recipes from Rotarians of District 5000

POI BISCUITS

1 cup poi, preferably several days old
⅓ cup shortening
1 egg
¼ cup milk
1½ cups flour
3 teaspoons baking powder
2 teaspoons sugar
½ teaspoon salt

Beat poi and shortening together. Add egg and milk. Stir in flour, baking powder, sugar, and salt.

Knead on lightly floured board. Pat to about an inch in thickness. Cut with a biscuit cutter and bake in a 425°F oven for 12 to 15 minutes. Serve hot with lots of butter.

KAY BOYUM
The Hele Mai, Ai (Come Eat) Cookbook, Flavors of Upcountry Maui

'ULU BREAD AND BISCUITS

In a mixing bowl put 1 egg, ⅓ cup cooking oil, 1 cup milk and beat thoroughly. Add 1 cup very ripe, soft breadfruit and beat until creamy. Combine 1 cup sifted white flour, 3/4 cup sifted whole wheat flour, 2 teaspoons baking powder, ¼ teaspoon baking soda, ¼ teaspoon mace, ½ teaspoon salt, and ½ cup sugar. Sift these dry ingredients into the liquids. Mix until smooth. Pour into an oiled, floured pan, 8½ x 4½ x 2-inches, and bake in 325°F oven for 1 hour.

DONNIE KLING
100 Years Sharing God's Love, United Community Church

SESAME BISCUITS

¼ cup soft butter
¼ pound grated cheddar cheese
½ cup flour
½ teaspoon salt
Dash of cayenne
Toasted sesame seeds

Combine all ingredients (except sesame seeds) and shape into rolls, 1½-inch in diameter, slice ⅜-inch thick, and roll in sesame seeds.

Place on cookie sheet. Bake in preheated oven 375°F for 12 to 15 minutes. Serve while warm.

NOTE: You may prepare in advance; wrap and freeze for future use.

MILLIE MESAKU
We, the Women of Hawaii Cookbook

BRAN MUFFINS

Makes 2 to 3 dozen

1 (15-ounce) box raisin bran cereal
2½ cups flour
1 teaspoon salt
½ cup sugar
2½ teaspoons baking soda
½ cup oil
2 eggs, well beaten
2 cups buttermilk
¾ cup nuts

Mix dry ingredients. In separate bowl, mix oil, eggs, buttermilk. Mix with dry ingredients. Can add nuts and more raisins, or glazed fruit for color. Bake in muffin pans ¾ full for 20 minutes or less at 400°F. (The dough may be kept in freezer for 3 months. If dough begins to dry add 1 or 2 tablespoons milk or yogurt before baking.)

CLEO H. BEATTY
Cook 'Em Up Kaua'i, The Kaua'i Historical Society Cookbook

MACADAMIA NUT MUFFINS

Makes 18 muffins

2 eggs, beaten
1 cup milk
4 tablespoons butter, melted
2 cups flour
4 teaspoons baking powder
½ teaspoon salt
3 tablespoons sugar
1 cup finely chopped macadamia nuts

Beat eggs and milk together. Beat in melted butter. Sift dry ingredients together and add to milk mixture. Add nuts. Mix quickly and thoroughly. Pour into buttered or paper-lined muffin pans. Bake at 450°F for 10 to 15 minutes.

TRISHA TATEYAMA
1988 4-H Local & Ethnic Food Show

QUEEN SURF BANANA MUFFINS

2 cups sugar
1 cup shortening
4 eggs
6 ripe bananas
2½ cups flour
1 teaspoon salt
2 teaspoons baking soda

Cream sugar and shortening. Add eggs and mashed bananas. Add dry ingredients, blend. Do not over-mix. Bake at 350°F for 25 minutes in muffin tins.

ALEX DYE
A Book of Favorite Recipes, Compiled by United Methodist Women of Wahiawa, United Methodist Church

TŪTŪ'S 'ONO POI MUFFINS

4 teaspoons baking powder
¾ teaspoon baking soda
2 cups sifted flour
½ teaspoon salt
1 tablespoon sugar
1 egg, well-beaten
2 tablespoons melted butter
2 quarts sour (bubbly) poi
¼ cup milk (optional)

Sift dry ingredients. Fold eggs and melted butter into poi. Add dry mixture. Stir to ensure complete mixing. DO NOT BEAT. If batter is soft, omit milk.

Bake at 425°F for 20 to 25 minutes. Serve warm with plenty of butter.

MELVA NAKI
From the Hawaiian Kitchens of the Molokai Lions

TARO PUFFS

½ cup flour
½ cup poi
3 teaspoons baking powder

Mix all ingredients and form into balls. Place them in refrigerator until firm. When ready to use, remove from refrigerator and drop the balls into deep fat heated to 375°F and fry until brown.

Favorite Island Cookery Book II, Honpa Hongwanji Buddhist Temple

RICOTTA PUFFS

Makes 3½ dozen

1 cup ricotta cheese
3 eggs
¼ cup sugar
1 cup regular all-purpose flour, unsifted
4 teaspoons baking powder
¼ teaspoon salt
Salad oil for frying
Powdered sugar

In a bowl, beat together the cheese, eggs, and sugar with a wooden spoon until blended and smooth. Stir together the flour, baking powder, and salt. Beat flour mixture in the cheese to form a smooth thick batter.

Pour salad oil in a pan to a depth of about 1½ inches and heat over medium-high heat until temperature registers 375°F on a deep-fat frying thermometer. Drop rounded teaspoonfuls of the batter in the oil, several at a time, and fry until golden brown on all sides, about 1½ minutes. Lift out puffs as cooked and drain well. Serve hot or reheated. Before serving, dust puffs with sifted powdered sugar.

To reheat, place puffs in a single layer on rimmed baking sheet and heat in 350°F oven for about 10 minutes.

Favorite Island Cookery, Book II, Honpa Hongwanji Buddhist Temple

PUFFY CORN FRITTERS

Makes 16 to 18 fritters

1 1/3 cups flour
1 1/2 teaspoons baking powder
3/4 teaspoon salt
1 tablespoon sugar
2/3 cup milk
1 egg, well-beaten
1 can whole kernel corn, well-drained

Sift together flour, baking powder, salt, and sugar. Blend milk and egg. Add gradually to dry ingredients. Stir in the drained corn and drop from tablespoon into deep hot fat (375°F). Fry until golden brown, 4 to 8 minutes. Serve with maple syrup.

MRS. SANDRA WILEY
A Book of Favorite Recipes, Compiled by United Methodist Women of Wahiawa, United Methodist Church

BREADFRUIT FRITTERS

Makes 4 to 6 servings

1 1/3 cups flour (unsifted)
3 teaspoons baking powder
1 teaspoon salt
1 cup breadfruit (uncooked), pulp or grated (depending on ripeness of fruit)
2 eggs, well-beaten
2/3 cup milk

Pour flour into sifter with baking powder and salt. Add to breadfruit and mix thoroughly. Beat eggs until light and fluffy and add milk. Combine with flour and breadfruit mixture. Drop from tablespoon or teaspoon into deep, hot fat, 365°F, 2 to 5 minutes. Drain on absorbent paper. Dust with powdered sugar or serve with honey or maple syrup.

May be served as part of main course, or when sweetened, as a dessert.

50th Anniversary Best of Our Favorite Recipes, Maui Association for Family and Community Education

POTATO CAKE DOUGHNUTS

1 cup sugar
2 tablespoons vegetable oil
2 eggs
1 teaspoon vanilla
1 cup buttermilk or sour milk
4 cups flour
1½ cups potato flakes
1 teaspoon baking soda
2 teaspoons baking powder
1 teaspoon salt
1 teaspoon cinnamon or nutmeg

Mix sugar, vegetable oil, and eggs; beat for 2 minute. Add vanilla and milk; mix. Add flour, potato flakes, baking soda, baking powder, salt, and cinnamon (or nutmeg); blend together and roll on floured board until 1/3-inch thick. Cut with doughnut cutter and fry in hot oil on both sides until brown. Leave plain or while doughnuts are still warm, roll in sugar or powdered sugar.

DORIS MORI
50th Anniversary Best of Our Favorite Recipes, Maui Association for Family and Community Education

COWBOY COFFEE CAKE

Mea ʻOno Paniolo

2½ cups sifted enriched flour
½ teaspoon salt
2 cups raw brown sugar
½ cup shortening
2 teaspoons baking powder
½ teaspoon soda
½ teaspoon cinnamon
½ teaspoon nutmeg
1 cup buttermilk
2 well-beaten eggs
½ cup macadamia nuts

Combine flour, salt, sugar, and shortening. Mix until crumbly. Reserve ½ cup of the mixture.

To remaining crumbs, add baking powder, soda, and spices. Mix thoroughly. Add milk and eggs. Mix well. Pour into 2 wax paper-lined 8 x 8 x 2-inch baking pans. Sprinkle with reserved crumbs. Sprinkle chopped nuts and cinnamon on top. Bake at 375°F for 25 to 30 minutes

FLORENCE KELLEY
The Friends of ʻIolani Palace Cookbook

YUMMY EASY SCONES

⅔ cup milk
1 tablespoon vinegar
1 teaspoon vanilla
2 cups flour
2 teaspoons baking powder
½ teaspoon nutmeg
¼ cup sugar
1 teaspoon baking soda
5 tablespoons cold butter
¾ cup raisins

Preheat oven to 450°F. First, in small bowl, mix vinegar and milk until milk curdles in large clumps. Or, use 1 (8-ounce) tub of plain yogurt. Add vanilla and set aside.

In a bowl, mix dry ingredients. Cut in butter with pastry cutter until it forms coarse crumbs. Add raisins; toss. Add curdled milk or yogurt. Lightly toss until it forms a mass. Roll or pat into a circle about 8 inches in diameter. Cut in 8 wedges. Place on greased cookie sheet. Bake at 450°F for 15 minutes or golden outside.

Ka'u Hospital Auxiliary, One More Time

CHEESE POP-OVERS

1 teaspoon salt
¼ teaspoon paprika
1 cup flour
⅞ cup milk
2 eggs
1 tablespoon grated cheese

Mix salt, paprika, and flour. Add milk gradually and beat until smooth. Beat eggs well and add. Then add cheese and beat 2 minutes. Bake 30 minutes 450°F at first, decreasing to 350°F. Heat muffin pans before putting butter into them.

The Hilo Woman's Club Cookbook

CROISSANTS

Makes 18

1 package dry active yeast
¾ cup warm milk
1 tablespoon sugar
1 tablespoon melted butter
2½ cups bread flour
1 teaspoon salt
½ cup butter, well-chilled

Mix yeast with warm milk and sugar; let rest 5 minutes. Add 1 tablespoon melted, cooled butter; put flour and salt in bowl and make well. Pour in liquids, mix and knead 5 minutes. Let rise 1 hour.

On floured board, roll out dough. Spread flakes of chilled butter over ⅔ of dough. Bring unbuttered part over, fold other ⅓ over and roll with rolling pin. Fold in thirds again, roll again, chill 30 minutes, roll and fold 3 times; chill another 30 minutes. Take out, fold, and roll twice. Leave overnight in icebox.

Take out, roll ¼-inch thick; make 9 x 4-inch squares. Cut each square in half into triangles; roll up from widest end. Place on baking sheet; brush with beaten egg and cream. Bake at 425°F for 20 minutes.

HELEN LANGI
1988 4-H Local & Ethnic Food Show

HOTEL HANA MAUI'S LAVOSH

8 cups bread flour
½ cup sugar
1¼ teaspoons baking soda
1¾ cups butter, softened
1½ cups buttermilk
¼ cup poppy seeds

Mix dry ingredients together; mix in butter until crumbly. Add buttermilk and mix until a ball forms. Divide dough into 6 equal portions. Roll out each portion on a floured surface to 1/16-inch thickness.

Cut into squares with a pizza cutter and place on a large baking sheet. Sprinkle with poppy seeds. Bake in a 400°F oven until golden brown.

Recipe may be cut in half.

Hana Maui Recipes from Then to Now

Good Friday, April 11, 1884,
There will be Ready
From 5 a. m. until 5 p. m.
THE FINEST
HOT ‡ CROSS ‡ BUNS
EVER MADE IN THIS CITY.
50 CENTS per Dozen,
At F. Horn's Steam Candy Factory & Bakery
Hotel Street. 41

HONEY ALMOND GRANOLA

4 cups Quaker Oats
⅓ cup firmly-packed brown sugar
½ cup wheat germ
½ cup flaked or shredded coconut
¼ cup sesame seeds
1 cup slivered almonds
⅓ cup vegetable oil
¼ cup honey (may use up to ½ cup)
1 teaspoon vanilla

Heat oats on an ungreased 13 X 9-inch pan in a preheated oven (350°F) for 10 minutes. Combine oats, brown sugar, wheat germ, coconut, sesame seeds, almonds, oil, honey, and vanilla until dry ingredients are well-coated.

Bake in an ungreased 13 x 9-inch pan in preheated oven (350°F) for 20 to 25 minutes, stirring mixture frequently (about every 5 minutes) to brown evenly. Cool, stir until crumbly. Serve with cold milk or cream. Store in tightly sealed container in fridge.

PATRICE PENDARVIS AND DAVID AND DYLAN GOODDALE
Hanalei School Collective Cook Book

SOUPS

DASHI

Makes 5 cups

1 square-inch konbu
5 cups water
1 cup katsuobushi
1 teaspoon shoyu
1 tablespoon salt
¼ teaspoon MSG

Rinse konbu. Bring to a boil. When large bubbles appear, remove konbu but continue boiling water. Add flaked katsuo. Remove pan from heat at once. Set aside for few minutes. Strain; season with shoyu, salt, and MSG.

Favorite Island Cookery Book II, Honpa Hongwanji Buddhist Temple

GAZPACHO WITH LĀNA'I PINEAPPLE

Makes 4 servings

1 cup cucumber, peeled and seeded
¼ cup red bell pepper
¼ cup yellow bell pepper
1 teaspoon jalapeño pepper, finely minced
⅛ cup sweet Maui onion
1 cup fresh pineapple, skin and core removed
1 tablespoon Italian parsley
½ cup pineapple cider or pineapple juice
Pinch salt

Coarsely chop cucumber, peppers, onion, pineapple, and Italian parsley. Place in a blender with pineapple cider and salt. Blend until mixture is smooth. Chill and serve.

CHARLENE AMORAL
Lana'i Cooks, Lana'i High & Elementary School

THAI PUMPKIN SOUP

1 small can pumpkin
2 small cans chicken broth
1 can Kern's mango nectar
½ cup peanut butter (creamy)
½ cup water
¼ cup scallions
2 teaspoons chopped fresh ginger
2 tablespoons fresh garlic
¼ cup cilantro

Bring pumpkin, chicken broth, mango, peanut butter, and water to a boil. Add scallions, ginger, and garlic. Simmer 30 minutes. Add cilantro. Serve. Really good.

LORI POLESKI
"No Ka Oi" The Best of Hawaii, Favorite Recipes from Rotarians of District 5000

CREAM OF TARO ROOT

Makes 2 gallons.

3 pounds taro root
2 ounces shallots, diced
1 stalk leeks
1 cup white wine
1½ gallons chicken stock or bouillon
2 quarts Avoset or heavy cream
Salt to taste
White pepper to taste

Peel and cut taro into chunks. Boil for 1 hour, drain, run taro through food processor or blender until smooth.

Sauté shallots, leeks, deglaze with wine, simmer with stock. Mix in taro, add avoset, season to taste.

BERT MATSUOKA, EXECUTIVE CHEF, SHERATON KAUAI RESORT
Cook 'Em Up Kaua'i, The Kaua'i Historical Society Cookbook

CHICKEN UDON SOUP

Makes 6 servings

1 chicken breast
5 cups Dashi (page 84)
¾ cup sliced mushroom
1 tablespoon mirin
2 teaspoons shoyu
1 cup udon, cooked
6 slices lemon peel

Skin chicken breast and slice think. Bring dashi to a boil; add chicken. Simmer 10 minutes. Add mushroom, mirin, and shoyu. Cook 3 minutes. Divide into 6 bowls. Add udon noodles and float lemon slices.

Favorite Island Cookery Book II, Honpa Hongwanji Buddhist Temple

CHICKEN PAPAYA SOUP

Makes 4 to 6 servings

2 pounds chicken (any type)
1 clove garlic
1 large tomato
1 medium round onion
1 (2-inch) fresh ginger or 8 to 10 leaves lemongrass
2 medium-size green papaya, peeled, seeds removed, and cut into bite-size chunks
Pepper to taste
Salt to taste (add only if you are not using shoyu; shoyu may be added at each serving)

Brown chicken with garlic. Add tomato and round onion until soft. Add ginger or lemon grass and cook until chicken is soft.

Add green papaya and simmer until soft. Add pepper and salt (if desired).

North Kohala Favorites

CHICKEN, LINGUISA, AND VEGETABLE SOUP

- 6 boned chicken thighs, skinned and fat removed
- ¾ pound linguisa (Portuguese sausage)
- 2 onions, thinly sliced
- 1½ cups thinly sliced carrots
- 2 cups thinly sliced celery
- 2 quarts chicken broth
- ½ pound Roma tomatoes, diced
- 2 cups thinly sliced cabbage
- 1 teaspoon lemon peel
- 1 package frozen peas
- 3 tablespoons lemon juice
- ⅓ cup mint leaves (fresh}
- Salt and pepper to taste

Cut chicken into 1 inch cubes. Cut linguisa into ½-inch slices.

In a 6-quart pressure cooker over high heat, brown Portuguese sausage over medium heat. Transfer to bowl. Discard all but 1 tablespoon of the drippings from pan. Add onions, carrots, and celery. Stir occasionally until onions are limp. Add broth, chicken, sausage, tomatoes, cabbage, and lemon peel. Bring to a boil and simmer for 45 minutes.

During last 15 minutes of cooking time, add peas, lemon juice, and mint, bringing mixture to a boil then reduce to simmer. Season with salt and pepper to taste.

MARIE HO

Our Favorite Recipes from the Portuguese Heritage Club of Hamakua

CURRIED CHICKEN SOUP

Makes 8 servings

1½ to 2 pounds chicken (boneless)
6 tablespoons butter
1 large onion, chopped
2 carrots, peeled and cut in ¼-inch rounds
1 tablespoon curry powder
5 cups chicken broth
6 sprigs parsley, chopped
¼ cup rice
1 cup half & half
1 (10-ounce) box frozen peas, thawed
Salt to taste
Pepper to taste

Remove skin from chicken and cut into 1-inch pieces. Melt butter in a large saucepan or stockpot. Add onion, carrots, and curry powder. Cook, covered, over low heat until vegetables are tender, about 15 minutes.

Add broth, parsley, chicken, and rice. Bring soup to a boil, reduce heat, and cover. Simmer until chicken is cooked and rice is tender.

Add half & half and peas; simmer for 15 minutes more.

ROSE MIZOKAWA
Puuloa Hawaiian Civic Club

HILO-STYLE CHICKEN GUMBO

¼ cup olive oil
3 to 4 slices bacon, diced
½ large onion, diced into 1-inch pieces
1 bell pepper, diced into 1-inch pieces
¼ cup cilantro (Chinese parsley)
3 tomatoes, diced
7 cups chicken stock
2 celery sticks, sliced
2 cups cooked rice
2 pounds chicken chunks
3 cups okra
Salt and pepper
4 Hawaiian chili peppers, diced

Sauté bacon, onion, and pepper. Add parsley, tomatoes, and stock. Simmer; add the rest and simmer for 30 minutes.

Our Favorite Recipes from the Portuguese Heritage Club of Hamakua

JHUK
Rice Soup

Makes 6 to 8 servings

Chicken or turkey bones
3 quarts water
1 cup raw rice, washed and drained
4 pieces dried shiitake mushrooms, softened in water and slivered
1½ teaspoons salt
½ teaspoon sherry
½ chung choi, minced
Minced green onion
Chinese parsley

In large pot, combine chicken or turkey bones and water; bring to boil and simmer 30 minutes. Remove bones and add rice, msuhrooms, salt, sherry, and chung choi; simmer additional 30 to 45 minutes. Garnish with green onion and Chinese parsley to serve.

The Tastes and Tales of Mōʻiliʻili,
A Collection of Recipes & Stories by Mōʻiliʻili Community Center

PORTUGUESE EGG SOUP

Makes 4 servings

1 cup chopped onions
1 clove garlic, minced
2 tablespoons olive oil
5 cups water
1 tablespoon salt
1 teaspoon powdered thyme
1 teaspoon celery salt
¼ teaspoon pepper
4 beef bouillon cubes
4 eggs
4 thick slices French bread, cut into 1-inch cubes

Sauté onions and garlic in olive oil. Add water, salt, thyme, celery salt, pepper, and bouillon cubes. Boil this mixture for 5 minutes. Turn to very low heat and poach eggs in soup until thoroughly cooked.

Dry French bread cubes in oven. Place bread cubes in bottom of soup bowl, pour soup broth on top, and place an egg in each bowl.

Cook 'Em Up Kaua'i, The Kaua'i Historical Society Cookbook

BURGER LONG RICE SOUP

1 package long rice
1 bunch watercress, mustard cabbage, or makina
1 pound ground round
1 small onion, sliced
2 cans chicken broth plus 1 can water
½ teaspoon salt or more to your taste
1 teaspoon shoyu
1 small piece of ginger, crushed
1 teaspoon liquor (wine or sherry)

Soak long rice in water, drain, and cut into 3 parts. Cut green vegetables into 1½-inch lengths. Sauté ground round and onion. Add broth, water, salt, shoyu, ginger, and liquor. Simmer for 20 minutes. Add long rice and simmer for 15 minutes. Add vegetables and turn off heat. If needed, add more stock.

Wisteria Delights, A Collection of Recipes by Pearl City Hongwanji Mission

EASY VEGETABLE SOUP

1 pound ground beef
1 cup chopped onions
1 clove garlic, minced
1 (15-ounce) can kidney beans
1 cup sliced carrots
1 cup sliced celery
1 cup diced potatoes
¼ regular rice (uncooked)
1 (16-ounce) can stewed tomatoes
5 cups water
4 beef bouillon cubes
1 tablespoon parsley flakes
1 teaspoon salt
¼ teaspoon basil leaves
½ teaspoon pepper
1 cup frozen green beans

Cook ground beef, onion, and garlic in pot until beef is browned. Add remaining ingredients, except the green beans. Bring to a boil. Reduce heat and simmer (covered) for about 40 minutes or until vegetables are done. Add beans and simmer for 10 minutes.

PATRICIA UYETAKE NISHIMURA
Our Daily Bread Centennial Cookbook, Iao Congregational Church

MORE HEINZ GOODS

New shipment just received by your grocer.

India Relish
Mince Meat
Tomato Ketchup

Pickles, sweet and sour; Malt Vinegar; Cider Vinegar; White Pickling Vinegar; Apple Butter; Red Kidney Beans

Horse Radish
Pearl Onions
Baked Beans

ALL THE FAMOUS "57"

VEGETABLE BEEF AND TORTELLINI SOUP

Makes 4 servings

1 pound ground beef
1 medium onion
1 carrot, chopped
1 clove garlic, chopped
Salt to taste
Pepper to taste
1/8 teaspoon cayenne pepper
1 cup chicken stock
2 bay leaves
1 (7-ounce) can cut tomatoes
3 cups water
1 package fresh tortellini

In a 3-quart Dutch oven, brown beef and drain the fat. Add onion, carrot, and garlic and sauté until limp. Add salt, pepper, and cayenne. Stir.

Add chicken stock to deglaze bottom of Dutch oven. Add bay leaves, cut tomatoes, and water. Bring mixture to a boil. Cover and reduce heat and simmer for 1 hour.

Add tortellini, take off heat and let stand for 15 minutes.

ADRIAN VERDUZCO
Cook 'Em Up Kaua'i, The Kaua'i Historical Society Cookbook

MINESTRONE SOUP

2 tablespoons olive oil
1 cup coarsely chopped round onion
2 cloves garlic, minced
Dash pepper
1½ pounds lean stewing beef
3 (10.5-ounce) cans beef broth
2 cans water
1½ teaspoons Italian herb seasoning
1 (16-ounce) can tomatoes
1 can kidney beans
1¾ cups sliced ripe olives
1½ carrots, cut into small dices
1 cup small shell macaroni
2 cups small diced zucchini
Parmesan cheese, grated (optional)

Add olive oil, onion, garlic, black pepper, stewing beef in large pot and brown. Add broth, water and Italian seasoning. Cover and cook for 1 hour until meat is tender.

Stir in tomatoes, kidney beans, olives, carrots, and macaroni. Add zucchini on top and cook until macaroni is done. Serve with cheese (optional).

NOTE: May use 2 cans of stewed tomatoes instead of a large can of whole tomatoes.

Wisteria Delights, A Collection of Recipes by Pearl City Hongwanji Mission

OXTAIL SOUP

Makes 8 servings

5 pounds oxtail, disjointed
3 quarts water
1½ cups shelled raw peanuts
1 piece star anise
2 small pieces orange peel (kwo pi)
8 pieces dried mushrooms, soaked and cut in 4
4 stalks celery, cut into 1-inch pieces
1 (1-inch) piece fresh ginger root, crushed
Salt to taste

Brown oxtail and discard oil. Add rest of ingredients and cook for 2½ hours until soft. Garnish with green onions and Chinese parsley.

BARBARA WONG
Family Favorites, Oahu Extension Homemakers Council

ANDRADE'S HAM HOCK SOUP

2 pounds ham hock
1 chopped onion
3 quarts water
4 (15-ounce) cans kidney beans
½ cup chopped celery
1 (8-ounce) package spaghetti
Salt and pepper to taste

Place ham hock, onion, and water in pot. Boil for 1½ to 2 hours until meat is tender enough to shred with a fork. Remove ham hock and shred and return to broth, with bone if desired. Add beans and celery and bring to a boil. Break up spaghetti and add to pot. Cook and stir until spaghetti is done. Simmer 20 minutes. Salt and pepper to taste. Serve with Portuguese white bread.

REBECCA ANDRADE
The Kahikolu Country Cookbook

PHO
Vietnamese Beef Noodle Soup

Makes 4 servings

Broth
5 cups beef stock
1-inch fresh ginger
3 star anise
2 green onions
3 tablespoons fish sauce

Soup
8 ounces rice sticks or cellophane noodles
1 onion
12 basil leaves
6 to 8 ounces beef tenderloin or sirloin, partially frozen

Garnish
2 cups fresh mung bean sprouts
8 sprigs fresh mint
2 jalapeño or Serrano chilies, thinly sliced
1 lime, quartered
Hoisin sauce
Hot chili sauce

Combine the beef stock, ginger, star anise, green onions, and fish sauce and gently simmer for 30 minutes. Remove the ginger, anise, and green onions.

Soak the rice sticks in warm water for 30 minutes.

Slice the green onions, onion, and basil leaves as thinly as possible. Slice the beef as thinly as possible across the grain. (Meat can be sliced using a meat slicer. It helps to partially freeze the meat before slicing.)

Bring 4 quarts water to boil. Arrange the sprouts, mint sprigs, chilies, and lime on a platter.

Just before serving, bring the broth to a boil. Cook the rice sticks in boiling water for 30 seconds, then drain. Divide the noodles among 4 large bowls. Arrange the scallions, onion slices, and beef slices on top. Spoon the boiling broth on top; the heat of the liquid should be sufficient to cook the meat.

Serve the soup at once, with the garnish platter on the side. Let each person add sprouts, mint, chilies, lime, and hoisin and/or chili sauce to taste.

LYNN NAKAMURA TENGAN
50th Anniversary Best of Our Favorite Recipes, Maui Association for Family and Community Education

OKINAWAN-STYLE SOUP

1 pound spareribs
7 cups boiling water
1 package nishime konbu, soaked
1 daikon or squash
1 small mustard cabbage, parboiled
2 tablespoons hondashi
½ cup miso

Have spareribs cut into 1½-inch lengths. Put into a large pot and add boiling water. Cook for 30 minutes and skim stock. Tie nishime konbu into knots and cut between knots. Peel daikon or squash into bite-size pieces. Add daikon, konbu, and cook for 20 minutes more. Parboil mustard cabbage for a few minutes in another pot. Cut into 1½-inch lengths. Add cabbage to soup just before serving. Before turning off heat, add hondashi and miso.

TETSUKO TOKIHIRO
Family Favorites, Oahu Extension Homemakers Council

PORTUGUESE BEAN SOUP

Makes 10 servings

½ pound dried kidney beans
2 to 3 ham hocks
1½ to 2 pounds hot Portuguese sausage, cut into ½-inch slices, sautéed and drained
1 (8-ounce) can tomato sauce
2 large baking potatoes, cut into ¾-inch cubes
1 onion, sliced
3 carrots, sliced
3 stalks celery, sliced
3 tablespoons minced parsley
1 clove garlic, minced
1 tablespoon lemon juice
½ head medium cabbage, shredded (optional)
½ cup uncooked macaroni (optional)
1 bunch watercress, chopped (optional)
Salt and pepper to taste
Allspice to taste

Cover beans with water and soak overnight; drain. Cover ham hocks with water and cook for 1 to ½ hours. Remove ham hocks; shred meat and discard bone and fat. Add beans to liquid and cook for 1 hour.

Return meat to soup along with Portuguese sausage. Cook for 10 minutes. Add tomato sauce, potatoes, onion, carrots, celery, parsley, garlic, and lemon juice. Simmer until vegetables are tender. Add cabbage, macaroni, watercress, salt pepper, and allspice. Simmer for 10 minutes or until macaroni is tender.

North Kohala Favorites

WON BOK AND PORK SOUP

Makes 6 to 10 servings

8 ounces ground pork
2 tablespoons chopped green onion
1 egg, slightly beaten
1 (1-inch) piece ginger, minced
1 teaspoon sherry or sake
½ teaspoon salt
2 (14.5-ounce) cans chicken broth
1 (6.5-ounce) can sliced mushrooms
16 ounces won bok, cut into 2-inch pieces

Combine pork, green onion, egg, ginger, sherry or sake, and salt. Shape into 1-inch balls.

In a 4-quart saucepan or stock pot, bring chicken broth to a boil. Reduce heat and add pork balls. Simmer covered for 20 minutes. Add mushrooms and won bok; continue to simmer for 5 minutes. Add 1½ teaspoon salt, if desired.

SHEILA BLACK
Lana'i Cooks, Lana'i High & Elementary School

EGG FLOWER SOUP

2 pounds pork butt, sliced
2 teaspoons wine, sherry or vermouth
2 teaspoons soy sauce
2 teaspoons cornstarch
4 tablespoons oil
½ stalk leek
8 cups broth, chicken or pork
2 cucumbers, sliced
Salt to taste
2 eggs, beaten

Dredge pork slices with wine, soy, and cornstarch. Heat oil and fry pork with leek. Add broth. When soup comes to a boil, add cucumber slices and salt. Slowly stir in beaten eggs.

MARITA BIVEN
The Hawai'i Youth Opera Chorus, Nā Mea 'Ai Punahele

HOT AND SOUR SOUP

4 cans chicken broth
¼ pound raw pork, slivered
½ cup diced tofu
⅓ cup shredded bamboo shoots
1 small can button mushrooms (approx. ⅓ cup)
2 teaspoons sesame oil
2 eggs, beaten

Optional
1 tablespoon wood ears
6 lily flowers, dried
6 small dried mushrooms
1 piece tangerine peel

Combine in small bowl and have ready:

4 teaspoons shoyu
1 teaspoon sugar
¾ teaspoon salt
¼ teaspoon pepper
1 teaspoon gin or vodka
2 tablespoons rice or cider vinegar

Combine and have ready:

2½ tablespoons cornstarch
¼ cup cold water

Place broth in pan. Add pork, tofu, bamboo shoots, mushrooms and sesame oil. Bring to boil, simmer 10 minutes. Add optional ingredients and seasonings; stir.

Stir in cornstarch mixture. Stir and remove from heat. Pour in eggs, stirring rapidly. Top with oil and serve.

Ono-Licious, Na Poe Humukuiki O Hawaii, Hawaii Quilt Guild

MANDARIN MUSHROOM SOUP WITH SINGING RICE

2 (13-ounce) cans chicken broth
1/3 pound lean pork, finely diced
1 garlic clove, crushed
1 tablespoon shoyu
1/4 cup sliced mushrooms
1/4 cup sliced water chestnuts
1 can green peas (frozen)
1 recipe for Singing Rice

Simmer chicken broth, pork, garlic, and shoyu for 10 minutes. Add mushrooms and water chestnuts and peas. Prepare Singing Rice as directed.

To serve: Pour half of rice in a warm casserole. Pour soup over the rice and serve. Serve remaining rice in a bowl.

Singing Rice

1 cup long grain rice
4 cups water
2 teaspoons salt

Combine rice, water, and salt in a 2 quart saucepan, and let stand for 30 minutes. Drain. Spread rice on well-greased cookie sheet. Bake for 8 hours at 250°F. Turn rice with spatula occasionally. Break rice into bite-size pieces. (May be stored in airtight containers in the refrigerator at this stage.) Heat salad oil in saucepan (2 inches deep) with a basket. Fry rice until golden brown about 4 minutes. Drain. Keep hot on a serving platter or in a bowl. Anything poured over the rice must be very hot to make the rice sing.

ADELE DAVIS
We, the Women of Hawaii Cookbook

MOCK BIRD'S NEST SOUP

1 bundle long rice
4 dried mushrooms
6 cups chicken broth
1/8 teaspoon aji (optional)
1½ teaspoons salt
1 cup ground pork
1 cup ground ham
½ cup water chestnuts, chopped
2 egg whites, slightly beaten
Chopped Chinese parsley

Cut long rice with scissors in ¼-inch lengths and soak in hot water for 30 minutes. Soak mushrooms in warm water until soft; wash thoroughly and remove stems. Chop mushroom caps fine. To the broth, add mushrooms, seasonings, meat, and water chestnuts; simmer for 30 minutes. Add drained long rice and simmer 5 minutes more. Remove from heat and stir in egg whites. Serve hot with chopped parsley sprinkled on top.

Ono-Licious, Na Poe Humukuiki O Hawaii, Hawaii Quilt Guild

BREADFRUIT CHOWDER

Makes 6 servings

2 thin strips bacon
1/3 cup sliced onion
2 cups diced raw green breadfruit
½ cup diced raw carrots
2 teaspoons salt
3 cups boiling water
1 1/3 cups milk

Cut bacon into small pieces and fry until light brown. Add onion and cook until light brown. Add vegetables, salt, and water. Boil until vegetables are tender. Add milk and serve hot.

50th Anniversary Best of Our Favorite Recipes, Maui Association for Family and Community Education

ISLAND CORN CHOWDER

½ pound bacon, sliced into ½-inch pieces
½ cup ham, diced
1 small round onion, diced
Pepper to taste
4 potatoes, diced
Pinch Hawaiian salt
1 can cream style corn
1 can kernel corn
1 can Carnation cream

Stir-fry bacon, ham, and round onion. Add some pepper to taste. Boil diced potatoes in enough water to cover the potatoes, add a pinch of Hawaiian salt. Add bacon mixture, cream style corn, and kernel corn to potatoes. Add Carnation cream just before you're ready to eat. Serve with crackers. Perfect on a cold day.

TRISHA TAMASHIRO
A Chorus of Recipes, Kamehameha School Children's Chorus

CLAM CHOWDER

4 tablespoons bacon grease
1 medium onion, chopped fine
1 medium carrot, shredded
1 cup diced celery
1 tablespoon chopped parsley
¼ teaspoon thyme leaves
2 cans minced clams
1 can cream of potato soup
3 cups liquid (water–milk–half & half)

Combine first six ingredients in a 3 quart saucepan and cook until limp. Add remaining ingredients and heat thoroughly. Season with salt and pepper to taste. For variation, add 1 (16-ounce) can stewed tomatoes.

ANNA HAMBLEY
We, the Women of Hawaii Cookbook

JULIET'S MAHIMAHI CHOWDER

- 1 or 2 onions, chopped (there should be equal amounts of onion and potato)
- 2 to 3 tablespoons butter
- 1 large potato, diced
- 6 slices bacon, cut in pieces and fried until most of the fat can be poured off
- 6 to 8 ounces of mahimahi fillet, uncooked
- 1½ pints half & half or 1 cup cream and 2 cups milk
- 2 Saloon Pilot crackers
- Salt and pepper to taste

In a 3-quart sauce pan, simmer the onions gently in butter until they turn light gold, then add diced potatoes and ¼ cup water. Cover saucepan and cook gently until the potatoes are just about done. Add the bacon and stir.

Then lay the whole piece of mahimahi on top of the potatoes and onions and bacon. Check the water and add a very little if it seems to need it. Cover the pot and on low heat, steam the fish until it is cooked through and flakes easily.

Break it up into generous pieces. Then add the half & half which has been warmed. Heat carefully. It must not come to a boil.

Thicken with crumbled Saloon Pilots and serve with extra crackers and Tabasco sauce for those who like it.

The Kauai Museum Presents Early Kauai Hospitality: A Family Cookbook of Recipes 1920-1920

LOBSTER MISO SOUP

1 lobster (raw), cut into serving pieces
Miso paste
9 cups boiling water
½ cup cubed tofu
Green onions, chopped (for garnish)

Put lobster in boiling water and cook for 30 minutes. Add miso according to your own taste. Just before serving, add cubed tofu and garnish with chopped green onions.

ETTA HELM
"Cooking with Lovely Hula Hands,"
Moana's Hula Halau, Kaunakakai

FISH SINIGANG

1 pound white fish, cut into 3 to 4 pieces
3 cups water
2 stalks green onion or 1 medium round onion, sliced
1 small tomato, cut into wedges
1 (1-inch) ginger root, crushed
1 tablespoon lemon juice
1 cup watercress
2 tablespoons miso
3 tablespoons patis
Salt to taste

Clean and cut fish into four pieces. Combine fish, water, onion, tomatoes, ginger, and lemon juice. Bring to a boil and cook for 20 minutes.

Reduce heat, and add watercress, miso, patis, and salt. Cover and cook only until leaves are wilted. Do not overcook. Serve hot.

Hawaii's Aloha Recipes, *The Japanese Women's Society of Honolulu*

PORTUGUESE FISH SOUP
Sopa De Peixe

Makes 6 servings

1 (2-pound) whole fish
¼ cup salad oil
2 onions, minced
2½ quarts water
1 tomato, chopped
1 to 2 teaspoons salt
¼ cup rice
2 potatoes, cubed
3 cloves garlic, minced
3 tablespoons white wine
Lemon wedges

Scale and clean fish. In a large saucepan, heat 3 tablespoons of the oil. Sauté onion until transparent. Add the water, fish, tomato, and salt. Cover; bring to a boil. Lower heat to medium; cook for 30 minutes. Carefully remove fish from pan. Strain broth; return to pan. Bring broth to a boil; add rice and potatoes. Cover and cook for 30 minutes or until rice is done.

In a skillet, heat remaining 1 tablespoon oil; sauté garlic and pan-fry fish with wine. Discard skin and bones; shred fish. Add to broth; simmer for 20 minutes. Serve with lemon.

50th Anniversary Best of Our Favorite Recipes,
Maui Association for Family and Community Education

BURI DAIKON
Yellowtail and Daikon Soup

2 pieces hamachi kama (yellowtail collar)
1 daikon
6 cups water
1 piece konbu, wiped off
1 (4-ounce) katsuo bushi (dried shaved bonito) or ½ package dashinomoto
½-inch ginger, sliced into a few thin slices
2 cups sake
2 to 3 tablespoons sugar
½ cup shoyu
½ cup mirin
1 yuzu citron or other lemon or lime

Cut the hamachi kama into bite-sized pieces and place into a large bowl or pot. Boil a pot of water. When the water is boiling, pour it over the hamachi to blanch the outer surfaces. Then immediately transfer the hamachi to cold water and wash off any remaining blood or dirt. Peel the daikon and cut it into oblique pieces 1 to 2 inches large. Boil the daikon in a pot of water until tender.

To make Katsuo-Dashi (soup stock): In a pot, boil the 6 cups water with konbu. Discard konbu just before boiling. Add katsuo bushi, turn off heat, and rest for five minutes. Then strain out the katsuo bushi, reserving the soup and returning it to heat. Alternatively, instead of using katsuo bushi, sprinkle ½ packet of dashinomoto into the water (no need for straining). Add the hamachi, daikon, ginger, and sake to the Katsuo Dashi. Bring it almost to a boil, then simmer at below boiling point. Add the sugar, shoyu, and mirin. Simmer for about 20 minutes, to ensure that the daikon absorbs the flavor of the yellowtail. Serve with thin slivers of yuzu rind. If yuzu is not available, add a few teaspoons of lemon or lime juice to the pot of soup before serving.

Wisteria Delights, A Collection of Recipes
by Pearl City Hongwanji Mission

OZONI

New Year's Mochi Soup

Osumashi (basic clear soup)
1 package katsuo dashinomoto
5 cups water
1 tablespoon shoyu
1 teaspoon salt
¼ teaspoon ajinomoto

Horenso, spinach, mizuna, or shingiku
Small pieces of mochi
Kamaboko, sliced
1 small can hokkigai, cut into ½-inch pieces
Nori, toasted

Make Osumashi: Add dashinomoto to boiling water. Add shoyu, salt, and ajinomoto. Bring to a boil.

Boil greens in salted water, drain, and cut in 1½-inch lengths. Broil mochi until soft. Place mochi, greens, kamaboko, hokkigai, and toasted nori into soup bowls and pour soup over all.

Favorite Island Cookery, Book I, Honpa Hongwanji Hawaii Betsuin

BILL'S FAMOUS MAUI ONION SEAFOOD GUMBO

2 tablespoons olive oil
1 pound Portuguese sausage, diced
1 cup chopped Maui onions
½ cup chopped green pepper
½ cup chopped celery
3 tablespoons minced garlic
1 medium tomato, chopped
1 tablespoon cayenne pepper or Cajun spice
4 bay leaves
6 cups fish stock or fish broth
2 tablespoons chopped thyme, fresh if possible
1½ teaspoons salt
½ teaspoon ground pepper

2 cups chopped fresh or frozen okra
2 tablespoons oregano
2 tablespoons Worcestershire sauce
1 pound fish, cut in 1-inch pieces
1 pound shrimp or crabmeat
¼ cup roux*

In a large pot, heat oil and add sausage, onion, green pepper, and celery. Sauté. Add garlic, tomatoes, cayenne, and bay leaves and cook 5 minutes. Add fish stock or broth, thyme, salt, and pepper. Bring to boil. Reduce heat and simmer 25 minutes. Stir in okra and cook 10 minutes. Stir in oregano and Worcestershire sauce. Add fish, shrimp, and/or crabmeat and cook 2 to 3 minutes. Add roux to thicken. Serve in bowls over rice.

*To make roux, mix ¼ cup flour and ¼ cup oil. Brown on low heat until dark brown 15 to 30 minutes. Do not burn.

BECKY SWAN AND BILL AND CODY GILLETTE
Hanalei School Collective Cook Book

KOREAN GREEN ONION SOUP

Makes 2 servings

¼ cup dried shrimps
3½ cups water
Shoyu
Ajinomoto
Sesame seeds
3 eggs, beaten
½ cup chopped green onions

Wash dried shrimp and add to 3½ cups of water and make a stock. Keep the flame very low after it boils. Add shoyu, ajinomoto, sesame seeds, and scrambled eggs. Just before serving, add chopped green onions. Do not overcook.

Cook 'Em Up Kaua'i, The Kaua'i Historical Society Cookbook

MOLOKAI OGO SEAWEED SOUP

Makes 4 servings

½ cup shiitake mushroom
8 cups water
1 tablespoon dashi (shrimp base)
1 small round onion
3 cups limu ogo
1½ cups won bok (Chinese cabbage)
½ cup green onions
4 sprigs Chinese parsley
4 pieces shrimp, cooked or dried

Soak mushrooms in water and let stand till softened. Put water into a pot and add dashi. Cut up small onion, 1-inch long and add to soup base. Bring to a boil, then lower heat to maintain high temperature. Cut ogo, mushroom, and won bok into 1½-inch pieces and set aside. Cut green onions in ¼-inch pieces. Divide ogo, won bok, and mushroom into four bowls. Add soup broth and garnish with green onions, Chinese parsley and shrimp. Serve hot.

Haili Congregational Church, 175th Anniversary

SCALLOP SOUP

1 cup (¼ pound) dried scallops
9 cups water, divided use
½ pound lean pork, slivered
1 cup bamboo shoots, slivered
3 tablespoons cornstarch
½ cup water
3 eggs, beaten
1¼ teaspoons salt

Garnish
Chinese parsley
Slivers of ham

Rinse scallops and soak in 3 cups of water for 2 hours. Add pork and the remaining 6 cups of water. Bring to a boil and simmer for 1½ hours.

Stir until scallops break into fine shreds. Add bamboo shoots and simmer for 15 minutes.

Mix cornstarch and water to make smooth paste. Stir in eggs and salt. Continue cooking and stirring for 1 minute. Top with slivers of ham and parsley before serving.

Ono-Licious, Na Poe Humukuiki O Hawaii, Hawaii Quilt Guild

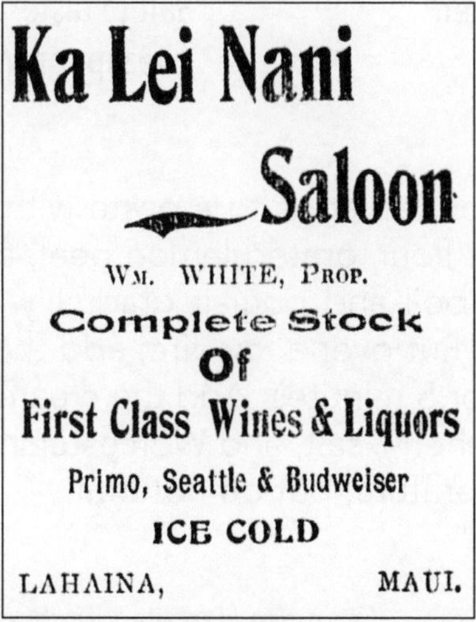

LEMON GRASS THAI SOUP

3 to 5 cups chicken stock
1 or 2 lemon grass stalks, crushed
½ pound straw mushrooms (canned or fresh)
½ pound fresh shrimp, deveined, with or without shells
2 tablespoons fish sauce
4 tablespoons lime juice
2 tablespoons chopped green onions
2 or more tablespoons Chinese parsley

Boil 3 to 5 cups chicken stock. Add lemon grass. Lower heat, then add straw mushrooms. Add the shrimp and fish sauce; simmer for 3 minutes. Later, add lime juice and top with green· onions and Chinese parsley. Serve.

SUESPEED HALL
Cooking with Honolulu Gardeners, Honolulu Community Recreational Garden Program

CRAB SOUP

2 hard-boiled eggs
1 tablespoon butter
1 tablespoon flour
1 lemon peel, grated
Pepper to taste
1 quart milk
½ to 1 pound crabmeat
½ cup cream
¾ cup sherry
Salt to taste
1 teaspoon Worcestershire sauce

Mash the hard-boiled eggs to a paste with a fork and add to them the butter, flour, grated lemon peel, and a little pepper. Bring milk to a boil and pour it gradually on the well-mixed pasted of eggs. Put over a low fire; add the crabmeat and allow to simmer for 5 minutes. Add the cream and bring to boiling again. Add sherry, salt, and Worcestershire sauce and heat to serving temperature, but do not boil.

ALICE J. DORSEY
From the Hawaiian Kitchens of the Molokai Lions

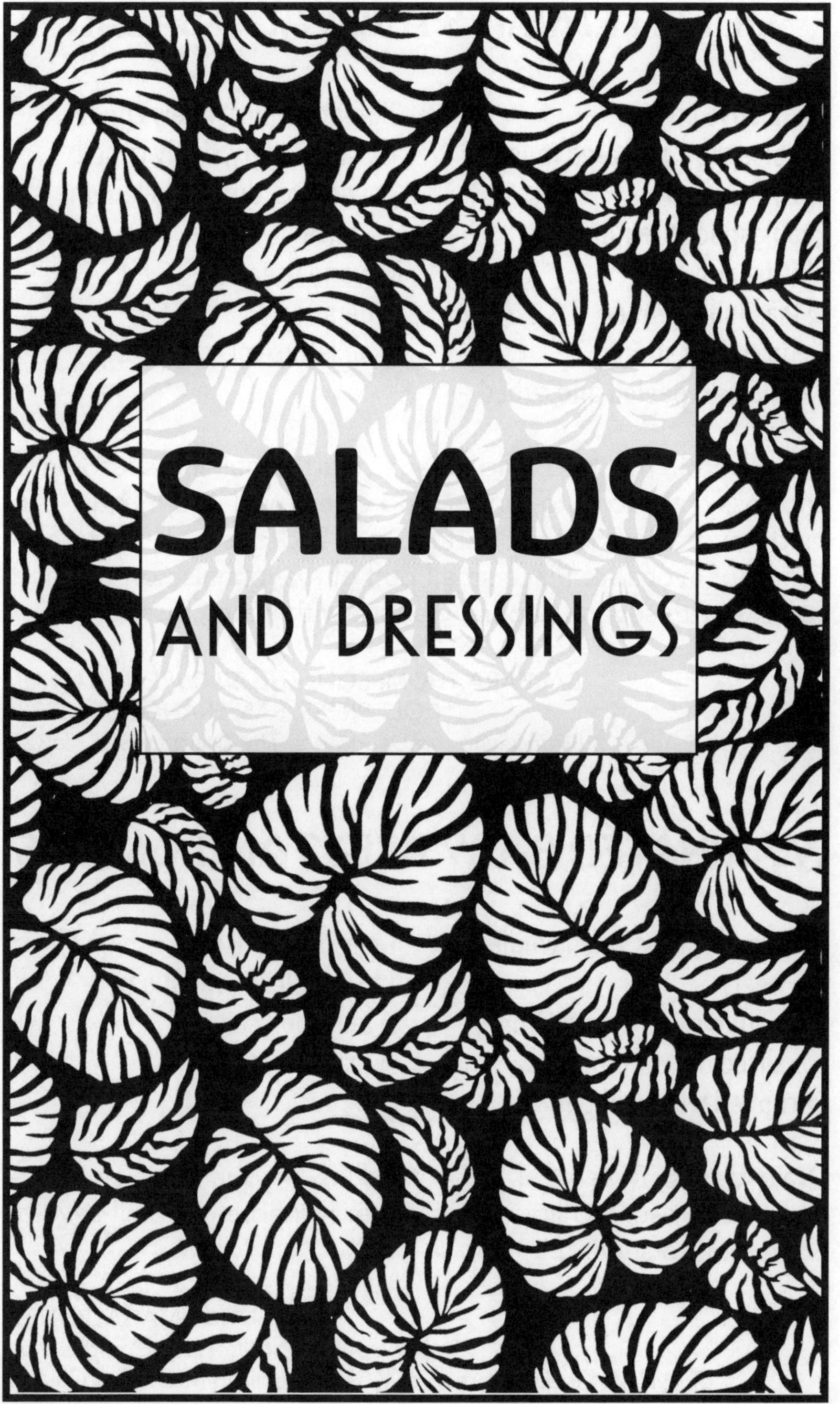

SALADS

AND DRESSINGS

QUEEN EMMA'S AVOCADO SALAD

1 cup olive oil
1 tablespoon prepared mustard
⅓ cup vinegar
2 tablespoons lemon juice
½ teaspoon salt
½ teaspoon pepper
1 cup crab or shrimp
2 tomatoes, peeled and cubed
2 green onions, finely cubed
1½ cups celery, finely cubed
3 avocados, dipped in lemon juice
Mayonnaise
Capers
Crisp lettuce or watercress

Mix olive oil, mustard, and vinegar; add remaining seasonings and toss crab, tomato, onion, and celery well into mixture. Arrange avocados on crisp lettuce leaf and pile crab mixture in center of avocado. Place small puff of mayonnaise on top and sprinkle with several capers. Garnish with watercress.

BARBARA THOMPSON, *THE EPICURE IN HAWAII*,
COLT PRESS, SAN FRANCISCO, 1938.
Dining with the Daughters, The Daughters of Hawaii

MARINATED BABY BEETS AND ONIONS

2 (1-pound) cans small whole beets
2 medium salad onions, thinly sliced or 1 (4-ounce) can
½ cup red wine vinegar
1 teaspoon dill seed
1 to 2 tablespoons sugar
½ teaspoon salt
¼ teaspoon pepper

Drain beets. Reserve 1 cup of liquid. In quart jar, combine beets and reserved liquid with other ingredients. Chill several hours before serving.

NOLA MAGALLONES
A Book of Favorite Recipes Compiled by United Methodist Women of Wahiawa United Methodist Church

BROCCOLI DELIGHT SALAD

4 cups broccoli, cut in pieces and blanched
¼ cup red round onions, diced
1 cup raisins
1 cup sunflower seeds
10 strips bacon, fried and crumbled

Dressing
4 tablespoons sugar
½ cup mayonnaise
1 tablespoon vinegar

Put broccoli, onions, raisins, seeds, and bacon in a bowl, then pour the dressing over. Toss and serve.

SCOTT LOPEZ
Food for the Body and Soul, West Kaua'i United Methodist Church

CUCUMBER NAMASU

Makes 3 to 4 servings

1 cucumber
2 stalks celery
¼ teaspoon salt

Vinegar Sauce
1½ tablespoons sugar
½ teaspoon salt
¼ cup vinegar
½ teaspoon MSG

2 radishes, for garnish

Cut cucumber in half lengthwise. Slice cucumber and celery in thin diagonal pieces. Sprinkle with salt. Let stand 10 minutes; rinse salt off, drain, then squeeze out excess water. Combine ingredients for vinegar sauce; pour over vegetables and mix. Garnish with thinly sliced radishes.

The Heritage of Hawaii Cookbook, Honolulu Gas Company, Ltd.

CORN SALAD

2 (16-ounce) cans whole kernel corn, drained
1 unpeeled cucumber, diced
1 tomato, diced
1 small onion, diced
½ teaspoon dried celery seed
½ teaspoon dry ground mustard

Dressing
1 cup mayonnaise
½ cup (scant) sour cream
2 tablespoons vinegar
Salt and pepper to taste

Combine drained corn kernels, diced vegetables, celery seed, and dry mustard. Toss well.

Make dressing. Combine mayonnaise, sour cream, and vinegar. Add to vegetables and toss. Season with salt and pepper. Chill for a few hours before serving.

Hilo Missionary Cooks

MAKE AHEAD CRUNCHY PEA SALAD

Makes 4 servings

⅓ cup mayonnaise
1 tablespoon Dijon mustard
½ teaspoon garlic salt
¼ teaspoon pepper
16 ounces peas, frozen, thawed and drained
2 eggs, hard-boiled and chopped
1 (8-ounce) can water chestnuts, sliced and drained
½ cup sliced celery
½ cup grated carrots

Mix first 4 ingredients. Stir gently into remaining ingredients. Chill 24 hours

Parks & Recreation Family Favorites

SPINACH SALAD WITH TOFU DRESSING

Dressing

4 ounces firm tofu, drained
¼ cup red wine vinegar
3 tablespoons vegetable oil
1 tablespoon sugar
1 tablespoon soy sauce
1 tablespoon sesame oil
1 tablespoon chili oil
1 teaspoon minced garlic

1 pound spinach, washed, stems removed and leaves torn into bite-sized pieces
5 strips bacon, crisp cooked, drained and crumbled
4 fresh shiitake mushrooms, thinly sliced
¼ cup sliced almonds, toasted

Place tofu in a blender. Add remaining dressing ingredients and process until smooth and creamy. Place spinach, bacon, mushrooms, and almonds in a salad bowl. Pour dressing over salad and toss until spinach is evenly coated. Serve immediately.

BARB WALLS
100 Years Sharing God's Love, United Community Church

FIRE AND ICE TOMATOES

4 large tomatoes
1 large green pepper
2 medium Maui onions
¾ cup white vinegar
1½ teaspoons celery salt
½ teaspoon salt
⅛ teaspoon cayenne
1½ teaspoons mustard seed
4½ teaspoons sugar
⅛ teaspoon black pepper
¼ cup water

Pare and quarter tomatoes. Slice green pepper into strips. Slice onions and separate into rings. Put vegetables into a bowl. In a saucepan combine vinegar, seasonings, and water. Bring to a boil and boil hard for one minute. Pour over vegetables and chill.

MIA KAJIYAMA
The Hele Mai, Ai (Come Eat) Cookbook, Flavors of Upcountry Maui

GREEK-STYLE SALAD

Makes 6 servings

3 tomatoes, cut into wedges
1 medium zucchini, cut into julienne strips
1 cucumber, sliced
1 red onion, cut into rings
1 cup pitted olives
½ pound feta cheese, cubed
1 (6-ounce) jar marinated artichoke hearts (undrained)
¼ cup red wine vinegar
Freshly ground pepper

In a large bowl, combine tomatoes, zucchini, cucumber, and onion rings. Add olives and feta cheese. Top with artichoke hearts. Pour vinegar over salad; sprinkle with pepper and toss well. Chill several hours, tossing occasionally.

50th Anniversary Best of Our Favorite Recipes, Maui Association for Family and Community Education

WON BOK SALAD

1 head won bok (Chinese cabbage), shredded
1 bunch green onions, chopped
2 tablespoons toasted sesame seeds
½ cup slivered almonds
1 package saimin (oriental flavor), break noodles into bite-size pieces
1 small package chow mein noodles

Dressing

3 tablespoons red wine vinegar
½ cup oil
1 package seasoning from saimin
2 tablespoons sugar
Salt to taste

Place won bok and green onions in large salad bowl. Add sesame seeds, almonds, saimin, and chow mein noodles. Combine Dressing ingredients and mix well. Just prior to serving, toss everything together with dressing. Cool, light, and delicious.

Hilo Missionary Cooks

HŌ‘I‘O FERN SHOOTS SALAD

1 bunch hō‘i‘o fern shoots
3 round onions
6 tomatoes
1 package dried shrimp
1 cup vegetable oil
2½ cups soy sauce
Dash pepper
Splash of patis to taste

Blanch fern shoots, chop into bite-size pieces. Drain and chop rest of ingredients. Add all ingredients together and toss well. Serve with white rice or poi.

KAWAILEHUA AHLOO, KAIULANI KAPUUAU
Hanalei School Collective Cook Book

BEAN SPROUT SALAD

Suk Chu Namul

Makes 6 servings

1 pound fresh bean sprouts
1 teaspoon salt
2 cups boiling water
1½ tablespoons finely chopped green onion
½ teaspoon sugar
1 tablespoon sesame or salad oil
1 tablespoon sesame seeds, toasted and ground
3 tablespoons shoyu
⅛ teaspoon finely chopped garlic
1/16 teaspoon cayenne

Clean bean sprouts and wash in cold water. Cook in salted, boiling water for 2 minutes and drain thoroughly. Add seasonings and mix well.

The Heritage of Hawaii Cookbook, Honolulu Gas Company, Ltd.

TERIYAKI TOFU-BEAN SALAD

Makes 4 to 5 servings

1 (16-ounce) package tofu, cubed
1 (15-ounce) can garbanzo beans, drained
2 cups sliced fresh mushrooms
⅓ cup sliced green onion
1 small green pepper, cut into bite-size pieces
1 small tomato, seeded and chopped
¼ cup snipped parsley
1 clove garlic, minced
¼ cup red wine vinegar
¼ cup olive or salad oil
2 teaspoons Dijon mustard
½ cup soy sauce, more or less to taste, depending on type of soy sauce
½ teaspoon ground ginger
½ teaspoon salt
Leaf lettuce
Sesame seeds (optional)

In a large bowl, combine tofu, garbanzo beans, mushrooms, green onion, green pepper, tomato, and parsley. Set aside.

In screw-top jar, combine garlic, wine vinegar, oil, mustard, soy sauce, ginger, and salt. Shake well. Pour over salad; toss.

Cover and chill several hours or overnight. To serve, use a slotted spoon to arrange mixture atop lettuce. Sprinkle with sesame seeds if desired.

50th Anniversary Best of Our Favorite Recipes,
Maui Association for Family and Community Education

CURRIED RICE SALAD WITH TOFU

Makes 6 servings

18 ounces tofu, pressed and broken into very small pieces; use 21-ounce tub
2½ cups cooked brown rice, chilled
3 tablespoons minced green onion or leek
2 tablespoons minced parsley

4 lettuce leaves
1 tomato, cut into wedges
2 green peppers, 1 slivered and 1 cut into rings

Dressing
6 tablespoons oil
⅓ cup rice vinegar
1 tablespoon lemon juice
1 teaspoon curry powder
¼ teaspoon (7-spice) red pepper
1 clove garlic, crushed
¾ teaspoon salt
Dash of pepper

Combine the first four ingredients with the slivered green pepper. Add dressing; mix lightly, and for best flavor, allow to stand for several hours.

Serve mounded on lettuce leaves in a large bowl; garnish with tomato wedges and green pepper rings.

The Hawai'i Youth Opera Chorus, Nā Mea 'Ai Punahele

TARO AND TOFU SALAD

Makes 4 servings

2 cups cooked and cubed taro
¼ cup finely grated carrot
¼ cup thinly sliced celery
¼ cup diced bell pepper
1 cup cubed firm tofu
2 tablespoons sesame seeds, toasted
½ cup mayonnaise
¼ cup sour cream
1 teaspoon salt
½ teaspoon pepper

Mix taro with vegetables and tofu. Add rest of ingredients to taro-vegetable mixture; mix well. Chill.

Favorite Island Cookery, Book IV, Honpa Hongwanji Hawaii Betsuin

KIM'S CABBAGE SLAW

Makes 8 servings

1 small tart green apple, cored and diced
¼ cup rice vinegar
1 small onion, thinly sliced
½ cup mayonnaise
¼ cup drained pickled, slivered ginger
1 tablespoon sugar
1 to 2 teaspoons caraway seed
½ teaspoon pepper
8 cups shredded napa cabbage
Thin apple slices, dipped in rice vinegar (optional)

In a large bowl, mix diced apple, rice vinegar, onion, mayonnaise, ginger, sugar, caraway seed (to taste), and pepper. Add cabbage and mix well. Pour into serving dish.

Garnish with apple slices if desired. Serve or cover and chill up to 4 hours.

Our Daily Bread Centennial Cookbook, Iao Congregational Church

SPAM® AND POTATO SALAD

3 pounds steamed potatoes
String beans (amount to your desire)
1 or 2 cans Spam®
6 hard-boiled eggs
1 cup chopped celery
1 medium round onion, chopped
1 cup packed shredded cabbage
1 cup grated carrots
1 pint mayonnaise
Salt and pepper to taste

Peel and slice potatoes in halves and steam for 20 minutes. Place washed and cleaned string beans in same steamer. When beans are just about done, add the Spam®, sliced in halves, above the beans. Turn heat of and let cool off.

While the potatoes, etc. are being steamed, prepare the rest of the vegetables. Combine all chopped veggies and eggs in a bowl; add sliced beans. Add mayonnaise and seasoning, then add cubed potatoes and Spam®, saving some Spam® for garnish.

GLADYS LAI
50th Anniversary Best of Our Favorite Recipes, Maui Association for Family and Community Education

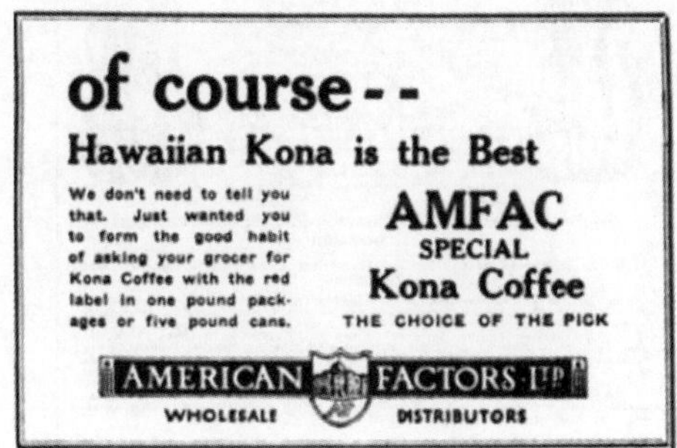

HOT GERMAN POTATO SALAD

2 pounds potatoes
1 pound regular yellow onions
1 pound thick sliced bacon
½ cup vinegar
Salt
Pepper
Chopped parsley

Boil potatoes, let cool, peel, slice into ¼-Inch slices and put aside. Chop onions. Cut up bacon in small pieces and fry till crisp. Drain bacon and put on paper towel. In bacon grease, simmer onions till glassy.

While simmering add vinegar, salt, and pepper. Mix with potatoes, leave room temperature. Before serving, mix in bacon pieces, put in serving dish and sprinkle parsley on top.

BEV & JUERGEN WILL
"No Ka Oi" The Best of Hawaii,
Favorite Recipes from Rotarians of District 5000

PURPLE POTATO SALAD

Makes 6 servings

This recipe won first-place blue ribbon at the Kaua'i Country Fair.

- 1½ pounds Okinawan sweet potatoes
- 2 eggs, hard-boiled and shelled
- 2 stalks celery, diced
- 1 small cucumber, peeled, seeded and diced
- 4 green onions, sliced diagonally
- ¼ cup diced sweet or dill pickles
- ½ each small red and yellow bell peppers, diced

Dressing

- ½ cup plain nonfat yogurt
- ¼ cup low-fat sour cream
- ¼ cup low-fat mayonnaise
- 1 tablespoon Dijon mustard
- Salt and pepper to taste
- ¼ cup chopped parsley

Boil purple potatoes in their skins until just barely tender, about 15 minutes (pierce center with wooden skewer to test). Plunge into cold water to stop cooking. When cool, peel and cut into large dice and put in a large bowl. Coarsely chop eggs and add to potatoes, along with celery, cumber, onions, pickles, and peppers.

Mix dressing ingredients in smaller bowl and pour over vegetables. Mix gently to coat potatoes. Serve at room temperature or chilled. Store in refrigerator.

GINI STODDARD
Island Flavors, Favorite Recipes of the Historic Hawai'i Foundation

ʻULU SALAD

Makes 4 to 6 servings

This salad is better the second day.

1 ʻulu (green and firm)
Italian dressing (bottled or homemade)
6 hard-boiled eggs, chopped
3 stalks celery, chopped fine
1 whole onion, chopped
½ cup chopped green olives or dill pickles
Mayonnaise to taste
1 teaspoon yellow mustard or to taste
Salt and pepper to taste

Boil ʻulu until tender. Peel and dice into cubes. Toss cubes with small amount of dressing, just enough to coat. Let cubes set for 1 hour. Toss with remaining ingredients and chill.

COILA EADE
Hana Maui Recipes from Then to Now

LEMON CHICKEN SALAD

½ cup salad dressing
2 teaspoons dried basil
1 teaspoon grated lemon peel
1 tablespoon lemon Juice
2 cups chopped chicken or turkey
1 cup halved red or green grapes
½ cup halved Chinese pea pods
½ cup thinly sliced red onion

Mix salad dressing, basil, lemon peel and lemon juice. Add chicken, grapes, pea pods, and onion. Refrigerate and serve on lettuce-lined platter.

JEAN HOES
100 Years Sharing God's Love, United Community Church

CHINESE CHICKEN SALAD

2 heads iceberg lettuce
¼ head won bok
2 to 3 cups shredded cooked chicken
1 to 2 stalks celery, sliced
1 package won ton chips
1 bottle unsalted peanuts

Dressing
1 cup oil
⅓ cup lemon juice
¼ cup white vinegar
⅔ cup sugar
¼ cup minced onions
1 clove garlic, minced
1 teaspoon dry mustard
2 to 3 tablespoons mayonnaise

Shred lettuce and won bok in large bowl. Add shredded chicken and celery. Crush won ton chips in package and sprinkle over chicken before serving.

Prepare dressing using a blender. Add oil, lemon juice, vinegar, and sugar. Blend well, making sure the sugar has blended with the other ingredients. Add onion, garlic, and mustard. Blend well. Add mayonnaise; blend. Just before serving, pour dressing over salad, then add peanuts. Toss and serve.

PATTI NAKAMOTO
"Pig Out" with Liholiho's Caring, Competent, Creative Cooks

CURRY CHICKEN SALAD

Makes 8 servings

The wonderful flavors in this salad need time to fully blend, so make it a day ahead.

2 cups mayonnaise
2 tablespoons lemon juice
2¼ tablespoons Chinese soy sauce
1 rounded tablespoon curry powder
1 tablespoon onion juice
1 tablespoon chopped chutney
3 cups diced white meat of chicken or turkey
1½ cups chopped celery
1 (6-ounce) can water chestnuts, drained and sliced
2 cups seedless white grapes
1 (1-pound) can pineapple chunks, well-drained
¼ cup slivered almonds, toasted

Combine mayonnaise, lemon juice, soy sauce, curry powder, onion juice, and chutney. Toss with remaining ingredients except almonds. Refrigerate overnight.

Sprinkle with almonds. Preparation time is 30 minutes.

North Kohala Favorites

THAI BEEF SALAD

Makes 6 servings

1 pound cooked roast beef
¼ ounce long rice
1 round onion, thinly sliced
1 cucumber, thinly sliced
1 stalk fresh lemon grass
¼ cup lime juice
2 tablespoons fish sauce
1 small red chili pepper, seeded and chopped
6 mint leaves
6 sprigs Chinese parsley, chopped

Slice roast beef into thin 2-inch strips. Soak long rice in warm water for 15 minutes. Drain long rice and cut into 3-inch lengths.

In a large bowl, combine roast beef, long rice, onion, cucumber, lemon grass, lime juice, fish sauce, red chili peppers, and mint leaves. Toss to mix well. Serve chilled or near room temperature.

ALLISON MA
1988 4-H Local & Ethnic Food Show

JOSEPH'S 'ONO TACO SALAD

Makes 10 servings

1 head lettuce (bite-size cut)
2 large tomatoes (cut fine)
1 avocado (optional, cut fine)
1½ cups cheddar cheese (grated)
½ bag regular-size Fritos
1 cup ripe olives (chopped)
1 bunch green onions (chopped)
1 pound ground beef (cooked, drained and chilled)

Sauce

⅓ cup mayonnaise
⅓ cup sour cream
3 tablespoons taco sauce

Place all ingredients in large bowl and toss with sauce. Serve immediately. If waiting to serve, keep all ingredients separate until ready to serve.

JOSEPH ZUKIN ALISA
1988 4-H Local & Ethnic Food Show

SALMON TOFU SALAD

1 block tofu, cubed and drained
1 bunch cut up watercress
2 tomatoes, diced
1 round onion, diced
1 package bean sprouts
1 can salmon or tuna

Sauce

½ cup canola oil
Minced garlic to your taste (optional)
⅔ cup minced green onions
½ cup shoyu

Garnish

Kamaboko, char siu pork, chicken (optional)

In 9 x 13-inch pan, place tofu on the bottom. Add watercress, tomatoes, onion, bean sprouts, and salmon or tuna.

To make Sauce, heat oil and garlic. When warm, add onions and shoyu.

Pour sauce over tofu and salmon mix before serving.

FLORENCE LANGAMAN
Food for the Body and Soul, West Kaua'i United Methodist Church

CRAB LONG RICE NAMASU

2 bundles long rice
1 egg
1 cucumber
2 slices boiled ham
2 head cabbage leaves
1 green onion, chopped
1 (7¾-ounce) can crab, flaked

Sauce
⅓ cup Japanese vinegar
½ cup sugar
2 tablespoons shoyu
1 teaspoon ginger, sliced thin in strips
2 tablespoons sesame oil
1 teaspoon ajinomoto

Cook long rice and cut. Fry egg in thin layer. Cut cucumber, egg, ham, and cabbage into thin strips; add long rice together with green onion and crab. Combine ingredients for sauce and pour over mixture. Serve cold.

Favorite Island Cookery, Book I, Honpa Hongwanji Hawaii Betsuin

FURIKAKE LINGUINE

1 package linguine
½ bottle (nori) furikake
1 tub taegu
1 cucumber, cut into strips
1 tomato, diced
½ bottle Tropics oriental dressing
½ stick kamaboko
1 package imitation crab

Boil linguine and cool. Add all other ingredients to linguine and mix. Refrigerate.

JORDAN
Ka'u Hospital Auxiliary, One More Time

POISSON CRU

Tahitian Fish Salad

2 pounds fresh fish (white-fleshed or 'ahi)
1 cup fresh lime juice
½ onion, diced
2 teaspoons salt
3 tomatoes, chopped
½ cup sliced scallions
¾ cup chopped green pepper
2 eggs, hard-boiled and chopped (optional)
1 cup coconut milk

Cut the fish in 1-inch cubes. In a non-metallic bowl, combine fish with lime juice, onion, and salt. Cover and marinate in refrigerator 2 to 4 hours, turning once or twice. Lime juice will "cook" the fish.

When ready to serve, drain the marinated fish and add the rest of the ingredients, blending gently. Serve cold as first course or for lunch.

MARCIE CARROLL
Island Flavors, Favorite Recipes of the Historic Hawai'i Foundation

CODFISH SALAD ALA PORTUGUESE

1 package dried codfish
1 onion
Tomato wedges
Avocado (optional)
Salad oil
Shoyu
Aji

Boil codfish until soft, changing water at least twice to extract most of the salty taste. Meantime, cut onions, tomatoes, and avocado in slices and put in bowl.

When codfish is soft, empty hot water and fill pot with cool water and shred fish. Add drained codfish to garnishes, adding oil and shoyu to taste. Add a dash of aji and toss.

JUDITH NOVIT
The Kahikolu Country Cookbook

PINEAPPLE AND LOBSTER SALAD

Meat of 1 lobster
½ cup celery
½ cup diced pineapple
¼ cup chopped almonds
Mayonnaise

Plunge lobster into rapidly boiling water and boil for 20 minutes. Remove meat from shell, cut into small pieces, and mix with celery, pineapple, almonds, and enough mayonnaise to moisten. Salad may be served in lobster shell and garnished with mayonnaise.

MRS. F.J. HARLOCKER
The Hilo Woman's Club Cookbook

SHRIMP AND SPINACH SLAW

4 cups finely shredded green cabbage
3 cups thinly sliced spinach leaves
1 medium cucumber, peeled and thinly sliced
2 medium celery stalks, thinly sliced
Yogurt Lemon Dressing (recipe below)
¾ to 1 pound shelled cooked tiny shrimp
Lemon wedges
Salt and pepper
About 12 large spinach leaves, crisped (optional)

In a large bowl, combine cabbage, slivered spinach, cucumber, and celery. If made ahead, cover and chill up until the next day. Add dressing to salad and mix well. Either garnish salad with spinach leaves, or arrange leaves on rim of a platter and mound salad in the center. Sprinkle shrimp onto slaw and add to taste, juice from lemon wedges and salt and pepper.

Yogurt Lemon Dressing

⅔ cup unflavored nonfat yogurt
3 tablespoons reduced calorie or regular mayonnaise
½ cup thinly sliced green onion
1 teaspoon grated lemon peel
2 tablespoons lemon juice
1 tablespoon sugar

Stir ingredients together and blend well. If made ahead, cover and chill up until next day.

100 Years Sharing God's Love, United Community Church

THAI MARINATED SHRIMP SALAD

2 cups sweet chili sauce
¼ cup rice vinegar
1 tablespoon chopped garlic
2 tablespoons grated ginger
2 tablespoon chopped cilantro
1 pound peeled and deveined shrimp
4 bunches watercress, blanched
½ pound bean sprouts, blanched
½ pound shredded carrots

Combine sweet chili sauce, vinegar, garlic, ginger, and cilantro. Divide in half. Marinate shrimp overnight. Grill shrimp until almost fully cooked or roast in oven. Cook and combine with remaining vegetables. Toss with remaining marinade.

ANTHONY C. VEA
Food for the Body and Soul, West Kaua'i United Methodist Church

OCEAN SOMEN SALAD

1 package somen
½ to ¾ pound ocean salad
1 medium carrot, grated
½ to ¾ block kamaboko, thinly sliced
Chopped lettuce (optional)
Celery (optional)

Dressing
2 tablespoons sugar
3 tablespoons Japanese vinegar
3 to 4 tablespoons vegetable oil
½ teaspoon salt

Cook somen according to instructions on package. Rinse under cold water. Drain thoroughly. Mix noodles with ocean salad, carrots, and dressing. Garnish with kamaboko, lettuce, celery, and more grated carrots for an appetizing appearance. May substitute Memmi Shoyu (noodle soup base) for dressing.

JANE NAKAMA
Our Daily Bread Centennial Cookbook, Iao Congregational Church

SEAWEED SOBA SALAD

½ cup hijiki
1 (25-ounce) package wakame
2 packages soba, cooked according to package
½ Maui onion, sliced thin
4 ounces kaiware
1 bunch watercress (1-inch pieces)

Sauce
6 tablespoons salad oil
6 tablespoons shoyu
2 tablespoons sugar
3 tablespoons lemon juice

Soak hijiki in warm water for 20 minutes and drain. Soak wakame in water for 15 minutes; drain and cut.

Break soba in half before boiling.

Toss squeezed hijiki in skillet with 1 tablespoon oil, 1 tablespoon shoyu, and 1 tablespoon sugar until juice is dissolved; cool.

Place soba in bottom of dish. Arrange other ingredients In layers: hijiki, onion, wakame, kaiware, and watercress. Refrigerate until ready to serve. Just before serving, pour sauce over and enjoy!

100 Years Sharing God's Love, United Community Church

24 HOUR SALAD

Makes 12 servings

1 head lettuce
½ cup chopped green onion
1 cup thinly sliced celery
1 (8-ounce) can water chestnuts, sliced
1 (10-ounce) package frozen peas
2 cups mayonnaise
2 teaspoons sugar
½ cup grated Parmesan cheese
1 teaspoon seasoned salt
¼ teaspoon garlic powder
½ pound bacon
3 hard-boiled eggs, chopped
2 medium tomatoes, quartered

In a salad bowl, place lettuce, onions, celery, water chestnuts, and frozen peas in layers. Spread mayonnaise evenly over the top of the vegetables. Combine the sugar, cheese, seasoned salt, and garlic powder, then sprinkle over mayonnaise. Cover and place in the refrigerator for 24 hours. Fry bacon until crisp, then crumble. Just before serving, sprinkle salad with eggs and bacon, then arrange tomatoes around salad.

NOTE: Bac-Os may substitute for bacon. You may use 1 package alfalfa sprouts, also.

AIKO ECKERD
Haleiwa Elementary School 115th Birthday

LONG RICE SALAD

Makes 6 servings

3 (1 7/8-ounce) package long rice
1 egg, beaten
1 cucumber
2 green onions
¼ pound thinly sliced ham
1 cup shredded cabbage
½ pound imitation crab legs, shredded
⅓ cup vinegar
⅓ cup sugar
2 tablespoons soy sauce
1 teaspoon ginger juice
2 teaspoons sesame oil

Cook long rice in salted boiling water until tender, about 10 to 15 minutes. Drain and rinse with cold water, cut into 3-inch lengths.

Fry egg in a thin sheet. Cut cucumber in half lengthwise; remove seeds. Cut egg, cucumber, onions, and ham into thin strips; mix with long rice. Stir in cabbage and crab. Combine remaining ingredients and pour over mixture, tossing gently.

North Kohala Favorites

VIETNAMESE-STYLE SOMEN SALAD

Dressing
1½ cups sugar
1 teaspoon salt
1 teaspoon chili sauce (optional)
½ cup vinegar
¼ cup water

1 package somen noodles, broken in halves and cooked
1 small Mānoa lettuce, chopped in 1-inch pieces
1 small cucumber, cut into matchsticks
¼ cup chopped chives, cut in 1-inch pieces
¼ cup chopped mint, cut in ¼-inch pieces
1 medium Chinese parsley plant, cut in ¼-inch pieces
¼ cup minced green onions
¼ cup chopped sweet basil leaves, cut in ¼-inch pieces
1 cup bean sprouts, cut in halves

Garnish
¼ cup ground peanuts
2 to 3 tablespoons shredded daikon
6 fried spring rolls, cut in halves (optional)
2 to 3 tablespoons shredded carrot
1 tablespoon crisp fried garlic or shallot flakes (optional)
½ cup sliced barbecue beef or pork (optional)

Cook Dressing ingredients until dissolved. Cool. Add 2 to 4 tablespoons Thai or Vietnamese shrimp or fish sauce to taste. Set aside.

Combine salad ingredients in a bowl (not Garnishes).

Toss salad with about ½ cooled dressing. Keep rest for next time. Garnish and serve.

KIM KAYODA
Cooking with Honolulu Gardeners,
Honolulu Community Recreational Garden Program

RAMEN SALAD

½ head cabbage
3 chicken breasts, cooked and shredded
1 package chicken ramen
3 tablespoons slivered almonds or unsalted peanuts
2 green onions, chopped
3 tablespoons sesame seeds, toasted

Dressing
2 tablespoons sugar
½ cup oil
3 tablespoons vinegar
1 teaspoon wine vinegar (optional)
1 flavor packet from ramen

Combine cabbage and chicken. Add ramen, nuts, green onions, sesame seeds, and dressing. Toss and serve.

North Kohala Favorites

MACARONI SALAD

1 cup uncooked macaroni (cook it)
2 hard-cooked eggs, chopped

Dressing
⅓ cup mayonnaise
1 tablespoon prepared mustard
1 tablespoon lemon juice
1½ cups sliced celery
2 tablespoons finely cut parsley
⅓ cup pickle relish, drained
⅓ cup chopped onion
2 tablespoons chopped pimiento

Mix dressing with macaroni and eggs and chill. (This is super).

DOROTHY TUTTLE
We, the Women of Hawaii Cookbook

CRUNCHY FRUIT SALAD

Makes 8 servings

2 (3-ounce) cans chow mein noodles
2 quarts assorted fresh fruit chunks and/or slices
½ cup Passion Fruit French Dressing

Put noodles on a platter. Arrange fruit on noodles. Before serving, pour dressing over fruit.

Passion Fruit French Dressing

Makes 1½ cups

1 (6-ounce) can frozen passion fruit juice, thawed
¾ cup salad oil
1 clove garlic
1 teaspoon paprika
½ teaspoon salt
½ teaspoon celery seed

Put all ingredients into blender. Cover and blend well.

50th Anniversary Best of Our Favorite Recipes, Maui Association for Family and Community Education

HAWAIIAN WALDORF SALAD

10 apples, diced
2 fresh pineapple, diced
1 (1-pound) can mandarin orange
1 pound fresh grapes
1 quart mayonnaise
½ quart whipped cream
1 pound celery, diced
½ cup coconut syrup (optional)
Juice from 2 lemons

Combine all ingredients and toss. Serve chilled.

ABELINA L. PABLO
Food for the Body and Soul, West Kaua'i United Methodist Church

RAZZLE DAZZLE FRUIT SALAD

4 apples, skinned and diced
2 cans fruit cocktail
1 (3-ounce) box wild strawberry Jell-O
1 (8-ounce) block cream cheese
2 (16-ounce) tubs Cool Whip
1 can mandarin oranges, drained
Frozen strawberries
Slivered almonds (optional)

Toss apples in syrup from fruit cocktail to prevent browning. Cream Jell-O powder with cream cheese. Fold in Cool Whip, followed by strained fruit. Chill until ready to serve. Garnish with almonds.

EMMA SMITH
Ka'u Hospital Auxiliary, One More Time

MANGO AND BEET SALAD

4 medium fresh beets
½ cup red onion, chopped, or green onions with leaves, chopped
Mango Vinaigrette Dressing (see below)
Beet leaves, chopped
1 bunch watercress, chopped
2 ripe mangoes, peeled and sliced

Cook the beets in boiling water for 30 minutes (or in microwave) or until tender; drain. When cool enough to handle, peel and chop into small cubes. In a bowl, toss the beets with the onions and 3 tablespoons of the vinaigrette. Set aside.

On a medium-sized serving platter, arrange chopped beet leaves around outer edge. Place chopped watercress in the center and spoon the beets and onions over it. Arrange mango strips decoratively in a ring around the beets. Serve remaining vinaigrette in a separate bowl with the salad.

Mango Vinaigrette Dressing

¼ cup cider vinegar
½ teaspoon curry powder
1 peeled and chopped fresh mango
1 tablespoon honey mustard
1 tablespoon fresh lime juice
Pinch Hawaiian salt
Dash cayenne pepper

Combine ingredients in food processor or blender and blend until smooth.

DION-MAGRIT COSCHIGANO
Island Flavors, Favorite Recipes of the Historic Hawai'i Foundation

LYCHEE FRUIT SALAD

Makes 6 servings

1 cup fresh lychee or canned, seeded
1 cup diced papaya
2 medium mangoes cut into slices
1 cup fresh figs, peeled & cubed
1 cup yogurt
1 teaspoon grated ginger root
1 tablespoon lemon juice
Chopped macadamia nuts

Place fruit in bowl or on individual salad plates lined with lettuce. Mix yogurt, ginger, and lemon juice. Pour dressing over salad just before serving. Sprinkle with macadamia nuts.

Ono-Licious, Na Poe Humukuiki O Hawaii, Hawaii Quilt Guild

THAI PINEAPPLE SALAD

Makes 6 servings

1/3 cup vegetable oil
2 tablespoons lemon juice
1 tablespoon soy sauce
1 to 2 teaspoons packed brown sugar
½ small pineapple, diced
2 small oranges, diced
1 small apple, diced
1 small bunch romaine, shredded
3 stalks green onions, chopped

Shake oil, lemon juice, soy sauce, and brown sugar in a tightly covered jar. Toss pineapple, oranges, and apple with dressing. Place shredded romaine in shallow bowl and mound fruit mixture in center. Garnish with chopped green onions.

ERINN MORISHITA
1988 4-H Local & Ethnic Food Show

GREEN PAPAYA SALAD

Makes 4 servings

1 clove garlic, minced
1 small red chili pepper, seeded and minced
1 tomato, thinly sliced
3 cups shredded green papaya
2 tablespoons fish sauce
2 tablespoons lime juice
8 Mānoa lettuce leaves
1 lime, cut into 8 wedges
2 large red chili peppers, thinly sliced

In a mortar, grind together minced garlic and minced chili pepper. In a bowl, mix together tomato and green papaya. Add fish sauce, lime juice, and garlic mixture. Toss lightly. Divide papaya mixture into 8 portions. Place a portion on a lettuce leaf, garnish with lime wedge and sliced chili peppers.

THOMAS CHUNG
1988 4-H Local & Ethnic Food Show

AVOCADO DRESSING

½ blender full of avocado
½ cup water
Dried onions as desired
4 cloves finely grated garlic
½ teaspoon lemon pepper
½ teaspoon sea salt
¼ cup lemon juice if meal has no dry carbohydrates

Leave the lemon juice out if serving cooked starches with the salad such as rice bread or potatoes. Avocado Dressing with no acid is a good alternative to regular salad dressings because of the lack of acid, making it more compatible with cooked foods.

Hanalei School Collective Cook Book

LEMON BLUE CHEESE DRESSING

Makes 5 cups

10 ounces blue cheese
2 cups salad oil
1 tablespoon grated lemon peel
½ cup lemon juice
2½ cups dairy sour cream
1 clove garlic, minced
2 teaspoons seasoned salt

Mash the blue cheese and blend in the oil, beating until smooth. Add the remaining ingredients and mix well. Cover and chill for several hours so flavors may blend. Bring to room temperature before tossing with salad.

Favorite Island Cookery, Book II, Honpa Hongwanji Buddhist Temple

BUTTERMILK DRESSING MIX

Makes 1 cup

1 cup nonfat dry milk
¼ cup sugar
4 teaspoons crushed dried basil
4 teaspoons instant minced onion
2 teaspoons dry mustard
1 teaspoon garlic powder
1 teaspoon salt
1 teaspoon lemon juice

Combine all ingredients. Store in airtight container.

To make 1½ cups dressing: Combine ¼ cup dressing mix with ½ cup cold water. Blend in ¾ cup mayonnaise or salad dressing. Shake well before serving.

A Lei of Recipes,
Kauai Association for Family and Community Education

"PERKINS" CAESAR DRESSING

1 tube anchovy paste
6 strips bacon, crisped
Juice from 1 lemon
1 tablespoon oregano, crumbled
1 egg
2 tablespoons minced onion
2 teaspoons salt
1 teaspoon ajinomoto
3 cups Wesson oil
¾ cup vinegar (if necessary, add ½ teaspoon salt to neutralize vinegar)

Combine all ingredients except the oil and vinegar. Beat with mixer at medium speed and slowly add the Wesson oil, 1 tablespoon at a time. Add vinegar last to control tartness and end with a thicker dressing. Parmesan cheese should be sprinkled on your finished salad.

MAVIS AKIYOSHI
A Book of Favorite Recipes, Compiled by United Methodist Women of Wahiawa, United Methodist Church

ORIENTAL DRESSING

2 tablespoons ground sesame seeds
2 tablespoons sugar
½ teaspoon salt
⅛ cup cooking oil
⅛ cup sesame oil
3 tablespoons white vinegar
2 tablespoons shoyu

Mix all ingredients well in a bottle. Refrigerate. Shake well before using and pour over salad. Good over somen salad.

WENDY TAKESONO
"Pig Out" with Liholiho's Caring, Competent, Creative Cooks

CREAMY TROPICAL SALAD DRESSING

Makes 2 cups

⅓ cup mayonnaise
⅓ cup salad oil
2 tablespoons tarragon vinegar
1 cup ketchup
¾ teaspoon dry mustard
2 tablespoons sugar
2 tablespoons honey
1½ teaspoons salt
1 teaspoon Worcestershire sauce
1 teaspoon lemon juice
1 teaspoon steak sauce
1 clove garlic, crushed
Dash of pepper
Dash of paprika

Put mayonnaise in a mixing bowl, slowing beat in salad oil. Combine remaining ingredients and blend into mayonnaise mixture.

Favorite Island Cookery, Book I, Honpa Hongwanji Hawaii Betsuin

FRENCH DRESSING

¼ teaspoon black pepper
¾ cup salad oil
1 (10¾-ounce) can tomato soup
⅔ cup sugar
⅔ cup cider vinegar
¼ cup finely chopped round onion, or less
½ to 1 teaspoon salt
2 teaspoons Worcestershire sauce
1 clove garlic, minced
Pinch of MSG (optional)

Combine ingredients in a quart bottle and shake well. Refrigerate.

Community Family Favorites, Community Church of Honolulu

FRUIT SALAD DRESSING

Makes 2 cups

2 eggs, beaten
¾ cup sugar
½ cup pear or pineapple syrup, drained from fruit
⅓ cup lemon juice
1 cup sour cream

In a saucepan, combine eggs, sugar, fruit syrup, and lemon juice. Cook over medium heat, stirring constantly until mixture thickens. Fold in sour cream and chill thoroughly before serving on fruit salad.

Favorite Island Cookery, Book II, Honpa Hongwanji Buddhist Temple

GUAVA DRESSING

1 cup mayonnaise
1 cup tomato ketchup
¼ cup vinegar
½ cup salad oil
1 teaspoon dry mustard
2 teaspoons lemon juice
½ cup guava jelly or jam
½ teaspoon garlic salt
1 teaspoon dried basil

Combine ingredients and beat with rotary beater or use blender. Chill. Serve on greens.

50th Anniversary Best of Our Favorite Recipes, Maui Association for Family and Community Education

PAPAYA SEED DRESSING

Makes 3 cups

1 cup sugar
1 teaspoon salt
1 teaspoon dry mustard
1 cup wine or tarragon vinegar
2 cups salad oil
1 small onion, chopped
3 tablespoons fresh papaya seeds

Place all dry ingredients and vinegar in blender. Mix, gradually adding oil and onion. When thoroughly blended, add papaya seeds. Blend only until seeds are consistency of coarse ground pepper. Good with fruit salad or greens. Keep refrigerated.

The Hawaii National Guard Auxiliary Cookbook

HONEY SESAME SALAD DRESSING

1 teaspoon paprika
½ teaspoon powdered mustard
½ teaspoon salt
½ teaspoon celery salt
½ cup honey
3 tablespoons lemon juice
¼ cup vinegar
½ cup water
1 tablespoon shoyu
1 tablespoon sesame oil
1 clove garlic, grated
1 teaspoon grated onion
1 tablespoon toasted sesame seeds, crushed

Shake ingredients in a jar.

Hilo Missionary Cooks

HERBAL SALAD DRESSING

1½ cups oil (part olive if possible)
Ground pepper to taste
½ teaspoon mustard seed
¼ cup water
1 tablespoon salt or soy sauce to taste
¼ teaspoon dill seed
1 tablespoon lemon juice
½ cup apple cider vinegar
2 to 3 cloves garlic
½ teaspoon finely chopped, fresh marjoram or ¼ teaspoon dried
½ teaspoon anise seed
1 handful fresh parsley
½ teaspoon finely chopped, fresh basil or ¼ teaspoon dried

Blend all ingredients in blender. Add 1 or all of these:

¼ sweet green bell pepper, chopped
½ to 1 seeded avocado
1 large green onion

Blend again and let flavors mingle before serving. Keep refrigerated and shake well before serving.

Cooking with Honolulu Gardeners,
Honolulu Community Recreational Garden Program

MAUI MISO DRESSING

1 cup rice vinegar
1 cup vegetable oil
2 tablespoons sesame oil
½ cup sugar
1 medium Maui round onion
2 tablespoons miso
1 teaspoon salt
1 teaspoon pepper
1 teaspoon crushed garlic
1 teaspoon grated ginger

Blend all of the ingredients for approximately 20 seconds. This dressing is excellent for somen salad and tossed salad.

Wisteria Delights, A Collection of Recipes
by Pearl City Hongwanji Mission

ROASTED SHALLOT VINAIGRETTE

5 roasted shallots
½ cup white wine vinegar
1 tablespoon honey
1 teaspoon salt
2 tablespoons Dijon mustard
1 cup safflower oil

To roast shallots: Drizzle whole shallot buds with a little oil, sprinkle with salt and pepper and bake in foil in a 300°F oven for 30 minutes. Cool. Squeeze cooked shallot out of peel and into food processor; blend with other ingredients, except oil. With processor on, add oil slowly in a stream until mixture is smooth and thick. Serve over fresh greens. Store in refrigerator.

DION-MAGRIT COSCHIGANO
Island Flavors, Favorite Recipes of the Historic Hawai'i Foundation

THOUSAND ISLAND DRESSING

Makes 1½ cups

1 cup mayonnaise
¼ cup chili sauce
1 tablespoon chopped onion
2 tablespoons chopped green pepper
1 egg, hard-boiled and chopped

Combine all ingredients. Mix well and chill.

ENID PARRISH
A Book of Favorite Recipes, Compiled by United Methodist Women of Wahiawa, United Methodist Church

KEOLU SALAD DRESSING

Makes 2 cups

1 cup salad oil
½ cup Japanese vinegar
¾ cup sugar
2½ teaspoons salt
½ teaspoon prepared mustard
Few slices of onion
2 to 3 bay leaves
¼ teaspoon black pepper
2 cloves garlic
½ teaspoon Worcestershire sauce

Place all ingredients into a blender and blend until well-mixed.

MICHELLE KIMURA VALENCIANO
Food for the Body and Soul, West Kaua'i United Methodist Church

LYONS SALAD DRESSING

¼ cup olive oil
3 tablespoons red wine vinegar
1 teaspoon dry mustard
¼ cup Parmesan cheese
½ teaspoon salt
½ teaspoon pepper (fresh ground best)

Mix all ingredients well. Add more wine vinegar to taste, if desired.

CAMILLE, JACKIE, KIM AND JOHN BRADY
Hanalei School Collective Cook Book

CANTONESE DRESSING

1 cup mayonnaise
¼ cup soy sauce
2 teaspoons curry powder
2 teaspoons powdered ginger
2 teaspoons fresh lemon juice

Prepare several hours before serving. Mix well and refrigerate before using. This may also be used as a marinade for chicken.

MARITA BIVEN
The Hawai'i Youth Opera Chorus, Nā Mea 'Ai Punahele

POPPY SEED DRESSING

½ cup sugar
2 teaspoons dry mustard
2 teaspoons salt
⅔ cup vinegar
3 tablespoons onion juice
2 cups salad oil
3 tablespoons poppy seeds

Mix together sugar, dry mustard, salt, and vinegar; add onion juice. Stir. Add oil slowly beating constantly with electric mixer at medium speed. Beat till thick. Add seeds and beat a bit more.

NELLA MAE KOETJE
Kalaheo Missionary Church Cookin' Book!

KAMUELA SALAD DRESSING

Makes 3½ cups

4 fat buds of garlic, pressed
1 teaspoon coarsely ground black pepper
3 teaspoons white sugar
⅓ cup tarragon vinegar
2 cups olive oil
1 cup saffola oil

Combine all ingredients in a large jar.

KAMUELA WHITE
A Chorus of Recipes, Kamehameha School Children's Chorus

THAI PEANUT SALAD DRESSING

Makes about ¼ cup

¼ cup corn syrup
2 tablespoons creamy peanut butter
1 tablespoon soy sauce
1 tablespoon cider vinegar
⅛ teaspoon crushed red pepper (optional)
1 tablespoon chopped cilantro or parsley

In small bowl with wire whisk or fork, stir corn syrup, peanut butter, soy sauce, vinegar, and crushed red pepper until smooth. Stir in cilantro. Serve over mixed greens. If dressing becomes too thick, stir in 1 to 2 teaspoons water until desired consistency.

KRISTIN J.P. TAITAGUE
A Chorus of Recipes, Kamehameha School Children's Chorus

MAUI HIGH DRESSING

1 cup ketchup
¼ cup vinegar
1⅛ teaspoons salt
Dash black pepper
¼ cup oil
½ cup sugar
Scant ½ teaspoon paprika
Dash MSG

Put all ingredients in blender and blend on Whip/Mix speed until well-blended. Chill and use as is or for a variation, mix equal amounts of mayonnaise and dressing—stir well and chill.

DORIS DOHN
The Hele Mai, Ai (Come Eat) Cookbook, Flavors of Upcountry Maui

GREEN GODDESS DRESSING

1 clove garlic
1 can anchovies
3 tablespoons chives
1 cup mayonnaise
1 tablespoon lemon juice
1 carton sour cream
⅓ cup chopped fresh parsley
¼ teaspoon salt
¼ teaspoon pepper
Pinch oregano and thyme

Blend all ingredients together in blender. Keeps a long time refrigerated.

PAT HODGINS
The Kahikolu Country Cookbook

PASSION FRUIT MAYONNAISE

Makes 1 pint

1 egg
¼ cup passion fruit juice
1 teaspoon dry mustard
1 teaspoon salt
1 tablespoon sugar
⅛ teaspoon paprika
1½ cups salad oil

Put all ingredients in blender except 1 cup oil. Add remaining oil gradually.

MONA KAHELE
The Kahikolu Country Cookbook

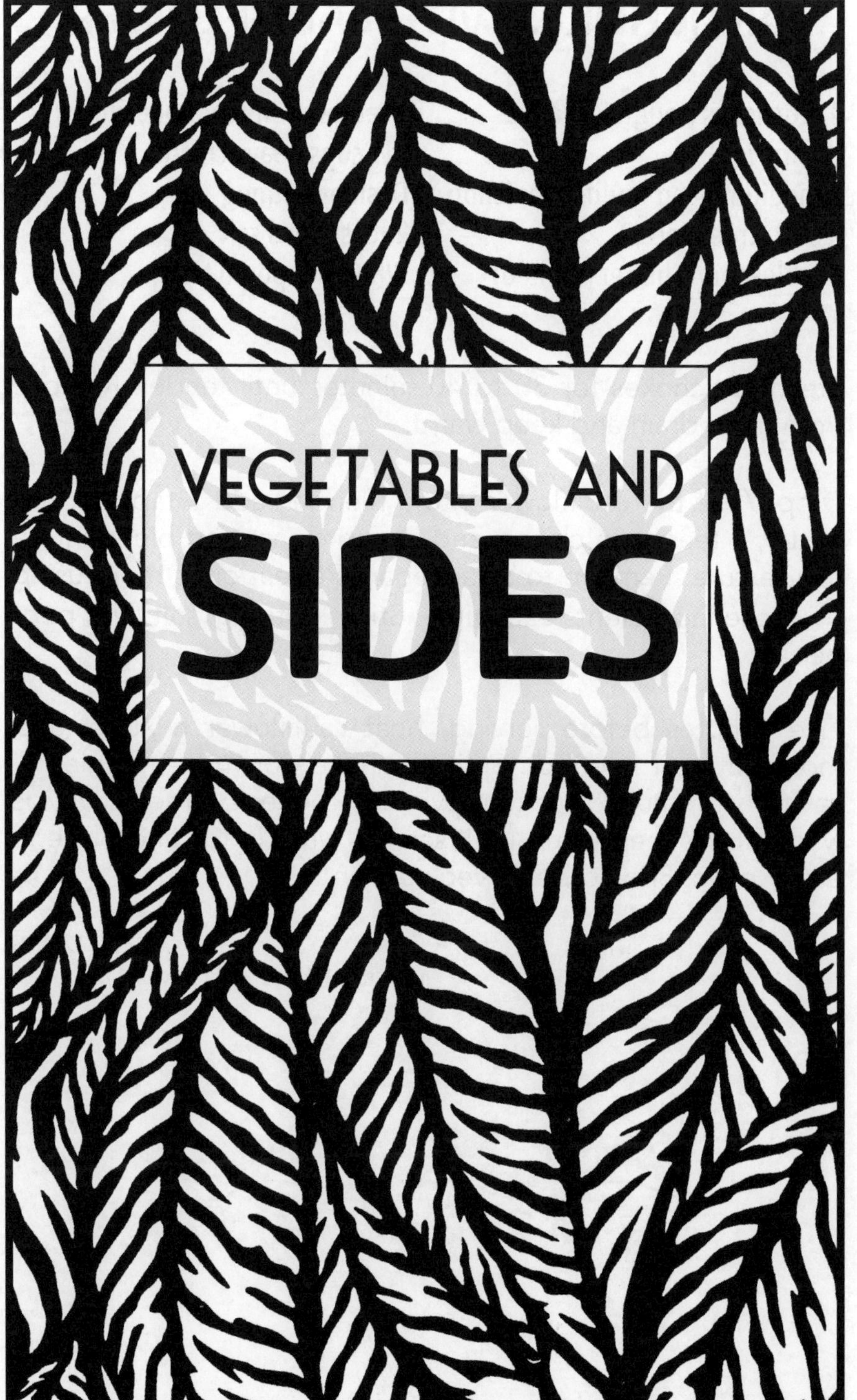

VEGETABLES AND SIDES

ARTICHOKES WITH CAULIFLOWER

4 artichokes (tough leaves removed)
1 medium head cauliflower (chop in large pieces)
6 tablespoons butter (melted)
3 tablespoons chopped chives
1½ cups heavy cream
Dash of nutmeg
2 teaspoons salt
White pepper to taste

Steam artichokes for 30 to 40 minutes until tender. Remove from heat, drain and keep warm.

Drop ⅓ of the cauliflower into a blender, add 2 tablespoons butter, 1 teaspoon chives, and ½ cup cream and blend into a rich texture. Remove to a saucepan. Repeat once more using ⅓ of the ingredients each time. Stir in nutmeg, salt, and pepper.

Five minutes before serving, heat cauliflower mixture (add more butter if needed). Split artichoke down the middle, fill cavity with cauliflower (remove the choke if larger cavity is wanted). To keep warm until served, wrap in foil and place in 200°F oven. Should be served very hot.

ADELE DAVIS
We, the Women of Hawaii Cookbook

ASPARAGUS, KAMA'ĀINA-STYLE

Makes 6 servings

2 pounds fresh asparagus
1 tablespoon cornstarch, mixed with tablespoon cold water
¾ cup chicken broth or 1 cube chicken bouillon dissolved in ¾ cup boiling water
1 clove garlic, finely chopped
Few grains black pepper
2 tablespoons vegetable oil
1 teaspoon lemon juice

1. Wash asparagus well. Break off tough lower stalks and cut into very thin slices.
2. Stir cornstarch and water mixture into chicken broth.
3. Cook liquid mixture until it thickens, stirring constantly to prevent scorching,
4. Add garlic and pepper, set aside.
5. Sauté asparagus slices in hot oil for 3 minutes or until tender, but not soft.
6. Add lemon juice to liquid mixture and pour over asparagus.
7. Stir ingredients and cook for 1 minute. Serve at once.

VARIATION: Combine ¼ teaspoon sugar, 1 teaspoon chopped green onions, and 1 tablespoon Chinese parsley together. Add to gravy. Soy sauce or salt may also be added to sauce, if desired.

KATHLEEN CHAN
Grandma & Grandpa's Hawaiian Island Cookbook, Honolulu Federal Savings and Loan Association

ASPARAGUS WITH PEANUT DRESSING

2¼ pounds fresh asparagus or 3 (10 ounce) packages frozen asparagus
3 tablespoons peanut butter
¼ cup sugar
¼ cup shoyu sauce
2 tablespoons sherry
1 small piece ginger, grated

If using frozen asparagus, cook as directed on package. For fresh asparagus, cut into 2-inch pieces. Cook simmering until tender. Drain and rinse in cold water. Mix peanut butter and sugar, add other ingredients slowly. Pour over chilled asparagus, stir to coat.

EVELYN STALEY
We, the Women of Hawaii Cookbook

BITTER MELON BLACK BEAN SAUCE

4 medium-sized bitter melon, sliced ¼-inch diagonally

Oil for frying
¼ cup chopped dried shrimp
1 teaspoon cornstarch
1 tablespoon water

Sauce
1 tablespoon oyster sauce
2 teaspoons soy sauce
1 tablespoon black beans, rinse and crush

Cut bitter melon lengthwise, remove seeds, and slice. Place in bowl, pour hot water over bitter melon and let stand for about 2 minutes. Drain and set aside. Mix Sauce ingredients together well and set aside. Heat oil in frying pan, add shrimps, bitter melon and stir-fry. Cover and simmer for 5 minutes. Add Sauce and simmer for a few more minutes. Add cornstarch mixed with water to thicken.

Favorite Island Cookery, Book IV, Honpa Hongwanji Hawaii Betsuin

BAKED BREADFRUIT

Makes 6 servings

1 very ripe breadfruit
1 cup water
½ cup butter or margarine

Place breadfruit in a shallow pan; add water. Bake at 350°F in oven for 1 hour or until tender. Pull out stem and core; cut breadfruit into 6 sections. Top with butter. If preferred, remove stem and core before baking. Put 1 tablespoon butter and 1 tablespoon sugar into cavity. Replace stem before baking.

50th Anniversary Best of Our Favorite Recipes, Maui Association for Family and Community Education

BREADFRUIT SOUFFLE

1 ripe breadfruit
2 eggs
Salt and pepper to taste
4 tablespoons butter, melted

Select a very ripe breadfruit and remove center. Scrap pulp from skin and force it through a sieve. Add well-beaten eggs, salt, pepper, and melted butter. Bake in a buttered, covered casserole, buttering cover as well as dish. Place baking dish in pan of water as for custard. Bake in 350°F oven for 45 to 50 minutes, or until a silver knife inserted in center comes out clean.

The Hilo Woman's Club Cookbook

SESAME BROCCOLI

2 pounds fresh broccoli (cut into 2-inch pieces)
2½ tablespoons sugar
2 tablespoons toasted sesame seeds
2 tablespoons oil
2 tablespoons vinegar
2 tablespoons shoyu

Cook broccoli in salted water until tender (do not overcook). Drain and keep warm. Combine remaining ingredients in saucepan and bring to a boil over medium heat. Pour over broccoli, turning spears to coat well. Garnish with chopped parsley.

NANCY EBSEN
We, the Women of Hawaii Cookbook

BRUSSELS SPROUTS WITH PECANS

2 quarts Brussels sprouts, trimmed
Boiling salted water
¼ cup sugar firmly packed brown
¼ cup butter or margarine
½ cup pecan halves

Cut a cross in stem end of each sprout for more even cooking. Cook in boiling salted water with enough water to cover sprouts, 5 to 10 minutes or until crisp-tender. Drain well.

In deep skillet over low heat, stir sugar and butter until sugar dissolves. Add Brussels sprouts and pecans; toss until well-glazed. Serve hot.

Favorite Island Cookery, Book IV, Honpa Hongwanji Hawaii Betsuin

CABBAGE KARASHI MISO

Makes 6 servings

½ small head cabbage

Karashi (mustard) Miso Sauce
4 tablespoons miso
2 tablespoons vinegar
2½ tablespoons sugar
2 teaspoons dry mustard

Shred and cook cabbage in boiling water for 5 minutes.

To make Karashi Miso Sauce, grind miso in suribachi. Add vinegar, sugar, and dry mustard mixed with a little water.

Mix Karashi Miso Sauce with cooked cabbage and serve.

Wisteria Delights, A Collection of Recipes
by Pearl City Hongwanji Mission

RED CABBAGE

2 pounds red cabbage
1 medium onion
4 ounces bacon, duck or goose fat
1 bay leaf
8 cloves
1 shot red wine or vinegar
1 cup water
3 to 4 medium sour apples
2 teaspoons salt
2 teaspoons sugar

Discard rough outer leaves of cabbage head, quarter, cut out white core, and shred finely. Dice onion, fry in fat until transparent, add all ingredients plus the peeled, cored, and roughly cut apples. Simmer for 1 hour until tender, tossing occasionally. Discard bay leaf and cloves if you can find them and bingo!

This is even better when warmed up. Bon appetit!

FRITZ H.H. BUTTGEN COLLECTION
The Kahikolu Country Cookbook

CAULIFLOWER IN SESAME SAUCE

Makes 4 servings

1 tablespoon tahini (sesame paste)
1 teaspoon soy sauce
½ teaspoon salt
¼ teaspoon ground pepper
1 tablespoon corn or peanut oil
1 small onion, thinly sliced
½ large head of cauliflower, cut into 1-inch florets

In a small bowl, stir together tahini, soy sauce, salt, and pepper until well-blended. Set sauce aside. In a large skillet, heat oil. Add onion and sauté over moderate heat, stirring occasionally until it begins to brown, about 3 minutes. Add cauliflower and stir-fry for 3 minutes. Add tahini sauce and toss to coat. Reduce heat to low, cover and cook until cauliflower is tender.

Favorite Island Cookery, Book IV, Honpa Hongwanji Hawaii Betsuin

EGGPLANT COOKED IN SAKE

Makes 3 to 4 servings

6 to 8 small eggplants (Lahaina size)
2 tablespoons vegetable oil
¼ cup sake
1 tablespoon shoyu
2 tablespoons sugar

Wash eggplants and cut the stem ends off. Then make criss-cross gashes on both sides. Sauté eggplants in vegetable oil. Add sake, shoyu, and sugar and cover tightly; cook over low heat until done and sauce is thickened.

Wisteria Delights, A Collection of Recipes by Pearl City Hongwanji Mission

LAHAINA NASUBI

2 cups water
¼ cup vinegar (Japanese)
¾ cup brown sugar
2 tablespoons Hawaiian salt
2 teaspoons baking soda
2 pounds nasubi (eggplant)

Boil and cool water, vinegar, brown sugar, and salt. Add baking soda. Soak nasubi for 2 days.

Hawaiian Hospitality,
American Business Women's Association Eleu Chapter

HOT AND SPICY EGGPLANT

1 pound eggplant
6 tablespoons vegetable oil
1 teaspoon chopped garlic
½ tablespoon chopped ginger
1 tablespoon hot bean paste
2 tablespoons soy sauce
1 teaspoon salt
1 teaspoon sugar
½ cup clear chicken soup
½ tablespoon vinegar
½ tablespoon sesame oil
1 teaspoon chopped scallions

Wash and cut eggplant (with skin) into thumb size pieces. Heat 6 tablespoons vegetable oil in wok till very hot. Add eggplant, turn heat to medium low, stir-fry till it's tender; press out oil and remove eggplant.

Add chopped garlic, ginger, and hot bean paste into wok with eggplant dripping. Stir-fry for a few seconds; add soy sauce, salt, sugar, and chicken soup and bring to a boil.

Return eggplant and cook one minute more until sauce is gone. Add vinegar, sesame oil, and chopped scallions; mix well and serve. Enjoy with a lot of rice.

MRS. PAUL TSO
Hawaii's Aloha Recipes, The Japanese Women's Society of Honolulu

EGGPLANT PARMESAN

¼ cup oil
1 minced onion
1 medium green pepper, chopped
¾ cup sliced fresh mushrooms
1 round eggplant sliced
1 large can tomatoes
1 teaspoon salt, basil, oregano and chopped parsley

Cheese mixture
2 eggs beaten
1 cup grated cheddar cheese
1 cup grated mozzarella cheese

Heat oil, sauté onion, pepper, mushrooms until limp. Add eggplant, tomatoes, salt, basil, oregano, and parsley. Cover and let simmer for 25 minutes. If too much liquid, turn up heat and uncover for a few extra minutes. Spoon layer of eggplant mixture into casserole with slotted spoon. Layer over with cheese mixture. Repeat layering and end up with cheese mixture on top. Bake uncovered at 375°F for 25 minutes.

NOTE: Cooked hamburger may be added to eggplant.

Hawaiian Hospitality, American Business Women's Association Eleu Chapter

MOCK OYSTERS

1 medium eggplant
3 cups brown rice flakes
3 tablespoons butter
½ pound grated cheddar cheese
1 tablespoon breadcrumbs
1 cup milk
Salt and pepper to taste

Cover whole eggplant with boiling water, add a pinch of soda. Cook 15 minutes. Wash in cold water. Butter casserole, chop eggplant. Layer eggplant and flakes, dot with butter and cheese. Top with breadcrumbs and add milk. Bake in preheated oven 375°F for 30 minutes.

ROBERTA CHATEAUNEUF
We, the Women of Hawaii Cookbook

SWEET AND SOUR GREEN BEANS

Makes 4 (1-cup) servings

3 strips bacon
1 small onion, sliced
1 (8-ounce) can water chestnuts, sliced
1 can French-style green beans
2 teaspoons cornstarch
¼ teaspoon salt
¼ teaspoon dry mustard
1 tablespoon brown sugar
1 tablespoon vinegar
3 tablespoons chopped pimento

In skillet, fry bacon until crisp. Remove bacon, drain and crumble. To the bacon fat in skillet, add onion and water chestnuts. Sauté until onion is golden, stirring frequently.

Drain green beans, reserving ½ cup liquid. Combine bean liquid, cornstarch, salt, mustard, brown sugar, and vinegar; add to skillet. Cook, stirring constantly, until mixture thickens. Add green beans and pimento; heat through.

Serve garnished with crumbled bacon.

PAT MERRILL
100 Years Sharing God's Love, United Community Church

GREEN BEANS NAMOOL

Makes 4 servings

½ pound green beans, sliced diagonally
½ cup sliced water chestnuts
½ cup sliced fresh mushrooms
1 clove garlic, crushed
1 teaspoon salad oil
1 teaspoon sesame oil
2½ teaspoons shoyu
½ teaspoon salt
Dash of pepper
1 teaspoon sugar
¼ teaspoon ajinomoto
2 teaspoons crushed roasted sesame seeds

Stir-fry beans, water chestnuts, mushrooms, and garlic in salad oil and sesame oil. Add the remaining ingredients; cover and cook until beans are tender, 4 to 5 minutes.

Favorite Island Cookery, Book I, Honpa Hongwanji Hawaii Betsuin

STUFFED LOTUS ROOT

Makes 4 servings

2 medium lotus root

Filling
½ cup miso
2 teaspoons grated ginger
2 tablespoons sugar

Batter
⅓ cup flour
Dash salt
½ teaspoon baking powder
2 tablespoons water

Pare skin from lotus roots. Mix Filling ingredients together and grind in a suribachi. Squeeze mixture into holes of lotus roots. (Pastry bag or paper cone would be helpful.) Prepare batter by mixing the batter ingredients. Dip lotus roots in batter and fry in deep fat for 10 to 20 minutes depending on size of lotus. Slice and serve.

Wisteria Delights, A Collection of Recipes by Pearl City Hongwanji Mission

STIR-FRY VEGETABLES WITH LUP CHONG

Lup chong (amount to your desire)
2 carrots
1 round onion
2 broccoli stems
4 celery tops with leaves
1 tablespoon oyster sauce

Slice lup chong. Stir-fry in pan. Drain oil and discard. Add carrots and onions, cut in thick julienne style. Cut other vegetables the same way. Stir-fry all together. If too dry, add a little water. Add oyster sauce. Serve.

You may also add string beans or any other vegetable you like. Use lup chong (how much you like), 1 per person or 1 per 2 people. Vegetables, you may add more or less, depending on how many you feed.

BEATRICE BARBOZA
50th Anniversary Best of Our Favorite Recipes,
Maui Association for Family and Community Education

MAUI ONION-SPINACH BAKED DISH

- 1 medium Maui onion, finely chopped
- 2 beaten eggs (room temperature is best)
- 1 (10-ounce) box frozen, chopped spinach, cooked and drained
- ½ to 1 full stick room temperature margarine (to taste, but I prefer ½ stick)
- 1 cup milk
- 1 cup flour
- 1 teaspoon salt
- 1 teaspoon baking powder
- Sprinkle of garlic powder
- 1 pound cubed Monterey Jack cheese
- ½ cup Parmesan cheese

Mix all ingredients together, then fold in both cheeses last. Pour into a 9 x 13-inch pan and bake at 350°F for 45 to 55 minutes. Let stand for 10 minutes before cutting and don't eat the whole pan alone!

SAM SHENKUS
"No Ka Oi" The Best of Hawaii,
Favorite Recipes from Rotarians of District 5000

ONION PIE

Makes 6 servings

1½ cups crushed soda crackers
½ cup oleo, melted (reserve small amount to pour over top)
2 cups chopped onion
1 cup milk
½ teaspoon salt
Dash of pepper
2 eggs, beaten
1 can mushrooms, drained
1½ cups grated cheddar cheese

1. Mix cracker crumbs and oleo (save a few to put on top).
2. Put in baking dish and make crust.
3. Sauté onions in oleo.
4. Warm the milk, salt, and pepper.
5. Add eggs, mushrooms, cheese, and onions.
6. Pour mixture on crust and bake at 350°F for 30 minutes.

DORIS WETTERS
50th Anniversary Best of Our Favorite Recipes,
Maui Association for Family and Community Education

JAPANESE-STYLE COOKED PUMPKIN

Makes 6 servings

½ medium pumpkin, seeded
2 tablespoons vegetable oil
1½ to 2 cups water
2 tablespoons sugar
½ (0.225-ounce) package dashinomoto (powdered soup base)
1 tablespoon soy sauce
1 teaspoon mirin
1 tablespoon sake

Cut pumpkin into 2-inch cubes and trim off skin. Heat oil in deep skillet or Dutch oven. Cook pumpkin in oil for approximately 1 minute on high heat, stirring quickly to prevent burning and sticking. Add water, sugar, and dashinomoto. Cover and cook until pumpkin is tender.

Combine soy sauce, mirin, and sake and add to the pumpkin. Stir to coat pumpkin. Cover and cook for 15 minutes on low heat. Turn heat off and let stand in pot for another 15 minutes to improve flavor before serving.

The Tastes and Tales of Mōʻiliʻili,
A Collection of Recipes & Stories by Mōʻiliʻili Community Center

COCONUT SPINACH

3 (10-ounce) packages frozen chopped spinach
$1\frac{1}{3}$ cups fresh coconut milk or 1 (12-ounce) can frozen coconut milk, thawed
Salt and pepper

Cook spinach according to package directions. Drain well, squeeze out all moisture with paper towel. Place spinach and coconut milk in a saucepan. Season to taste with salt and pepper and heat to just boiling (do not overcook). Serve in bowl with some grated coconut and a dash of nutmeg.

CHARLENE DO
We, the Women of Hawaii Cookbook

SCALLOPED SQUASH CASSEROLE

3 pounds yellow summer squash
3 slices onion
1 bay leaf
1/8 teaspoon thyme
1 cup water
2 teaspoons salt
3 tablespoons dry breadcrumbs
4 tablespoons butter
3 tablespoons flour
1/8 teaspoon white pepper
1½ cups light cream
3 egg yolks
¾ cup grated Swiss cheese

Lightly scrape the squash and slice paper thin. In a saucepan, combine squash, onion, bay leaf, thyme, water, and 1 teaspoon salt. Bring to a boil, cover, and cook over low heat of 10 minutes. Drain, discarding the onion and bay leaf.

Melt the butter in a saucepan, blend in flour, pepper, and remaining salt. Add the cream gradually, stirring steadily to the boiling point; cook over low heat 5 minutes.

Beat egg yolks in a bowl; gradually add the hot sauce, stirring steadily to prevent curdling. Mix in half of the cheese, then the squash. Turn into a buttered baking dish; sprinkle with a mixture of the breadcrumbs and remaining cheese. Bake in a 325°F oven for 30 minutes.

REBECCA DIXON
We, the Women of Hawaii Cookbook

STEAMED STUFFED SUMMER SQUASH

4 small or medium summer squash
½ teaspoon Worcestershire sauce
¼ teaspoon or 1 clove of garlic or onion minced
¼ teaspoon salt or Lawry's
Pinch of herbs
1 tablespoon butter
3 tablespoons dry breadcrumbs (Italian style Progresso recommended)
¼ cup grated Parmesan cheese
⅛ teaspoon Spice Island New Orleans Creole Spice
3 tablespoons Brautweiser spread
¼ teaspoon dry basil

Wash squash thoroughly and cut the stem ends of squash. Steam squash but leave whole. When almost tender, drain and cool. Scoop out centers of squash leaving a shell about ½-inch thick. Chop the removed pulp into small bits.

Mix all the remaining ingredients and add chopped pulp to mixture. Preheat oven to 400°F. Generously refill squash shells with mixture. Place stuffed shells in a pan on a rack above ¼ inch of water. Bake until hot, about 10 minutes. Serve one stuffed shell per person. This vegetable recipe is rich, but unusual and delicious even if you are not a squash lover. This recipe originated with my great aunt, Mrs. Marcella Fenton.

MARITA COLLINS BIVEN
Dining with the Daughters, The Daughters of Hawaii

POTATO PIE

1 cup cream or 2% milk
24 ounces frozen hash browns, thawed for 20 minutes
½ cup butter
½ cup minced onion
1 teaspoon salt
½ teaspoon pepper
¼ cup grated Parmesan cheese

Preheat oven to 350°F. Bring cream to a boil and add potatoes. Cook until cream is absorbed. Mix in remaining ingredients except cheese. Put mixture into a greased pie plate. Cover with cheese. Bake uncovered for 1 hour.

JASON FRANK
A Chorus of Recipes, Kamehameha School Children's Chorus

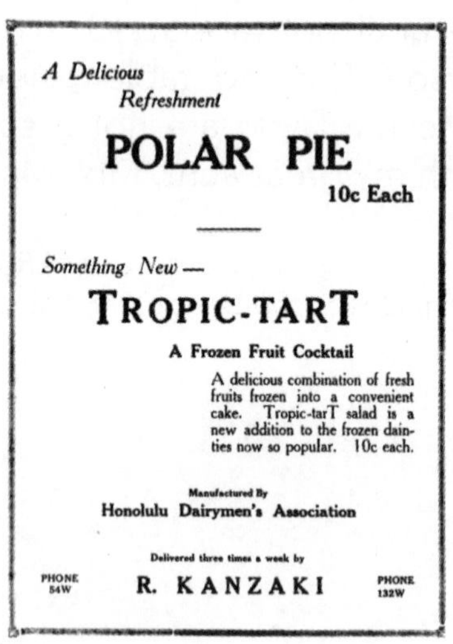

SCALLOPED POTATOES

Makes 6 servings

1 medium onion, minced
¼ cup butter
¼ cup flour
½ teaspoon dried dill weed
½ teaspoon salt
⅛ teaspoon pepper
2 cups skim milk
6 medium red skin potatoes, sliced ¼-inch thick

Preheat oven to 375°F. Spray shallow, 2-quart glass baking dish with nonstick cooking spray.

In small saucepan over medium-high heat, cook onion in butter 2 to 3 minutes until tender. Reduce heat to medium and stir in flour, dried dill weed, salt and pepper until combined. Gradually stir in milk. Bring to boiling, stirring frequently. Boil 2 minutes until thickened, stirring constantly.

Arrange potato slices in prepared baking dish. Spoon onion-milk sauce over potato slices. Cover with aluminum foil and bake 45 minutes. Remove foil and bake 30 minutes more until potatoes are tender and golden brown.

Ono-Licious, Na Poe Humukuiki O Hawaii, Hawaii Quilt Guild

HĀMĀKUA PLANTATION SWEET POTATO CASSEROLE

Makes 10 to 12 servings

A family favorite for Thanksgiving; can be made ahead and chilled, but not frozen.

3 cups sweet potatoes
2 eggs, beaten
1/3 cup milk
1/3 cup butter, melted
1 teaspoon vanilla

Topping
1/3 cup butter, melted
1 cup light brown sugar
½ cup flour
1 cup chopped macadamia nuts (or pecans)

Preheat oven to 350°F.

In a large bowl, peel, boil, and mash potatoes (or mash well-drained canned potatoes). With a mixer, beat in eggs, milk, butter, and vanilla. Beat until mixture is light and fluffy on medium speed. Spread lightly in an ungreased 13 x 9-inch or large round baking dish.

Mix Topping ingredients and crumble mixture onto potatoes. Bake 25 to 30 minutes.

MRS. EMIL A. (PATRICIA) OFFER
Island Flavors, Favorite Recipes of the Historic Hawai'i Foundation

FRIED TARO SLICES

Another delicious taro dish. Sweet potatoes could be substituted. Scrub one medium-sized taro. Parboil in salted water until tender (about one hour). Peel the taro and slice in ½-inch slices. Heat fat in a frying pan; bacon fat is particularly good. Fry the slices until brown on each side. Salt to taste. Serve immediately.

Cook 'Em Up Kaua'i, The Kaua'i Historical Society Cookbook

TARO PATTIES

Makes 4 servings

- 1 large taro root
- 4 to 5 cloves garlic
- 1 medium to large zucchini
- 1 medium to large red onion
- 1½ teaspoons dry Italian seasoning
- 1 teaspoon vege-sal or salt
- ½ cup each of cornmeal and unbleached flour
- ¼ cup gomasio (a sesame-salt seasoning), can be found in health food stores

Cube and steam taro. In food processor (or by hand), chop garlic zucchini and onion, finely. After taro cools, place in blender and mix until smooth. Then add taro to veggie mix in a bowl and add seasonings. On large plate, mix cornmeal, flour, and gomasio. Take some taro mix and form patty on the plate—coat both sides. If taro mix needs to be drier, add some of the flour to it. Cook on nonstick surface with a small amount of oil. Cook each side until brown.

CHRISTINE MELAMED

Hanalei School Collective Cook Book

BAKED TOMATOES

Tomatoes a la Provencale

Makes 6 to 8 servings

6 to 8 medium tomatoes, sliced
2 tablespoons salad oil
2 tablespoons finely chopped garlic
2 tablespoons chopped parsley
2 tablespoons fine dry breadcrumbs
Dash of pepper
Dash of salt

Core tomatoes and cut in half horizontally. Gently squeeze out juice and seeds. Arrange tomatoes, cut-side up, in shallow 3-quart baking dish. Drizzle with oil. Bake uncovered in 400°F oven for 10 minutes. Meanwhile, combine garlic, parsley, breadcrumbs, and pepper. Sprinkle mixture over tomatoes and continue baking uncovered for 15 minutes, or until tomatoes are soft throughout. Season with salt to taste.

ASA WAKABAYASHI
1988 4-H Local & Ethnic Food Show

STUFFED TOMATOES

Makes 6 servings

6 large firm tomatoes
6 eggs, hard-boiled and cooled
1 cup white sauce
¼ cup fresh minced parsley
Salt and pepper
½ cup grated Gruyere cheese
½ cup melted butter

Slice tops off tomatoes and carefully hollow out. Salt insides lightly. Cut eggs into thick slices and combine with white sauce. Add parsley, salt, and pepper. Stuff tomatoes with this mixture and sprinkle with grated cheese. Place tomatoes in a Pyrex dish, pour over the melted butter and brown in hot oven, 425°F. Cook for 15 minutes.

GINI STODDARD
Cook 'Em Up Kaua'i, The Kaua'i Historical Society Cookbook

CHINESE UNG CHOY

Makes 4 servings

1 tablespoon sesame oil
¼ cup sesame seeds
2 tablespoons soy sauce
3 quarts ung choy leaves, washed and still dripping
½ cup cheddar cheese, cut into ½-inch cubes

Heat oil and sesame seeds in pan until seeds are lightly browned. Add soy sauce and leaves, stirring constantly until leaves are wilted. Remove from heat and toss with cheese cubes.

COMMUNITY GARDEN COUNCIL
Cooking with Honolulu Gardeners, Honolulu Community Recreational Garden Program

MAKINA AND WATERCRESS IN SESAME SAUCE

8 large leaves of makina (Chinese won bok cabbage)
1 bunch watercress

Wash makina and watercress and boil separately until just tender. Drain and cool. Spread 4 makina leaves on "su" (bamboo mat), alternating and overlapping stem and leaves. Place ½ bunch watercress in center and roll like jelly roll. Press lightly and let stand for 10 minutes. Unroll "su" and cut into 1-inch pieces and place them upright on a dish. Serve cold with Goma Sauce.

Goma Sauce

1 tablespoon goma (sesame seeds)
½ cup shoyu
2 tablespoons sugar

Pan roast goma well. Grind slightly in a suribachi (corrugated bowl for grinding) and add shoyu, sugar, and mix well.

Wisteria Delights, A Collection of Recipes
by Pearl City Hongwanji Mission

ZUCCHINI-FETA CASSEROLE

¾ cup boiling water
¾ cup bulgur
2 cups sliced onions
4 garlic cloves, minced/pressed
2½ tablespoons vegetable oil
6 cups thinly sliced zucchini rounds
½ teaspoon dried oregano
½ teaspoon dried basil
½ teaspoon dried marjoram
⅛ teaspoon black pepper
2 eggs
1 cup (5 ounces) grated feta cheese
1 cup cottage cheese
½ to 1 cup fresh chopped parsley
2 tablespoons tomato paste
1 tablespoon tamari soy sauce
1 cup (3 ounces) grated cheddar cheese
2 medium tomatoes, thinly sliced
1½ tablespoons sesame seeds

Grease 9 x 9-inch casserole dish. Pour boiling water over bulgur. Cover. Set aside until water is absorbed and the bulgur is chewable.

Sauté onions and garlic in oil until translucent. Add zucchini, herbs, and pepper. Sauté until zucchini is tender but not falling apart. Lightly beat eggs in a bowl. Mix in feta and cottage cheeses. Add parsley, tomato paste, and soy sauce to the bulgur and mix well. Layer in casserole: bulgur mixture, sautéed vegetables, feta mixture, and top with cheddar cheese, tomato slices, and sprinkling of sesame seeds.

Bake at 350°F for 45 minutes (30 minutes cover, 15 minutes uncovered).

LEE ALDEN JOHNSON
"No Ka Oi" The Best of Hawaii,
Favorite Recipes from Rotarians of District 5000

VEGETABLE STRUDEL

12 spinach leaves
2 tablespoons olive oil
1 medium onion, finely sliced
1 medium red pepper, cut in strips
1 medium green pepper, cut in strips
2 medium zucchini, sliced
2 eggplants, sliced
Salt and pepper
6 sheets filo pastry
1⅓ ounces butter, melted
⅓ cup finely sliced fresh basil
½ cup grated Cheddar cheese
2 tablespoons sesame seeds

Preheat oven to 415°F. Brush a cookie sheet with melted butter or oil. Wash spinach and steam or microwave until just softened. Squeeze out excess moisture and spread out to dry. Heat oil in fry pan. Fry onions 3 minutes. Add peppers, zucchini, and eggplants; cook, stirring, for another 5 minutes until vegetables are soft. Season and set aside to cool. Brush 1 sheet of filo with butter; top with second sheet. Repeat with remaining filo, brushing with butter between each layer. Place spinach, vegetables, basil, and cheese along one long side of pastry about 2 inches from edge. Fold the sides over the filling. Fold short end over and roll tightly. Place seam down on pan; brush with remaining butter and sprinkle with sesame seeds. Bake 25 minutes, until golden brown and crisp. Serve immediately.

KELLEY TACHIBANA
"Cooking with Lovely Hula Hands,"
Moana's Hula Halau, Kaunakakai

JAI
Monk's Food

Makes 8 servings

½ (1-ounce) package kam choi
½ (1-ounce) package chien gee
4 stalks foo chuck
1 bundle long rice, soaked
10 dried mushrooms, soaked
3 tablespoons salad oil
1 small piece ginger, sliced
1 (3½-ounce) can nam yoy
2 tablespoons dau fu mui
½ cup fatt choi, soaked
1 (10½-ounce) can bamboo shoots, sliced
2 pieces jow dou fu, sliced
1 (6½-ounce) can water chestnuts, sliced
1 can gingko nuts
5 cups water
2 tablespoons wine
1 tablespoon sugar
1 cup funn teu, soaked
1 cup Chinese peas
3 tablespoons oyster sauce

Soak overnight the kam choi, chien gee, and foo chuck; clean, rinse, and drain. Cut foo chuck and long rice into 2-inch pieces. Remove stems from mushrooms; cut caps and chien gee into pieces.

In a large saucepan, heat oil. Add ginger, nam yoy, and dau fu mui. Fry ½ minute. Add kam choi, chien gee, foo chuck, mushrooms, fatt choi, bamboo shoots, jow dou fu, water chestnuts, gingko nuts, water, wine, and sugar. Cover; simmer 1½ hours.

Add funn teu and long rice; simmer 15 more minutes. Add peas and oyster sauce; simmer uncovered for 5 more minutes.

Favorite Island Cookery, Book I, Honpa Hongwanji Hawaii Betsuin

CRUSTLESS VEGETABLE PIE

1 medium eggplant, peeled and cubed
2 medium zucchinis, cubed
1 large onion, chopped
¼ cup olive oil
4 medium tomatoes, peeled and chopped
3 eggs
¾ cup grated Parmesan cheese
1 tablespoon minced parsley
½ teaspoon basil
Salt and pepper
¼ pound thinly sliced mozzarella cheese

Sauté eggplant, zucchini, and onion in the oil until vegetables are softened about 10 minutes. Add tomatoes, cover and simmer for 25 to 30 minutes until mixtures is soft. Transfer to a mixing bowl and let cool. Preheat oven to 350°F. Beat eggs with ¼ cup Parmesan cheese, parsley, and basil. Add to the vegetables with salt and pepper to taste.

Pour half of mixture into greased 9-inch pie pan and top with ¼ cup Parmesan cheese. Layer with remaining ingredients, top with mozzarella cheese and bake 40 to 45 minutes or until pie is set and cheese is golden brown.

ADELE DAVIS
We, the Women of Hawaii Cookbook

COSMO CASSEROLE

1 medium green breadfruit
1 pound string beans
½ cup bacon fat
1 cup toasted breadcrumbs
2 medium sized zucchini squash
6 ripe tomatoes
12 green onions
1 teaspoon salt

Peel green breadfruit and cut into ½-inch cubes and boil until tender. Cut and boil string beans. Rub casserole with a little bacon fat and dust on some breadcrumbs. Then place a layer of thinly sliced squash (not peeled) then a layer of sliced tomato, a layer of diced breadfruit and chopped onions, a layer of string beans. Then pour two tablespoons of bacon fat over and repeat, each time sprinkling a little salt or a teaspoon of shoyu (according to taste). Cover with remaining breadcrumbs and 4 slices of bacon and bake in oven 375°F for 45 minutes.

MRS. L.W. BRYAN
The Hilo Woman's Club Cookbook

KOREAN VEGETABLE DISH

Jhap Chae

3 tablespoons soy sauce
5 cloves garlic, minced
2 tablespoons sugar
1 teaspoon sesame seed oil
1 tablespoon sesame seeds
1 teaspoon sake
¾ pound pork or beef, cut into thin strips
4 pieces dried mushrooms, soaked, thinly sliced
3 medium round onions, sliced
½ teaspoon sugar
¼ teaspoon salt
¼ teaspoon MSG (optional)
1 carrot, julienned
10 pieces string beans, julienned
1 bunch watercress, cut into 2-inch pieces
1 cucumber, julienned
1 bunch green onion, cut into 2-inch strips
1 tablespoon oil
2 bundles long rice, cooked in boiling water for 2 to 3 minutes and drained well
3 tablespoons soy sauce
Dash MSG (optional)

Combine soy sauce, garlic, sugar, sesame seed oil, sesame seeds, sake, and MSG. Soak meat and mushrooms in mixture. Set aside. Heat 2 tablespoons of oil in pan. Cook onions; season with sugar, salt, and MSG. Spoon into large pot. Do the same for the other vegetables. Cook meat. Combine with vegetables in the pot. Add oil in pan and cook long rice. Season with 3 tablespoons soy sauce and dash of MSG. Add this to vegetable and meat mixture in pot. Mix well and serve.

PEGGY LAI
Community Family Favorites, Community Church of Honolulu

VEGETARIAN LASAGNA

Makes 8 servings

- 9 lasagna noodles
- 2 (8-ounce) cans tomato sauce
- 1 clove garlic, minced
- 1 teaspoon fresh oregano (or ½ teaspoon dried)
- 1 (10-ounce) package frozen chopped broccoli, thawed and drained
- 1 cup shredded carrot
- 1 (15 to 16-ounce) container ricotta cheese
- ¼ cup grated Parmesan cheese
- 1 cup shredded mozzarella cheese

Preheat oven to 350°F. Spray a 13 x 9-inch baking dish with vegetable cooking spray. Set aside.

Cook lasagna noodles according to package directions with no salt. Drain noodles in colander.

In a small bowl, combine tomato sauce, garlic, and oregano. Mix well. In a medium bowl, combine broccoli, carrots, ricotta, and Parmesan cheese. Mix well. Spread ½ cup tomato sauce in prepared dish. Place 3 noodles on top. Spread ½ the broccoli mixture over noodles. Spoon ½ cup of tomato sauce over broccoli; place 3 noodles on top. Spread with the remaining broccoli mixture, top with ½ cup of tomato sauce. Top with remaining noodles and tomato sauce; sprinkle mozzarella over top. Bake until bubbling, about 45 minutes. Cook for about 15 minutes. Cut into squares.

IVY TAKUSHI

Lana'i Cooks, Lana'i High & Elementary School

VEGETABLE FRITTERS

1 large carrot
1 (10-ounce) medium zucchini
1 (10-ounce) medium yellow squash
⅓ cup all-purpose flour
⅓ cup freshly grated Parmesan cheese
½ teaspoon salt
⅛ teaspoon ground pepper
1 large egg
½ cup vegetable oil

With coarse shredder, shred carrot, zucchini, and squash. Pat very dry with paper towels. In medium bowl, mix shredded vegetables with flour, cheese, salt, pepper, and egg. In 10-inch skillet, heat oil over medium heat. Gently drop ⅛th of mixture at a time (¼ cup) into oil in skillet, flattening slightly to about 3-inch round. Cook three fritters at a time, turning once, 5 minutes, until golden brown. With pancake turner, transfer to paper towels to drain. Keep warm in low oven while cooking remainder. ENJOY!

PHYLLIS KO
The Hawai'i Youth Opera Chorus, Nā Mea 'Ai Punahele

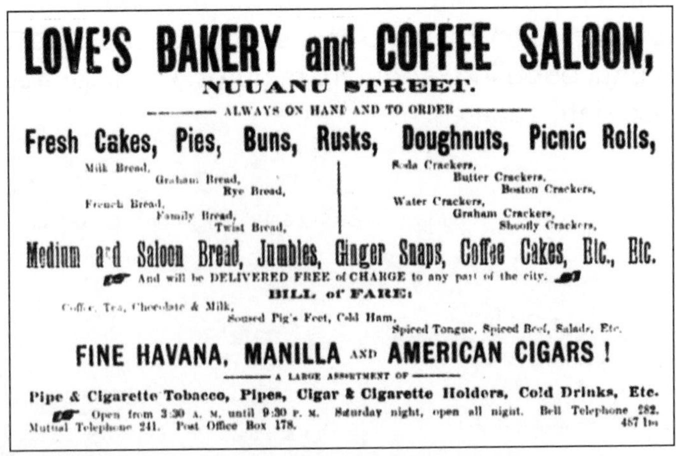

NISHIME

2 strips nishime konbu
3 pieces dried mushrooms (shiitake), soaked, washed, and cut in 1-inch pieces
¼ pound cut up pork
2 tablespoons oil
1¼ cups water
3 aburage (fried tofu), cut In 1-inch pieces
½ cup shoyu
⅓ cup sugar
¼ teaspoon salt
1 teaspoon ajinomoto
1 cup daikon (turnip), cut in stew pieces
2 konyaku, sliced
1 cup carrots, cut in stew pieces
1 cup gobo (burdock), cut in ¼-inch thick diagonal slices and soaked in water until ready to use
2 cups araimo (Japanese taro), cut in 1¼-inch pieces

Soak konbu and mushroom in water for 10 minutes or until soft. Wash and strip konbu down center, lengthwise, if too wide (more than 3 inches). Tie in knots about 2 inches apart. Cut between knots. Fry pork in oil until light brown. Add water, mushroom, aburage, and konbu. Cover; cook for 10 minutes. Add seasonings and cook for 5 minutes. Add daikon, konyaku, carrots, and gobo; cook another 15 minutes. Add taro and cool until taro is done (about 15 minutes).

KATSUKO MATSUO
Our Daily Bread Centennial Cookbook, Iao Congregational Church

RATATOUILLE

½ pound long eggplants
½ pound zucchini
4 tablespoons olive oil (more if needed)
½ pound thinly sliced onions
2 green bell peppers, sliced
2 cloves garlic, crushed
1 pound firm ripe tomatoes, peeled and juiced
Salt and pepper to taste
3 tablespoons minced fresh basil
3 tablespoons minced fresh parsley

Peel eggplants and cut into slices ³/₈-inch thick. Scrub zucchini and cut into slices ³/₈-inch thick. Place vegetables in bowl and sprinkle with salt. Toss and let stand for 30 minutes. Drain. Dry each slice in paper towel.

Sauté eggplants and zucchini, a small amount at a time, in hot olive oil about a minute on each side to brown very lightly. Remove to dish.

In the same skillet, sauté onions and peppers for about 10 minutes or until tender, but not browned. Add more oil to pan as necessary. Stir in garlic; season to taste with salt and pepper.

Slice the tomato pulp into ³/₈-inch strips. Lay them over the onions and peppers. Season with salt and pepper. Cover skillet and cook over low heat for 5 minutes or until tomatoes begin to render their juice. Uncover. Baste tomatoes with the juices. Raise heat and boil for several minutes until juice has almost evaporated.

Place ¹/₃ of tomatoes-onions-peppers mixture in bottom of a 2½ quart casserole; sprinkle 1 tablespoon basil and parsley over it. Arrange half of the eggplant and zucchini mixture on top. Add half of the remaining tomato mixture, basil, and parsley. Put in remaining eggplants-zucchini on top, then top with remaining tomatoes, basil, and parsley.

Cover casserole and bake in moderate oven 45 minutes. Uncover. Baste with rendered juices and bake an additional 15 minutes.

NOTE: Reheat slowly at serving time or serve cold. Also freezes well.

WIN BURGESS
Cooking with Honolulu Gardeners, Honolulu Community Recreational Garden Program

PAPAYA AS A VEGETABLE

- 4 green papayas, peeled and diced
- 5 tablespoons margarine
- 1 Maui onion, chopped
- 4 tomatoes, peeled, seeded, chopped
- 1 chicken bouillon cubes
- ¼ cup freshly grated Parmesan cheese
- ¼ cup chopped macadamia nuts
- Salt and pepper to taste

Combine first five ingredients in a large saucepan and cook until papaya is soft. Add cheese and nuts, mix and serve. Some chopped parsley can be sprinkled on top for color.

ANNA HAMBLEY
We, the Women of Hawaii Cookbook

PIGEON PEA WITH RICE

1¼ cups rice, pre-soaked
¼ cup melted butter or margarine
1 medium onion, chopped
1 clove garlic, minced
1½ teaspoons salt
1 teaspoon basil, dried
1 teaspoon oregano, dried
1½ cups peas or beans (such as pigeon peas, winged beans, etc., pre-cooked)
2½ cups chicken bouillon or broth

Clean, wash, and soak rice for ½ hour. Heat butter and fry onions until golden. Fry garlic; add drained rice, salt, basil, oregano, and peas. Continue to cook for 5 minutes, stirring. Gradually add hot bouillon. Mix thoroughly and bring to a boil. Simmer, covered, for 20 to 25 minutes or until liquid has been absorbed and rice is tender.

NOTE: Any of the following spices can be used: cloves, cinnamon, caraway seeds, turmeric, ginger, red pepper, coriander, parsley, or cumin.

COMMUNITY GARDEN COUNCIL
Cooking with Honolulu Gardeners, Honolulu Community Recreational Garden Program

CHINESE PEAS

Makes 4 to 6 servings

2 tablespoons oil
1 large can button mushrooms
1 pound water chestnuts, cut into halves
Salt to taste
1 cup chicken broth
1 teaspoon cornstarch
1 teaspoon shoyu
1 pound Chinese peas, remove strings and leave whole
1 cup green onion, cut into 1-inch lengths

Heat oil in pot. Stir in mushrooms and water chestnuts. Add salt and chicken broth. Simmer for 10 minutes. Combine cornstarch and shoyu and add to the gravy. Add peas and green onions, stirring constantly for 3 to 5 minutes so that peas will be cooked but not soft. Serve immediately.

Favorite Island Cookery, Book II, Honpa Hongwanji Buddhist Temple

JAPANESE-STYLE HIBISCUS GREENS

Makes 4 to 6 servings

3 tablespoons sesame oil
3 tablespoons sesame seeds
2 tablespoons shoyu
2 tablespoons vinegar
½ pound young tender Sunset Hibiscus leaves
1 tablespoon sugar

Heat sesame oil in large skillet or wok. When oil is hot, add sesame seeds and cook until the seeds pop. Add shoyu and vinegar. Toss in the greens and stir-fry until soft. Add sugar and mix well with the greens.

Cooking with Honolulu Gardeners,
Honolulu Community Recreational Garden Program

VEGETABLE TEMPURA

1 cup flour
1 teaspoon sugar
1 teaspoon salt
1 teaspoon baking powder
¾ cup water
1 egg
½ cup julienned carrots
1 cup julienned string beans
½ cup julienned gobo
¼ cup chopped parsley
¼ cup chopped chives
3 stalks green onion, chopped
½ kamaboko (red), julienned
Oil (for deep-frying)

Heat oil. In a fairly large bowl (2-quart size), add dry ingredients. In ¾ cup water, add egg and stir to mix. Add to dry ingredients and mix until well-blended. Add prepared vegetables and kamaboko. Mix until vegetables are coated with batter. Drop by spoonfuls or hashi (chopsticks) into hot oil. Drain on paper towel. Serve hot.

YOSHIKO MAEDA
50th Anniversary Best of Our Favorite Recipes,
Maui Association for Family and Community Education

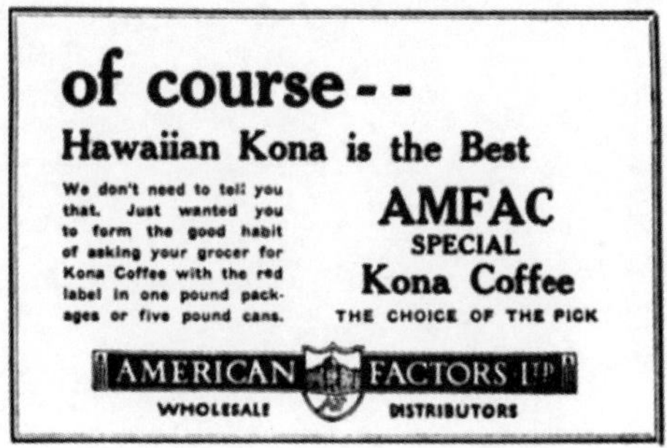

OKARA

2 cups water
1 envelope, dashinomoto
3 dried mushrooms (medium size), soaked and chopped
¼ cup chopped shio konbu
½ cup chopped green beans, or peas
Salt to taste
¼ cup oil
⅓ cup chirimen iriko
2 cups okara
¼ cup carrot, minced
4 stalks chives, chopped

1. In a saucepan, boil water; add dashinomoto and bring to a boil.
2. Add mushrooms, konbu, carrots and cook about 5 minutes.
3. Lastly, add beans and set aside. (Add salt to taste.)
4. In another larger saucepan, heat the oil and brown the iriko. Add okara and stir-fry.
5. Add cooked vegetables and add chives last.

TAMAE KON
Grandma & Grandpa's Hawaiian Island Cookbook, Honolulu Federal Savings and Loan Association

RICE
AND NOODLES

THAI FRIED RICE

Makes 4 servings

2 tablespoons soybean oil
1 clove garlic, minced
1 onion, minced
3 cups cooked rice
¾ cup sliced water chestnuts
1 tomato, halved and quartered
1 tablespoon tomato sauce
⅓ cup pineapple chunks
⅓ cup grated carrots
½ teaspoon salt
1 cucumber, sliced
4 stalks green onion, chopped
4 sprigs Chinese parsley.
1 small red chili pepper, seeded and sliced

In a wok, heat oil. Brown garlic. Add onion and stir-fry for 1 minute. Stir in rice, water chestnuts, tomato, tomato sauce, pineapple, carrots, and salt. Mix well and stir-fry for 3 minutes. Serve with cucumber slices, chopped green onions, Chinese parsley, and sliced chili pepper.

PETER CHANG
1988 4-H Local & Ethnic Food Show

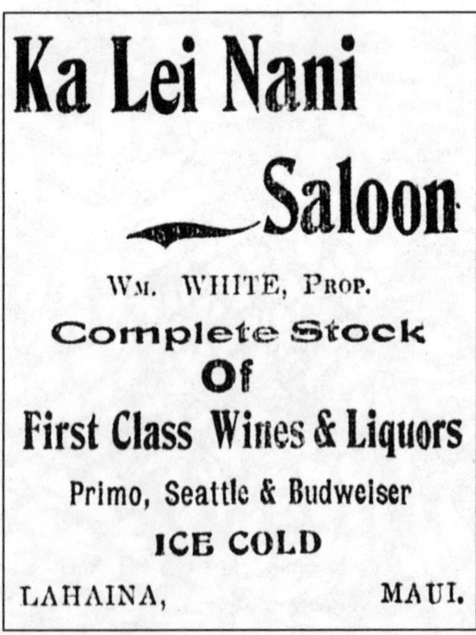

KOREAN-STYLE FRIED RICE

Makes 6 to 8 servings

¼ pound pork, thinly sliced
¼ teaspoon sesame seed oil
¼ teaspoon sugar
1½ tablespoons soy sauce
1 clove garlic, pressed
2 tablespoons canola oil
1 (12-ounce) package bean sprouts, washed and drained
3 cups cold, cooked rice
3 tablespoons soy sauce
1 cup minced green onion

Marinate pork in sesame oil, sugar, soy sauce, and garlic for 15 minutes. Stir-fry pork in hot oil for 2 to 3 minutes or until cooked through. Add bean sprouts and rice; stir-fry additional 2 minutes or until rice is heated through. Add soy sauce and green onion; toss until well-mixed. Serve hot.

The Tastes and Tales of Mōʻiliʻili,
A Collection of Recipes & Stories by Mōʻiliʻili Community Center

FRIED RICE

3 slices bacon, cut into ½-inch pieces
3 cups cooked rice
1 cup diced ham
½ cup chopped onion
¼ cup slivered water chestnuts
2 tablespoons shoyu
2 tablespoons oyster sauce
¼ teaspoon black pepper
2 tablespoons oil
2 eggs, beaten
2 stalks green onion, thinly sliced

In a large skillet, fry bacon for 2 minutes. Add remaining ingredients except for eggs and green onions. Stir-fry for 4 minutes until mixture is thoroughly heated. Add beaten eggs and stir-fry until eggs are cooked. Remove from heat; toss with green onions and serve.

DONNA SLATER
Food for the Body and Soul, West Kauaʻi United Methodist Church

KEDGEREE

3 slices bacon
1 (6½-ounce) can tuna, or leftover cooked fish
3 cups boiled short-grain rice
Salt and freshly ground pepper
3 hard-boiled eggs

Dice and fry bacon and remove bacon bits. Over low heat, stir in fish to warm it. Add rice, breaking it up by dragging two forks through it in opposite directions. This, and the fat, will break the rice up into individual grains. Season with ¼ teaspoon salt and lots of freshly ground pepper. Add bacon back and mix thoroughly. Grate 2 or 3 eggs into mixture, and mix thoroughly. Grating the last egg over the mixture in the serving dish is a "pretty-for-nice" touch.

EDITH RICE PLEWS
Dining with the Daughters, The Daughters of Hawaii

OYAKO DONBURI

Makes 1 serving

⅔ cup soup stock (sea weed or iriko fish)
1 tablespoon sugar
1 tablespoon mirin
3 tablespoons shoyu
¼ round onion, chopped
Several pieces chicken, bite-size
2 eggs
Crushed nori (for garnish)

Heat soup stock, sugar, mirin, and shoyu. Add onion and chicken. Beat eggs and pour over the cooking chicken sauce. Cook until eggs become firm. Slide this sauce over hot rice in a large rice bowl (donburi). Sprinkle crushed nori over oyako donburi rice.

TAKAKO DICKINSON
Our Daily Bread Centennial Cookbook, Iao Congregational Church

SEKIHAN
Red Bean Rice

½ cup azuki (Japanese dried red beans)
4 cups water, divided use
1 teaspoon salt
½ teaspoon ajinomoto (optional)
2 cups rice
2½ cups mochi rice
Salt to taste
Sesame seeds, roasted

In a pot, combine azuki with 3 cups water; bring to a boil, then add another cup of cold water. Simmer for about 1 hour until azuki is soft. Do not overcook. Remove from heat; add salt and ajinomoto. Drain, reserving liquid. Add enough water to azuki liquid to measure 4½ cups.

Wash and soak the rice and mochi rice for 1 hour. Drain water and place rice in a rice cooker. Add the 4½ cups reserved liquid to the soaked rice; top with the cooked azuki. Cook according to manufacturer's directions. When rice is done, gently stir to mix rice and azuki.

Just before serving, sprinkle with salt and roasted sesame seeds.

JANICE TOGUCHI
50th Anniversary Best of Our Favorite Recipes, Maui Association for Family and Community Education

NAGAKURA'S MOCHI RICE

4 cups mochi rice
8 shiitake mushrooms, soaked and sliced
4 lup chong, sliced
¼ pound char siu, sliced
2 stalks green onion, chopped
2 csns chicken broth

Soak mushrooms, slice and SAVE juice. Stir-fry mushrooms, lup chong, char siu, and green onions. Wash rice and drain water. Add cut-up ingredients to rice. Fill rice pot with chicken broth and shiitake water to 8 cup line. You may use a regular rice cooker for this dish.

LORI NAGAKURA
"Pig Out" with Liholiho's Caring, Competent, Creative Cooks

SHISO RICE

3 cups rice (rice measure)
3 cups water
1 (1-ounce) package Chirimen Iriko
2 tablespoons oil
¼ cup shoyu
2 tablespoons raw brown sugar
1 package dashinomoto
1 handful chopped shiso

Wash rice and add water and leave aside. Sauté the iriko in heated oil. Add the shoyu, sugar, dashinomoto, and shiso. Add this mixture to the rice. Mix well and cook in your automatic rice cooker. Mix well before serving.

SUE KANESHINA
Our Daily Bread Centennial Cookbook, Iao Congregational Church

SPANISH RICE

Makes 6 to 8 servings

½ pound lean ground beef
1 medium onion, chopped
Bell pepper, chopped (optional)
Celery, chopped (optional)
Garlic, chopped (optional)
1 to 2 (8-ounce) cans tomato sauce
3 cans cooked brown rice
1 can kidney beans
1 cup grated or sliced cheese
Salt and pepper, if desired

In large skillet, brown beef and drain excess fat. Add onion, bell pepper, celery, and garlic; cook until tender-crisp. Add tomato sauce and rice and mix well. Add kidney beans. Cover and heat on low until hot. Add cheese until melted. Season as desired. Serve with vegetable or fruit salad and a glass of milk to complete the meal.

TOSHIKO YOGI
Family Favorites, Oahu Extension Homemakers Council

SAVORY RICE PILAF

Makes 6 servings

2 cups long grain rice
1 tablespoon olive oil
4 cups stock
½ cup apple juice
1 large onion, diced
2 cloves garlic, minced
1 teaspoon lemon juice
½ teaspoon dried thyme

In a 2-quart saucepan, combine the rice and oil. Stir over medium heat until the rice is golden brown, about 5 minutes. Add the stock, apple juice, onion, garlic, lemon juice, and thyme. Bring to a boil. Reduce the heat to low, cover the pan, and simmer until all the liquid has been absorbed and the rice is tender, about 20 minutes. Fluff with a fork before serving.

Parks & Recreation Family Favorites

WILD RICE

Makes 8 servings

1 cup wild rice
½ (14½-ounce) can chicken broth
⅓ cup minced round onion
½ block butter
1 (5-ounce) can mushrooms, sliced
2 tablespoons minced parsley
1 (8-inch) Portuguese sausage, chopped

Rinse rice and soak in hot water, covered, for ½ day. Drain and dry well. Cook in rice cooker with chicken broth for 25 minutes. Sauté remaining ingredients in butter. Mix with rice and season to taste. Garnish and serve.

Hawaii's Aloha Recipes, The Japanese Women's Society of Honolulu

PORTUGUESE HARD RICE

2 tablespoons oil
½ onion, sliced
1 potato, sliced
1 carrot, sliced
Parsley, chopped
½ can tomato sauce
1 can kidney beans
Shredded cabbage (optional)
2 cups rice, washed
3 cups water
½ to 1 teaspoons vinegar
Salt
Pepper
Allspice
Ajinomoto
Shredded kale (optional}

Put oil in soup pot and heat. Add sliced onion, potato, carrots, and parsley. Brown a little. Add tomato sauce, kidney beans, and cabbage. Add rice and water. Add rest of seasonings. Turn to high. Bring to boil with cover on. Remove cover and let water dry up. Turn stove to medium. Put cover back on and cook until rice is done (15 minutes). Remove from stove and let set for several hours.

MILO B. FERREIRA
Our Favorite Recipes from the Portuguese Heritage Club of Hamakua

GANDULE RICE
Puerto Rican Red Rice

½ pound pork, spareribs, or chicken, diced
5 cloves garlic, minced
½ cup achiote oil
4 cups rice
1 cup chopped green onions
½ cup chopped round onions
¾ cup chopped bell pepper
½ cup Chinese parsley
1 can tomato sauce
1 cup gandule beans
Salt to taste
1 can olives
½ teaspoon MSG

Cook or brown meat with minced garlic and achiote oil. Cook rice separately in rice cooker or pot. When the meat is well-done; add in green and round onions, bell pepper, Chinese parsley, and tomato sauce.

With a pot of water cook gandule beans (separate from all other ingredients), boil till the beans are soft. Drain all the water.

Combine all ingredients, including the olives and gandule beans. Simmer for about 10 to 15 minutes, then combine with the rice another 10 to 15 minutes. Stir till dry on low heat.

SHARON SANCHEZ
Haleiwa Elementary School 115th Birthday

JAMBALAYA

Makes 6 to 8 servings

A delicious Cajun-type dish that is enjoyed by many—try it, you'll like it!

1 cup chopped onion
1 cup chopped green bell pepper
1 clove garlic, minced
2 tablespoons canola oil
2 (1-pound) cans whole tomatoes, undrained and chopped
1 (6-ounce) can tomato paste
1 (4-ounce) can sliced mushrooms, undrained
1 cup cooked rice
¾ teaspoon salt
⅛ teaspoon ground thyme
⅛ teaspoon cayenne pepper
1 bay leaf
½ pound cooked shrimp, peeled and deveined
¾ cup chopped fresh parsley

In a large skillet, sauté onion, green pepper, and garlic in hot oil. Add tomatoes, tomato paste, mushrooms, rice, seasoning, and bay leaf. Cover and bring to a boil. Reduce heat and simmer on low for 30 to 45 minutes.

Remove from heat and let stand 5 minutes. Remove bay leaf; stir in shrimp and parsley just before serving.

MURIEL MIURA KAMINAKA
The Tastes and Tales of Mō'ili'ili, A Collection of Recipes & Stories by Mō'ili'ili Community Center

MIXED RICE
Pi-Bium Pahb

Makes 4 to 5 servings

½ pound beef, thinly sliced
4 cups rice, cooked

Beef Marinade
2 stalks green onions, minced
1 clove garlic, minced
Dash pepper
1 tablespoon toasted and crushed sesame seeds
2 tablespoons soy sauce
2 teaspoons sesame oil

Mix beef well in marinade. Stir-fry over high heat. Set aside.

2 cucumbers: Wash and without peeling, cut into 1½-inch lengths. Shred finely. Sprinkle with 1 teaspoon salt and let stand 10 minutes. Squeeze out liquid. Add 1 tablespoon, chopped green onions, ajinomoto, 1 teaspoon toasted and crushed sesame seeds, and stir-fry lightly. Chill.

1 package fresh bean sprouts: Clean bean sprouts. Wash and cook in hot water until tender. Drain. Add 1 tablespoon soy sauce, 1 tablespoon minced green onions, ½ clove minced garlic, 1 tablespoon toasted and crushed sesame seeds and ajinomoto. Mix well and stir-fry quickly.

1 carrot: Wash and peel carrot. Finely shred lengthwise into 1-inch pieces. Cook in boiling, salted water for 3 minutes. Drain. Add 1 tablespoon chopped green onions, ajinomoto and 1 teaspoon toasted and crushed sesame seeds. Stir-fry lightly.

2 eggs: Beat lightly with a pinch of salt. Make a thin omelet and cut into strips.

To serve, put cooked rice on plate or bowl and ingredients on the top. Mix and serve.

Hawaii's Aloha Recipes, The Japanese Women's Society of Honolulu

RICE AND PORTUGUESE CABBAGE

1½ cup rice
2 cups water
½ teaspoon salt
7 ounces Portuguese sausage, sliced
¾ cup chopped Portuguese cabbage
½ cup chopped potatoes
½ cup chopped carrots

Bring rice and water to a boil over medium-high heat. Stir in remaining ingredients. Cook over low heat until rice is tender. Do not stir too often.

MARIE S. HO
Our Favorite Recipes from the Portuguese Heritage Club of Hamakua

BREAK DA MOUTH SPAM® MUSUBI

1 (12-ounce) can Spam®
4 tablespoons water
4 tablespoons sugar
4 tablespoons shoyu
2 tablespoons mirin
1 package yaki sushi nori
6 cups cooked rice, 3 cups raw
1 jar furikake

Cut Spam® into 10 slices. Heat water, sugar, shoyu, and mirin in flat frying pan until sugar dissolves. Place Spam® in mixture and simmer for a while until it gets sticky, turn frequently. Remove and let Spam® cool.

Cut nori into ½-inch widths. Dampen sides of musubi maker—fill maker ⅓ with rice then press with cover. Spread thin layer of furikake to cover rice. Place a piece of Spam®, cover with more rice, and press down with cover firmly. Lift maker and fold nori over rice. Salt rice a little while still warm.

Ono-Licious, Na Poe Humukuiki O Hawaii, Hawaii Quilt Guild

SUSHI RICE

6 cups rice
6 cups water less 1 tablespoon
1 tablespoon sake

Awase-zu
⅔ cup sugar
2½ tablespoons salt
1 tablespoon ajinomoto
1 cup vinegar

Cook rice with water and sake.

Put Awase-zu ingredients in a sauce pan and bring to a boil. Cool.

To the cooked rice, gradually sprinkle the Awase-zu, stirring lightly. Cool rice with a fan as it is being stirred. Barazushi or chirashi zushi can be made by adding carrots, string beans, shiitake, etc. to the sushi rice.

Carrots
2 medium carrots
3 tablespoons water
2 tablespoons sugar
1 tablespoon shoyu

Cut carrots into small, thin pieces. Add remaining ingredients and cook at high heat until all the liquid has evaporated, stirring constantly.

String beans
15 string beans
1 tablespoon water
1 tablespoon sugar
¼ teaspoon salt

Cut string beans diagonally into very thin strips. Add remaining ingredients and cook at high heat until all the liquid has evaporated, stirring constantly.

Shiitake

8 medium dried shiitake (soaked in water for about 1 hour)
4 tablespoons water
3 tablespoons sugar
1 tablespoon shoyu

Cut soaked shiitake into small and very thin pieces. Add the remaining ingredients and cook in moderate heat for 10 minutes. Then increase heat and cook while stirring constantly until all the liquid has evaporated.

Eggs

1½ tablespoons cornstarch
2 tablespoons water
3 eggs
½ teaspoon salt
1 teaspoon sugar
Dash of ajinomoto

Mix cornstarch and water well. Beat eggs, add cornstarch-water mixture, salt, sugar, and ajinomoto. Fry thin in a flat, slightly greased pan. Put pan under a broiler for about 10 seconds to cook the top. This will eliminate turning the egg mixture over. Remove from pan, cool, and cut into thin strips.

Garnish

The barazushi may be garnished with fried eggs, toasted nori, and pickled ginger root (benishoga).

Favorite Island Cookery, Book I, Honpa Hongwanji Hawaii Betsuin

NORI MAKI SUSHI

Makes 8 rolls

Sushi Rice
3 cups rice
3 cups water

Cook rice and set aside.

Vinegar Sauce
½ cup Japanese rice vinegar
1 teaspoon MSG
2 tablespoons sake (rice wine)
½ cup sugar
1 teaspoon salt

Combine ingredients. Sprinkle over hot rice and mix. Cool. Rice is now ready to make Nori Maki Sushi.

10 sheets nori (seaweed)

Filling
1 (2-ounce) packages kanpyo (dried gourd)
1 small carrot, cut into ½-inch strips
4 pieces shiitake (dried mushroom), soaked and cut into ½-inch strips
10 sprigs watercress, blanched
1 (3½-ounce) can eel

To prepare kanpyo: Soak in water 10 to 15 minutes, wash thoroughly. Cook in 2 to 3 cups water or broth until tender, about 20 to 30 minutes. Season with 2 tablespoons shoyu, 1 tablespoon sugar, and dash of MSG. Cut into the length of nori.

To prepare dried mushroom and carrot: Cook 5 to 10 minutes, or until tender in 1 tablespoon dried shrimp, 1 cup water, and 1½ teaspoons salt.

Method of rolling: Place a sheet of nori on the sudare (bamboo mat) with edge nearest you even with the edge of the sudare. Spread sushi rice over nori to a thickness of about ½-inch leaving 1½-inch margin on end farthest from you.

Arrange 1 inch from edge nearest you, 5 strands of kanpyo, 1 row each of dried mushroom, carrot, watercress, and eel, split lengthwise on the rice.

Roll away from you, being careful to hold the vegetables in place with your fingers. When the sudare touches the rice, lift the mat and continue to roll, like you would for jelly roll, until completely rolled.

Roll again in the sudare and apply slight pressure to tighten the roll.

To serve, cut each roll into 7 or 8 pieces. Arrange on plate, cut side up.

The Heritage of Hawaii Cookbook, Honolulu Gas Company, Ltd.

BROILED SUSHI

9 shiitake mushrooms, chopped, soaked in water until soft, then drained
10 sticks imitation crabmeat, shredded
1 cup sour cream or cream cheese
1 cup mayonnaise
3 cups cooked rice
Furikake
Korean nori (the wasabi nori at Daiei is really good, too)

Mix together the mushrooms, crabmeat, sour cream OR cream cheese and mayonnaise. (I use sour cream.) Place cooked rice in a 9 x 13-inch pan. Sprinkle furikake over rice. Top with crabmeat mixture. Broil for approximately 10 to 15 minutes. Spoon on nori.

IAN FITZ-PATRICK
"No Ka Oi" The Best of Hawaii, Favorite Recipes from Rotarians of District 5000

BUCKWHEAT NOODLE SUSHI

Soba Sushi

Makes 3 servings

1 cup soup stock (dashi)
¼ cup soy sauce
⅓ cup Japanese sweet cooking wine (mirin)
10 ounces green tea buckwheat noodles (cha soba)
1 package fresh water eel (unagi)
1 roll thick-cooked egg (atsuyaki tamago)
Beefsteak leaves (shiso)
2 to 3 sheets nori
Green horseradish (wasabi)

In a bowl, combine dashi, soy sauce, and mirin for a dipping sauce; chill. Cook soba according to package directions. Do not overcook. Heat unagi in package in boiling water; cool and cut into 3 long strips. Cut tamago roll into long strips. Finely chop shiso leaves.

Place a sheet of nori, shiny side down, on bamboo mat. Spread a layer of noodles over ¾ of the nori, leaving 1 inch uncovered at the farthest end. Two inches from the nearest edge, arrange unagi, tamago, and shiso leaves crosswise on noodles. To roll, bring the edge of nori up and over the noodles, encasing the center ingredients. Roll like jelly roll, lifting mat until nori completely surrounds roll. Leave in bamboo mat for 2 to 3 minutes to hold shape. Slice each roll into 6 pieces. Serve with wasabi and dipping sauce.

50th Anniversary Best of Our Favorite Recipes,
Maui Association for Family and Community Education

QUICKIE LAYER SUSHI

4 tablespoons vinegar
4½ cups short grain rice, washed and cooked
2 cans tuna
3 tablespoons brown sugar
2 tablespoons soy sauce
½ teaspoon salt
Furikake nori

Sprinkle the vinegar over the rice; mix. Line a 14 x 10 x 1-inch pan with a double layer of waxed paper. Spread half of hot rice on the waxed paper. In a frying pan, stir in the tuna, brown sugar, soy sauce, and salt. Cook until somewhat dry; tuna should not be wet. Spread tuna over rice layer. Spread the second half of the rice over the tuna layer. Lay double waxed paper on top of the rice. Place a second pan of the same size on top of the waxed paper and weigh the pan down with a heavy weight for two hours or until rice has cooled. Remove weight. Put a tray large enough to cover on top of the rice and flip rice over onto tray. Remove waxed paper. Cut rice into 2-inch squares. Sprinkle furikake nori (in bottle) over rice and serve.

NOTE: May use diced takuwan in place of tuna.

Community Family Favorites, Community Church of Honolulu

INARI SUSHI

5 packages aburage
15 pieces string beans
1 or 2 carrots
6 cups rice (rice cooker cup)

Vinegar mixture
¾ cup white sugar
1¼ tablespoons salt
½ cup Japanese vinegar

Stock for aburage
¾ cup raw brown sugar
1 tablespoon salt
4 tablespoons Kikkoman memmi soup base
3 cups water
2 tablespoons white sugar
1 teaspoon salt
¾ cup water

Cut aburage in halve; split open and pour boiling water to remove some of the oil. Bring stock ingredients to a boil, then add the aburage. Cook for 20 minutes; mix gently with wooden spoon in between cooking time.

Slice string beans and carrots into small pieces. Cook carrots with the white sugar and water. When half cooked, add the string beans and 1 teaspoon salt and cook until done.

Season the cooked rice with the string beans, carrots, and slowly add the vinegar mixture. Season to suit your taste. You may add some of the aburage broth to the rice mixture. Fill aburage with rice mixture.

SUE KANESHINA
Our Daily Bread Centennial Cookbook, Iao Congregational Church

CHICKEN LONG RICE

Makes 6 to 8 servings

2½ pounds chicken thighs
3 quarts water, divided use
1 tablespoon salt
1½ tablespoons ginger root
8 ounces long rice
5 chicken bouillon cubes
3 green onions, chopped

Put chicken into 5-quart saucepan. Add 2 pints of the water, salt, and ginger. Bring to a boil, skim, lower heat, and simmer for 40 minutes. Remove from heat and drain, saving broth.

Remove meat from chicken, discarding bones. Shred meat and set aside. Put broth into saucepan. Bring to a boil. Add long rice and bouillon cubes, then lower heat and cook covered or 5 minutes. Turn off heat and let stand about 30 minutes.

With kitchen shears, cut long rice into approximately 3 or 4 inch lengths. Stir in chicken and heat briefly, if desired, before serving. Sprinkle with green onions.

Hilo Missionary Cooks

KOREAN LONG RICE

1 pound pork
1 cup string beans
1 large carrot, cut diagonally
cooking oil
1 cup thinly sliced bamboo shoots
4 dried mushrooms, soaked in water and cut into thin slices
1 teaspoon grated ginger
1 tablespoon chopped garlic
1 small onion, chopped
1 bundle long rice
½ teaspoon pepper
¼ cup shoyu
1 cup bean sprouts
1 tablespoon sesame seeds

Cut pork in thin slices. Fry string beans and carrots in a little oil and set aside. Fry pork well. Add bamboo shoots, mushrooms, ginger, and garlic, and cook well.

Add carrots, beans, onions, long rice, pepper, and shoyu. Cook for 5 minutes. Add bean sprouts and cook for a few more minutes. Sprinkle with sesame seeds.

Wisteria Delights, A Collection of Recipes
by Pearl City Hongwanji Mission

CHINESE GON LO MEIN

2 teaspoons oyster sauce
1 teaspoon sugar
1 teaspoon sesame oil
2 (12-ounce) packages fried noodles
1 package bean sprouts
1 carrot, diagonally sliced
1 round onion, diagonally sliced
1 head broccoli, diagonally sliced
3 stalks celery, diagonally sliced
1 (4-ounce) can sliced mushrooms
Salt and pepper to taste
1 cube chicken bouillon
1 tablespoon cooking oil
1 cup cooked chicken, shredded
Chinese parsley or green onion for garnish

Mix oyster sauce, sugar, and oil and pour over noodles. Put noodles into 250°F oven to warm.

Lightly stir-fry vegetables in hot oil. Season vegetables with salt, pepper, and bouillon cube. Combine vegetables with noodles and shredded chicken. Put in serving dish and garnish with green onions/parsley.

JENNIE S. WUNG
100 Years Sharing God's Love, United Community Church

LOOK FUN
Chow Fun

Makes 6 servings

1½ pounds lean pork
1 tablespoon corn oil
2 rolls look fun noodles, cut into ¼-inch strips
2 cups finely sliced string beans
1 medium size carrot, finely sliced
1 (10-ounce) package bean sprouts
1 stalk celery, sliced diagonally
4 stalks green onions, cut in 1-inch lengths

Chinese parsley, for garnish

Marinade for pork
1 (½-inch) slice ginger, pressed
¾ teaspoon salt
2 teaspoons shoyu sauce
1 teaspoon sugar

Seasoning for ingredients
¼ to ½ cup chicken broth
2 teaspoons salt
¼ teaspoon white or black pepper
1 teaspoon oyster sauce
1 teaspoon sherry
¼ teaspoon MSG

Slice pork in thin strips and marinate for 15 minutes. Sauté pork in oil until brown (pork should be cooked through).

While pork is cooking, steam look fun noodle strips in a colander. Add look fun noodles and stir-fry 1 minute. Add vegetables and seasonings and stir-fry for another minute or so. For those who like Chinese parsley, garnish with parsley.

Still Many More of Favorite Recipes,
Maui Association for Family and Community Education

BEEF BROCCOLI WITH NOODLES

Makes 6 servings

¾ pound beef
1 teaspoon finely grated ginger
2 tablespoons shoyu
2 tablespoons salad oil, divided use
2 cups sliced broccoli
1 medium onion, sliced
4 stalks green onion

Gravy mixture
1 teaspoon sugar
½ teaspoon salt
¼ teaspoon MSG
Dash pepper
1 tablespoon cornstarch
2 cups chicken broth
Crisp or soft-fried noodles

Slice beef thinly; marinate in ginger and shoyu for ½ hour. Heat 1 tablespoon of the oil and sauté broccoli for 1 minute; remove broccoli.

Heat remaining oil; sauté beef and sliced onions until browned.

Combine gravy mixture and stir into meat mixture. Add broccoli and green onions; cook until sauce thickens. Serve over hot noodles.

Favorite Island Cookery, Book II, Honpa Hongwanji Buddhist Temple

XIAN NOODLE SALAD WITH PEANUT SAUCE

Makes 6 servings

½ pound linguine or thin spaghetti noodles
2 tablespoons vegetable oil
1 cup shredded lettuce
1 cup bean sprouts
1 cup mushroom (enoki, button, shiitake)
1 red bell pepper, thinly sliced
1 cup thinly sliced asparagus or green vegetable

Dressing

¼ cup sesame seeds
½ cup chicken broth
½ cup peanut butter
¼ cup red wine
2 tablespoons dark soy sauce
2 tablespoons sesame seed oil
1 tablespoon dry sherry
1 tablespoon sugar
½ to 1½ teaspoons Chinese chili sauce, according to taste
½ teaspoon salt
½ cup chopped green onion
2 tablespoons minced ginger
1 large clove garlic, minced

Cook noodles until al dente. Drain, cool, and mix with oil. In large bowl place lettuce, sprouts, mushrooms, and pepper. Set aside. Slice asparagus on a slant in 1-inch lengths. If green vegetables are used, cut in 2-inch lengths. Parboil until crisp tender; drain and cool. Add to lettuce mixture in bowl.

In an unoiled skillet, brown sesame seeds and pour into another bowl. Add other dressing ingredients; mix. Add noodles to vegetables and combine with dressing. Serve immediately.

If this is prepared early, place in the refrigerator but let it stand outside and return to room temperature because the sauce thickens when cooled.

Community Family Favorites, Community Church of Honolulu

CHICKEN CANTON NOODLES

1 (14-ounce) package Canton noodles
1 package black fungus
1 (1-inch) piece ginger, crushed
½ teaspoon salt
¼ cup wine
4 to 5 chicken breasts, boned
1 pound Chinese peas
1 tablespoon oil
1 clove garlic
1 piece ginger, crushed
3 carrots
½ cup soup stock
1 tablespoon soy sauce
1 tablespoon sugar
2 tablespoons oyster sauce
1 tablespoon cornstarch

Boil noodles for 10 minutes or until done (do not add salt). Drain and keep warm. Soak fungus for 1 hour, then wash in running water.

Combine ginger, salt, wine, and chicken; marinate for 30 minutes. Parboil Chinese peas in salted water containing drop of oil to give glossiness. Sauté garlic and ginger; add chicken and stir-fry until cooked.

Remove chicken and add carrots, fungus, stock, and seasoning (do not overcook vegetables). Return chicken to pot and add Chinese peas. Thicken sauce with cornstarch.

Mix noodles with vegetables and serve hot.

Hawaii's Aloha Recipes, The Japanese Women's Society of Honolulu

YAKISOBA

Makes 4 servings

2 tablespoons oil
2 cups slivered cabbage
½ cup slivered carrots
½ cup slivered Spam®, char siu, or ham
1 package yakisoba (contains 2 bags)
4 tablespoons Ikari brand steak sauce
3 tablespoons Ikari brand Worcestershire sauce
½ cup sliced green onion, cut into ½-inch lengths
½ stick kamaboko, slivered

Heat oil over medium heat, add cabbage and carrots, stir-fry half a minute. Add Spam® and stir-fry until hot. Add yakisoba and sauces; mix until the noodles are separated. Stir-fry until well-mixed and hot. Mix in green onion and kamaboko.

VARIATIONS: Other vegetables may be added. Garnishes of slivered fried eggs, other meats, and/or Chinese parsley may be sprinkled on top.

Community Family Favorites, Community Church of Honolulu

FRIED SOMEN WITH SAKE-CHILI SAUCE

Makes 6 servings

1 (9-ounce) package somen
3 tablespoons salad oil, divided use
1 teaspoon salt, divided use
Dash of white pepper
¼ pound lean pork, cut in thin strips
2 cloves garlic, minced
3 cups shredded cabbage
1 tablespoon soy sauce
¼ teaspoon hondashi (fish flavored soup granules)
2 green onions, cut into 1-inch lengths
½ cup sake
3 Hawaiian red peppers, seeded and minced

Cook somen according to package directions; rinse and drain.

In a large skillet, heat 2 tablespoons of the oil. Fry somen; season with ½ teaspoon of the salt and the pepper. Place on a platter. Add the remaining tablespoon oil to the skillet. Lightly brown pork. Add garlic; cook for 30 seconds. Add cabbage, soy sauce, hondashi, and the remaining ½ teaspoon salt; cook for 1 minute. Add green onions; cook for 30 seconds.

Arrange pork and vegetable mixture over somen. Combine sake and red peppers; use sparingly on somen.

50th Anniversary Best of Our Favorite Recipes,
Maui Association for Family and Community Education

SAIMIN

Makes 4 to 6 servings

A favorite snack or light meal for all of us! Prior to the days of instant soup bases and frozen, ready-to-eat saimin, saimin was prepared as follows:

Soup Stock
9 cups water
¼ cup dried shrimp
1 (6-inch) piece dashi konbu
2 to 3 small pork bones
Dash pepper
2 teaspoons soy sauce
1½ teaspoons salt

2 (9½-ounce size) fresh saimin noodles
½ cup chopped green onions
¼ pound char siu, cut into strips
8 to 12 slices kamaboko

Combine water, shrimp, konbu, bones, pepper, soy sauce, and salt in large pot to prepare Soup Stock; bring to a boil over high heat. Lower heat and simmer 30 minutes; strain.

Cook noodles according to package directions. Pour into colander; drain and place noodles in soup bowls. Pour hot soup stock over noodles and garnish with green onions, char siu, and kamaboko.

NOTE: Cooked bean sprouts or cabbage may be placed atop the noodles, if desired.

The Tastes and Tales of Mōʻiliʻili,
A Collection of Recipes & Stories by Mōʻiliʻili Community Center

FAMILY-STYLE PANSIT

Makes 6 servings

1 (7½-ounce) package long rice
4 large dried mushrooms
½ pound lean pork
¼ pound shrimp
2 tablespoons salad oil
4 cloves garlic, minced
2 (14½-ounce) cans chicken broth
2 tablespoons patis
¼ teaspoon pepper
2 (4-ounce) packages fried egg noodles
Lemon wedges

Soak long rice and mushrooms in warm water for 30 minutes; drain. Cut long rice in 3-inch lengths. Remove stems from mushrooms; dice caps. Slice pork thinly. Shell, clean, and cut shrimp into small pieces.

In a large skillet, heat oil. Sauté garlic and brown pork. Stir in shrimp and mushrooms; sauté 1 minute. Add broth, patis, and pepper; bring to a boil. Add long rice and noodles, stirring lightly until noodles are cooked. Serve with lemon wedges.

North Kohala Favorites

PAD THAI NOODLES

1 pound Wet Sen Lek Noodles (found at Kilauea Farmer's Market or Asian section in supermarket)
1 teaspoon minced garlic
1 teaspoon minced chili pepper
½ pound pork or chicken, chopped, or shrimp, peeled and deveined; rinse and drain or ¼ pound combination of any two
2 eggs (more if desired)
1½ tablespoons fish sauce
1½ tablespoons tamarind juice (can substitute tamarind soup mix)
1 tablespoon sugar
¼ teaspoon paprika
¼ cup shredded ginger (fresh is best, but minced works well, too)
⅓ pound bean sprouts
1 tablespoon crushed peanuts
Shredded carrots and lime juice garnish (optional)

Heat 1 tablespoon oil, then stir-fry noodles (already boiled and drained) until hot. Remove, set aside.

Heat 2 tablespoons oil, add garlic and chili pepper. Cook until fragrant; add meat and/or shrimp and stir-fry until color changes. Add eggs and stir-fry until nearly dry. Add the rest of the ingredients in order, stirring well. Add noodles and stir until blended well.

For extra zest, heat and blend in a sauce pan coconut milk and either red (hot) or yellow (mild) curry past to pour over pad Thai noodles.

ERIC, SHERI, HOLLY HAMM
Hanalei School Collective Cook Book

FETTUCCINE WITH PEPPER SAUCE

Makes 4 servings

1½ cups broccoli florets
1 medium apple, pear OR pear-apple, chopped
1 medium green pepper, cut in ¾-inch pieces
1 medium onion, chopped
¾ medium Anaheim pepper, chopped fine
1 to 2 tablespoons cooking OR olive oil
12 ounces skinless/boned chicken in strips
1 (10¾-ounce) can cream of chicken soup
½ cup water
1 teaspoon dried basil
1 teaspoon ginger
1 teaspoon garlic salt
½ teaspoon pepper
1 teaspoon oyster sauce
1 teaspoon shoyu
1 teaspoon aromatic bitters (If available)
2 large mushrooms, sliced
½ cup shredded cheddar cheese
8 ounces fettuccine (I use fresh)

Spray a wok or large skillet with cooking spray. Preheat wok on medium to high heat. Stir-fry broccoli, apple, pepper, onion, and Anaheim pepper for 3 to 4 minutes. Remove from wok. Add oil to wok. Stir-fry chicken for 3 to 4 minutes or until no longer pink. Add soup, water, basil, ginger, garlic salt, pepper, oyster sauce, shoyu, and bitters and mix thoroughly. Stir in sweet pepper mixture. Add mushrooms; bring to a boll. Reduce heat, add cheese, cook until cheese is melted. Serve over hot cooked pasta.

JOHN WALLS
100 Years Sharing God's Love, United Community Church

EASY OVEN LASAGNA

½ pound ground beef
½ cup water
2 (15-ounce) cans marinara sauce
1 teaspoon salt
1 (8-ounce) package lasagna
1 cup ricotta or cottage cheese
12 ounces mozzarella cheese
¼ cup grated Parmesan cheese

Brown ground beef, drain. Add water, marinara sauce, and salt; bring to boil. In a 2-quart (11¾ x 7½-inch) baking dish, layer hot sauce, uncooked lasagna, ricotta, and mozzarella cheese; repeat layers, ending with sauce. Garnish with mozzarella and Parmesan cheese.

Cover tightly with foil. Bake at 375°F for 1 hour, or cover dish with waxed paper and microwave approximately 25 minutes, turning once. Let stand 5 to 10 minutes before cutting into squares.

NOTE: Freeze after and reheat later for baking for best results.

COLLEEN UEDA
"Pig Out" with Liholiho's Caring, Competent, Creative Cooks

TOFU LASAGNA

1 (16-ounce) box lasagna noodles
¼ cup butter
1 pound mushrooms, sliced
3 cloves garlic, chopped
½ teaspoon salt
¼ teaspoon pepper
2 large jars prepared spaghetti sauce
¾ cup wheat germ
1½ blocks tofu, drained and mashed
½ cup Parmesan cheese
1 pound mozzarella cheese
½ cup chopped parsley
Cheddar cheese, grated (optional)

Cook lasagna noodles according to package directions. Drain and set aside.

In a large skillet, melt butter and sauté mushrooms and garlic. Season with salt and pepper. Add prepared spaghetti sauce and wheat germ. Heat thoroughly and set aside.

In a small bowl, combine the tofu and Parmesan cheese. In another bowl, mix mozzarella cheese and parsley. In a deep 9 x 13-inch greased pan, layer: ½ of noodles, ½ of tofu mixture, ½ of sauce, ½ of mozzarella mixture. Repeat layers; end with noodles, sauce, and mozzarella mixture. Grated cheddar cheese may be sprinkled on top.

Bake in a 350°F oven for 45 minutes to 1 hour. Let stand for 15 minutes before cutting. If prepared ahead and refrigerated, increase the baking time by 15 minutes.

Wisteria Delights, A Collection of Recipes
by Pearl City Hongwanji Mission

LINGUINE WITH CHICKEN AND PEANUT SAUCE

Makes 6 servings

- 1 pound skinned, boneless chicken breast
- 1 (14½-ounce) can chicken broth
- 2 tablespoons soy sauce
- 2 tablespoons dry white wine or water
- 1 tablespoon cornstarch
- ⅛ to ¼ teaspoon ground red pepper
- ½ cup peanut butter
- 1 tablespoon peanut oil or cooking oil
- 2 cloves garlic, minced
- 1 teaspoon grated ginger root
- 1 medium onion, thinly sliced and separated into rings
- 8 ounces linguine, cooked and drained
- 2 green onions, sliced
- Papaya slices (optional)

Cut chicken into bite-size pieces; set aside. For sauce, in a medium mixing bowl, stir together chicken broth, soy sauce, wine or water, cornstarch, and red pepper. Blend in peanut butter. Set aside.

Preheat a large skillet over high heat. Add peanut oil. (Add more oil as necessary during cooking.) Stir-fry garlic and ginger root in hot oil 15 seconds. Add onion; stir-fry 2 to 3 minutes or till onion is crisp-tender. Remove vegetables from skillet. Add half of the chicken to the skillet. Stir-fry about 3 minutes or till done. Remove chicken. Repeat with remaining chicken. Return all chicken to skillet. Push chicken from center of skillet.

Stir sauce; add to center of the skillet. Cook and stir till thickened and bubbly. Cook and stir 2 minutes more. Return vegetables to skillet; stir to coat with sauce. Heat through. Serve atop hot cooked linguine. Sprinkle with sliced green onions. Serve with sliced papaya if desired.

50th Anniversary Best of Our Favorite Recipes,
Maui Association for Family and Community Education

ORIENTAL CLAM LINGUINE

1 tablespoon oil
4 cloves garlic, minced
2 (6.5-ounce) cans clams
3 tablespoons oyster sauce
¼ cup chopped parsley
½ pound linguine, cooked
1 tablespoon sesame oil

Heat oil, cook garlic; avoid burning. Add clams with juice, oyster sauce, and parsley. Simmer. Add noodles and sesame oil. Mix well and serve.

Wisteria Delights, A Collection of Recipes
by Pearl City Hongwanji Mission

'AHI PASTA

3 tablespoons olive oil
4 thin slices Maui onion
½ pound 'ahi, cut in 1-inch cubes
2 small tomatoes, cut in ¼-inch slices
¼ cup sliced olives
2 tablespoons fresh minced basil
2 tablespoons minced garlic
Salt and pepper
1¼ pounds linguine
2 tablespoons capers
Parsley

Heat oil in heavy skillet over medium/low heat. Add onions; cook until translucent. Add 'ahi, tomatoes, olives, basil, garlic, salt, and pepper. Cook until fish is opaque, stirring often.

Cook linguine in large pot of boiling water with salt. Drain. Spoon 'ahi mixture over linguine and serve. Garnish with capers and parsley.

RONNIE ODA
A Chorus of Recipes, Kamehameha School Children's Chorus

CRAB PASTA

1 package rigatoni
⅛ cup olive oil
3 cloves garlic, minced
1 large tomato, diced
½ (3-ounce) jar marinated artichoke hearts, diced and drained
2 tablespoons basil, chopped (optional)
½ cup fresh crabmeat, cooked
3 teaspoons Parmesan cheese
Salt and pepper

Boil rigatoni and drain. Rinse in cool water. Sauté garlic, tomato, artichoke hearts, and basil in olive oil for 5 minutes. Fold in crabmeat. Add to noodles and serve with Parmesan cheese.

DEBBIE ISHADO
Haili Congregational Church, 175th Anniversary

HAMBURGER MACARONI CASSEROLE

1 onion, chopped
2 stalks celery, chopped
1 pound ground beef
1 can condensed cream of mushroom soup
1 can condensed tomato soup
1 can cream corn
2 tablespoons ketchup
1 tablespoon salad oil
1 teaspoon ajinomoto
1 teaspoon salt
2 tablespoons mayonnaise
1 (8-ounce) package macaroni, cooked

Fry onions, celery, and ground beef until done. Turn off heat. Add condensed cream of mushroom soup, tomato soup, and cream corn. Add seasonings and mix well. Add cooked macaroni and mix well. Pour into quart casserole dish or a 9 x 14 x 2-inch pan. Bake 350°F for 20 minutes.

Wisteria Delights, A Collection of Recipes by Pearl City Hongwanji Mission

MANICOTTI WITH FLORENTINE-STYLE MEAT FILLING

1 box manicotti or Stuff-a-roni pasta (about 12 shells)
1 package frozen spinach
1 pound ground beef
½ cup minced onion
½ cup Italian style breadcrumbs
½ cup grated Parmesan cheese
2 eggs, slightly beaten
1 teaspoon salt
¼ teaspoon pepper
2 cup bottled or canned spaghetti sauce
4 ounces grated Mozzarella cheese

Cook pasta shells according to package directions. Thaw spinach and squeeze out excess water.

In large bowl, mix together ground beef, onion, breadcrumbs, spinach, Parmesan cheese, eggs, salt, and pepper. Garlic salt may be substituted for part of the salt.

Spray baking dish with nonstick cooking spray and cover bottom with 1 cup of the spaghetti sauce. Fill manicotti shells with ground beef mixture and arrange filled shells in single layer in baking dish. Completely cover filled shells with the remaining cup of sauce; use more sauce if necessary or desired. Cover dish with foil and bake for 35 minutes at 350°F.

Take dish out of the oven and sprinkle mozzarella cheese evenly over baked manicotti and return to oven uncovered. Turn oven off and take manicotti out when cheese topping starts to melt. Use more cheese if you like a lot of cheese topping. Parmesan cheese may also be sprinkled on top along with the mozzarella. Cover and keep warm if not serving right away.

Wisteria Delights, A Collection of Recipes
by Pearl City Hongwanji Mission

PASTA WITH PROSCIUTTO AND ASPARAGUS

1½ pounds fresh asparagus
1 (1-pound) box farfalle (bow-tie) pasta
6 ounces prosciutto ham, cut in thin strips
2 tablespoons butter
1 cup heavy cream
Grated Parmesan cheese

Break the woody ends of the asparagus off and cook it in a saucepan or skillet with just enough water to cover. When it is just tender, drain it and rinse with cool water to prevent it from over-cooking and to set its bright green color.

Cook the pasta. As it is cooking, sauté the prosciutto ham in the butter in a wide shallow skillet. Add the asparagus when the ham is beginning to darken, but do not allow the ham to brown. Toss the asparagus and ham together for half a minute and add the cream. Turn the heat up and stir the sauce until it thickens.

When the pasta is done, drain it and add it to the hot sauce and toss it with the Parmesan cheese. Serve immediately with red wine, a salad, and a baguette.

STEPHEN H. WILSON
"No Ka Oi" The Best of Hawaii,
Favorite Recipes from Rotarians of District 5000

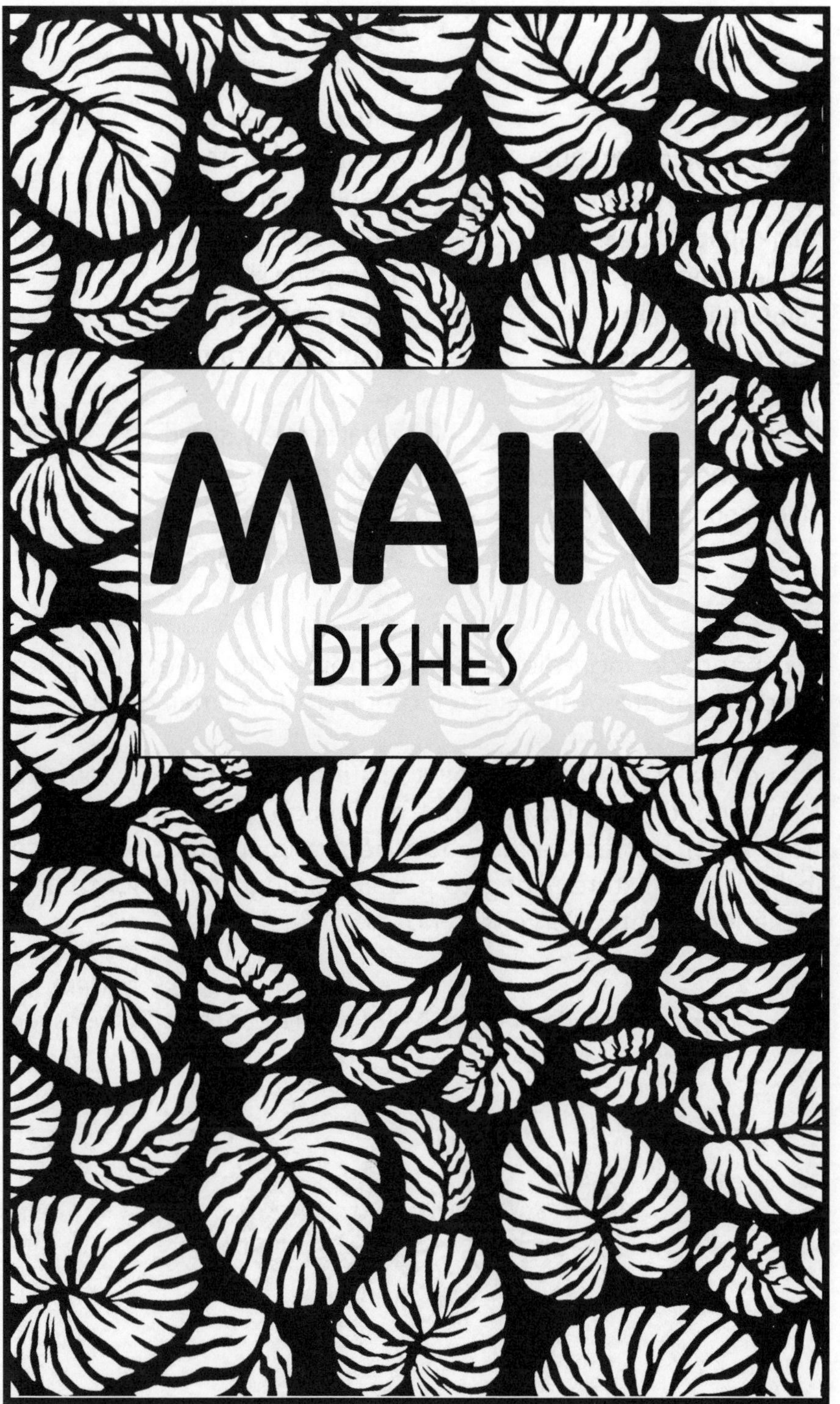
MAIN
DISHES

BEEF TOMATO

Marinade
1 tablespoon oyster sauce
2 tablespoons shoyu
2 tablespoons sugar
1 tablespoon cornstarch
1 tablespoon sake
1 clove garlic, crushed
1 slice ginger, crushed

1 pound beef, thinly sliced
2 tablespoons oil

Sauce
½ cup beef broth
1 tablespoon oyster sauce
1 tablespoon shoyu
1 teaspoon sherry
1 teaspoon salt
1 tablespoon cornstarch

2 stalks celery, sliced
1 bell pepper, sliced
1 onion, sliced
3 tomatoes, quartered

Mix marinade ingredients and combine with beef slices; let stand 20 minutes. Mix Sauce ingredients in a small bowl.

In a hot wok or skillet, heat oil and stir-fry beef quickly; remove from pan. Stir-fry celery, pepper, and onion for a couple of minutes. When almost tender, add beef and tomato. Stir sauce and add to mixture. Bring to a boil, stirring until smooth and thickened slightly. Serve with hot rice.

PATSY TAMEKAZU
Island Flavors, Favorite Recipes of the Historic Hawai'i Foundation

BEEF WITH CRISP LONG RICE

1 pound beef, sliced into 2-inch thin strips

Marinade
2 tablespoons cornstarch
1 teaspoon grated ginger
½ teaspoon salt
1 tablespoon sugar
3 tablespoons shoyu

Gravy
2 teaspoons cornstarch
¼ teaspoon MSG
½ teaspoon salt
1 tablespoons shoyu
¾ cup water

Rice
1 (4-ounce) bundle long rice
1 cup cooking oil
½ head shredded lettuce

½-inch piece ginger, thinly sliced
1 clove garlic
2 medium yellow onions, sliced,
1 stalk green onion, cut thin for garnish

Mix Marinade ingredients together and marinate beef; set aside. Mix Gravy ingredients together and set aside.

Cut dry long rice into 3-inch lengths. Heat oil in skillet. When hot, deep-fry long rice, a small handful at a time. Rice will instantly becoming puffy and crispy. Watch carefully. Drain on paper towels. Line serving platter with shredded lettuce. Arrange puffed long rice on top of lettuce. Set side.

Heat oil in skillet. Fry ginger and garlic till brown. Discard and fry onions till limp. Remove. Fry meat for 2 minutes. Mix with onions, put on long rice. Boil gravy, pour over meat, garnish and serve with rice.

The Hele Mai, Ai (Come Eat) Cookbook, Flavors of Upcountry Maui

GINGER BEEF WITH PAPAYA

1 fresh papaya, peeled, sliced in strips, and soaked in salted ice water for 1 hour
1 small red onion, thinly sliced
4 small pieces fresh ginger, sliced thin
1½ pounds beef tenderloin, sliced paper thin
2 cups beef broth
½ teaspoon salt
1 teaspoon oyster sauce
1 teaspoon shoyu
½ cup water
1 teaspoon cornstarch

Rinse papaya and drain.

Sauté onion in oil until soft. Add papaya, ginger, beef, and sauté 2 to 3 minutes. Stir carefully to not break up papaya. Add broth and salt. Bring to boil.

In saucepan, mix oyster sauce, shoyu, water, and cornstarch. Add to papaya-beef mix and stir until thickened. May garnish with watercress.

The Kahikolu Country Cookbook

CANTONESE BEEF STIR-FRY WITH HOISIN SAUCE

Makes 6 servings

1 pound boneless beef sirloin
¼ cup soy sauce
2 tablespoons cream sherry
2 tablespoons hoisin sauce
2 teaspoons sugar
¾ teaspoon chili paste
¾ teaspoon sesame oil
1 to 2 corners star anise
3 medium carrots
1 tablespoon cornstarch
½ cup water
3 tablespoons salad oil
1 quart broccoli florets
8 ounces Chinese snow peas
2 to 3 stalks green onion, sliced
½ cup roasted cashews

Slice beef across the grain into thin, bite-size pieces. In a bowl, combine the soy sauce, sherry, hoisin sauce, sugar, chili paste, sesame oil, and star anise. Add sliced beef to this sauce and marinate 2 to 3 hours. Cut carrots into thin diagonal slices. Combine cornstarch and water; set aside. Drain the beef, reserving the marinade. Heat wok on high. Add 1 tablespoon oil to the wok. Just before the oil begins to smoke, add the broccoli and prepared carrots; stir-fry for 3 to 4 minutes. Add in pea pods and green onion; stir-fry 2 minutes more. Remove vegetables from wok. Add 1 tablespoon salad oil to wok. Stir-fry half of the beef at a time for 2 to 3 minutes on high heat, adding more oil as necessary. Remove from wok. Stir-fry the remaining beef; remove from wok. Add the remaining marinade from the beef to the work and the cornstarch mixture. Cook until mixture begins to boil. Add cooked beef, vegetables, and cashews. Stir-fry for 1 minute or until heated through. Serve with hot rice.

ARLENE CHANG
Community Family Favorites, Community Church of Honolulu

CHAVEZ'S ORIGINAL ENCHILADA

1½ pounds ground beef
1 medium onion
1 small green pepper, diced
1 package taco seasoning (optional)
3 small cans Las Palmas or La Victoria brand enchilada sauce
1 package corn tortillas
1 can Parmesan
1 small head lettuce, finely shredded
1 large can black olives (pitted or unpitted)
Sour cream (optional)
2 blocks cheese (Monterey jack and yellow cheddar), grated and mixed
Chopped Chinese parsley (optional)

Fry ground beef with onion, green pepper, and taco seasoning mix. Set aside. Heat enchilada sauce till hot. Set aside.

Deep-fry each tortilla in hot oil quickly on each side, will be very soft. Dip individually in hot sauce. Place on pan and sprinkle inside tortilla with Parmesan. Fill with hamburger, lettuce, 2 olives, sour cream, and some sauce. Add a generous amount of cheese, roll up lengthwise and continue to fill and set side-by-side in casserole dish. Pour remaining sauce over enchiladas and decorate with leftover olives. Sprinkle with more Parmesan.

Bake at 350°F for 15 minutes. Add remaining cheese on top and continue to bake till cheese melts and is hot.

Haleiwa Elementary School 115th Birthday

CHILI VERDE

3 tablespoons salad oil
3 pounds round steak or boneless chuck, cut in ½-inch cubes
1 green pepper, chopped
1 large clove garlic, minced
2 large cans tomatoes
1 large (7-ounce) can California green chilies, seeded, chopped
½ cup chopped parsley
½ teaspoon sugar
¼ teaspoon ground cloves
2 teaspoons ground cumin
1 cup dry red wine
2 cups pinto, if you wish
Salt to taste

Brown about a quarter of meat at a time on all sides in heated oil; remove with a slotted spoon and reserve. In pan drippings sauté green pepper and garlic till soft. In 5-quart pan, combine tomatoes and liquid, green chilies, parsley, seasonings, and wine. Bring to boil, then return heat to simmer. Add meats, juices, and vegetables. Cover and simmer 2 hours, stirring occasionally. Remove cover and simmer for about 45 minutes till sauce reduced to thickness desired and meat is very tender. Taste, add salt.

LEANNA STODD
The Hele Mai, Ai (Come Eat) Cookbook, Flavors of Upcountry Maui

HAMBURGER CURRY

2 pounds hamburger
1 medium onion
¾ teaspoon curry powder
1 teaspoon salt
½ teaspoon black pepper
2 medium-sized potatoes, cubed
1 to 2 carrots, cubed
Flour or cornstarch

Brown hamburger; remove as much of the fat as possible. Add onion and fry until golden brown; add seasonings. Add 4 to 5 cups of water to the cooked mixture, as in making stew. Add carrots and potatoes and cook until done. Thicken with flour or cornstarch mixture.

ANN CATANIA
Family Favorites, Oahu Extension Homemakers Council

MONGOLIAN BEEF

1 pound flank stake (1-inch thick), scored and pounded

Marinade
¼ teaspoon Chinese Five Spice
1 teaspoon Worcestershire sauce
½ teaspoon slivered ginger
1 clove garlic
¼ cup shoyu
1¼ teaspoons sugar
1 teaspoon sesame seed oil

Marinate steak for 15 to 30 minutes. Broil. Sirloin, T-bone, or top round may be used.

100 Years Sharing God's Love, United Community Church

TAMALE CASSEROLE

1½ pounds ground beef
½ cup chopped onion
½ cup chopped green pepper
1 (1½-ounce) package chili seasoning mix
1 (16-ounce) can tomatoes
1 (12-ounce) can whole kernel corn
¾ cup pitted ripe olive halves
1 cup yellow cornmeal
1 teaspoon salt
2½ cups cold water

In large skillet, brown meat and drain. Stir in onions, green pepper, seasoning mix, and tomatoes. Simmer 10 minutes. Add corn and olives. Mix lightly. Spoon into 11¾ x 7½-inch casserole.

In 2-quart pot, combine cornmeal, salt, and water. Cook, stirring constantly over medium heat until thickened. Spoon or pipe corn meal around edges of ground beef mixture. Bake at 350°F for 40 minutes. Serve with cheddar or jack cheese, if desired.

TERRY LEONG
Community Family Favorites, Community Church of Honolulu

BEEF STROGANOFF

1 pound fillet of beef, beaten flat
1 medium size onion, chopped
1 cup fresh mushrooms or
 1 medium-size can
Salt and pepper
Sour cream (small)

Cut fillet of beef into long strips. Fry quickly in hot fat. Remove from skillet.

Sauté onions and mushrooms in butter. Add fried beef to the sautéed mushrooms and onions. Sprinkle generously with salt and pepper. Cover with sour cream and serve on nest of rice, mashed potatoes, or noodles.

Hawaiian Hospitality,
American Business Women's Association Eleu Chapter

TERIYAKI STICKS

2 flank steaks
1¼ cups shoyu
¼ to ½ cup sugar to taste
3 cloves garlic, chopped
1 to 2 inch chunk ginger
2 stalks green onion, chopped
4 tablespoons oil

Slice flank steak against the grain. Mix remaining ingredients together. Add sliced meat. Let meat marinate for several hours. Skewer meat onto bamboo sticks. Cook on charcoal grill.

MAVIS AKIYOSHI
A Book of Favorite Recipes, Compiled by
United Methodist Women of Wahiawa, United Methodist Church

CABBAGE ROLLS

Makes 6 servings

12 large cabbage leaves
1 pound ground beef
1 cup cooked rice (raw rice can also be used)
1 teaspoon minced parsley
1 egg
½ cup milk
¼ cup finely chopped onions, divided use
1 teaspoon salt
Pepper to taste
2 tablespoons brown sugar
1 can condensed tomato soup
½ cup water
1 bay leaf
4 whole cloves

Carefully remove outer leaves of a large head of cabbage. Pour boiling water over them, let stand until wilted; drain well. If center stalks are large, pare down with a sharp knife.

Combine ground beef, rice, parsley, egg, milk, half of onions, salt, and pepper. Place heaping tablespoon of mixture into center of each cabbage leaf, wrap tightly, envelope fashion, securing overlap with toothpicks (if necessary). Place rolls in greased baking dish, sprinkle with brown sugar, cover with soup and water, remaining onions, bay leaf, and cloves.

Bake in moderate oven at 350°F for about 1½ hours adding more water if necessary to keep rolls nearly covered with sauce. Serve with sour cream.

MARTHA MOKEPHUA
Family Favorites, Oahu Extension Homemakers Council

BUTTER YAKI

4 tablespoons butter
1½ pounds sirloin tip, sliced very thin
5 stalks green onion, cut in 2-inch lengths
5 leaves won bok, cut in 2-inch lengths
12 fresh mushrooms, cut in half
½ package been sprouts
1 round onion, sliced ¼-inch thick

Any other vegetables that require little cooking may be used.

In an electric skillet, melt 1 tablespoon butter. Cook meat and vegetables as desired, adding more butter when necessary. Do not overcook; vegetables should be crisp-tender. Dip in sauce before eating.

Butter Yaki Sauce

Juice of 1 lemon
¼ cup shoyu
1 teaspoon Ko Choo Jung
1 teaspoon sesame seed oil
½ teaspoon Japanese instant stock

Sauce is sufficient for 4 people. Serve in individual dishes with grated turnip (daikon) and chopped green onion.

Hawaiian Hospitality, American Business Women's Association

SHABU SHABU NABE

Makes 4 servings

1½ pounds top sirloin, cut in paper thin slices
1 bunch watercress, cut in 1½-inch length
1 medium round onion, sliced
12 stalks green onion, cut in 1½-inch length
1 box frozen broccoli spears, cut in 1½-inch length
6 cups chicken or beef broth
½ pound cooked udon (noodles)

Ponzu (Shoyu-vinegar sauce)
1 cup shoyu
¼ cup Japanese rice vinegar
¼ teaspoon ko choo jung sauce

Arrange beef, vegetables, and noodles on a platter and place on dining table. Combine ingredients for ponzu and pour into four small dishes and set before diner. Bring broth to boil. Dip beef in the boiling broth until it turns light pink. Cook vegetables in the same manner. Add the noodles last and cook only until reheated. Each guest cooks a choice of beef or vegetables in the broth. Dip in ponzu before eating.

NOTE: The broth may be served as the last course, if desired. Any combination of vegetables may be used.

Favorite Island Cookery, Book I, Honpa Hongwanji Hawaii Betsuin

SUKYAKI WITH MISO

⅔ pound boneless beef sirloin or tenderloin
1 yaki dofu, cut into 1¼-inch squares
1 (8-ounce) carton shirataki
3 stalks green onion, cut diagonally into 2-inch lengths
2 fu, soak in water
4 dried shiitake, soak in water and slice
1 gobo, scrape and soak in vinegar water
⅓ bunch watercress, cut into 2-inch lengths

Slice beef thinly. Prepare Sukiyaki Miso Sauce.

Sukiyaki Miso Sauce

½ cup soup stock
½ cup red (aka) miso
4 tablespoons sugar
4 tablespoons sake
3 tablespoons mirin
Shichime togarashi (red pepper)
Konasansho (ground black or white pepper)
Daikon oroshi (grated turnip)

Bring first five sauce ingredients to a boil in sukiyaki nabe. Add meat to sauce and cook rest of ingredients as in sukiyaki. Serve with chili pepper, ground pepper, grated turnip.

Wisteria Delights, A Collection of Recipes by Pearl City Hongwanji Mission

BULGOGI

Korean Marinated Barbecue Meat

4 teaspoons toasted and ground sesame seeds
½ cup soy sauce
2 tablespoons sugar
3 stalks green onion, minced
½ teaspoon pepper
4 tablespoons sesame seed oil
1 teaspoon MSG (optional)
1 large clove garlic, minced
1 to 2 hot chili peppers
3 pounds beef, sliced thin

Mix together all ingredients except beef. Add beef, mix, and let stand a few hours. Broil over hot coals in a broiler oven or in a skillet on top of stove.

ESTHER AHUNA
Community Family Favorites, Community Church of Honolulu

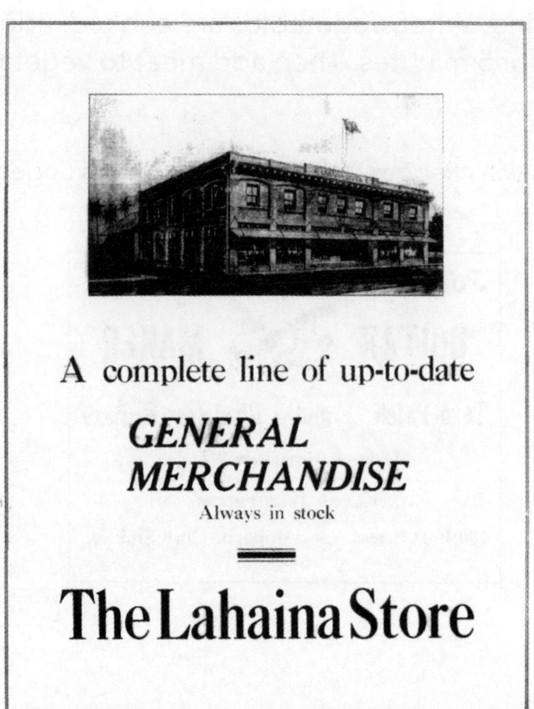

POCHERO

2 pounds beef, cut into serving pieces
2 cups beer
Water
Salt, pepper, and ajinomoto to taste
2 tablespoons oil
1 clove garlic, minced
1 onion
⅓ cup tomato sauce
1 medium size potato, quartered
1 pound cabbage, quartered
½ pound green beans, cut into 1-inch lengths
½ cup garbanzos

Boil beef in beer and add enough water to cover. Simmer meat until tender. Season with salt, pepper, and ajinomoto. Set aside.

Heat oil and brown garlic. Add onion, tomato sauce, potato, cabbage, and beans with enough water to make a thick sauce after simmering. When vegetables are cooked, add garbanzos and simmer for 5 minutes. Then add meat to vegetables. Serve hot.

Hawaii's Aloha Recipes, The Japanese Women's Society of Honolulu

KOREAN FLANK STEAK

1 (about 1¼-pound) flank steak
½ cup sugar
½ cup shoyu
1 clove garlic, minced
Flour for coating
2 stalks green onions, minced or chopped
2 eggs, well-beaten
Oil for frying

Flank steak should be tenderized twice (you must have the butcher at the market put the meat through the tenderizer twice when buying the meat).

Make marinade of sugar, shoyu, and garlic. Cut meat into 4 or 5 pieces about the size of large hamburgers for easier handling. Marinate 30 minutes to an hour, or less.

Coat meat with flour, then dip into mixture of chopped green onions and eggs. Fry in oil, using medium heat (shoyu burns easily). Turn over once when bottom half is nicely browned. Remove to pan lined with paper towels after both sides are nicely browned.

Slice thinly and arrange on platter to serve. For best results, slice with an electric knife, or chill before cutting with a very sharp knife (to prevent coating from falling off and giving a messy look). This is a good potluck dish, as it is good hot or cold and makes a lot for the amount of meat used.

Wisteria Delights, A Collection of Recipes
by Pearl City Hongwanji Mission

PEPPER STEAK

Makes 6 servings

1½ pounds sirloin tip or round steak
2 tablespoons oil
⅓ cup chopped onions
1 teaspoon salt
Dash of pepper
1 beef bouillon cube
1 cup hot water
1 (#2½) can stewed tomatoes
1 green pepper, sliced
3 tablespoons cornstarch
½ cup cold water
3 tablespoons soy sauce

Cut meat into ¼-inch serving pieces. Brown meat in oil; add onions, salt, pepper. Dissolve bouillon in hot water; add to meat. Simmer 25 minutes.

Add tomatoes and green pepper; cook 5 minutes. Combine rest of ingredients; stir into meat mixture. Cook 5 minutes, stirring constantly until thickened. Serve with hot rice or noodles.

The Hawaii National Guard Auxiliary Cookbook

MANGO STEAK

Makes 4 to 6 servings

The mango gives this steak an exotic flavor.

2 tablespoons oil
1½ pounds round beef steak
2 lemons, thinly sliced
3 tomatoes, peeled and sliced
2 mangoes
1 bottle of beer
Salt and pepper

In a pan, heat the oil and brown the steak on both sides. In a casserole, arrange the sliced lemons and tomatoes, overlapping them. Set steak on top.

Peel the mangoes and cut flesh away from pit. Make as many slices as possible. Crush remaining flesh to a pup. Arrange the mango slices on top of the steak. Pour pulp and beer over top of steak and mango slices. Sprinkle with salt and pepper.

Cover casserole and bake in a 350°F oven for 1½ to 2 hours, or until tender.

Hana Maui Recipes from Then to Now

DAVE MATTO'S PRIME RIB

Soak at room temperature, 7-pound roast in 1 cup vodka (wrap in cheese cloth). Baste every 10 to 15 minutes. Dump off drippings at 1 hour, add fresh cup of vodka, soak for additional hour, basting every 10 to 15 minutes.

During The First Hour: Slice onions in rings, lay flat on pan, pour ½ cup white wine, garlic powder, and 1 stick of butter (slice thin and place on each ring.) Cook at 350°F until wine evaporates and rings tum golden brown (approximately 35 to 40 minutes).

Prepare the following seasonings:

2 tablespoons coarse ground pepper
2 teaspoons garlic salt
2 teaspoons sage
½ teaspoon dry Chinese or Coleman's mustard
5 tablespoons flour

Mix thoroughly and set aside.

During The Second Hour: Light charcoals; keep a backup of lite coals going separately.

Drip Pan
1 cup red wine
1 cup water
1 Maui onion, sliced
2 cloves garlic, sliced
1 carrot, sliced

Attach drip pan so that it hangs under the grill, directly under the roast. Prepare Weber for indirect heating, place approximately 10 coals on each side. Cover grill and monitor temperature, adjusting coals to reach 225°F on an oven thermometer. Remove roast from cheese cloth; cover roast with olive oil, rub seasoning mixture on roast, coat heavily. Place some of the sautéed onion rings on top. Insert meat thermometer into center of roast. Place in Weber, monitor Weber temperature closely and keep it at 225°F constantly. Cook until meat temperature reaches 130°F , approximately 4½ hours. Make au jus with the drippings and serve with remaining sautéed onions.

GARY SIRACUSA
"No Ka Oi" The Best of Hawaii,
Favorite Recipes from Rotarians of District 5000

HAWAIIAN TERIYAKI BURGER

Makes 6 to 8 servings

1½ pounds ground round
¼ cup sugar
1 small onion, chopped
1 egg
¼ cup soy sauce
2 cloves garlic, minced
½ teaspoon minced ginger
2 tablespoons sesame oil
2 stalks green onion, chopped

Combine all ingredients and form into patties (about ¼ pound each). Fry, grill, or broil to preference.

The Tastes and Tales of Mōʻiliʻili,
A Collection of Recipes & Stories by Mōʻiliʻili Community Center

KOREAN MEAT PATTIES

Makes 6 servings

1 egg, slightly beaten
2 tablespoons milk
2 teaspoons sugar
½ teaspoon (or more) salt
⅛ teaspoon black pepper
1 tablespoon plus 1½ teaspoons shoyu
1 tablespoon sesame seeds, toasted and crushed
1 small clove garlic, minced
¼ cup chopped onions
¾ cup day old breadcrumbs
1 pound ground round or meat of your choice

Combine all ingredients, except ground meat, and mix thoroughly. Add ground meat and blend; handle mixture lightly. Shape into 6 patties and broil.

Still More of Our Favorite Recipes,
Maui Association for Family and Community Education

WHITE RUSSIAN MEATBALLS

Makes 6 to 8 servings

2 pounds ground beef
2 cups breadcrumbs
2 eggs, slightly beaten
½ cup milk
½ cup minced onion
1 to 2 cloves garlic, minced
1 teaspoon Worcestershire sauce
2 teaspoons salt
1 large green pepper
5 tablespoons butter
5 tablespoons flour
4 cups canned tomatoes
2 cups sour cream

Combine first 8 ingredients, shape into 2-inch size balls, and brown in butter. Remove to large casserole. Brown chopped peppers in butter, add flour, and cook a minute. Add tomatoes, stirring until thick and smooth. Add cream and pour all over meatballs. Bake in 300°F oven for 45 minutes. Serve over rice or noodles

JUDITH NOVIT
The Kahikolu Country Cookbook

SWEET SOUR MEATBALLS

Makes 4 servings

Meatballs
1 pound ground beef
1 teaspoon ajinomoto
¾ teaspoon salt
1 tablespoon chopped onion
½ cup soft breadcrumbs
¼ cup milk
1 tablespoon flour
2 tablespoons butter

Sauce
¼ cup vinegar
¼ cup ketchup
1/16 teaspoon cayenne
¼ teaspoon oregano
¼ cup molasses

Mix meatballs, roll in flour and brown in butter. Combine sauce. Pour over balls, simmer 10 minutes or so, stirring occasionally. Serve with rice or hot noodles.

GEORGIA REMALY
A Book of Favorite Recipes, Compiled by United Methodist Women of Wahiawa, United Methodist Church

WAIKĪKĪ MEATBALLS

Makes 6 servings

2 pounds ground beef
⅔ cup cracker crumbs
⅓ cup minced onion
1 egg
1½ teaspoons salt
¼ cup evaporated milk
1 tablespoon vegetable oil
1 (13½-ounce) can pineapple, chunks
2 tablespoons cornstarch
½ cup brown sugar
⅓ cup vinegar
1 tablespoon soy sauce
⅓ cup chopped green pepper
⅓ cup thinly sliced carrots

Mix first seven ingredients. Shape into balls about 1½-inch in diameter. Heat oil in pan. Brown and cook meatballs. Remove and keep warm. Drain oil.

Combine syrup from pineapple, cornstarch, sugar, vinegar and soy sauce until smooth. Pour into skillet along with green pepper and carrots. Cook until mixture thickens and boil. Add meatballs and pineapple. Stir until meatballs are well-coated with sauce.

RUSSELL KUNANE TORRES
A Chorus of Recipes, Kamehameha School Children's Chorus

EVERYDAY MEATLOAF

Makes 4 to 6 servings

¾ cup dry breadcrumbs
1 cup milk
1½ pounds ground beef
2 eggs, beaten
¼ cup grated onion
1 teaspoon salt
¼ teaspoon sage
¼ teaspoon pepper

Piquant Sauce
6 tablespoons brown sugar
½ cup ketchup
½ teaspoon nutmeg
2 teaspoons mustard

Soak breadcrumbs in milk. Add meat, eggs, onion, and seasonings; mix together well. Place in a loaf pan. Combine Piquant Sauce Ingredients and spread over top of meatloaf. Bake at 350°F for 45 minutes.

The Tastes and Tales of Mō'ili'ili,
A Collection of Recipes & Stories by Mō'ili'ili Community Center

TERIYAKI LOAF

Makes 6 to 8 servings

1 pound ground pork
1 pound ground chuck
1 cup soft breadcrumbs
2 eggs, beaten slightly
½ cup chopped onions
1 clove garlic, minced
½ teaspoon ground ginger
2 tablespoons soy sauce
2 tablespoons lime or lemon juice
2 tablespoons brown sugar

For basting
1 tablespoon soy sauce
1 tablespoon honey

Preheat oven to 350°F. Combine all meatloaf ingredients, shape in loaf in baking pan. Bake 30 minutes; blend basting ingredients together and baste. Bake 30 minutes more.

VIRGINIA HILKER
The Hele Mai, Ai (Come Eat) Cookbook, Flavors of Upcountry Maui

CHINESE POT ROAST

Garlic, minced
Ginger, minced
1 teaspoon salt
1½ teaspoons Chinese Five Spice seasoning
4 pounds chuck roast
2 tablespoons oil
1 tablespoon sherry
2 tablespoons brown sugar
3 tablespoons shoyu
1½ cups water, divided use
3 carrots, cut into serving pieces
1 onion
3 potatoes
1 stalk celery
2 tablespoons cornstarch
2 stalks green onion, chopped

Rub garlic ginger, salt and Chinese Five Spice on meat. Mix sherry, sugar, and shoyu and pour on meat. Let stand and 20 to 30 minutes. Turn once.

Brown meat in oil. Pour marinade over roast and add 1¼ cups of the water. Cover and simmer for 2 hours. Peel and cut vegetables into serving size pieces, add to roast and simmer for 30 minutes. Remove meat and vegetables from pot.

Combine cornstarch and remaining ¼ cup water. Add green onions and add to sauce left in pot; stir and cook until mixture thickens. To serve, pour gravy over meat and vegetables.

Wisteria Delights, A Collection of Recipes
by Pearl City Hongwanji Mission

PORTUGUESE POT ROAST

½ cup vinegar
½ cup water
1 teaspoon salt
1 teaspoon pepper
1 pound chuck steak
3 medium potatoes, quartered
2 stalks celery, sliced
1 carrot, sliced
3 cloves garlic
1 round onion, cut into ¼-inch slices
1 can tomato sauce

Combine vinegar, water, salt, and pepper. Cut meat into strips. Marinate for 45 minutes to 1 hour.

Brown meat; simmer until meat is tender over medium heat. Add vegetables and tomato sauce. Cook over medium heat until vegetables are done.

HELEN BOTELHO
Our Favorite Recipes from the Portuguese Heritage Club of Hamakua

KANAKA BEEF STEW

Makes 4 to 6 servings

1½ pounds stewing meat
2 cups water
2 teaspoons Hawaiian salt
1 large taro, peeled and diced
½ cup round onion, cut in wedges
3 tomatoes, peeled and cut wedges (or 1 can whole tomatoes)

Lightly brown beef in a 3 quart saucepan to sear and retain juice. After browning, add water and simmer for 2 hours or until beef is tender. Add salt, taro and onions. Cook 20 minutes; add in another cup of water as needed. Add tomatoes and bring stew to a boil. Serve hot.

EDITH YEE
Family Favorites, Oahu Extension Homemakers Council

LUNCH WAGON CURRY STEW

2½ pounds stew meat, cut into 1-inch cubes
3½ cups water
1 (14-ounce) can beef broth
1 large onion, quartered
3 stalks celery, chopped
2 large carrots, roll cut
2 medium potatoes, 1-inch cubes
2 tablespoons (or less) curry powder
2 teaspoons salt to taste
½ cup cornstarch

In a large pot, heat oil and brown meat on all sides. Add water and beef broth. Cover and cook for 1 hour. Add onion, celery, carrots, potatoes, curry powder, and salt. Bring to a boil, then sinner for about 3 hours. Add some water to cornstarch and mix to blend, then add to stew (slowly) to thicken.

For beef stew, add 1 (8-ounce) can tomato sauce instead of curry powder.

TRACY OSHIRO
Hugs & Kisses of Aloha, Aloha Airlines Flight Attendant Cookbook

TRIPE STEW

1 package tripe
½ onion, sliced
1 bay leaf
1 teaspoon Hawaiian salt
1 can tomato soup
1 (15½-ounce) can stewed tomatoes
1½ stalk celery and leaves
½ bell pepper, sliced
1 carrot, sliced

Parboil tripe for 5 to 10 minutes. Rinse and cut off excess fat. Cut into strips and add enough water to cover. Add onions, bay leaf, and salt. Boil for 30 minutes.

Add soup and stewed tomatoes. Boil for 30 minutes. Add celery leaves and bell pepper. Boil for 1 hour or until tripe is tender. Add more salt if needed. Then, add sliced celery and carrots. Simmer until carrots are tender. Thicken if desired.

TEKLA ING
Hugs & Kisses of Aloha, Aloha Airlines Flight Attendant Cookbook

HAWAIIAN POI STEW

Makes 6 to 8 servings

2 tablespoons oil
Ginger
3 pounds chuck roast, cubed
1 medium onion, diced
3 medium tomatoes, diced
Salt and pepper
5 cups water
1 (17-ounce) package poi
4 stalks green onion, 1-inch pieces
1 small Hawaiian red pepper, minced (optional)

Brown ginger in oil; add meat and brown 3 minutes. Add onion, tomatoes, salt, pepper, and water. Water should cover meat. Bring to boil and simmer 45 minutes or until meat is tender. Skim off fat. Gradually add poi; stir to thicken stew. Add green onions just before serving. Pass red pepper at table.

Cooking with Honolulu Gardeners,
Honolulu Community Recreational Garden Program

OXTAIL

3 pounds oxtail
1 (8-ounce) package dried mushrooms (shiitake)
1 (1-ounce) package pepeias (black fungus)
1 (8.5-ounce) can bamboo shoots
1½ cup roasted peanuts (shell and lining removed)
Salt to taste
½ teaspoon MSG

Cut oxtail at joints. Put into pot with enough water to cover. Bring to boil; lower heat. Cover and simmer until tender. Check after 3 hours. Add more water, if necessary. When tender, add remaining ingredients and cook until done. Serve with hot rice.

EVANGELINE INABA
From the Hawaiian Kitchens of the Molokai Lions

TERIYAKI SHORT RIBS

Makes 4 servings

4 pounds meaty short ribs, deboned

Sauce

½ cup sugar
½ cup shoyu
3 tablespoons sake
½ teaspoon salt
1 teaspoon grated ginger
1 clove garlic, grated
2 tablespoons oil
2 tablespoons sesame seeds, toasted and ground
1 stalk green onion, chopped
1 teaspoon ajinomoto

Marinate ribs in sauce 1 hour. Turn at least once. Place on cold broiler pan. Broil 3 inches from heat for 5 minutes. Dip each rib in sauce, turn and broil 4 to 5 minutes longer.

Favorite Island Cookery, Book I, Honpa Hongwanji Hawaii Betsuin

MOLOKAI SHORT RIBS

4 pounds short ribs
¼ cup vinegar
½ cup water
1 cup ketchup
3 tablespoons brown sugar
1 clove garlic, minced
4 tablespoons shoyu

Brown ribs in large pot with a little pepper and salt. Add other ingredients and simmer. Pour in roasting pan and cover with foil. Bake at 325°F for 2 hours or until tender.

SHIRLEY RAWLINS
From the Hawaiian Kitchens of the Molokai Lions

KALBI

Korean Short Ribs

2½ pounds short ribs, sliced thin

Sauce

¾ cup shoyu
¼ cup sesame oil
3 cloves garlic, crushed (or use 1 teaspoon prepared crushed garlic)
⅔ cup sugar
⅔ cup honey
¾ cup chopped green onion

Mix Sauce ingredients and marinate beef for one hour.

Barbecue on grill, but don't overcook kalbi.

Wisteria Delights, A Collection of Recipes
by Pearl City Hongwanji Mission

PLANTATION HASH

1 tablespoon cooking oil
1 medium onion, chopped
1 small head cabbage
1 inch-long piece ginger root, chopped fine
1 cup cooked corned beef, chopped
Dash soy sauce to taste

Heat oil in large skillet. Add chopped onion and cook until semi-soft. Chop and add cabbage; continue to cook to desired crispness. Add chopped ginger and chopped corned beef. Simmer until heated through. Add soy sauce to taste.

NOTE: Quantities and cooking method can be adjusted to individual taste.

LEE MCCASLIN
Island Flavors, Favorite Recipes of the Historic Hawai'i Foundation

CORNED BEEF PATTIES

1 can corned beef
1 medium onion, minced
6 eggs, slightly beaten
Salt and pepper to taste
1/3 cup minced parsley

Combine and stir all ingredients until well-blended. Drop by teaspoonfuls into a well-greased frying pan and fry.

Hawaiian Hospitality,
American Business Women's Association Eleu Chapter

PULEHU RIBS

3 pounds beef short ribs
1 tablespoon sugar
1 tablespoon Hawaiian rock salt
1½ tablespoons shoyu
1½ teaspoons chili pepper water
1 teaspoon sesame oil

Combine ingredients and rub into ribs. Let stand for 3 to 4 hours. Grill over charcoal.

PRISCILLA BADUA
Food for the Body and Soul, West Kaua'i United Methodist Church

RIBS IN PINEAPPLE-MUSTARD SAUCE

Makes 4 to 6 servings

3 pounds pork spareribs
½ teaspoon salt
½ teaspoon garlic powder
¼ teaspoon pepper
2 tablespoons butter
1 small onion, chopped
¼ cup packed brown sugar
¼ cup Dijon mustard
¼ cup dry white wine
2 cups chopped Dole fresh pineapple
2 tablespoons chopped parsley

Place ribs on rack in baking pan. Sprinkle with salt, garlic powder, and pepper. Roast in 375°F oven about 45 minutes. Remove to baking dish.

Melt butter in skillet and sauté onion until tender. Stir in sugar, mustard, and wine. Boil rapidly about 2 minutes, reduce and heat slightly. Stir in pineapple and spoon over ribs. Bake in 375°F oven for 15 minutes. Sprinkle with parsley.

DOLE PINEAPPLE, CASTLE & COOKE, INC.
Hawaii's Aloha Recipes, The Japanese Women's Society of Honolulu

PANIOLA BARBECUED RIBS (MO BETTAH)

4 pounds pork spareribs
1 large onion, sliced
1 lemon, sliced
1 cup ketchup
4 tablespoons Worcestershire sauce
1 teaspoon chili powder
1 teaspoon salt
Dash of Tabasco sauce
2 cups water

Cut ribs into serving-size pieces lengthwise. Place in shallow pan, meat side up. Place a slice of onion on each rib. Roast in 400°F oven for 30 minutes. While ribs are baking, put lemon, ketchup, Worcestershire sauce, chili powder, salt, Tabasco, and water in saucepan and bring to a boil. Cook until slightly thick. Pour over ribs and bake in 350°F oven for 45 minutes or until tender. Baste every 15 minutes.

Hana Maui Recipes from Then to Now

SPARERIBS WITH BLACK BEANS

Makes 3 to 4 servings

1 pound spareribs
1 teaspoon black beans
1/8 teaspoon baking powder
1 teaspoon black soy sauce
½ teaspoon soy sauce
½ teaspoon sesame seed oil
1 tablespoon oyster sauce
1/8 teaspoon pepper
1 clove garlic, minced

Have butcher cut ribs into 1-inch pieces. Trim off excess fat, rinse and drain well. Rinse, drain, and mash black beans. Add baking powder to ribs and allow to marinate while preparing sauce. In a small bowl, mix the black beans with the remaining ingredients. Mix ribs with this black bean sauce and allow to marinate about 30 minutes. Steam for 30 minutes.

MARIA CHAN
Community Family Favorites, Community Church of Honolulu

SWEET SOUR SPARERIBS, KAMUELA-STYLE

20 pounds pork spareribs
2 handfuls Hawaiian salt
Sprinkle of garlic salt
3 large round onions
3 large bell peppers
2 cups cider vinegar
2 cups brown sugar
¼ cup shoyu
2 large pineapple, diced 1-inch

Rub ribs with Hawaiian salt, then put in a large pot. Brown spareribs, then cover and cook for ½ hour on medium heat.

Add onions and bell peppers; stir occasionally. No need to add water—natural juices will finish cooking ribs. Cook for 1 to 1½ hours on low heat or until ribs are tender.

Mix together vinegar, brown sugar, and shoyu until sugar is dissolved. Add to pot. Stir. Add pineapple. Simmer for 10 minutes, stirring occasionally.

ELAINE FLORES
Puuloa Hawaiian Civic Club

PORTUGUESE SAUSAGE
Linguisa

Makes 8 servings

2 pounds lean pork
¼ cup water
1 tablespoon vinegar
8 cloves garlic, minced
2 Hawaiian red peppers, minced
1 teaspoon salt
¼ teaspoon pepper
⅛ teaspoon paprika
⅛ teaspoon MSG
Few drops of liquid smoke

Chop pork into ¼-inch pieces. In a bowl, combine remaining ingredients. Add meat and refrigerate for 2 days, stirring occasionally. Form into small thin patties and fry until browned on both sides and cooked throughout.

50th Anniversary Best of Our Favorite Recipes,
Maui Association for Family and Community Education

BAKED BEANS WITH PORTUGUESE SAUSAGE

Makes 10 servings

1 pound Portuguese sausage
1 (1 pound, 15-ounce) can pork and beans
1 (15-ounce) can kidney beans
1 large onion, sliced
1 cup ketchup
½ teaspoon vinegar
2 tablespoons Worcestershire sauce
⅓ cup brown sugar
3 tablespoons dark molasses
1 tablespoon prepared mustard

Cook sausage in water for 10 minutes; drain and slice. Put sausage, beans, and onions into a 3-quart baking dish. Combine remaining ingredients and stir into bean mixture. Bake, uncovered, in electric oven at 350°F for 1 hour.

North Kohala Favorites

DEEP-FRIED ALMOND PORK

Makes 4 to 6 servings

1 pound pork, cut in ½-inch cubes
½ cup flour

Batter
½ cup flour
½ cup cornstarch
Dash of Ajinomoto
½ teaspoon sugar
1 egg, slightly beaten
¾ cup water
1 quart oil for frying

Sauce
½ cup water
2 tablespoons ketchup
1 teaspoon Worcestershire sauce
2 tablespoons vinegar
Drop of hot sauce
2 tablespoons sugar
1 tablespoon cornstarch
¼ teaspoon salt
¼ cup blanched and slivered almonds

Dredge pork cubes in flour. Combine flour, cornstarch, ajinomoto, and sugar. Add egg to water and mix thoroughly; add to dry ingredients. Stir only until flour mixture is moistened. Coat pork cubes with batter and deep-fry in oil heated to 375°F until golden brown. Drain on absorbent paper.

Combine sauce ingredients and simmer over low flame until thick and clear. Pour over fried pork. Sprinkle slivered almonds over pork before serving.

Favorite Island Cookery, Book I, Honpa Hongwanji Hawaii Betsuin

BIVA'S FAMOUS ADOBO

4 cloves garlic
2 trays belly pork

Sauce
¼ cup vinegar
½ cup shoyu
3 bay leaves
1 stick cinnamon, broken in half
1 teaspoon cracked peppercorns
2 chili peppers, sliced

Mix Sauce ingredients and set aside. Sauté chopped garlic in a little oil. Add cut 1 x 1-inch pork and brown (leave skin on when cutting) about ½ hour. Drain oil. Add Sauce.

Cook on medium fire until sabao (sauce) goes down and slowly lower fire. Cook about a half hour.

JOY ESPIRITU
"Cooking with Lovely Hula Hands," Moana's Hula Halau, Kaunakakai

OVEN KĀLUA PIG

14 to 16 ti leaves, stems cut off
4 to 6 pounds pork butt
2 to 3 tablespoons Hawaiian salt
2 tablespoons liquid smoke
Heavy aluminum foil

Wash ti leaves and arrange them in a circular pattern overlapping leaves. In a container, place butt and rub all sides with salt and liquid smoke. Place butt fat side up on the ti leaves. Fold or wrap butt with ti leaves to completely cover and tie securely with string. Place the wrapped butt on foil and seal well so no steam escapes. Place the prepared butt in a shallow roasting pan and roast in a preheated 450°F oven. After one hour, reduce heat to 400°F and cook from 3 to 4 hours longer or until done.

HAWEA WAIAU
Haili Congregational Church, 175th Anniversary

KĀLUA PIG

Kālua pig is the favorite way of serving pork at an old fashioned lūʻau.

Imu or Underground Oven

Dig oblong hole 4½ inches long by 3 inches wide and 2½ inches deep. Make it larger if pig is large size. Lay kindling in bottom. Put long stick upright in center of imu. Lay firewood around it using 3 to 4 bags of wood. Cover wood with imu (round porous) stones, about 40 to 50, more if necessary. Make a light by wrapping rag around end of long stick. Dip in kerosene. Light. Remove center pole and light kindling through the hole. Burn until wood becomes glowing coals and stones are very hot.

The Pig

1 pig dressed. Slit between shoulders and ribs to backbone and up to head, being careful not to cut through the skin. Rub 1 handful Hawaiian (coarse) salt in slits. Rub 4 handfuls salt inside pig. Put hot stones in slits and opu (abdomen) as many as they will hold. Tie the 4 legs together.

Line a 4 x 4 foot piece of chicken wire with ti leaves. Place pig on it. Then cover hot stones in imu (pit) with 4 banana trunks that have been cut 2 feet long and crushed with blunt side of an axe. Lay netting containing pig on banana stalks. Cover with 2 dozen banana leaves or 6 to 8 dozen ti leaves.

Completely Cover With This

1 dozen burlap bags. Cover bags with sand. Allow pig to cook 2½ to 3 hours according to size. Remove sand, bags, leaves, and stones inside pig. Put pig in large container. Cut in generous servings. Serve at once.

Cook ʻEm Up Kauaʻi, The Kauaʻi Historical Society Cookbook

PORK CHOP SUEY

Makes 2 servings

1 cup chopped celery
½ cup chopped onion
½ cup sliced mushrooms
1 cup chopped cooked pork
½ cup green pepper strips
1 cup canned bean sprouts
1 teaspoon cornstarch
2 tablespoons cold water
1 cup chicken broth
2 teaspoons shoyu

Sauté celery, onion, mushrooms, and pork in butter for 3 minutes. Add pepper, bean sprouts, cornstarch diluted in water, chicken broth, and shoyu. Bring to boiling point and simmer for 4 minutes. Serve with fluffy white rice.

Cook 'Em Up Kaua'i, The Kaua'i Historical Society Cookbook

OKINAWAN SHOYU PORK

6 pounds pork butt
1 can beer or ½ cup water
3 tablespoons Hawaiian salt
1 cup raw sugar
½ cup shoyu
2 thumb-sized pieces of ginger, sliced
3 good-sized cloves garlic, mashed with knife

Simmer pork in sauce until done. Next day, skim off fat; slice pork. Thicken sauce with 3 tablespoons cornstarch and 3 tablespoons water. Pour sauce over sliced pork.

Before serving Okinawan Pork, line serving platter with cooked somen or won bok that has been blanched in hot water. Arrange pork on top of somen, then pour hot (heated) sauce.

NOTE: Shoyu pork can be used as garnish on somen salad, stir-fry with vegetables, use for sandwiches, in omelets, etc.

TOMI KANESHIRO
Kalaheo Missionary Church Cookin' Book!

PORK HASH WITH WATER CHESTNUTS

Makes 4 servings

1 pound ground pork
10 water chestnuts, chopped
3 dried mushroom, soaked, squeezed, chopped
1 onion, chopped
3 tablespoons soy sauce
½ teaspoon salt
1 teaspoon cornstarch
2 tablespoons oil

Mix pork, chestnuts, mushrooms, and onion. Add remaining ingredients. Put in deep bowl and steam 25 minutes.

PATSY GREENWELL
The Kahikolu Country Cookbook

PICKLED PORK
Porco Em Vinha D'Alhos

Makes 6 servings

1½ pounds boneless pork
1½ cups vinegar
2 cloves garlic, crushed
6 Hawaiian red peppers, seeded and chopped
1 bay leaf, crushed
2 teaspoons salt
6 whole cloves
¼ teaspoon thyme
⅛ teaspoon sage
2 tablespoons salad oil

Cut pork into 1½ x 2-inch pieces. Combine vinegar, garlic, red peppers, bay leaf, salt, cloves, thyme, and sage. Pour over pork and let stand overnight in refrigerator. Cook pork in marinade for 20 minutes; drain. Heat oil in skillet. Add pork and sauté slowly for 10 to 15 minutes until browned.

The Hawaii National Guard Auxiliary Cookbook

BASIC CHAR SIU

1½ pounds pork (butt)

Marinade
1 tablespoon whiskey or rice wine
2 tablespoons sugar
1 tablespoon soy sauce
1 tablespoon hoisin sauce
½ tablespoon salt

Cut meat into slabs approximately 2-inches thick and marinate for at least 1 hour. Bake at 350°F in oven on rack with drip pan below for 30 to 45 minutes.

JANE AKITAKE
Our Daily Bread Centennial Cookbook, Iao Congregational Church

PORK ESTOFADO

Makes 5 servings

¼ cup cooking oil
3 cloves garlic
½ kilo lean pork, cut in serving pieces
½ cup vinegar
¼ cup soy sauce
⅓ cup sugar
½ cup water
1 bay leaf
8 peppercorns
1 carrot, cut in strips
2 soba bananas, cut diagonally 1-inch thick, fried
2 pieces pan de sol or French bread, cut in squares and fried

Brown garlic in hot oil. Drop in pork pieces; fry until brown. Add vinegar, soy sauce, sugar, water, bay leaf, and peppercorns. Allow to boil without stirring. Lower heat and cook until pork is almost done. Add carrots and continue cooking until pork is tender. Before serving, add fried bananas and pan de sol or French bread.

FLORA CARRANCHO
From the Hawaiian Kitchens of the Molokai Lions

PIG'S FEET

1 handful black beans
2 chili peppers (optional)
2 cloves garlic, crushed
2 tablespoons peanut or vegetable oil
2 to 3 pounds pig's feet, chopped
1 teaspoon salt
½ cup vinegar
1 cup water
1 tablespoon shoyu
3 teaspoons raw sugar

Mash washed black beans, chili pepper, and garlic and stir-fry in heated peanut oil. Add chopped pig's feet and stir-fry until browned.

Add salt, vinegar, water, shoyu, and sugar. Cook, covered, until done.

LILLIAN MAEDA
Our Daily Bread Centennial Cookbook, Iao Congregational Church

PORK AND PEAS GUISANTES

Makes 4 to 6 servings

2 pounds chopped pork
1 clove garlic
1 medium round onion, chopped
1 medium whole tomato
2 medium cans sweet peas
1 small bottle chopped red pimentos
1 can tomato sauce
1 bay leaf
Salt and pepper to taste

Brown pork with garlic. Add round onion and tomato until cooked. Add peas, pimentos, and tomato sauce and let simmer for 10 to 15 minutes on low heat. Two minutes before ending simmering, add bay leaf.

North Kohala Favorites

MOO SHOO PORK

Moo Shoo Pork is traditionally served with Peking Doilies (aka Mandarin Pancakes) with or without additional sauces, such as hoisin, plum sauce, or hot mustard.

¼ cup lily buds (30)
2 tablespoons cloud ear mushrooms
½ pound lean pork
1 tablespoon soy sauce
1 teaspoon sugar
1 scallion
2 slices fresh ginger root
2 eggs
1½ tablespoons oil
½ cup bamboo shoots, shredded
½ teaspoon salt

Soak lily buds and cloud ear mushrooms in water to cover in separate containers.

Shred pork against grain. Combine soy sauce and sugar and toss with pork.

Remove hard parts of cloud ear mushrooms and shred. Shred scallion, with top, into 2-inch lengths. Mince ginger root.

Beat eggs lightly; heat 1½ tablespoons oil. Scramble quickly and remove from pan while still moist. Heat remaining oil; add ginger root and stir-fry a second. Add pork and bamboo shoots and stir-fry until pork loses its pinkness. Add salt, scallion, lily buds and cloud ear mushrooms. Stir-fry 1 minute. Cover; cook 2 minutes longer over medium heat.

Add scrambled eggs and stir just to reheat. Serve immediately.

NADINE WILLIAMS
From the Hawaiian Kitchens of the Molokai Lions

CANTONESE-STYLE SWEET-SOUR PORK

Makes 6 servings

2 teaspoons sherry (cooking wine)
1 teaspoon salt
½ teaspoon white pepper
1 pound pork butt, cut in 1-inch cubes
2 eggs, beaten
2 tablespoons all-purpose flour
¼ cup cornstarch
1 cup diced cooked carrots
½ cup cut onion, cut in wedges
1 cup diced cucumber

Sauce
¼ cup oil
1 clove garlic, crushed
6 tablespoons brown sugar
2 tablespoons cornstarch
6 tablespoons cider vinegar
2 teaspoons soy sauce
6 tablespoons ketchup or chili sauce
1 cup water

Combine sherry, salt, and white pepper; add pork and let stand for 15 minutes. Mix beaten eggs, flour, and cornstarch; coat pork with this mixture.

Heat oil, drop in pork cubes and deep-fry until well-done; drain. Stir-fry carrots, onions, and cucumbers for 1 minute; drain.

Heat oil in saucepan, fry garlic. Combine with remaining Sauce ingredients; simmer until thickened. Add pork and vegetables and stir until they are coated with sauce.

NOTE: 1 cup diced green pepper and 1 cup pineapple chunks, drained may be substituted for vegetables.

The Hawaii National Guard Auxiliary Cookbook

PORK WITH CUMIN, LEMON, AND CILANTRO

Minho Rojoes a Cominho

2 tablespoons ground cumin
1½ tablespoons minced garlic
2 teaspoons pepper
1 teaspoon salt
7 tablespoons chopped fresh cilantro (fresh coriander), divided use
2 tablespoons fresh lemon juice
Grated zest (1 lemon)
1 cup dry white wine
2 pounds pork shoulder or butt, cut into 1½-inch cubes
2 tablespoons olive oil
Chicken stock as needed
4 paper thin lemon slices, cut into quarters

In small bowl, stir together cumin, garlic, pepper, salt, 4 tablespoons cilantro, lemon juice, zest, and wine. Place pork in glass container and rub with cumin mixture in the meat. Cover and refrigerate overnight.

The next day, drain pork, reserving marinade. Pat meat dry. In heavy saucepan over high heat, warm olive oil. Add pork and sauté until golden, 8 to 10 minutes. Add reserved marinade and enough chicken broth just to cover meat. Bring to boil on high heat. Reduce heat to low, cover and simmer until very tender.

Add lemon slices during last 10 minutes of cooking. Season with salt and pepper. Transfer to a warm serving bowl. Sprinkle with remaining 3 tablespoons of cilantro and serve.

Our Favorite Recipes from the Portuguese Heritage Club of Hamakua

PORTUGUESE PORK WITH RED PEPPERS AND CLAMS

2½ pounds lean boneless pork, cut in 1-inch cubes
2 tablespoons salad oil
2 medium onions, thinly sliced
2 medium tomatoes, peeled and chopped
⅛ teaspoon crushed red pepper
1 to 1½ dozen clams in the shell, well-scrubbed
2 large red bell peppers, seeded and cut into strips (or 1 jar sliced pimentos)
¼ cup fresh cilantro, chopped

Wine Marinade
1½ cups dry white wine
2 bay leaves
1 teaspoon salt
1 teaspoon paprika
3 cloves garlic, minced

Combine marinade and pork cubes in a large plastic bag and chill for 6 to 8 hours. Stir several times. Lift out pork and drain well. Reserve marinade. Heat oil in a wide frying pan over medium to medium-high heat. Add about half the pork at a time and brown well on all sides; remove from the pan as browned. Add more oil to pan if needed, then add onions and cook, stirring until limp; remove from pan.

Pour in reserved marinade (discard bay) and boil, stirring to loosen browned bits from pan bottom until reduced by half. Return pork and onions to pan. Stir in the tomatoes and crushed red pepper. Cover and simmer until pork is tender (about 30 minutes). Add the clams and fresh bell pepper (if used). Cover and simmer gently until clams pop open, about 20 minutes. If using the canned peppers, stir them in now, along with the cilantro. Serve immediately.

MARIE HO
Our Favorite Recipes from the Portuguese Heritage Club of Hamakua

MANAPUA

Pork Filling
1 cup roast pork (may use fresh pork, fried)
4 fresh shrimps, boiled and chopped
4 water chestnuts, chopped
1 stalk green onion, chopped
1 teaspoon oyster sauce
1 teaspoon shoyu
Salt to taste

Mix together and let stand for 10 minutes.

Buns
¾ cake yeast
1¼ cups warm water
1 tablespoon shortening
⅔ tablespoon sugar
1 teaspoon salt
4½ cups flour
Red food coloring

Dissolve yeast in warm water; add shortening, sugar, salt, and flour. Knead until smooth (slightly). Dough must be stiff. Then cut dough into approximately 2-inch balls, flatten in the palms of hands and fill them with about 2 teaspoons of the above pork filling, placing them on white paper 2½ x 2½-inch square. Let rise for about 1½ to 2 hours. Steam 20 minutes. Use red food coloring for design on top of each bun after it is steamed.

Favorite Island Cookery, Book I, Honpa Hongwanji Hawaii Betsuin

TARO JAMBALAYA

Makes 4 servings

3 slices bacon, diced
1 pound chop suey pork (lean)
2 cloves garlic, minced
1 medium onion, chopped
1 large green pepper, chopped
¾ cup sliced water chestnuts
3 cups diced cooked taro
2 tablespoons chopped chives
1 teaspoon salt
1 teaspoon MSG
½ teaspoon pepper
3 tablespoons sherry
1 tablespoon shoyu
½ cup chopped green onion

Heat electric skillet to 300°F. Add bacon and fry until almost crisp. Push to side of skillet. Add pork and garlic and stir-fry 3 minutes. Add onion, green pepper, and water chestnuts; continue cooking 3 minutes. Push to side with bacon. Add taro, chives, and seasonings; stir-fry 5 minutes longer. Combine with bacon and vegetables. Lower temperature to 275°F.

Add sherry and shoyu and cook until liquid is absorbed. Garnish with green onion. Serve with tossed green salad and hot garlic French bread.

Favorite Island Cookery, Book II, Honpa Hongwanji Buddhist Temple

KOREAN CHAP CHEY
Chop Sin

Makes 6 servings

1 pound pork
1 cup string beans
1 large carrot
2 pieces bamboo shoots
3 big dry mushrooms
1 teaspoon ginger root
1 tablespoon garlic
1 bundle long rice
1 teaspoon ajinomoto
½ teaspoon pepper
¼ cup shoyu
½ pound bean sprouts
1 small onion
1 tablespoon sesame seeds

Cut pork in thin slices. Cut vegetables diagonally in 2-inch length strips. Heat pot. Fry string beans and carrots. Put aside. Fry pork well. Add bamboo shoots, mushrooms, ginger root, and garlic. Cook well. Add fried carrots, beans, long rice, seasonings and shoyu. Ten minutes before serving, add bean sprouts, onion, and sesame seeds.

Cook 'Em Up Kaua'i, The Kaua'i Historical Society Cookbook

LAULAUS

Makes 8 servings

24 taro leaves or fresh spinach leaves
1 pound salted butterfish or similar substitute
1⅓ tablespoons rock salt
2 pounds fresh pork, shoulder or leg
8 ti leaves (corn husks or parchment paper may be substituted)
4 cooking bananas
4 sweet potatoes

Wash taro leaves thoroughly. Remove stem and fibrous part of vein. If fish is very salty, soak it in cold water for a few hours. Work rock salt into pork thoroughly. Arrange 5 to 6 taro leaves in palm of hand placing the largest leaf on the bottom. Place piece of pork, fat side up, on leaves. Place piece of butterfish on top of pork. Fold leaves over pork and fish to form a bundle.

Prepare each ti leaf by cutting the stiff rib partially through and stripping it off by rolling the leaf vertically over the finger. Place laulau on the end of a tie leaf and wrap it tightly. Wrap another ti leaf in the opposite direction to form a flat package. Tie securely with string or the fibrous part of the ti leaf. Steam the laulaus four to six hours. Add the sweet potatoes and bananas for the last hour. In steamer, place laulaus on a rack above the water and replenish water when necessary.

Cook 'Em Up Kaua'i, The Kaua'i Historical Society Cookbook

SITAW
(Very Long String Beans)

1 tablespoon oil
2 cloves garlic
1 small round onion, sliced
10 medium pieces shrimp, peeled and chopped
1 cup chopped pork
1 tablespoon patis
1½ cups water
3 cups sitaw (when cut)
Salt to taste

Fry garlic in oil. When browned, add the onion, shrimp, pork, and patis. Stir and cook until the pork begins to brown. Add water and let it boil. Then add the string beans and cook until tender. Add salt to taste.

Hawaii's Aloha Recipes, The Japanese Women's Society of Honolulu

PORK AND SHRIMP STIR-FRY FILIPINO-STYLE

4 bitter melons, medium size
1½ round onions
¾ pound green beans
¾ pound tiger shrimp
1½ pounds pork slices
1 tablespoon vegetable oil
4 large cloves garlic
1 bay leaf
2 tablespoons patis
Salt and pepper
Ajinomoto
2 large tomatoes

Prep ingredients: Wash and clean vegetables. Remove the core of the bitter melons and cut into 3-inch slivers. Cut onions into slices. Divide into 3 groups. Cut string beans into 3-inch strings. Shell the shrimps. Wash pork thoroughly.

Let's cook: Brown pork in a large pan with vegetable oil, garlic, and bay leaf. Add ⅓ of the onion slices, patis, salt, pepper, and ajinomoto. Blend in one tomato to create a tasty sauce. Simmer until some of the water evaporates. The sauce should now be thick and have a tomato orange color. In a separate pan, stir-fry the shrimps with butter or margarine and set aside. Remove pork and most of the sauce from the pan. Stir-fry the beans followed by the bitter melon and remaining onions until half cooked. Remove from pan. Finally, stir-fry everything together: the pork, sauce, vegetables, shrimp, and the remaining tomatoes.

RECIPE NOTE: Awarded "Most Original" to Noel and his dad, Mariano, in Cub Scout's Father/Son cook off.

NOEL AND MARIANO TORRES
Food for the Body and Soul, West Kaua'i United Methodist Church

CHORIZO

5 pounds coarse ground pork butt
3 teaspoons salt
1 teaspoon ground cumin
1 teaspoon cayenne pepper
2 tablespoons fresh oregano
8 cloves garlic, pressed
1 large onion, finely chopped
¼ cup crushed chili peppers
1 cup wine vinegar

Mix all together and stuff into hog casing, or make patties. Wait 24 hours before cooking. After stuffing the sausage into the casing, place it overnight in the refrigerator to insure proper blending of the spices.

NOTE: Be sure you work with cold meat (not freezing). You will be using your hands to mix. Since the meat is very cold, you may want to every so often between mixing spices thoroughly to put the meat back in the freezer or refrigerator and warm up your hands.

North Kohala Favorites

TAIWAN MUSHI

1 pound ground pork hash
1 medium onion, chopped
1 can takenoko, slivered
2 or 3 large dried shiitake, slivered
1 tablespoon sake
2 tablespoons shoyu
1 teaspoon salt
2 tablespoons sugar
2 blocks tofu
2 eggs

Sauté ground pork in skillet with 1 tablespoon oil; add onion, takenoko, and mushroom; sauté for few minutes. Add seasoning to taste. Cut tofu in 1-inch block and lay in 9 x 13-inch pan. Pour the hash mixture over tofu. Beat eggs and pour over hash mixture. Bake ½ hour at 235°F.

A Lei of Recipes, Kauai Association for Family and Community Education

THE GOVERNOR'S PORK STEW

Makes approximately 4 servings

2½ pounds meaty pork belly, cut in 1-inch cubes
2 cups water
1 small round onion, minced
2 tablespoons minced garlic
½ cup water
¼ cup white vinegar
1 teaspoon salt
1 cup tomato sauce
4 potatoes, quartered
1 (6-ounce) can black olives, pitted
½ cup sliced pimientos
¼ cup breadcrumbs
1 cup frozen peas, thawed
Chinese parsley for garnish

In a 4-quart pot, brown belly cubes over medium heat till lightly brown.

Drain fat from pot, add 2 cups water, and cook over medium heat, covered, approximately 40 minutes. Remove cover and continue to cook until most of the liquid is reduced. Add onion and garlic; cook 2 minutes.

Add ½ cup water, vinegar, salt, tomato sauce, potatoes, olives, and pimientos. Cover and cook 20 minutes or until potatoes are tender. Stir in breadcrumbs and peas. Transfer to serving platter; garnish with Chinese parsley.

BENJAMIN CAYETANO (FORMER GOVERNOR)
Island Flavors, Favorite Recipes of the Historic Hawai'i Foundation

LŪ'AU WRAPPED PORK CHOPS

Pork chops
Rock salt
Chicken bouillon concentrate
Large lū'au leaves, 2 per pork chop

Rub pork chops with salt and chicken bouillon to taste. Place each pork chop in center of lū'au leaves and fold over to make packages. Steam for 4 hours. Serve topped with Creamy White Sauce, if desired.

Creamy White Sauce
6 tablespoons margarine
6 tablespoons flour
2 cups chicken broth
¼ cup dry white wine (optional)
¼ cup cream cheese
Salt and pepper

Melt margarine, stir in flour; add chicken broth and wine, simmer 20 minutes. Add cream cheese and stir. Season with salt and pepper.

Favorite Island Cookery, Book IV, Honpa Hongwanji Hawaii Betsuin

PORK CHOPS WITH MUSTARD SAUCE

Makes 4 servings

4 large pork chops
2 tablespoons butter or margarine
2 tablespoons vinegar
1 teaspoon Dijon mustard
Salt and pepper
½ cup cream
1 or 2 tablespoons finely chopped parsley or chives

Cook chops slowly in skillet in 2 tablespoons butter or margarine until well-browned on both sides (30 to 40 minutes). Remove chops and keep warm.

Lift glaze in pan with 2 tablespoons vinegar. Add mustard, salt, and pepper. Blend in ½ cup cream and stir until mixture comes to a boil. Simmer 2 or 3 minutes. Pour over chops, sprinkle with parsley or chives.

PAT SPILLANE
Cook 'Em Up Kaua'i, The Kaua'i Historical Society Cookbook

MISO PORK ROAST

1 piece ginger, crushed
2 cloves garlic, crushed
¾ cup miso
½ cup sugar
¼ cup shoyu
4 pounds pork butt or chicken thighs

Combine ginger, garlic, miso, sugar, and shoyu. Marinate the pork overnight. Place pork in a dish fat-side down. Cook on high for 6 to 8 minutes, covered. About halfway through cooking time, turn the pork over; cover and let stand 15 minutes before slicing.

NOTE: 1 cup of each miso, sugar, and shoyu can be used.

A Lei of Recipes, Kauai Association for Family and Community Education

INDONESIAN PORK ROAST

3 pounds pork butt
1 chicken bouillon cube
1 cup water
1 clove garlic, grated
¼ cup sugar
½ cup soy sauce
⅓ cup vinegar

Brown pork on all sides.

Dissolve chicken bouillon in 1 cup hot water. Combine remaining ingredients and add to chicken stock. Pour sauce over pork. Simmer for 3 hours.

Cooked pork freezes well. You may also shred the pork and cook it with cabbage in the manner of kālua pork and cabbage.

Wisteria Delights, A Collection of Recipes by Pearl City Hongwanji Mission

BAKED HAM WITH KONA COFFEE SAUCE

6 to 8 pounds precooked ham
Whole cloves
2 pounds brown sugar
½ cup dry mustard
1½ cups vinegar
¼ cup Worcestershire sauce
1 heaping tablespoon cornstarch
2 to 3 tablespoons water
2 cups V-8 juice
2 cups brewed Kona coffee
2 cups Sauterne wine

Score ham and place cloves in ham. Combine brown sugar, dry mustard, vinegar, and Worcestershire sauce in a small bowl. Put ham in a deep baking pan and cover with brown sugar mixture. Bake at 375°F for 1 hour, basting occasionally. Remove ham from oven; place on platter.

Return drippings to the oven; stir occasionally until sugar foams and turns golden brown. Turn drippings into a saucepan. Combine cornstarch and water into a smooth paste. Add V-8 juice, coffee, and wine to the cornstarch mixture and pan drippings. Bring to a boil and cook for 10 minutes. Strain sauce and remove excess fat. Slice ham and serve with sauce.

Community Family Favorites, Community Church of Honolulu

LĀNA'I BAKED BEANS

Makes 4 servings

1 (1 pound 4-ounce) can crushed Hawaiian pineapple
2 cups cooked ham strips (turkey ham may be used)
1 to 2 tablespoons butter or margarine
1 (1 pound 12-ounce) can baked beans
½ cup hickory smoked BBQ sauce
1 large green bell pepper, cut into chunks
¼ cup chopped green onions

Drain pineapple. Sauté ham strips in butter in skillet until golden. Combine beans, barbecue sauce, green pepper, onions, and pineapple. Pour into casserole and bake in 350°F oven for 20 to 30 minutes.

RAE LINDQUIST
Hana Maui Recipes from Then to Now

ROAST LAMB

4 pounds leg of lamb
Salt and pepper
1 carrot
1 cup of ordinary coffee with cream and sugar

Salt and pepper the leg of lamb. Put lamb in roasting pan with a carrot. Roast in a 325°F oven; for medium rare 15 to 20 minutes per pound, for well-done 25 to 30 minutes per pound. Baste with the cup of coffee with cream and sugar. Place lamb on platter.

For Gravy: Use the proportion of ½ cup drippings to 3 tablespoons flour, with 1 to 1½ cups water. Blend in a blender. Pour into roasting pan, stir constantly until smooth and thickened. Simmer for at least 5 minutes, stirring most of the time. Add salt and pepper to taste.

VIRGINIA DOMINIS KOCH
Dining with the Daughters, The Daughters of Hawaii

NI'IHAU LAMB SHANKS

Makes 6 servings

⅔ cup ketchup
½ cup vinegar
½ cup water
¼ cup soy sauce
8 ounces crushed pineapple, undrained
¼ cup brown sugar
1 teaspoon salt
½ teaspoon nutmeg
2 teaspoons grated fresh ginger
1 onion, thinly sliced
6 lamb shanks (about 6 pounds)

Mix together everything except lamb, simmer uncovered over low heat about 30 minutes.

Place lamb tightly in oven-proof dish, pour on sauce, cover, bake at 350°F for 2½ to 3 hours until lamb is tender. Place lamb on serving platter. Pour sauce through strainer. Skim off fat. Bring to boil; add 2½ tablespoons cornstarch mixed with 2½ tablespoons water. Cook, stirring until thickened and clear. Spoon over meat.

MARY ANNE ZOOK
Cook 'Em Up Kaua'i, The Kaua'i Historical Society Cookbook

KOREAN-STYLE BARBECUE CHICKEN

Makes 4 to 6 servings

2 to 3 pounds chicken, cut into serving pieces

Sauce

½ cup soy sauce
½ cup sugar
¼ cup sake
1 teaspoon salt
1 tablespoon sesame oil
1 teaspoon toasted sesame seeds
1 slice fresh ginger, crushed
1 clove garlic, crushed

Combine Sauce ingredients and marinate chicken 1 to 2 hours. Place in saucepan, cover, and bring to a boil. Continue cooking on low heat, turning once, 30 minutes or until tender and done. If desired, chicken may be broiled or grilled instead, turning over once during cooking until brown on both sides and done.

The Tastes and Tales of Mōʻiliʻili,
A Collection of Recipes & Stories by Mōʻiliʻili Community Center

BAKED MANDARIN CHICKEN

2 pounds chicken thigh or breast
1 teaspoon salt
½ teaspoon slivered ginger
⅓ cup hoisin sauce
¼ cup cider vinegar
¼ cup sugar (or less)
¼ cup chopped green onion
2 tablespoons salad oil

Combine ingredients and soak overnight. Bake at 350°F for 30 minutes covered with foil and basting often. Double recipe for 5 pounds of chicken.

Wisteria Delights, A Collection of Recipes
by Pearl City Hongwanji Mission

HAWAIIAN STICKY CHICKEN

Makes 4 to 6 servings

1 fryer, cut into serving pieces
1 cup pineapple tidbits
1 cup pineapple juice
2 tablespoons cornstarch
1 cup water
Salt and pepper to taste
2 tablespoons vegetable oil
1 tablespoon sugar
2 tablespoons lemon juice
1 teaspoon salt
¼ teaspoon thyme
¼ teaspoon marjoram
¼ teaspoon paprika
¼ teaspoon curry powder
Parsley
¼ cup slivered almonds

Fry chicken in oil until brown on all sides. Drain and place in greased 13 x 9-inch baking pan. Place pineapple and juice in medium bowl. Dissolve cornstarch in water; add to pineapple and blend well. Stir in remaining ingredients. Pour sauce over chicken.

Cover and bake in 350°F oven 30 to 35 minutes or until chicken is done. Place chicken with sauce on serving platter. Garnish with fresh parsley and slivered almonds.

Hana Maui Recipes from Then to Now

AZORES CHICKEN

½ pound Portuguese sausage, slice ⅛-inch thick
2 large whole chicken breasts, split
Salt and pepper to taste
6 tablespoons butter, divided use
½ cup thinly sliced green onion, divided use
½ cup dry white wine, divided use
1 pound cabbage, finely shredded
½ teaspoon salt

In skillet, brown sausage over medium heat. Drain well and set aside. Pour off fat from skillet. Season chicken breasts with salt and pepper. In same skillet, brown chicken in 2 tablespoons of butter. Arrange chicken and sausage in shallow baking dish. Sauté half the onions in skillet (just to coat with drippings).

Add ¼ cup wine and stir to loosen. Spoon onions and wine drippings over chicken. Cover and bake at 375°F for 45 minutes or until chicken is tender.

Just before serving, melt remaining 4 tablespoons butter in skillet over medium heat. Add cabbage and remaining onions. Salt to taste and sauté tossing just to heat cabbage through, keeping it crisp. Add remaining ¼ cup wine and heat. Serve at once, spooning a bed of cabbage onto each plate and topping with chicken and sausage mix.

MARIE HO
Our Favorite Recipes from the Portuguese Heritage Club of Hamakua

SESAME CHICKEN

4 tablespoons flour
8 tablespoons cornstarch
4 tablespoons sugar
1½ teaspoons salt
2 cloves garlic, chopped
1 tablespoon sesame seeds
5 teaspoons shoyu
2 stalks green onion
2 eggs
5 pound box chicken thighs

Mix all together and soak chicken for at least ½ hour. Deep-fry.

KELLEY TACHIBANA
"Cooking with Lovely Hula Hands," Moana's Hula Halau, Kaunakakai

CHICKEN HEKKA

Makes about 8 servings

2 tablespoons canola oil
1 (2-inch) piece of ginger root, crushed
1½ pounds chicken, sliced
¾ cup shoyu
¾ cup sugar
¾ cup mirin
3 medium carrots, julienne
2 sweet onions, sliced
1 (14-ounce) can shredded bamboo shoot, drained
½ pound fresh mushrooms, sliced
1 bunch watercress, cut in 2-inch length
1 (8-ounce) long rice, soaked and cut in 2-inch length

Heat oil in a large skillet or wok. Stir-fry ginger until brown then discard. Add chicken on high heat. Add shoyu, sugar, and mirin. Cook for 2 more minutes then add one vegetable at a time; stir-fry after each addition. Add long rice; cook for a few more minutes or until done.

HAWEA WAIAU
Haili Congregational Church, 175th Anniversary

CHICKEN KATSU

5 pounds chicken thighs, deboned
4 tablespoons flour
8 tablespoons cornstarch
4 tablespoons sugar
1¼ teaspoons salt
1 tablespoon sesame seed
1 teaspoon shoyu
¼ teaspoon ajinomoto (optional)
Green onions
3 cloves garlic, chopped
2 eggs
1¼ package panko flakes

Combine chicken, flour, cornstarch, sugar, salt, sesame seed, shoyu, ajinomoto, green onions, garlic, and eggs. Soak for awhile. Roll in panko flakes and deep-fry. Slice when cool.

Sauce
½ cup ketchup
2 tablespoons Worcestershire sauce
⅓ teaspoon dry mustard

North Kohala Favorites

TERI YAKITORI

Makes 4 to 6 servings

1 pound boneless chicken
⅓ cup soy sauce
¼ cup sugar
1 clove garlic, crushed
1 small piece fresh ginger root, crushed
Bamboo skewers

Remove skin from chicken and cut into 1-inch pieces. Thread 3 to 4 pieces of chicken on each bamboo skewer. Combine soy sauce, sugar, garlic, and ginger and marinate skewered chicken for at least 30 minutes before grilling. Grill on outdoor grill or broil in oven-broiler until done.

The Tastes and Tales of Mō'ili'ili, A Collection of Recipes & Stories by Mō'ili'ili Community Center

CHICKEN KELIGUIN

Makes 9 servings

1 whole chicken
½ cup vinegar
2 tablespoons salt
2 tablespoons pepper
5 whole lemons
½ cup chopped white onion
½ cup chopped green onion
Salt to taste
¾ cup fresh grated coconut
Chili peppers (optional)

Cut chicken in half. Then marinate chicken with vinegar, salt, and pepper for 2 hours. Put the chicken on the broiler and broil in oven at 400°F for 40 minutes, turning the chicken occasionally.

Debone the chicken, then chop finely and put into a large bowl. Squeeze fresh lemon and add the lemon juice, not the pits. Add chopped onion, green onion, salt, and finely shredded coconut. Add chili peppers, finely crushed, to add a spicy taste to your dish.

NOTE: Always taste the mixture while adding.

KAANEHE KOREA
1988 4-H Local & Ethnic Food Show

CHICKEN MACADAMIA

3½-ounce jar macadamia nuts
2 tablespoons butter
2 eggs
2 tablespoons oil
2 tablespoons soy sauce
1-inch ginger root, minced or 1 teaspoon powdered ginger
¼ teaspoon pepper
2 tablespoons brandy
1 medium sized onion, minced
¼ cup cold water
½ cup flour
¼ cup cornstarch
3 whole chicken breasts
Peanut oil or other salad oil

Place macadamia nuts in shallow pan with butter. Bake in 350°F oven, stirring frequently until lightly browned, about 15 minutes. Avoid scorching.

In mixer or blender, blend well the eggs, oil, soy sauce, ginger, pepper, brandy, onion, water, flour, and cornstarch.

Cut chicken breasts in half lengthwise, then cut each in half crosswise. Soak chicken in batter for 20 minutes, then fry in electric skillet containing ¼-inch peanut oil heated to 350°F. Cook until medium brown on both sides. Sprinkle nuts over chicken on serving platter.

LENORE KNOBLE
The Hele Mai, Ai (Come Eat) Cookbook, Flavors of Upcountry Maui

CHICKEN SATAY

6 cloves garlic, chopped
4 teaspoons coriander
4 teaspoons light brown sugar
1 tablespoon black pepper
2 teaspoons salt
2½ pounds boneless chicken breasts, cut into 1½ to 2-inch cubes
½ cup shoyu
4 teaspoons chopped ginger
2 tablespoons lime juice
6 tablespoons oil
¼ cup chopped fresh coriander (for garnish)

Peanut Sauce
1 cup chunky peanut butter
1 to 2 teaspoons hot chili sauce
2 cloves garlic, crushed
3 tablespoons honey
1 teaspoon cayenne pepper
¼ cup lime juice
¼ cup shoyu
½ cup peanut oil

Combine garlic, coriander, brown sugar, pepper, and salt. Rub mixture on chicken pieces. Place on tray and marinate 45 minutes. Combine shoyu, ginger, lime juice, and oil in shallow NON-ALUMINUM pan. Add chicken and marinate covered in refrigerator for 6 hours or overnight. Turn several times during marinating process.

To make peanut sauce, place peanut butter in food processor. Add chili sauce, garlic, honey, cayenne pepper, lime juice, shoyu, and peanut oil until smooth, thick paste is formed. Sauce can be made ahead. Cover and refrigerate, but bring to room temperature before serving. Grill or broil chicken on skewers soaked in water. Cook until tender (8 to 10 minutes). Sprinkle with fresh coriander and serve with peanut sauce. Absolutely ‘ono!

Ono-Licious, Na Poe Humukuiki O Hawaii, Hawaii Quilt Guild

COLD CHICKEN WITH GINGER-ONION SAUCE

Makes 6 servings

3 to 4 pounds chicken fryer
Water
3 or 4 stalks green onion
Fresh ginger (scraps and skins)
2 tablespoons shoyu
2 tablespoons salt
2 tablespoons vegetable oil

Sauce

¾ cup peanut oil
¾ cup minced fresh ginger
1¼ cups chopped green onion (green and white parts)
1 teaspoon MSG (optional)
1 teaspoon sesame oil
3 tablespoons sherry
¼ teaspoon white pepper
1 tablespoon salt
½ clove garlic, minced

Garnish

Chopped greens
Chinese parsley

Place chicken in pot and fill with enough water to cover chicken by at least 2 inches. Add green onions, ginger, shoyu, and salt. Bring to a vigorous boil. Turn heat down and simmer covered for 45 to 50 minutes. (Giblets can be boiled for broth for later use.)

Heat peanut oil; cool. Add remaining sauce ingredients; mix well, and let stand 10 minutes. Transfer cooked chicken to another pot and cool in tap water. Pat dry, rub whole chicken with vegetable oil, and refrigerate a few hours before serving.

To serve, cut into 1 x 2-inch pieces and place on bed of chopped greens. Stir sauce mixture and spread evenly over pieces. Garnish with Chinese parsley.

GENJI SANTOKI
Country Cookbook,
Compiled by the Wahiawa General Hospital Auxiliary

DYNASTY CHICKEN

Makes 4 servings

4 pieces chicken breasts
1 teaspoon salt
2 teaspoons honey
2 teaspoons water
10 ounces cooked broccoli

Gravy
1 cup chicken broth
1½ teaspoons oyster sauce
¼ teaspoon salt
¼ teaspoon sugar
4 teaspoons cornstarch
Dash of pepper

Clean and salt chicken. Combine honey and water; brush on chicken. Broil chicken 8 to 10 minutes on each side.

Combine Gravy ingredients and bring to a boil, stirring constantly. Pour over chicken and broccoli to serve.

Favorite Island Cookery, Book I, Honpa Hongwanji Hawaii Betsuin

GUAVA CHICKEN

Makes 6 to 8 servings

5 pounds chicken thighs
½ cup ketchup
½ cup sugar
½ cup oyster sauce
¼ cup plum wine
¼ teaspoon Chinese Five Spice
1 clove garlic, mashed
1 teaspoon oil
½ cup frozen guava nectar base
½ teaspoon salt

Combine ingredients and marinate chicken overnight. Line pan with foil. Place chicken, skin side down, in pan. Bake at 325°F for 30 minutes. Turn and continue baking for 30 minutes.

Hawaii's Aloha Recipes, The Japanese Women's Society of Honolulu

DIJON CHICKEN AND ARTICHOKES

4 chicken breasts, boneless, skinless and pounded flat
2 tablespoons butter
½ cup thinly sliced onions
1 cup sliced fresh mushrooms
2 garlic cloves, minced
1 (6-ounce) jar marinated artichoke hearts, drained
2 tablespoons Dijon mustard
1 cup dry white wine
½ cup whipping cream
2 tablespoons fresh parsley, chopped (optional)

Brown chicken breasts in butter in sauté pan. Remove from pan and keep warm. Add onion, mushrooms, and garlic and sauté lightly. Add artichoke hearts and mustard. Add wine; allow to simmer until reduced by half. Stir in cream.

Return chicken to pan, cook 5 to 10 more minutes or until no longer pink in middle. Check for doneness. Remove chicken to serving dish. Pour sauce over and sprinkle with parsley, if desired. Serve with pasta or rice and rolls to sop up the delicious sauce!

PAT HARRELL-LAKATOS
A Chorus of Recipes, Kamehameha School Children's Chorus

EASY CHICKEN PARMESAN

Makes 4 servings

4 skinless, boneless chicken breasts
1 egg
½ cup dry breadcrumbs
2 tablespoons oil
2 cups Prego or any kind a spaghetti sauce
½ cup shredded mozzarella cheese
4 cups cooked spaghetti (angel hair works nicely)

Dip chicken into egg and coat with breadcrumbs. Heat oil in skillet. Cook chicken 10 minutes or until done. Set aside.

In same pan, heat Prego to a boil. Return chicken to skillet.

Cover and cook over low heat 5 minutes or until chicken is hot. Top chicken with cheese and heat until cheese is melted. Serve with spaghetti. To with Parmesan cheese.

DICK AND HAPPY PACKS
"No Ka Oi" The Best of Hawaii,
Favorite Recipes from Rotarians of District 5000

GINGER SPICY CHICKEN

Makes 4 servings

2 whole chicken breasts, split, boned, and skinned
Salt as desired
2 tablespoons vegetable oil
1 medium red pepper, cut into ¼ x 2-inch strips (1½ cups)
1 medium green pepper, cut into ¼ x 2-inch strips (1½ cups)
1 (8-ounce) can juice pack pineapple chunks (undrained)
½ cup picante sauce
2 tablespoons chopped fresh cilantro or parsley
2 to 3 teaspoons grated fresh ginger

Lightly salt chicken. Cook in oil over medium heat until lightly browned and cooked through, about 5 minutes. Remove and reserve.

Add peppers, pineapple, picante sauce, cilantro, and ginger to skillet. Cook, stirring frequently, 5 to 7 minutes or until peppers are tender and sauce is thickened. Return chicken to skillet; heat through.

MARION Y. MURAOKA
50th Anniversary Best of Our Favorite Recipes,
Maui Association for Family and Community Education

HONG KONG CHICKEN

Makes 6 servings

- 3 chicken breasts, halved, boned, skinned, and cut into 1-inch squares
- ⅓ cup corn oil
- 2 green peppers, cut into ½-inch squares
- 1 can bamboo shoots, sliced and drained
- 2 tablespoons honey
- ½ cup cashews

Sauce

- ¼ cup shoyu
- 1 tablespoon sugar
- 1 tablespoon dry sherry
- 1½ teaspoons MSG
- 1 teaspoon salt
- 1 teaspoon cornstarch
- ¼ teaspoon garlic powder
- ¼ teaspoon ground ginger
- ⅛ teaspoon pepper

Mix sauce ingredients in deep bowl and add chicken, tossing gently to coat pieces. Drain and reserve liquid.

Heat 1 tablespoon corn oil in 10-inch pan over medium heat. Add chicken, stirring constantly until browned on all sides. Remove chicken, place on platter. Cover with aluminum foil. Drain liquid from pan.

Add remaining corn oil; heat. Stir in peppers, bamboo shoots, and reserved sauce. Cook uncovered for 3 to 4 minutes, until peppers are crisp. Return chicken to pan; stir gently to combine with vegetables. Add honey and cook uncovered for 2 to 3 minutes. Add cashews just before serving.

Favorite Island Cookery, Book II, Honpa Hongwanji Buddhist Temple

SHOYU CHICKEN

¼ cup corn oil
¼ cup shoyu
¼ cup brown sugar
1 clove garlic, crushed
½ teaspoon grated ginger
8 broiler-frying chicken pieces(thighs are best)

Mix together oil, shoyu, sugar, garlic and ginger. Line a baking pan with aluminum foil. Place chicken in pan; pour sauce over chicken and bake in 325°F oven 1 hour; or until done, turning chicken twice during baking. Skim fat from sauce, if desired. Serve sauce with chicken.

Hawaiian Hospitality, American Business Women's Association

IMPERIAL CHICKEN

5 pounds chicken thigh, deboned
1½ blocks butter, melted
1½ cups breadcrumbs
¼ teaspoon black pepper
½ cup Parmesan cheese
¼ cup parsley flakes
1 clove garlic, crushed
2 teaspoons salt

Dip chicken in butter, combine other ingredients and dip chicken into mixture.

Bake 45 minutes at 325°F.

CAROL SUEHIRO
Hawaiian Hospitality,
American Business Women's Association Eleu Chapter

KIKILA CHICKEN

Makes 6 servings

In November 1974, the Board of Directors of the Daughters of Hawaii went for an extraordinarily interesting and productive 2-day "think tank" at Kikila, the lovely von Holt-Burkland-White country house at Lā'ie on O'ahu. Husbands, children, and grandchildren were all left behind by the ladies who arrived with bathing suits, paddle tennis apparel, scratch paper, sharpened pencils and open minds. The inspiration for this event came from "KC" Perkins and her cousin Ellin Burkland. "KC" spelled out the terms of this goal-seeking occasion; the group, without inhibiting itself with "means," was to concentrate on the raison d'etre *of the Daughters of Hawaii, past, present and most specifically, future.*

For two fabulous days, the assemblage produced a grand number of directional arrows, many of which have been subsequently followed. The meeting times were intense. They were interspersed with plunges into the sea at "Pounders," lively games of paddle tennis, immersion by a few into the cold waters of the swimming pool, and of course, eating.

There were memorable meals. The one recorded here astonished many members of the group as the cooks, "KC" and Ellin had not been isolated in the kitchen for any discernible length of time. The assemblage went to the dining room to joyously eat extraordinarily tasty chicken thighs and douse onto their rice the sauce, in which the thighs swam. A fullsome salad rounded out the meal. The ingredients seemed hard to believe.

12 chicken thighs
1 package dried onion soup mix
1 jar apricot jam
1 bottle Russian dressing

Put the chicken thighs into a baking pan. In a bowl, mix together all the above listed ingredients. Pour this mixture over the chicken thighs. Bake at 350°F for one hour.

J. PATRICIA MORGAN SWENSON
Dining with the Daughters, The Daughters of Hawaii

KUNG PAO CHICKEN

1 pound boned chicken breast
1 egg white
2 teaspoons cornstarch
1 cup peanut oil
1 teaspoon minced garlic
1 teaspoon crushed red pepper
3 teaspoons oil
⅔ cup roasted peanuts

Sauce
2 tablespoons hoisin sauce
1½ tablespoons brown bean sauce
1½ tablespoons dark brown sugar
1 tablespoon cooking sherry
1 tablespoon red wine vinegar
2 tablespoons water

Cut chicken into ½-inch squares and combine with egg white and cornstarch.

Combine Sauce ingredients and set aside.

Heat wok or pot with peanut oil. Sauté chicken quickly and remove from pot. Pour out oil. Sauté garlic in oil, add red pepper (more may be added if desired), chicken, and sauce. Stir together for 1 minute. Add ⅔ cup roasted peanuts. Garnish with Chinese parsley.

Hawaii's Aloha Recipes, The Japanese Women's Society of Honolulu

LEMON CHICKEN

5 pounds chicken thighs, deboned and cut into bite-size pieces
4 tablespoons sherry
4 tablespoons shoyu
2 teaspoons salt
2 teaspoons sugar

Batter
2 eggs
¼ cup cornstarch
½ teaspoon baking powder
Deep oil

Lemon Sauce
1 tablespoon oil
1 teaspoon salt
3 tablespoons sugar
1 tablespoon cornstarch
1 to 2 tablespoons lemon juice
1 cup chicken broth

Marinate chicken in sherry, shoyu, salt, and sugar for 15 minutes. Combine Batter ingredients and mix well. Roll chicken in batter and deep-fry till golden brown. Cook Lemon Sauce ingredients together over low heat until thick. Drizzle Lemon Sauce over chicken before serving.

LYNN SAGUCIO
Kalaheo Missionary Church Cookin' Book!

MAYONNAISE CHICKEN

2 pounds chicken thighs
½ cup mayonnaise
½ cup water
¼ teaspoon salt
Pepper
Bread or corn flake crumbs

Slit the meaty portion of the thighs so that the seasoning will penetrate. Sprinkle salt on the chicken. Combine mayonnaise, water, salt, and pepper. Dip chicken in the mayonnaise mixture and coat with breadcrumbs. Line cookie sheet with tin foil and line the chicken on sheet. Bake in 350°F oven, uncovered, for ½ hour. Turn chicken and continue cooking the other side for another ½ hour.

A Lei of Recipes,
Kauai Association for Family and Community Education

MISOYAKI GARLIC CHICKEN

5 pounds chicken thighs, skinless, boneless
1 pound shinshu miso
½ pound white miso, local
⅔ cup mirin
⅔ cup sake
5 ounces minced garlic
1½ cup sugar
1 ounce dashinomoto

Combine all ingredients, marinate overnight. Broil chicken until browned on both sides, then cook in a 350°F oven for 10 to 15 minutes longer.

Wisteria Delights, A Collection of Recipes
by Pearl City Hongwanji Mission

MOA MA PUA KALA

Garlic salt
2 jars marinated artichoke hearts (or more, or use frozen kind or canned), sliced
3 or 4 chicken breasts, cubed, cooked, and drained
2 cans cream of mushroom soup (hemo the can–I know, but some people, you gotta tell)
½ cup mayonnaise
2 or more teaspoons curry powder
1 teaspoon lemon juice
4 slices sourdough bread (any kind bread is OK)
¼ cup melted butter

Get one rectangular 9 x 13-inch glass or steel baking pan. Put butter on top your lima and smear it around the sides and bottom of the pan. Wash your hand with hot water and soap so the spoon no slip. Put garlic salt (plenty) all over the pan. Put the chopped artichoke hearts in the bottom of the pan; spread it out, not one lump. Spread the precooked chicken on the layer of artichokes. Put garlic salt again. Mix up the soup, mayo, curry, and lemon juice in a separate bowl. Taste it, should have slightly curry taste. Slather all that on top the chicken. Sprinkle the shredded cheese on the soup stuff.

Strategically place the bread cubes over the cheese so no can spock the cheese. Take a picture and send to Terry Shintani so he cannot see the cheese underneath the bread—tell him 'as bread and broccoli casserole (make his day). Put away the camera. Pour the melted butter all over the bread.

Bake at 350°F for 25 to 30 minutes or till the cheese stay melt and the bread come little bit brown. This one can make ahead of time and freeze. Taste better the second day anyway, but not going last. Serve with rice. Some people—the ones that live on the moku East of Hawai'i—try use macaroni, but junk. Go rice, kaikaina.

Low-calorie alternative: Use broccoli instead of artichokes. No put mayonnaise. No put mushroom soup. No put butter. No put garlic salt. No put cheese. Eh, you know what—just pulehu the gonfonit chicken and whack with rice (brown) and broccoli.

BETTY JENKINS
Puuloa Hawaiian Civic Club

MOCHIKO CHICKEN

½ cup mochiko
½ cup cornstarch
½ cup sugar
1 teaspoon salt
½ cup soy sauce
2 cloves garlic, chopped
1 teaspoon grated ginger
2 eggs
¼ cup chopped green onion
MSG (optional)
5 pounds chicken drumettes
Panko (Japanese flour meal for breading)

Combine all ingredients except panko and chicken. Mix well.

Add drumettes and soak for 1 hour in refrigerator. Coat chicken pieces with panko and deep-fry until golden brown.

CONNIE BARCELONA
Kalaheo Missionary Church Cookin' Book!

ORANGE CHICKEN

Makes 6 servings

3 whole chicken breasts, split
½ cup oil
Juice of one lemon
1 teaspoon crushed basil
Salt and pepper to taste
2 tablespoons oil
1 medium onion, chopped
1 cup orange marmalade
¼ cup soy sauce
¼ cup brown sugar
1½ teaspoons crushed basil
1 (11-ounce) can mandarin oranges, drained (reserve juice)

Place chicken in large glass baking dish or broiler pan and coat evenly with oil, lemon juice, basil, salt, and pepper. Bake in a 375°F oven for 15 minutes on each side.

In saucepan, combine remainder of ingredients except oranges, but including juice and heat until marmalade is melted.

Cook 'Em Up Kaua'i, The Kaua'i Historical Society Cookbook

SESAME TERIYAKI CHICKEN

6 cloves garlic
1 ginger, thumb size
1 cup sugar
1 cup shoyu
¼ cup sesame oil
½ can beer
½ cup chopped green onion
Sesame seeds
5 pounds chicken thighs, boneless

Crush the garlic and ginger. Make marinade with all the ingredients. Marinate the chicken overnight. Cook on a hibachi (or broil).

Parks & Recreation Family Favorites

PAPER-WRAPPED CHICKEN

1 tablespoon white wine OR sherry
1 tablespoon hoisin sauce
1 tablespoon sodium reduced soy sauce
1 tablespoon finely minced cilantro
1 teaspoon finely minced green onion (white part only)
¼ teaspoon finely minced fresh ginger
¼ teaspoon finely minced garlic
1 teaspoon ketchup
¼ teaspoon sesame oil
1 tablespoon cornstarch
6 boneless chicken thighs OR 4 boneless chicken breasts, cut into bite-size pieces
24 (6 x 6-inch) parchment paper squares OR foil
Cilantro for garnish

In medium bowl, combine all ingredients except chicken and garnish, stir in chicken and cover and refrigerate; allow to marinate 1 to 2 hours.

To assemble, place 2 tablespoons chicken on lower half of parchment paper and wrap in envelope fold. Fold lower corner to center. Fold left and right corners to center. Fold top corner to center and tuck into pocket envelope style. Place packet on large cookie sheet and bake in 350°F oven for 30 minutes. Serve on tray, garnish with cilantro.

NYIT-MEE CHONG HOM
100 Years Sharing God's Love, United Community Church

ROAST CHICKEN WITH GUAVA GLAZE

Makes 6 servings

1 to 4 pounds chicken skinned and trimmed of fat
1 teaspoon ground cumin
Salt and fresh ground pepper to taste
2 large cloves garlic, minced
1 tablespoon olive oil
2 tablespoons fresh lime juice

Guava Glaze

¾ cup guava jelly
¾ cup guava nectar or juice
¼ cup fresh lime juice
3 tablespoons jalapeño jelly
1½ teaspoons Worcestershire sauce
1½ teaspoons red wine vinegar
1 teaspoon paprika
½ teaspoon ground cumin
2 cups diced fresh papaya
1 cup guava topping

Season chicken with cumin, salt, and pepper. Mix together the garlic and oil and rub over the chicken. Set chicken in a shallow glass dish and sprinkle with lime juice. Cover and marinate for 2 to 3 hours in the refrigerator. Preheat oven to 350°F. Meanwhile, make Guava Glaze.

Guava Glaze: In small saucepan, combine guava jelly, guava nectar, and next 6 ingredients. Bring to a boil. Reduce heat to low and simmer, stirring often, about 10 to 15 minutes. Remove from the heat.

Roasting and glazing chicken: Set chicken in roasting pan, cover loosely with aluminum foil and roast for 45 minutes. Brush chicken with hot glaze and return to the oven. Roast, uncovered, brushing with glaze every 10 minutes for 20 or 30 minutes or until the juices run clear when pierced with a fork.

Transfer the chicken to a warmed platter and brush with glaze one last time. Bring the remaining glaze to a simmer. Remove from the heat and stir in papaya. Serve the chicken with the glaze alongside.

VARIATION: If using chicken breasts, season 4 breasts with cumin, salt, pepper, garlic, oil, and lime juice. Bake in 350°F oven. Before serving, slice chicken and pour fruits and glaze over chicken.

100 Years Sharing God's Love, United Community Church

PRIZE-WINNING TARO CHICKEN

Makes 4 to 6 servings

½ thumb fresh ginger, grated
1 tablespoon liquor (optional)
2 tablespoons shoyu sauce
1 teaspoon salt
1 clove garlic, grated
2 pounds chicken thighs or a whole fryer, cut up
Flour
2 tablespoons oil
1 teaspoon salt
1 clove garlic, grated
Pinch of sugar
½ pound carrots, cut up
1 round onion, cut up
2 stalks celery, cut up
1½ pounds Hawaiian taro, cooked, peeled, diced in serving pieces
2 tablespoons cornstarch
2 tablespoons water
Salt and pepper to taste

Mix ginger, liquor, shoyu, salt, and garlic. Put chicken in mixture; marinate 15 minutes. Remove chicken from marinade.

Sprinkle chicken with flour. Heat oil in pan; brown chicken only.

Transfer to a heavy pot, adding enough water to cover. Add prepared vegetables; cook until vegetables are tender. Add taro, stir occasionally. Thicken gravy with cornstarch and water. Season to taste. Turn off heat.

EDITH YEE
Family Favorites, Oahu Extension Homemakers Council

POLYNESIAN BAKED CHICKEN

Makes 8 servings

½ cup butter or margarine
1 cup flour
1 teaspoon seasoned salt
4 pounds chicken pieces
1 cup orange juice
2 tablespoons lemon juice
½ cup brown sugar
1 tablespoon cornstarch
1 tablespoon soy sauce
½ teaspoon salt
2 cups sliced papayas

Melt butter in large baking pan. Combine flour and seasoned salt. Dredge chicken pieces in flour mixture; arrange in baking pan, skin side down. Bake in oven at 350°F for 40 minutes; turn and bake 20 more minutes.

In saucepan, combine orange juice, lemon juice, sugar, cornstarch, soy sauce, and salt. Cook until mixture thickens. Gently stir in papaya and pour mixture over chicken. Bake for 10 more minutes.

LILLIAN MAEDA
Our Daily Bread Centennial Cookbook, Iao Congregational Church

SINGAPORE CHICKEN CASSEROLE

Makes 4 servings

This mildly spiced curry dish is a busy cook's dream.

- 1 tablespoon olive or vegetable oil
- 4 teaspoons curry powder
- 2 cups sliced onion
- 1 pound chicken cutlets, cut into 3 x 1-inch strips
- 1 (8-ounce) can pineapple chunks, drained and juice preserved
- 1 tablespoon cornstarch
- 1 cup fresh or canned mung bean sprouts, rinsed and dried
- 2 tablespoons soy sauce

In a deep 3-quart microwave-safe casserole dish, mix oil and 3 teaspoons of the curry powder. Microwave on high for 1 minute. Stir in onion, cover with lid, and microwave for 6 to 9 minutes, stirring twice, until tender. Stir in chicken; cover and microwave on high for 3 to 4 minutes, stirring once.

Blend reserved pineapple juice and cornstarch until smooth and stir into chicken mixture. Cover and microwave on high for 1 to 1½ minutes, stirring once after 40 seconds, until juices are slightly thickened. Stir in pineapple chunks, bean sprouts, soy sauce, and remaining 1 teaspoon curry powder. Cover and microwave 2 minutes until heated through, stirring once after 1 minute. Let stand covered 5 minutes before serving.

SUGGESTION: Serve with mango chutney, raisins, chopped green onion, almond slices, and flaked coconut as condiments.

Community Family Favorites, Community Church of Honolulu

SMOKED CHICKEN, PEKING-STYLE

1 tablespoon peppercorn
1 tablespoon coarse salt
5 pieces chicken thighs

4 cups water
1 stalk green onion
2 slices ginger
1 star anise
¼ teaspoon cinnamon
½ cup shoyu

Fry peppercorn with coarse salt. Sprinkle this mixture on chicken (use as much or as little salt to taste). Let this stand for a couple of hours.

Combine rest of ingredients in a pot and bring this to a boil. Let simmer for 10 minutes. Add chicken and simmer another 10 minutes. Remove and let cool.

For the smoking process, use a heavy pan. (I use my old pressure cooker which no longer works as a pressure cooker.) Line the bottom of pan with foil. Put ½ cup sugar, ½ cup tea leaves, and ½ cup flour into pan and mix well. Place a rack over this. Place the cooked thighs on it; cover and smoke at low heat for 8 minutes. Then turn thighs over and smoke for another 5 minutes. Thighs should turn nice and brown. To serve, chop into bite-size pieces.

NOTE: Smoked chicken or fish is a very popular dish in old Peking. The chicken may be done several days ahead and served cold, if so desired. The liquid mixture in which the thighs are simmered may be used a second or third time.

ROSE KWAILIN MAU
Community Family Favorites, Community Church of Honolulu

EASY CHICKEN POT PIE

Makes 6 servings

1⅔ cups frozen mixed vegetables, thawed
1 cup cut-up cooked chicken
1 (10.75-ounce) can condensed cream of chicken soup
1 cup Bisquick Original baking mix
½ cup milk
1 egg

Heat oven to 400°F. Mix vegetables, chicken, and soup in ungreased 9-inch pie plate. Stir remaining ingredients with fork until blended. Pour into pie plate. Bake for 30 minutes or until golden brown.

LEE HU
Ka'u Hospital Auxiliary, One More Time

THAI CHICKEN CURRY

Makes 3 servings

¾ pound boneless chicken
1 round onion
2 medium-size potatoes
2 tablespoons vegetable oil
2 tablespoons yellow curry paste
2 cups coconut milk
2 tablespoons fish sauce or nam pla
2 teaspoons brown sugar
1 to 5 yellow chili peppers
1 cup peas (optional)

Slice chicken into strips. Cut onions into eighths. Cut potatoes into 1-inch cubes. Stir-fry the chicken in the oil and set it aside. Then stir-fry the curry paste in oil until it bubbles. Add the potatoes, round onion, coconut milk, fish sauce, brown sugar, and peppers; stir and simmer for about 5 minutes. Add the chicken and simmer until potatoes are cooked.

RENEE TAKARA
1988 4-H Local & Ethnic Food Show

WEST KAUA'I CURRY

2 large onions, halved and sliced
1 tablespoon finely chopped fresh ginger
2 cloves garlic, peeled and pressed
½ teaspoon cumin powder
3 tablespoons butter or olive oil
3 tablespoons flour
3 tablespoons curry powder or to taste
½ cup milk
2 cups coconut milk
1 teaspoon salt
2 cups cooked diced chicken or cooked shrimp

Sauté onions, ginger, garlic, and cumin in butter until lightly browned; remove from heat. Add flour mixed with curry powder and stir to blend. Add milk, stirring constantly. Add coconut milk slowly and stir until smooth. Put back on heat and stir until it boils. Simmer slowly for a few minutes. Let stand to blend flavors. Before serving, add salt and chicken and heat slowly. Serve with rice and condiments: chopped hard-boiled eggs, chopped crisp bacon, chopped peanuts or mac nuts, grated fresh coconut, sliced green onions, and mango chutney.

LOPAKA MANSFIELD
Food for the Body and Soul, West Kaua'i United Methodist Church

THAI CHICKEN BASIL STIR-FRY

Makes 4 servings

1 pound boneless, skinless chicken
6 dried shiitake, soaked
3 tablespoons oil
¼ onion, thinly sliced
2 cloves garlic, minced
1 tablespoon minced ginger
2 tablespoons soy sauce
2 tablespoons rice vinegar
1 tablespoon fish sauce (nam pla)
¼ teaspoon crushed red pepper
¼ cup thinly sliced basil

Cut chicken and mushrooms into thin slices. Heat 2 tablespoons oil in skillet over medium-high heat. Add onion, mushrooms, garlic, and ginger; stir-fry until onion is transparent. Remove vegetables and set aside.

Combine soy sauce, vinegar, fish sauce, and pepper; set aside.

Add remaining oil to skillet and stir-fry chicken until lightly browned, about 3 minutes. Add soy sauce mixture and cook for 1 minute. Stir in basil and serve over hot rice.

LILLIAN MAEDA
Our Daily Bread Centennial Cookbook, Iao Congregational Church

WAI'OLI FRIED CHICKEN

Makes 2 serving

2 broiler chicken halves
2 teaspoons salt
1½ teaspoons MSG (optional)
¼ teaspoon pepper
1 cup flour
1 egg, beaten
½ cup milk
1½ cups breadcrumbs
¼ cup shortening
¼ cup butter

Rinse chicken and pat dry. Combine salt, MSG, pepper, and flour in paper bag; shake to mix well. Place chicken in bag; shake vigorously; remove and dip in mixture of egg and milk. Roll in crumbs. Fry in hot mixture of shortening and butter until brown on both sides. Place in heavy pan with 2 tablespoons water; cover tightly and bake at 350°F for 50 to 60 minutes.

THE ORIGINAL WAIOLI TEA ROOM RESTAURANT, 1974
The Tastes and Tales of Mōʻiliʻili,
A Collection of Recipes & Stories by Mōʻiliʻili Community Center

CHICKEN TINOLA

Makes 8 servings

2 tablespoons cooking oil
4 cloves garlic, crushed
1 teaspoon sliced ginger (strips)
½ cup chopped onion
1 stewing chicken, cut into pieces
1 tablespoon patis
10 cups rice water
1 small sliced green papaya
1 teaspoon salt
1 teaspoon ajinomoto
1 cup sili (pepper) leaves

Fry the garlic in hot cooking oil until brown. Add the ginger and chopped onion. Cook until soft.

Drop in pieces of chicken. Season with patis; cover and let it simmer for 5 minutes.

Add the rice water; simmer until chicken is tender. Add the sliced papaya and cook until papaya is tender.

Just before removing from the fire, season with salt and ajinomoto. Add the pepper leaves. Serve hot.

FLORA CARRANCHO
From the Hawaiian Kitchens of the Molokai Lions

CHICKEN THIGHS WITH PAPAYA SEED DRESSING

2 pounds chicken thighs, deboned
1 bottle of papaya seed dressing
1 teaspoon minced garlic
1 tablespoon chopped cilantro
Salt, pepper, flour

Sprinkle salt and pepper lightly on chicken thighs. Mix papaya seed dressing, garlic, and cilantro and pour over chicken. Marinate the chicken overnight.

Coat chicken well with flour and fry in hot oil until golden brown.

RECIPE NOTE: Mom's favorite to make for family potlucks.

BETTY ISHIBASHI
Food for the Body and Soul, West Kaua'i United Methodist Church

FRIED CHICKEN DRUMMETTES

Makes 6 to 10 servings

Dipping Sauce
½ cup soy sauce
3 tablespoons sugar
1 teaspoon togarashi (Oriental hot pepper)
1 clove garlic, minced
2 drops sesame oil
1 stalk green onion, minced

5 pounds chicken drummettes
2 eggs, well beaten
1 cup flour
½ gallon canola or vegetable oil (for frying)

Mix together all ingredients for Dipping Sauce and set aside. Dip chicken in beaten eggs and then roll in flour until well-coated. Deep-fry in 375°F oil until browned. Drain on absorbent paper. While hot, dip into Dipping Sauce.

ETTA HELM
"Cooking with Lovely Hula Hands," Moana's Hula Halau, Kaunakakai

CHAR SIU HOT WINGS

Makes 10 to 12 servings

Sauce
½ cup honey
1 tablespoon red food coloring
1 teaspoon Chinese Five Spice
¼ cup thick soy sauce
1 teaspoon salt
1 tablespoon oyster sauce
2 tablespoons wet bean curd (red)
¼ cup sherry
3 cloves garlic, minced
2 cups brown sugar

5 pounds hot wings

Mix sauce thoroughly until sugar dissolves. Marinate wings overnight, turning wings occasionally. Bake at 350°F for 1 hour.

Favorite Island Cookery, Book IV, Honpa Hongwanji Hawaii Betsuin

SPICY KOREAN CHICKEN WING

Makes 8 servings

5 pounds chicken wingettes
Cornstarch for coating
1 tablespoon ko choo jang (Korean-style hot sauce)
2 eggs, beaten
1½ tablespoons soy sauce
⅔ cup cornstarch
¼ cup sugar
1½ tablespoons salt
2 stalks green onions, thinly sliced
1 clove garlic, minced
1 tablespoon toasted sesame seeds
Oil for deep-frying

Coat chicken with cornstarch. Combine chicken wingettes with all the remaining ingredients, except oil for deep-frying; mix well. Marinate, refrigerate overnight. Heat oil for deep-frying to 375°F. Deep-fry chicken until done.

DAVID KAWAMURA
Puuloa Hawaiian Civic Club

FRIED DUCK WITH CHINESE SAUCE

Makes 6 to 8 servings

1 (3 to 4 pounds) duck

Sauce

¼ teaspoon Chinese cinnamon
¼ teaspoon pepper
½ teaspoon salt
½ teaspoon liquor
1 tablespoon shoyu
1 tablespoon sugar
4 tablespoons chopped parsley
3 pieces star anise
3 pieces ginger, minced

Cornstarch
Oil for frying
Chinese Five Spice seasoning

Rub duck with the sauce. Place duck in a large pan and steam for 45 minutes. When cool, chop duck into 4 large pieces. Sprinkle cornstarch over them. Fry in deep fat until brown. Chop into small chunks. Sprinkle Chinese seasoning. Serve over hot wun tun if desired, or use shredded lettuce or won bok.

Favorite Island Cookery, Book II,
Honpa Hongwanji Buddhist Temple

PEKING DUCK

1 Long Island duckling (4 to 6 pounds)
6 to 7 stalks green onion
1 small piece ginger root
2 tablespoons dry sherry
4 tablespoons hoisin sauce
2 tablespoons honey
2 tablespoons shoyu

Wash and clean duck. Rub salt on skin and cavity and let stand for 30 minutes. Wash and clean onion and ginger, crush them together. Mix all ingredients together and let stand for about 10 minutes. Marinate duck, pouring sauce over and inside, and let stand for at least 1 hour until time for cooking in either oven or a charcoal fire drum. The latter is preferred.

When using drum, coals should be red hot with vents slightly open when duck is hung. Duck should be ready to serve in an hour by this method of roasting.

Oven roasting requires three temperatures—start at 375°F for 30 minutes, reduce heat to 250°F for 1 hour, and then increase heat to 400°F for 30 minutes.

Favorite Island Cookery Book II,
Honpa Hongwanji Buddhist Temple

ORANGE BASIL CORNISH GAME HENS

Makes 4 servings

½ cup orange juice
½ cup fresh basil leaves
2 tablespoons fresh lemon juice
1 tablespoon olive oil
3 cloves garlic, crushed
1 teaspoon grated orange zest (rind)
½ teaspoon salt
¼ teaspoon freshly ground pepper
2 Cornish game hens, backbone removed and halved

1. In food processor or blender, place the orange juice, basil, lemon juice, olive oil, garlic, orange zest, salt, and pepper.
2. Place the Cornish hen halves in a noncorrosive baking pan in a single layer. Pour the marinade over the hens. Refrigerate, covered, 1 hour, turning once after 30 minutes.
3. Preheat the broiler. Arrange the hen halves on the broiler pan skin side down. Broil 6 inches from the heat, basting with the marinade until browned, 8 to 10 minutes. Turn skin side up. Baste and broil until the skin is browned and juices run clear when thigh is pricked with fork, 8 to 10 minutes longer. Serve warm, or at room temperature.

BRENDA SPEAK
Cooking with Honolulu Gardeners, Honolulu Community Recreational Garden Program

TURKEY OR CHICKEN TETRAZZINI

1 medium onion, chopped
2 tablespoons butter or margarine
3 cups chicken broth
1½ cups water
Salt and pepper
8 ounces uncooked spaghetti, broken
1 can sliced mushrooms, drained
2 tablespoons grated Parmesan cheese
¾ cup milk
3 cups cooked, diced turkey

In large pot or Dutch oven, sauté onion in butter. Add broth, water, salt, and pepper. Bring to boil. Add spaghetti, boil until done, about 20 minutes. Add more water, if necessary, to keep from sticking. Add remaining ingredients. Cover and heat for about 45 minutes on low. Turn into serving dish. Garnish with parsley and pimentos.

PEGGIE BAREFOOT
A Book of Favorite Recipes, Compiled by United Methodist Women of Wahiawa, United Methodist Church

DILL AND LEMON FISH BAKE

Makes 6 servings

- 2 teaspoons dill weed, divided use
- 1 teaspoon grated lemon peel
- 1/16 teaspoon ground black pepper
- 1½ pounds (6) flounder fillets or another white fish
- 1 cup water
- ½ cup dry vermouth or apple juice
- 3 tablespoons fresh lemon juice

Preheat oven to 350°F.

Combine 1 teaspoon of the dill with lemon peel and black pepper; rub into both sides of each fillet. Roll up fillets from the narrow ends; secure with toothpicks if needed. Place in a shallow 1½-quart casserole dish.

Combine water, vermouth, lemon juice, and remaining 1 teaspoon dill. Pour over fish. Cover with foil. Bake until fish flakes easily when tested with a fork, 15 to 20 minutes. Serve with sauce spooned over fish.

LUDVINA ABREW
50th Anniversary Best of Our Favorite Recipes, Maui Association for Family and Community Education

BUTTERFISH TERIYAKI

4 fillets of butterfish
1 teaspoon salt

Sauce No. 1
1/3 cup shoyu
3 tablespoons mirin
¼ teaspoon ajinomoto

Sauce No. 2
1/3 cup shoyu
3 tablespoons mirin
1 tablespoon sugar
2 tablespoons water
¼ teaspoon ajinomoto
1 teaspoon cornstarch

Sauce No. 1: Combine ingredients in a saucepan and boil down to 1/3 of its original volume.

Sauce No. 2: Combine ingredients, except cornstarch, and bring to a boil. Thicken it with cornstarch paste.

Salt fish and let stand for 10 minutes. Pan broil, brushing sauce heavily. Reduce heat, continue broiling until sauce is used up.

Favorite Island Cookery, Book I, Honpa Hongwanji Hawaii Betsuin

BAKED FISH FILLETS WITH WINE

2 or 3 medium tomatoes, peeled and sliced
1 small onion, very thinly sliced
1 to 1½ pounds fish fillets (sole, halibut, haddock)
½ cup white wine (sauterne)
1 cup grated American cheese
Salt and pepper to taste
Paprika

Arrange tomato slices over the bottom of a greased baking dish. Over this, arrange onion slices, sprinkle with salt and pepper. Arrange fish fillets over onions, pour wine over fish, and again sprinkle with salt and pepper. Top fish with the grated cheese and dust with paprika. Bake in a moderately hot oven 375°F for 25 minutes.

HELEN HISERMAN COLE
Dining with the Daughters, The Daughters of Hawaii

RED SNAPPER WITH GINGER SAUCE

Make 2 to 4 servings

1½ pounds whole red snapper
1 tablespoon dark soy sauce
1 tablespoon sesame oil
2 tablespoons medium dry sherry, divided use
1 tablespoon shredded ginger root
2 stalks green onion, finely chopped
½ teaspoon cornstarch

Cut 3 shallow incisions on each side of fish. Place fish on a large platter that will fit into a deep roasting pan.

Combine soy sauce, sesame oil, and 1 tablespoon of sherry. Spoon sauce over fish. Put half of ginger and green onion in cavity of fish. Arrange remainder on top of fish.

Mix cornstarch in remaining sherry to make a binder. Fill roasting pan with about 3 inches of water. Put platter, with fish, on a high-legged rack above water level.

Bring water to boil over high heat, reduce the heat to moderate, cover, and steam for 15 minutes or until eyes bulge. Pour juices accumulated on platter into saucepan. Bring to a boil over high heat; reduce heat to moderate. Stir binder and stir into sauce. Cook, stirring constantly, until sauce thickens. Pour over fish and serve immediately.

Favorite Island Cookery, Book IV, Honpa Hongwanji Hawaii Betsuin

DAD'S LOCAL-STYLE BAKED FISH

1 fresh fish (pāpio, kūmū, or reef fish) cleaned
1 stalk lemon grass, crushed
1 small ginger, slivered
2 cloves garlic, crushed
Hawaiian salt
Pepper
Peanut oil
Green onion

Stuff fish belly with lemon grass, ginger, garlic, Hawaiian salt, and pepper. Sprinkle Hawaiian salt and pepper on outside of fish also. Wrap fish with ti leaf and tie with string. Bake in covered pan at 375°F for about 45 minutes. When done baking, drizzle fish with hot peanut oil. Garnish with green onion. Soooooo 'ono!

TIANA HOKUTAN
A Chorus of Recipes, Kamehameha School Children's Chorus

BUTTERFISH MISO-STYLE

8 slices butterfish
Lemon juice

Sauce
⅔ cup white miso
1 tablespoon vinegar
2 tablespoons shoyu
2 tablespoons sugar
Green onions, chopped
1 clove garlic, grated
1 piece minced ginger

Sprinkle lemon juice on butterfish and pour miso sauce. Let stand for 15 minutes. Wrap each butterfish in foil with some sauce. Bake at 350°F for 25 to 30 minutes.

LIMA HANA
Family Favorites, Oahu Extension Homemakers Council

FISH AND CHIPS

2 pounds fish (paka) fillets
¼ cup milk
1 cup crushed Maui Potato Chips
¼ cup grated Parmesan cheese
¼ teaspoon dried thyme, crushed
¼ cup melted butter

Dip fish in milk, then into potato chips to which you have mixed in the cheese and thyme, coating fish well. Place in greased baking dish. Sprinkle with any extra crumbs. Drizzle the melted butter over the top. Heat oven to 500°F. Bake for 12 to 15 minutes.

MRS. C.N. OVERMAN
The Hele Mai, Ai (Come Eat) Cookbook, Flavors of Upcountry Maui

BALINESE BROILED FISH

Sauce
1 (6-ounce) can frozen grapefruit juice concentrate, thawed
2 tablespoons lime or lemon juice
¾ teaspoon salt
½ teaspoon dry mustard
¼ teaspoon Tabasco
¼ teaspoon thyme
2 to 3 pounds fish

Combine all ingredients and use as marinade, then brush on fish while broiling. A 1-pound whole fish serves one person. A 1-pound fish steak or fillet serves 3 people.

The Kahikolu Country Cookbook

TAKARA BUNE

Stuffed Fish Treasure Ship

1½ pounds whole red fish preferred
⅓ cup carrot
⅓ cup bamboo shoot
⅓ cup water chestnuts
½ cup shiitake, softened in water
⅔ cup soup stock or shiitake water
½ teaspoon salt
1 teaspoon sugar
1½ teaspoons shoyu
¼ teaspoon ajinomoto
1 egg
1 to 2 stalks green onion, chopped
⅓ cup frozen peas
Sake
Aluminum foil

Scale fish thoroughly and cut on both sides of backbone. Break backbone near tail and near head; remove. Take out entrails and wash. Dry with paper towel and sprinkle salt inside and out.

Cut carrot, bamboo shoot, water chestnuts, and shiitake into ¼-inch cubes. Cook carrot in stock or shiitake water for 3 minutes. Add bamboo shoot, water chestnuts, and shiitake. When carrot is tender, season with salt, sugar, shoyu, and ajinomoto. Cook over medium heat until almost dry.

Break egg into bowl. Add green onion and peas. Pour into vegetable mixture. Sprinkle sake on fish and stuff cavity with vegetable mixture. Lift tail up and use bamboo stick to keep tail in place. Cut a square of aluminum foil and grease. Place fish in center of foil, bringing up sides to help keep fish in shape. Lay foil wrapped fish in baking pan and bake. Place on platter; open and fold back foil. Garnish with parsley.

MRS. KEIKO ENOMOTO
WIFE OF FORMER CONSUL GENERAL OF JAPAN
Hawaii's Aloha Recipes, The Japanese Women's Society of Honolulu

FISH BAKED IN TI LEAVES

1 red snapper (about 4 to 5 pounds)
1 teaspoon salt
1 tablespoon minced onion
1 teaspoon minced parsley
¼ cup minced celery
2 tablespoons melted butter
½ teaspoon salt
¼ teaspoon paprika
½ teaspoon dill seed
2 cups ½-inch bread cubes
1 (10½-ounce) can chicken broth, divided use
Ti leaves or foil
1 lemon, sliced
2 ounces salt pork, cut into thin strips

Clean and scale snapper; wash and pat dry. Rub inside and out with salt. Combine onion, parsley, celery, butter, salt, paprika, dill seed, bread cubes, and ½ cup chicken broth. Mix together and use to stuff fish. Sew or use toothpicks to close opening. Line pan with ti leaves or foil. Place fish on top of ti leaves or foil.

Place fish on top of ti leaves. Pour remaining chicken broth over fish. Top fish with lemon slices and salt pork. Wrap ti leaves at 350°F for 1 to 1½ hours or until fish flakes. Place on platter and serve with lemon wedges.

Hana Maui Recipes from Then to Now

SZECHWAN PEPPER CRUSTED 'AHI ON CRISP TARO SHRIMP CAKE

4 tablespoons ground toasted Szechwan peppercorns
2 tablespoons ground toasted mustard seeds
½ tablespoon hichimi togarashi
4 ounces (1 x 1-inch) 'ahi block

Combine peppercorns, mustard seed, and togarashi. Coat 'ahi block on all sides. Sear 'ahi in hot pan. Slice 'ahi and set aside.

8 ounces cooked and diced taro
2 ounces diced Maui onion
1 ounce rinsed and chopped ogo
4 ounces cooked and diced tiger prawns
2 cups panko
1 pound taro leaves, cooked and drained

Combine taro, onions, ogo, and tiger prawns. Form into patties, bread with panko and fry in hot pan.

2 tablespoons miso paste
½ cup Hanalei poi

Mix ingredients well and set aside.

4 ounces mango chutney
2 ounces diced fresh papaya
3 tablespoons water
2 tablespoons ume purée
½ ounce diced red bell peppers
½ ounce minced green onions

Combine ingredients well and set aside. Place cooked taro leaf on plate. Top with taro shrimp cake. Place sliced 'ahi on top of shrimp cake. Add a teaspoon of mango papaya chutney in the center of 'ahi slice. Drizzle with sweet soy and miso poi sauce. Garnish with tobiko, tatsoi, chives and friend taro chips.

ANTHONY C. VEA
Food for the Body and Soul, West Kaua'i United Methodist Church

FRESH TUNA (AKU) PORTUGUESE-STYLE

½ cup vinegar
½ cup water
1 clove garlic, crushed or minced
¼ teaspoon MSG (optional)
1½ pounds fresh tuna (aku)
1 teaspoon salt
¼ teaspoon pepper
¼ cup oil
Flour (in shaker)

Mix together vinegar, water, garlic, and MSG. Pour over fish slices and let stand for 1 hour. Spoon marinade over fish occasionally. Remove fish from marinade and pat dry with paper towels.

Heat oil in frying pan. Sprinkle fillets with salt, pepper, and flour. Cook in oil until lightly browned.

Serve with sourdough French bread. Use stale bread as fresh bread gets soggy.

Pour the remaining oil from frying pan. Add the leftover marinade and bring to a boil. Dip pieces of bread in marinade. 'Onolicious.

Still More of Our Favorite Recipes,
Maui Association for Family and Community Education

TUNA BURGERS

1 can tuna, drained and flaked
½ cup fine fresh breadcrumbs (2 slices)
½ cup chopped celery
2 tablespoons minced onion
2 tablespoons chili sauce
1 teaspoon lemon juice
4 hamburger buns or as desired
Lettuce and tomato slices
⅓ cup mayonnaise

Combine first 4 ingredients. Blend next 3 ingredients, stir into tuna mixture. Form into 4 patties. Fry in lightly oiled skillet over medium heat for 5 minutes or until browned. Serve on hamburger buns with lettuce and tomatoes.

SANDRA WILEY
A Book of Favorite Recipes Compiled by United Methodist Women of Wahiawa United Methodist Church

SPANISH FISH BALLS

1 pound minced aku
1 medium onion, chopped
1 stalk celery, chopped
1 small green pepper, chopped
1 small tomato, chopped
1 potato, grated and excess water removed
1 egg
Salt and pepper to taste

Mix above ingredients, shape into round balls, and pan-fry. Set aside.

Sauce

1 (15-ounce) can whole tomatoes
½ cup water
2 stalks celery, sliced
1 medium onion, sliced
3 cloves garlic
2 teaspoons brown sugar
Salt and pepper to taste

Break tomatoes in saucepan and add rest of ingredients. Bring to a boil, then simmer 10 to 15 minutes.

Add fish balls to sauce and simmer 10 minutes. Garnish with parsley.

AGNES GROFF AND LUDVINA ABREW
50th Anniversary Best of Our Favorite Recipes, Maui Association for Family and Community Education

BACALHAU A GOMES DE SA
Cod Casserole

Makes 6 servings

2 pounds salted cod
2 large onions
¾ cup olive oil
1 clove garlic, minced
3 large potatoes, cooked
4 hard-boiled eggs, sliced
½ cup pitted, sliced ripe olives
⅓ cup chopped parsley

Soak cod in cold water overnight. Drain, rinse with fresh water. Add water to just cover cod and simmer covered for 15 minutes. Drain, flake into large pieces.

Sauté onion in oil, stir in garlic and sliced potatoes. In a 2-quart casserole dish, layer half the potatoes, half the cod, and half the onions. Repeat. Bake for 10 minutes at 350°F until lightly browned. Garnish with eggs, olives, and parsley. Serve with wine vinegar, olive oil, and freshly ground black pepper.

MICHELLE CARDOZA
The Kahikolu Country Cookbook

MISOYAKI SALMON

2 tablespoons miso
2 tablespoons Japanese rice vinegar
¼ cup sake
¼ cup sugar
½ tablespoon minced ginger
2 (6-ounce) salmon fillets

Mix together all ingredients, except salmon. Pour mixture over salmon and marinate for a few hours or overnight. To cook salmon, place in a well-oiled pan on medium heat, searing each side. Bake for about 10 minutes at 425°F.

Wisteria Delights, A Collection of Recipes by Pearl City Hongwanji Mission

SAVORY SALMON LOAF

½ cup buttered breadcrumbs
2 eggs, beaten
½ cup milk
1 (1-pound) can salmon, flaked
1 teaspoon lemon juice
½ teaspoon salt
Dash of pepper
½ teaspoon ground sage
2 teaspoons chopped onion
1 tablespoon chopped parsley
1 tablespoon butter, melted

Mix together and bake in greased loaf pan for 30 to 40 minutes at 350°F. Garnish with cooked, sliced hard-boiled eggs; sprinkle with paprika.

Kalaheo Missionary Church Cookin' Book!

SALMON TERIYAKI

1 pound salmon fillets
¼ cup soy sauce
½ cup sake
3 tablespoons sugar
1 teaspoon minced garlic
1 tablespoon minced ginger

Wash fish fillets and pat dry.

Combine soy sauce, sake, sugar, garlic, and ginger. Marinate fish in mixture 30 minutes. Drain fish. Broil 6 inches from heat source 4 minutes on one side and broil other side 2 minutes. Squeeze lemon juice over fish and serve hot.

Hawaiian Hospitality,
American Business Women's Association Eleu Chapter

COCONUT FISH

2 pounds mahimahi or ono
¼ cup butter
¼ cup flour
½ cup milk
½ cup light cream
1 cup coconut milk
¼ cup dry white wine
Salt and pepper to taste
1 (3½-ounce) jar salted chopped macadamia nuts
Chopped parsley and lemon wedges

Rinse fish and pat dry. Arrange in single layer in greased baking dish 8 x 12-inches. In saucepan, over moderate heat melt butter, stir in flour and cook until bubbly. Gradually add milk, cream, and coconut milk, stirring constantly. Add wine and season to taste. Cook until thick. Pour sauce over fish. Top with nuts and bake uncovered at 350°F for 25 minutes or until fish flakes. Garnish with chopped parsley and lemon wedges.

JODY BALDWIN
The Hele Mai, Ai (Come Eat) Cookbook, Flavors of Upcountry Maui

MAHIMAHI (OR SHRIMP) WITH CHILI SAUCE

1½ pounds mahimahi, cut into 1½ to 2-inch squares or 1½ pounds peeled and cleaned shrimp

Batter

1 cup flour
1 egg
1 teaspoon baking powder
¾ cup water
Salt to taste

Chili Sauce

1 teaspoon cornstarch
¼ cup apple cider vinegar
½ cup sugar
½ cup chicken broth
½ teaspoon Worcestershire sauce
1 teaspoon soy sauce
2 tablespoons ketchup
2 tablespoons chili sauce
1 clove garlic, minced
1 small piece ginger, crushed
Dash of MSG (optional)

Garnish (optional)

1 teaspoon toasted sesame seeds
1 tablespoon minced green onions

Mix batter ingredients together. Coat fish or shrimp with batter and deep-fry until golden brown. Drain on paper towels, then place on platter. Blend Sauce ingredients in small pot and simmer 10 to 15 minutes. Pour sauce over cooked fish and sprinkle with garnish just before serving.

NOTE: This Chinese-style sweet sour sauce may be made ahead and reheated before serving. If taking this dish somewhere, keep sauce hot in a thermos or reheat just before serving.

Wisteria Delights, A Collection of Recipes by Pearl City Hongwanji Mission

CURRIED MAHIMAHI

1 pound mahimahi, without bone
3 tablespoons oil
1 medium onion, chopped fine
1 clove garlic, crushed
½-inch slice ginger, crushed or grated
1 small bay leaf
1 teaspoon powdered coriander
1 teaspoon powdered turmeric
½ teaspoon powdered fenugreek, if available
1½ cups coconut milk
1 teaspoon salt
¼ teaspoon black pepper
Dash cayenne
1 tablespoon lemon juice
Fresh Chinese parsley, chopped

Cut mahimahi into large chunks or cubes. Sauté lightly in oil over moderate heat about 2 minutes each side. Set aside. Increase heat and sauté onions, garlic, ginger, and bay leaf. When it begins to get brown, add the coriander, turmeric, and fenugreek. Continue frying for a few minutes. Add coconut milk, salt, pepper, and cayenne. Simmer over very low heat until well-blended, about 20 minutes. Slide fish carefully into sauce. Sprinkle with lemon juice and continue cooking very gently barely simmering for 15 minutes or so, basting occasionally. Sprinkle generously with Chinese parsley at last minute so it stays bright green. Serve with rice and Cucumber Raita or fresh chutney.

Cucumber Raita
1 cup plain yogurt
½ cup diced drained cucumber
1 clove garlic, crushed
Salt

Mix. Delicious on curry.

NOTE: The spices can be substituted with curry powder, if desired.

RAE PATTISON
Haleiwa Elementary School 115th Birthday

STEAMED 'ŌPAKAPAKA WITH LEMON SOY SAUCE

Makes 1 serving

8 ounces fresh 'ōpakapaka
2 ounces peanut oil
4 green onion stems, cut into 1-inch pieces
½ ounce fresh ginger, grated
Green onion strips (white part only), sliced thin in 1-inch long strips
Pinch of sugar, to taste
1½ teaspoons soy sauce
Juice of ½ lemon
Sprinkling of white pepper
2 sprigs Chinese parsley for garnish

Coat fish with a little peanut oil. Line onion stems in a row on a plate. Place fish on stems to give it a lift. Place plate in a steamer and spread no top of fish with grated ginger. Cook until done. Remove from steamer and drain excess liquid from plate.

Place thin onion strips on fish; spread them out. Mix sugar and soy sauce together and pour over fish and onions. Squeeze lemon juice over the fish.

Heat remaining peanut oil until it starts to smoke. Pour oil over fish (it must sizzle). Serve immediately with a little white pepper sprinkled on top. Garnish with Chinese parsley.

North Kohala Favorites

ESCABECHE

2 pounds fish steaks
Salt and pepper to taste
⅓ cup flour
Oil
2 cloves garlic, minced
1 round onion, sliced
1 to 2 bell peppers, cut into rings
¾-inch piece ginger, minced
1 (5½-ounce) can pineapple chunks (save liquid)

Sauce

¼ cup vinegar
¼ cup sugar
1 cup water
Liquid from pineapple

1 tablespoon cornstarch

Lightly salt and pepper fish. Dredge with flour. Brown fish on both sides in hot oil. Set fish aside on a large platter and keep warm. Remove all but 2 tablespoons oil from skillet. Sauté garlic, onion, bell peppers, and ginger for about 2 minutes.

Mix Sauce ingredients (except cornstarch); add to skillet. Cover and simmer for 3 minutes. Add pineapple chunks. Dissolve cornstarch in ¼ cup water. Gradually pour cornstarch mixture into pan and stir until thickened. Pour over fish and decorate with bell peppers. Serve with rice.

MELECIA SHORT
Family Favorites, Oahu Extension Homemakers Councils

BIRD'S NEST WITH SHRIMP

Makes 2 to 4 servings

Chinese Taro Nest

1 large Chinese taro, peeled and shredded
Salt to taste
½ teaspoon cornstarch
Vegetable oil

Place taro in colander. Sprinkle generously with salt. Rinse under cold water. Pat taro dry. Mix with cornstarch. Heat oil in deep-fryer. Spray 9-inch strainer with nonstick spray. Press taro into bottom and sides of strainer. Fry taro in strainer until golden brown, 12 to 15 minutes. Carefully remove nest from strainer. Repeat with remaining shredded taro to form nests.

Shrimp-Vegetable Filling

1 tablespoon cornstarch
1 egg
8 shrimps, shelled and deveined
2 pieces bamboo shoot chunks, drained
8 pieces straw mushrooms, drained
8 Chinese peas

Blend cornstarch and egg. Stir in shrimps to coat completely. Add shrimps to oil and deep-fry 2 minutes. Remove shrimps using slotted spoon. Deep-fry vegetables 30 seconds. Remove vegetables using slotted spoon.

Sauce

1½ teaspoons cornstarch
1½ teaspoons water, divided use
4 teaspoons vegetable oil
⅔ cup water
⅔ cup soy sauce
4 teaspoons sugar
1 tablespoon white wine vinegar
½ teaspoon crushed garlic
¼ teaspoon minced ginger root

Blend cornstarch and ½ teaspoon water. Heat oil in wok over high heat. Mix water, soy sauce, sugar, vinegar, garlic, and ginger root into oil. Add shrimps, vegetables, and cornstarch mixture and stir until thickened, about 1 minute. Spoon into potato nest. Serve immediately. Nest and filling should be consumed together.

VARIATIONS: Baking potatoes may be used in place of taro. Chicken, skinned and boned, and scallop may be used in place of shrimps.

Favorite Island Cookery, Book IV, Honpa Hongwanji Hawaii Betsuin

THAI SHRIMP WITH GARLIC

Makes 4 servings

¼ cup soybean oil
4 cloves Asian garlic, minced
¾ pound shrimp, shelled and deveined
¼ cup coconut milk
¼ cup straw mushrooms
¼ teaspoon ground black pepper
2 teaspoons fish sauce
3 cups shredded cabbage
3 sprigs Chinese parsley
2 red chili peppers, seeded and sliced

In a wok, heat oil and brown garlic. Stir in shrimp, coconut milk, mushrooms, black pepper, and fish sauce. Cook until shrimp are done, about 3 minutes. Serve over shredded cabbage and garnish with parsley and chili peppers.

PATRICK CHUNG
1988 4-H Local & Ethnic Food Show

SAFFRON AND SHRIMP RISOTTO

6 to 8 cups low-sodium vegetable or chicken stock
24 medium shrimp, peeled, deveined, cut into thirds, reserve shells
3 tablespoons olive oil
½ cup finely chopped shallots
Pinch of saffron threads
1 cup Arborio rice
½ cup white wine
4 to 6 tablespoons unsalted butter
½ cup grated Parmesan cheese (optional: more for grating or shaving)
¼ cup chopped fresh flat-leaf parsley
Salt and freshly ground pepper

Heat stock in pan over high heat. Add shrimp shells to stock. Cover and simmer for 15 minutes. Pour stock through fine sieve discarding solids left in the pan. Return stock to stove; keep at simmer over medium heat.

Heat oil in heavy-bottomed saucepan over medium heat. Add shallots and saffron, continue stirring until translucent. Add rice, stirring until rice begins to sound like glass beads, 3 to 4 minutes. Add wine, stirring until wine is absorbed. Using a ladle, add ¾ cup of hot stock to rice. Using a wooden spoon, stir rice constantly at a medium speed. When rice has absorbed most but not all of the liquid, and mixture is just thick enough to leave a clear wake behind the spoon when stirring, add another ¾ cup stock. Continue adding stock in this manner, stirring constantly until rice is mostly translucent but still opaque and slightly crunchy in center.

Add shrimp, continue stirring and adding stock until rice is al dente but not crunchy and shrimp is cooked through, about 3 minutes. As rice nears doneness, watch carefully and add smaller amounts of liquid. The mixture should be thick enough that grains of rice are suspended in liquid about the consistency of heavy cream. It will thicken slightly when removed from heat. Remove from heat. Stir in butter, Parmesan cheese, and parsley. Season with salt and freshly ground pepper. Grate or shave Parmesan cheese over risotto. Serve immediately.

MONICA KALAHUI
Hugs & Kisses of Aloha, Aloha Airlines Flight Attendant Cookbook

SHRIMP SINGAPORE

Makes 6 to 8 servings

2 pounds shrimp, cleaned
2 tablespoons butter or margarine
4 tablespoons flour
2 teaspoons curry powder
1 teaspoon salt
1/8 teaspoon cayenne pepper
2 cups chicken broth
4 apple bananas

Cook shrimp in boiling salted water until barely done. Drain well. Set aside. Melt butter or margarine in a skillet or saucepan. Remove from heat and stir in flour, curry powder, salt, and cayenne pepper. Gradually add the chicken broth, stirring until smooth. Return to heat and cook, stirring until the sauce is thickened. Peel the bananas; cut them in half crosswise, then in thirds lengthwise. Add them to the sauce. Cover and simmer 5 minutes, stirring occasionally. Add shrimp and heat. Serve over rice.

SUELYN TUNE
Community Family Favorites, Community Church of Honolulu

BEER BATTER COCONUT SHRIMP

12 pieces jumbo shrimp
1 teaspoon salt
1 teaspoon white pepper
2 cups panko
2 cups shredded coconut
3 cups beer
3 cups all-purpose flour
2 teaspoons baking powder
2 teaspoons garlic salt
1 egg

Peel, devein, and butterfly the shrimp. Soak shrimp in iced water with the salt and white pepper for 15 minutes. Mix panko and coconut and set aside. Blend remaining ingredients to make a fresh beer batter. Dip shrimp in beer batter, then roll in coconut and panko mix. Deep-fry until golden brown. Serve with your choice of sauce.

GARY SIRACUSA
"No Ka Oi" The Best of Hawaii,
Favorite Recipes from Rotarians of District 5000

ABSOLUTE PURITY IN 

PRIMO BEER

Ask your physician about Primo Beer and he will tell you of its purity.

Not fortified like imported beers to preserve it.

ORDER A TRIAL CASE FOR HOME USE.

PRAWNS WRAPPED IN RICE PAPER

1 pound fresh frozen prawns
1 egg white, lightly beaten
1 teaspoon salt
½ teaspoon sugar
2 teaspoons cornstarch
3 ounces fatback, cut into size of matchsticks
3 ounces lean ham, cut into size of matchsticks
4 ounces bamboo shoots cut into size of matchsticks
4 to 6 scallions, cut into tiny rounds
15 sheets rice paper
Peanut oil for frying

Chop prawns roughly. Put in a bowl. Add egg white, salt, sugar, and cornstarch to the prawns. Stir until well-coated. Add fatback, ham, and bamboo shoots. Mix in scallions. Cut the rice paper sheets into 30 squares, each 4 inches.

Spread about 1 tablespoon of the filling, almost to the edges of rice paper. Fold over and roll into a small cigar, leaving both ends open, seal with a little water smeared on the edge. Fry in deep oil for about 3 minutes until filling is cooked and the rice paper is crisp. Drain on paper towels.

Ono-Licious, Na Poe Humukuiki O Hawaii, Hawaii Quilt Guild

WHITE CRAB WITH BLACK BEAN SAUCE

3 pounds white crab
2 cans chicken broth
1 piece ginger
2 tablespoons Lee Kum Kee black bean sauce with garlic
2 teaspoons sugar
1 tablespoon cornstarch
1 cup water
1 bunch green onions

Clean white crab and cut in halves. Simmer crab in 2 cans of chicken broth. Slice ginger and add into broth. Add 2 tablespoons of black bean sauce when crabs turn red. Add sugar (until taste is preferred). Add cornstarch and water to thicken broth. Chop green onions and sprinkle over crabs. Ready to serve.

SARAH WONG
A Chorus of Recipes, Kamehameha School Children's Chorus

CRAB SUPREME

8 slices bread
2 cups crabmeat
Salt to taste
1 onion, chopped
½ cup mayonnaise
½ cup chopped green pepper
1 cup chopped celery
4 eggs, beaten
3 cups milk
1 cup canned cream of mushroom soup
Grated cheese
Paprika to taste

Dice half of bread into baking dish. Mix crab, salt, onions, mayonnaise, green peppers, and celery and spread over bread. Dice other slices of bread and place over crab mixture. Mix eggs and milk together and pour over all. Cover and place in refrigerator overnight. Bake for 15 minutes at 325°F. Then spoon soup over the top. Sprinkle with cheese and paprika. Bake 1 hour more, covered. Bake uncovered 15 minutes more.

JANET ALLEN
The Hele Mai, Ai (Come Eat) Cookbook, Flavors of Upcountry Maui

HAWAIIAN LOBSTER

2 tablespoons butter
2 tablespoons flour
2 teaspoons curry powder
1 cup milk
Meat of medium-sized lobster
1 cup grated coconut
Salt

Melt butter. Mix flour and curry powder and cook in butter over slow heat for 5 minutes. Add milk and cook two or three minutes after it begins to boil. If too thick, thin with a little more milk. Add lobster, coconut, and salt just before taking from stove. Serve in rice ring with chutney.

Rice ring is made by rinsing ring mold in cold water, pressing in warm rice, and turning it out on serving dish.

MRS. KENNETH BYERLY
The Hilo Woman's Club Cookbook

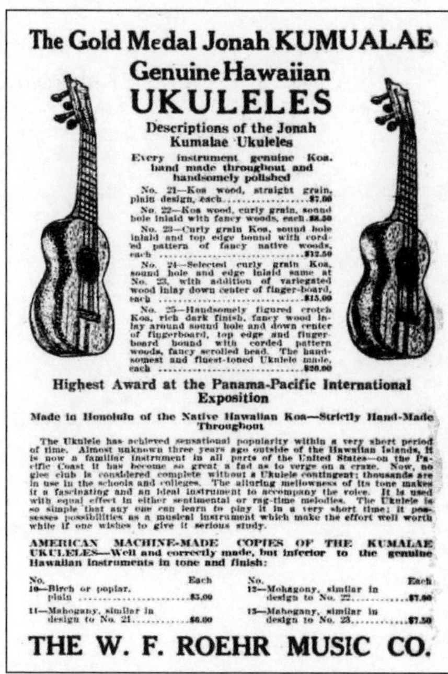

LOBSTER TAIL CANTONESE

6 frozen lobster tails
¼ cup oil less
1 clove garlic, chopped fine
½ pound ground pork
2 teaspoons cornstarch
¼ cup shoyu
1½ teaspoons sugar
1 teaspoon salt
½ teaspoon pepper
2¼ cups boiling water
2 eggs
½ cup chopped green onion
Aji

Chop lobster tails in 2-inch pieces. Heat oil in pot. Add garlic and pork and sauté until pork is no longer pink. In small bowl, make smooth mixture of cornstarch and ¼ cup water, stir into pork the cornstarch, shoyu, sugar, salt, pepper, and boiling water. Reduce heat and simmer stirring until thick and translucent, about 10 minutes. Add lobster, cook covered over low heat 10 minutes. In small bowl, beat eggs slightly. Blend some pork, lobster sauce, and stir all at once into lobster mixture. Add onion and serve immediately. Add aji.

JUDITH NOVIT
The Kahikolu Country Cookbook

SCALLOPS IN SAKE

1 pound scallops
½ teaspoon salt
2 tablespoons sake
1 tablespoon olive oil
1 tablespoon lemon juice
Pinch of paprika
Pinch of oregano
Pinch of white pepper
Pinch of dried parsley
1 tablespoon butter or oil for cooking

Wash and dry scallops. Mix ingredients, except butter or oil. Marinate scallops in mixture at least 15 minutes. Sauté scallops on both sides until golden brown.

Our Daily Bread Centennial Cookbook, Iao Congregational Church

OYSTERS WITH GINGER AND GREEN ONION

Makes 6 servings

Light and healthy

1 teaspoon wine
1 tablespoon low sodium soy sauce
2 teaspoons Chinese or wine vinegar
½ teaspoon sugar
Pepper to taste
2 tablespoons oil
1 inch ginger, sliced into ⅛-inch slices and smashed
½ cup green onion or leeks, 2-inch length
1 (10-ounce) jar oysters, rinsed, drained well
1 teaspoon cornstarch, mixed with 2 tablespoons water

Combine wine, soy sauce, vinegar, sugar, and pepper to make sauce. Heat the oil in a wok or pan over high heat. Add ginger and stir-fry for half a minute. Add onion and stir-fry for half a minute. Put in the oysters and stir-fry for 2 minutes. Pour in the sauce and stir-fry for 1 minute. Add cornstarch mixture and cook until thickened, 15 seconds. Garnish with Chinese parsley, if desired. Serve immediately.

Community Family Favorites, Community Church of Honolulu

OCTOPUS IN WINE SAUCE

Polvo em Molho de Vinho

Makes 6 servings

1 large (2½ pound) octopus
2 cups white wine, divided use
2 cups red wine
1 (12-ounce) can beer
3 cloves garlic, minced
2 teaspoons paprika
2 tablespoons minced parsley
2 teaspoons ground fresh mild red pepper
1 teaspoon salt
1 large onion, minced
3 tablespoons olive oil
3 potatoes, cubed
French bread

To clean octopus, turn body inside out. Remove internal organs and sac containing black secretion. Rinse thoroughly; slice.

In a large bowl, combine 1 cup of the red and white wines with 1 cup beer, garlic, paprika, parsley, red pepper, and salt. Add octopus; marinate for 2 hours.

In a large saucepan, sauté onion in olive oil until transparent; add octopus and marinade. Cover; cook over medium heat for 45 minutes, stirring frequently. Add potatoes, remaining wine, and beer. Cook for 20 more minutes or until potatoes are done. Serve with French bread and wine.

50th Anniversary Best of Our Favorite Recipes,
Maui Association for Family and Community Education

HAWAI'I KAI BOUILLABAISSE

Makes 4 to 6 servings

½ pound bacon, cut into ½-inch pieces
¼ cup olive oil
1 large onion, diced
4 cloves garlic, minced
1 medium bunch celery, chopped into ½-inch pieces
3 (6.5-ounce) cans chopped clams with juice
1 (16-ounce) can crushed tomatoes
½ package dried onion soup
2 tablespoons basil leaves
2 bay leaves, broken in half
1 teaspoon marjoram
1 pound mahimahi fillets
Salt and pepper to taste
½ cup flour
½ cup white wine (optional)

Sauté bacon pieces in Dutch oven until just starting to crisp; remove from pan and drain on paper towels; set aside. Discard bacon drippings leaving residue in pan; add 1 tablespoon olive oil and sauté onions, garlic, and celery on medium heat. When onions begin to brown, add clams with juice, tomatoes, onion soup, bacon, basil, bay leaves, and marjoram. Stir well and simmer on low heat for at least one hour.

While bouillabaisse is simmering, cut mahimahi into 1-inch cubes and sprinkle with salt and pepper. Dredge fish in flour and sauté in remaining olive oil until fish just begins to brown on all sides. Remove from pan and drain on absorbent paper. Add fish to bouillabaisse during last 5 to 10 minutes of cooking. If bouillabaisse is too thick, add white wine. Serve with hot French bread and salad.

The Tastes and Tales of Mō'ili'ili,
A Collection of Recipes & Stories by Mō'ili'ili Community Center

FISHERMEN'S STEW

Makes 6 servings

4 stems saffron or ¼ teaspoon turmeric or 1 teaspoon tea, powdered instant
1 teaspoon coriander seeds
2 pounds mahimahi, sea bass or any white fish
4 onions, sliced
6 medium potatoes, thinly sliced
3 tablespoons olive oil
3 cloves garlic, minced
½ bunch parsley, chopped
1 (16-ounce) can whole tomatoes
1 bay leaf
1 cup dry white wine
Salt and pepper to taste

Simmer saffron and coriander seeds in 2 cups water for 20 minutes. Set aside.

Cut fish in 1-inch cubes. Prepare onions and potatoes.

In a very large saucepan or Dutch oven, heat olive oil, lightly sauté onions, garlic, and parsley. Add fish, potatoes, tomatoes, bay leaf, wine, and seasonings.

After removing the saffron and coriander seeds, add the water to the above; add additional water to cover ingredients, if needed. Bring to a boil. Cover pan and simmer 20 to 25 minutes.

Parks & Recreation Family Favorites

POLYNESIAN 'ULU SEAFOOD SUPREME

This won second prize in Hāna's cook-off contest.

1 green breadfruit, cut into 1-inch cubes
¼ cup butter
½ cup coconut milk
1 pound quartered scallops
15 medium raw shrimp, chopped
6 ounces crabmeat
1 lobster tail, chopped
2 cans coconut milk, heated
1 tablespoon sugar
Salt to taste
½ cup fresh grated coconut
½ cup grated cheddar cheese

Boil breadfruit in salted water until soft. Mash 4 cups breadfruit until soft. Mix breadfruit with the ¼ cup butter and coconut milk. Set aside.

Cook seafood until pink; drain. Mix together the 2 cans coconut milk, ½ cup mashed breadfruit, 1 tablespoon sugar, salt and seafood.

Pour mixture into a casserole dish. Sprinkle ¼ cup coconut over top of mixture. Spread remaining breadfruit on top of coconut. Sprinkle top with ¼ cup each coconut and cheddar cheese. Put under broiler until golden brown.

SINA FOURNIER
Hana Maui Recipes from Then to Now

DESSERTS

7-UP CAKE

1 package Lemon Supreme cake mix
1 small package instant lemon pudding
1½ cans 7-Up
4 eggs
¼ cup oil

Icing
1 cup sugar
3 tablespoons flour
1 cube butter
2 eggs
1 can crushed pineapple
1 package coconut

Cake: Mix well and bake at 305°F for 30 to 35 minutes.

Icing: Cook until slightly thick. Cool and add coconut. Spread over cake.

MARY HUMPHRIES
Kalaheo Missionary Church Cookin' Book!

BAKED BUTTER MOCHI CAKE

2 cups mochiko
2 cups brown sugar
1 tablespoon baking soda
1 (12-ounce) can coconut milk
1 (12-ounce) can evaporated milk
2 eggs
¼ cup melted butter
1 teaspoon vanilla

Mix mochiko, brown sugar, and soda.

Beat with mixer the coconut milk, evaporated milk, eggs, melted butter, and vanilla. Add wet mixture to dry ingredients. Beat and pour into greased 9 x 13-inch pan. Bake at 350°F for 1 hour.

KAREN OYAMA AND BETSY SAITO
Family Favorites, Oahu Extension Homemakers Council

BLACK RUSSIAN CAKE

Makes 12 servings

1 package Duncan Hines yellow cake mix
1 small package instant chocolate pudding
1 cup oil
4 eggs
¼ cup vodka
¼ cup Kahlua
¾ cup water

Glaze
¼ cup Kahlua
¼ cup powdered sugar

Mix all dry ingredients together. Mix all wet ingredients together. Then mix them both together. Spray bundt pan with Pam. Bake at 350°F for 50 minutes. Leave in pan for 15 minutes, then turn over. Glaze with Kahlua and powdered sugar.

LORRAINE SCHLEMMER HOWELL
Dining with the Daughters, The Daughters of Hawaii

CHOCOLATE DOBASH CAKE

3 eggs, separated
1¼ cups sugar, divided use
1½ cups flour
¾ teaspoon soda
¾ teaspoon salt
⅓ cup cocoa
⅓ cup salad oil
1 cup milk, divided use

Beat egg whites until frothy; gradually beat in ½ cup sugar. Beat until stiff. Sift dry ingredients together. Make a well in the flour mixture, add salad oil and half of milk. Beat until well-blended on medium speed on mixer. Add remaining milk and egg yolks. Beat until smooth. Fold in meringue. Pour into 2 layer pans. Bake in 350°F oven for 30 to 35 minutes. Cool. Slice each layer in half to make 4 layers. For frosting, combine the following and heat until thick.

2 cups water
½ cup sugar
¼ cup butter or margarine
½ cup cocoa
⅓ cup cornstarch
Salt

A Lei of Recipes,
Kauai Association for Family and Community Education

CHRISTMAS CAKE

2½ cups self-rising flour
1 cup buttermilk
1½ cups vegetable oil
1 teaspoon baking soda
1 teaspoon vanilla
¼ cup red food color (2 [1-ounce] bottles)
1½ cup sugar
1 teaspoon cocoa
2 eggs
1 teaspoon white vinegar

Heat oven to 350°F. Mix all ingredients with electric mixer. Bake in 3 pans sprayed with nonstick coating. Bake for 20 minutes.

Frosting
⅓ pound butter, softened (1⅓ sticks)
10 ounces cream cheese
1 (1-pound) box confectioners' sugar
2 cups chopped pecans

Combine butter, cream cheese, and powdered sugar in bowl. Beat until fluffy. Then fold in 1½ cups pecans. Use to fill and frost cake. Decorate top of cake with remaining ½ cup pecans. Refrigerate at least 1 hour before serving.

JUDY CALHOUN
100 Years Sharing God's Love, United Community Church

COCONUT CAKE

½ pound butter
1 cup sugar
3 large eggs, separated
2 cups cake flour
2½ teaspoons baking powder
¾ teaspoon salt
1 teaspoon vanilla
¾ cup milk

Cream butter and sugar. Add egg yolks one at a time and beat well after each addition. Sift flour once and then measure. Add baking powder and salt and sift three times. Add vanilla to milk. Gradually combine the flour and milk to egg mixture, beating lightly after each addition. Pour cake batter into two 8-inch cake pans that have been well-buttered.

Bake at 375°F in preheated oven for about 25 minutes. Test with toothpick or clean broom straw. Set upright on rack for 5 minutes then turn out to cool and frost.

Coconut Frosting
2 cups white sugar
1 cup water
3 egg whites
1 teaspoon lemon extract
1 cup freshly grated coconut, divided use

Boil sugar and water until it forms a ball when dropped into a cup of cold water.

Beat the 3 egg whites until stiff, then pour the boiled sugar-water into it slowly and stir well. Add lemon extract and ½ cup coconut.

Spread between cake layers and pour over cake, finishing with sprinkling remaining coconut over all.

The Kauai Museum Presents Early Kauai Hospitality: A Family Cookbook of Recipes 1920-1920

FRESH GINGER CAKE

Makes 8 to 10 servings

The flavor bursts in your mouth.

1½ cups sifted flour
1 teaspoon baking soda
¼ teaspoon salt
7 tablespoons vegetable oil
½ cup plus 1 tablespoon apple juice
½ cup brown sugar
¼ cup light molasses
¼ cup dark corn syrup
1 egg
3 tablespoons grated fresh ginger

Sift together the flour, baking soda, and salt. In a mixing bowl, combine the oil and apple juice. Beat in the sugar, molasses, and corn syrup. Beat in the egg. Add the ginger and the flour mixture and mix well.

Pour into a greased and floured 9-inch square pan; bake in 350°F oven for 30 to 35 minutes or until cake springs back when touched. Cool cake in pan 5 minutes, then take out of pan and cool on wire rack. Cut cake into squares and serve topped with ice cream or whipped cream.

Hana Maui Recipes from Then to Now

HAUPIA CAKE
Island Coconut Cake

Makes 10 servings

A delicious dessert served at lū'aus.

1 cup shortening
2 cups sugar
4 eggs, separated
½ teaspoon vanilla extract
½ teaspoon lemon extract
3 cups all-purpose flour
3 teaspoons baking powder
¼ teaspoon salt
1 cup milk
Coconut Cream Filling (recipe follows)
Light as a Cloud Frosting (recipe follows)
1½ cups shredded fresh or packaged coconut

Grease and flour three 8-inch round cake pans and set aside.

Cream shortening and sugar; add egg yolks, vanilla extract, and lemon extract. Beat well. Sift flour with baking powder and salt; add alternately with milk to creamed mixture. Beat egg whites until stiff peaks form; fold into batter.

Pour into prepared pans. Cool thoroughly. Fill with Coconut Cream Filling and frost with Light as a Cloud Frosting. Sprinkle top and sides with coconut.

Coconut Cream Filling

½ cup sugar
⅓ cup flour
¼ teaspoon salt
1½ cups milk
2 eggs, beaten
1 teaspoon vanilla extract
3 tablespoons butter or margarine
½ cup shredded coconut

Blend sugar with flour and salt in a saucepan; add milk and stir, making sure there are no lumps. Cook until mixture starts to thicken. Pour some of hot mixture into eggs. Mix well. Pour back into pot and cook until thick. Remove from heat and stir in vanilla, butter, and coconut. Cool completely before filling cake.

Light as a Cloud Frosting

This frosting is delicious, easy to make, and fat-free. It can be used on any cake.

1½ cups sugar
½ teaspoon cream of tartar
⅛ teaspoon salt
½ cup hot water
4 egg whites (room temperature)
½ teaspoon almond extract
½ teaspoon coconut extract

Combine sugar, cream of tartar, salt, and water in a saucepan. Cook over medium heat, stirring until clear. Continue cooking without stirring until it reaches soft-ball stage (240°F).

In a bowl, beat egg whites until it forms soft peaks. Slowly pour in syrup mixture and continue beating. Add flavorings. Beat until stiff enough to spread.

For vanilla frosting, use 1 teaspoon vanilla extract instead of coconut.

NICOLE STRIEGL
Hana Maui Recipes from Then to Now

FUNNEL CAKE

1¼ cups all-purpose flour
¼ teaspoon salt
½ teaspoon baking soda
2 tablespoons sugar
¾ teaspoons baking powder
1 egg, beaten
⅔ cup milk (more if batter is too thick)
1 small funnel

Sift flour, salt, baking soda, sugar, and baking powder together in separate bowl. Mix egg and milk together; add to dry ingredients. Beat until smooth. Hold finger over the "puka" of the funnel; pour in some batter. Remove finger; move funnel in a circle motion over a pan filled with 1 inch hot oil (375°F). Fry until golden brown, turning once. Remove from pan and drain on a paper towel. Sprinkle with powdered sugar and serve hot.

ETHELREDA R. KAHALEWAI
Puuloa Hawaiian Civic Club

HAWAIIAN BANANA CAKE

½ cup butter
1½ cups sugar
1 cup mashed ripe banana
2 eggs, beaten
4 tablespoons sour cream
1 teaspoon baking soda
1 teaspoon baking powder
1¾ cups flour
1 cup broken nut meats

Cream butter and sugar, add banana, beaten eggs, sour cream, soda, baking powder, flour, and nut meats. Bake 50 minutes in spring form pan, medium oven. Cover with icing made of 1 ½ cups powdered sugar, 3 tablespoons melted butter, grated rind of half an orange, and orange juice to make soft enough to spread.

The Hilo Woman's Club Cookbook

HAWAIIAN WEDDING CAKE

1 cup oil
2 cups sugar
3 eggs
2 teaspoons vanilla
2 small jars strained carrots (baby food)
2 cups flour
1 teaspoon cinnamon
½ package shredded coconut
2 teaspoons baking soda
1 teaspoon salt
1 cup chopped nuts
1 can medium size crushed pineapple, drained

Mix the oil, sugar, eggs, vanilla, and carrots. Combine flour, cinnamon, coconut, baking soda, and salt. Add flour mixture to egg mixture. Add 1 cup chopped nuts and 1 can medium size crushed pineapple (drained). Mix well. Pour into greased 9 x 13 x 2-inch pan. Bake in 350°F oven for 50 minutes.

Frosting

1 package vanilla Instant pudding
¾ cup cold milk
1 cup heavy cream
1 teaspoon vanilla

Whip together until thickened.

Family Favorites, Oahu Extension Homemakers Council

ISLAND FAMOUS CARROT CAKE

4 eggs
1½ cups oil
2 teaspoons vanilla
2 cups sugar
2 cups flour
1 teaspoon salt
2 teaspoons baking soda
2 teaspoons baking powder
2 teaspoons cinnamon
2 cups grated carrots
¾ cup finely chopped coconut
1 small can crushed pineapple
1 cup diced walnuts or pecans
8 ounces cream cheese
1 box powdered sugar
1 stick (block) margarine
1 teaspoon vanilla

Beat together eggs, oil, and vanilla. Sift together the next 6 dry ingredients and add to egg mixture, then fold in carrots, coconut, crushed pineapple including juice, and the nuts. Bake for 45 to 60 minutes at 350°F.

For icing, blend together cream cheese, powdered sugar, margarine, and vanilla. Spread on cake and serve.

GWEN FURUKAWA
Our Daily Bread Centennial Cookbook, Iao Congregational Church

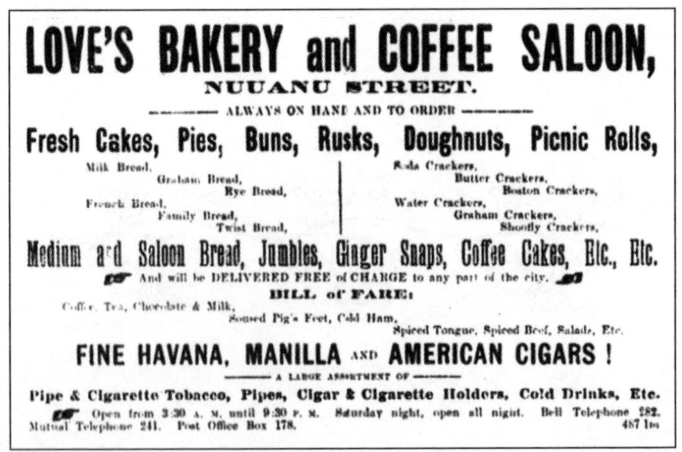

KONA COFFEE SPICE CAKE

1 cup butter
2 cups sugar
3 eggs, separated
1 cup cold strong Kona coffee
¼ teaspoon allspice
¼ teaspoon cloves
⅛ teaspoon nutmeg
¼ teaspoon ginger
¾ teaspoon cinnamon
5 teaspoons baking powder
4 cups flour
2 tablespoons molasses
½ cup currants
½ cup thinly sliced citron
¾ cup chopped raisins
1 teaspoon vanilla

Cream butter and gradually add sugar. Beat egg yolks into coffee and add to first mixture. Sift spices, baking powder, and flour (except ¼ cup) then add molasses and beat well. Fold in stiffly beaten egg whites. Dredge fruit with the remaining flour and add with the vanilla. Bake in deep pan for 45 minutes at 350°F. Sprinkle with powdered sugar or make your favorite icing.

JEAN KEYS
We, the Women of Hawaii Cookbook

MANGO CAKE

3 eggs
1 teaspoon vanilla
½ cup Wesson oil
½ block margarine, melted
1½ cups sugar
2 cups cubed mango
2 cups flour
2 teaspoons cinnamon
2 teaspoons baking soda
½ teaspoon salt
½ cups raisins
¼ cup chopped walnuts

Beat eggs, vanilla, oil, and margarine for 2 minutes on medium speed. Add sugar and beat till smooth. Stir in mango cubes, dry ingredients, and slightly floured raisins and nuts. Mix well. Pour into pan. Bake at 350°F for 45 minutes in 9 x 13 x 2-inch pan.

Our Daily Bread Centennial Cookbook, Iao Congregational Church

MOLOKAI CREAM CAKE AND CREAM CHEESE FROSTING

1 cup buttermilk
1 teaspoon soda
½ cup shortening
2 cups sugar
1 stick butter or oleo
3 eggs, separated
2 cups flour
1 teaspoon vanilla
1 cup chopped nuts
1 can coconut

Preheat oven to 325°F.

Mix buttermilk and soda. In a separate bowl, cream shortening, sugar, and butter; add egg yolks one at a time, beating well after each. Alternate buttermilk mixture and flour to cream mixtures. Stir in vanilla. Beat egg whites until stiff; gently fold into cream mixture. Stir in ¾ of the nuts and ¾ of the coconut.

Bake in 3 round cake pans for 25 minutes.

Cream Cheese Frosting
1 stick butter or oleo
1 (8-ounce) package cream cheese
1 teaspoon vanilla
1 box powdered sugar

Cream butter, cream cheese, and vanilla. Beat in sugar, little at a time.

Frost and sprinkle remaining nuts and coconut on top and sides.

RON CARLISLE
From the Hawaiian Kitchens of the Molokai Lions

PINEAPPLE PLANTATION CAKE

3 tablespoons margarine or butter
½ cup brown sugar
6 slices canned pineapple
10 to 12 maraschino cherries
Ginger cake mix*

Melt butter or margarine in an 8 x 8 x 2-inch square pan. Add brown sugar and well-drained pineapple slices and cherries. Fill ⅔ full with ginger cake batter and bake at 350°F for 40 minutes.

*May substitute white or yellow cake mix.

50th Anniversary Best of Our Favorite Recipes, Maui Association for Family and Community Education

RED VELVET CAKE

1½ cups sugar
½ cup shortening
2 eggs
2 cups flour
1 teaspoon salt
1 tablespoon cocoa
1 cup buttermilk
1 teaspoon vanilla
2 ounces red food coloring
1 teaspoon soda
1 tablespoon vinegar

Cream sugar and shortening; add eggs and beat well. Sift flour, salt, and cocoa three times; add alternately to creamed mixture with buttermilk. Add vanilla and coloring. Fold in soda mixed with vinegar. Bake in three 8-inch pans at 350°F for 25 minutes or until done. Fill layers with coconut filling or serve with your favorite frosting. (Can also be made in 9 x 13-inch pan.)

PINKY THOMAS
The Hele Mai, Ai (Come Eat) Cookbook, Flavors of Upcountry Maui

‘ULU CAKE

½ cup butter
1½ cups sugar
¾ cups mashed ripe ‘ulu (breadfruit)*
1 egg
2 teaspoons vanilla
2 cups flour
1 teaspoon baking powder
¼ teaspoon salt
1¼ teaspoon soda
½ cup buttermilk

Cream butter and sugar until light and fluffy. Add breadfruit, egg, and vanilla; mix well. Sift dry ingredients together; add dry ingredients alternately with buttermilk, mixing after each addition. Bake in greased and floured loaf pan for 1 hour in 350°F oven.

* If breadfruit is unavailable, mashed potatoes may be substituted.

CHRIS CHIU
Hana Maui Recipes from Then to Now

TOMATO SOUP CAKE

Makes 1 (8 x 4 x 3-inch) loaf

- 2 cups sifted flour
- 1 teaspoon baking soda
- 2 teaspoons baking powder
- 1 teaspoon cinnamon
- ½ teaspoon cloves
- 1 teaspoon nutmeg
- ½ cup shortening
- 1 cup sugar
- 1 cup condensed tomato soup
- 1 cup chopped walnut meats
- 1 cup raisins

Sift flour, soda, baking powder, and spices together 3 times. Cream shortening with sugar until fluffy. Add sifted dry ingredients and tomato soup alternately in small amounts, beating thoroughly after each addition. Stir in nuts and raisins. Pour into small greased tube pan or loaf pan and bake in moderate 350°F oven for 50 to 60 minutes. Let stand 24 hours before cutting. Cover with cream cheese frosting.

ALICE BOTELHO

Our Favorite Recipes from the Portuguese Heritage Club of Hamakua

FROSTING FOR CAKES

Butter Frosting

Makes 2 cups

1/3 cup butter
3 cups sifted confectioner's sugar
1 egg yolk, beaten
3 tablespoons light cream
1½ teaspoons vanilla extract

In a bowl, combine butter and sugar. Blend in egg yolk. Stir in cream and vanilla. Beat until smooth.

Chocolate Butter Frosting

1/3 cup butter
3 cups sifted confectioner's sugar
1 egg yolk, beaten
3 tablespoons light cream
1½ teaspoons vanilla extract
3 ounces melted unsweetened chocolate

In a bowl combine butter and sugar. Blend in egg yolk and cream. Stir in vanilla and chocolate. Blend thoroughly.

Lemon Butter Frosting

1/3 cup soft butter
3 cups confectioner's sugar, sifted
1 egg yolk, beaten
3 tablespoons lemon juice
1½ tablespoons grated lemon rind

In a bowl, combine butter and sugar. Blend in egg yolk. Add lemon juice and rind. Blend thoroughly.

Hawaiian Hospitality,
American Business Women's Association Eleu Chapter

KALAPAKI JELLY ROLL

One of our family favorites. But once an adventurous cook used mint jelly instead of guava—it was a disaster!

4 eggs
¾ cup sugar
1 teaspoon vanilla
¾ cup cake flour
¼ teaspoon salt
¾ teaspoon baking powder
1 cup guava jelly, mashed up for ease in spreading

Beat eggs whole until very light yellow. Add sugar and vanilla and continue beating until smooth and creamy. Fold in the flour sifted with salt and baking powder.

Line bottom of a greased shallow jelly roll pan with brown or waxed paper and grease again.

Bake in preheated oven at 400°F for 13 to 15 minutes. Invert the pan at once on a dish towel (linen), sprinkled with powdered sugar. Remove paper. Cut off all four edges. Spread evenly with guava jelly and roll up in the cloth. You should work fairly fast, not letting the cake cool.

Served sliced.

The Kauai Museum Presents Early Kauai Hospitality: A Family Cookbook of Recipes 1920-1920

PUTO

Steamed Cupcakes

Makes 16 to 18 cupcakes

1½ cups margarine or butter
2¼ cups sugar
1 cup milk, divided use
3 cups flour
1 tablespoon baking powder
4 large eggs
2 tablespoons mayonnaise
½ teaspoon vanilla

Optional topping
Fresh shredded coconut

Boil water in a steamer. Line muffin pans with baking cups. Beat margarine under medium speed until fluffy, adding sugar and ½ cup of the milk alternately.

Add flour, baking powder, eggs, and the rest of the milk alternately. Continue beating under medium speed for about 1 minute. Add mayonnaise and vanilla. Continue beating until batter is smooth.

Pour into muffin pans and steam for about 15 minutes. Test for doneness by inserting toothpick in the center of a cupcake; if it comes out clean, then it's done.

Serve hot with melted butter or serve cold with fresh shredded coconut topping.

SABINA SIQUIG
Country Cookbook,
Compiled by the Wahiawa General Hospital Auxiliary

GUAVA CREAM CHEESECAKE

Makes 12 to 16 servings

Crust

1¼ cups graham cracker crumbs
3 tablespoons sugar
¼ cup melted butter

Filling

2 (8-ounce) packages cream cheese
4 eggs
¾ cup sugar
1 tablespoon lemon juice
½ teaspoon lemon rind

Topping

1 cup sour cream
2 tablespoons sugar

Glaze

1 tablespoon cornstarch
¼ cup water
⅔ cup frozen guava concentrate

Final topping

1 ounce chopped nuts

Combine Crust ingredients. Press mixture into bottom of a 9 x 13-inch pan. Chill. In a large bowl, beat cream cheese until smooth. Add eggs 1 at a time, beating well after each addition. Gradually add sugar, lemon juice, and lemon rind. Pour into prepared Crust. Bake at 350°F for 30 minutes.

Blend Topping ingredients together. Spread over warm cake and return to oven for 10 minutes. Prepare Glaze by combining ingredients and cooking over medium flame, stirring constantly for 2 to 3 minutes. Cool to room temperature; spread over cheesecake. Sprinkle with chopped nuts.

STACEY ANN FUKUSHIMA
1988 4-H Local & Ethnic Food Show

LILIKO'I CHEESECAKE

Makes about 8 servings

Crust

1⅔ cups crumbs (22 squares graham crackers finely rolled)

3 tablespoons honey

¼ cup butter or margarine, softened

Mix together crumbs, honey, and margarine and press firmly in 9-inch pan.

Cheesecake

1 envelope or 1 tablespoon gelatin (unflavored)

½ to ¾ cup raw sugar*

½ cup boiling water

½ cup liliko'i juice

2 (8-ounce) packages cream cheese, softened

In a large bowl, mix unflavored gelatin and sugar. Add boiling water and liliko'i juice and stir until gelatin is completely dissolved. With electric mixer, beat in cream cheese until smooth. Pour into crust, chill until firm. (About 2 hours.)

*For a sweeter cake, use 3/4 cup of sugar.

KARL AND CATHERINE LO

Cook 'Em Up Kaua'i, The Kaua'i Historical Society Cookbook

ARARE COOKIE CRUNCH

¾ cup butter
¾ cup margarine
1½ cups powdered sugar
2⅔ cups flour
1½ teaspoons vanilla extract
2 cups crushed arare (Japanese rice crackers)

Preheat oven to 325°F. In large bowl of electric mixer, cream butter, margarine, and sugar. Add flour and vanilla, mix well. Stir in arare. Drop dough by teaspoonfuls onto ungreased baking sheets and flatten slightly. Bake for 20 minutes or until golden brown.

SHANE KELI'IA'A
A Chorus of Recipes, Kamehameha School Children's Chorus

COWBOY COOKIES

Makes about 70 cookies

1 cup shortening
1 cup brown sugar
1 cup sugar
2 eggs
1 teaspoon vanilla
2 cups flour
1 teaspoon baking powder
1 teaspoon baking soda
1¾ cups oatmeal
1½ cups corn flakes
1 cup salted Spanish peanuts

Combine shortening, sugars, eggs, and vanilla. Then add other ingredients. Roll into walnut size balls. Bake on ungreased cookie sheet. Bake at 350°F for about 13 to 15 minutes.

Ono-Licious, Na Poe Humukuiki O Hawaii, Hawaii Quilt Guild

BISCOTTI A LA LĀNA'I

Makes approximately 40 biscotti

- 2 cups plus 2 tablespoons all-purpose flour
- 1½ teaspoons baking powder
- ¼ teaspoon salt
- ½ cup soft butter
- ¾ cup sugar
- 3 eggs
- 1 tablespoons macadamia liqueur
- 1 teaspoon vanilla extract
- ¼ cup dried pineapple
- ½ cup grated coconut, fresh or packaged
- 1 thumb-sized ginger, peeled and grated

Preheat oven to 350°F.

Combine flour, baking powder, and salt; set aside. In a large mixing bowl, cream butter and sugar until fluffy. Beat eggs into mixture one at a time. Mix in liqueur and vanilla. Stir in flour mixture, pineapple, coconut, and ginger until just well-combined; do not over-mix.

Divide dough into two portions, form into loaves, and place 2½ inches apart on an ungreased cookie sheet. Bake at 350°F for 25 minutes or until light brown. Cool for 5 minutes. On a cutting board, slice each loaf diagonally into ½-inch-thick slices. Place slices cut side up on cookie sheet and bake for an additional 8 to 12 minutes. Cool on wire rack and store in airtight container.

DOLORES FABRAO
Lana'i Cooks, Lana'i High & Elementary School

BLACK PEPPER COOKIES

1 cup sugar
1 cup dark corn syrup
1 cup butter
1 tablespoon vinegar
2 eggs, slightly beaten
½ teaspoon ground black pepper
1 teaspoon ground .ginger
1 teaspoon ground cloves
1 teaspoon ground cinnamon
1 teaspoon baking soda
5 cups flour

Combine sugar, corn syrup, butter, and vinegar in small pan and bring almost to a boil. Cool to room temperature, then stir in eggs. Sift together dry ingredients and stir into mixture, blending well. Chill overnight. Divide dough into 8 or 9 equal portions and roll each out very thin on floured board. Cut into desired shapes and bake on greased cookie sheet.

Favorite Island Cookery, Book IV, Honpa Hongwanji Hawaii Betsuin

CHINESE NOODLE COOKIES

1 (12-ounce) package peanut butter chips
1 (5-ounce) can chow mein noodles
⅓ chopped pecans
⅓ cup miniature marshmallows

Heat peanut butter in top of double broiler until melted. Gently stir in noodles. Divide mixture into thirds. Stir pecans into one portion. Blend marshmallows into another (remainder is plain). Drop all 3 mixtures by rounded teaspoon onto waxed paper. Let cookie set until cooled.

RUTH TUFTE
We, the Women of Hawaii Cookbook

ENGLISH TOFFEE COOKIES

1 cup butter or margarine
1 cup sugar
1 egg, separated
1 teaspoon vanilla
2 cups flour
½ cup chopped nuts

Cream butter and sugar until light and fluffy, add egg yolk and vanilla and beat well. Mix in flour. With a spatula, spread the cookie dough evenly on an oiled cookie sheet, 12 x 14-inches. Brush with beaten egg white and spread nuts on top. Bake at 300°F for 40 to 45 minutes. Cool 5 minutes, then cut when warm.

Favorite Island Cookery, Book I, Honpa Hongwanji Hawaii Betsuin

FORTUNE COOKIES

3 tablespoons butter or margarine
½ teaspoon vanilla
3 tablespoons sugar
1 egg white
⅓ cup flour

Beat all ingredients EXCEPT flour until well-blended. Stir in flour. Spread rounded teaspoonful batter in 3-inch circle on greased cookie sheet. Bake in preheated oven. Fold cookie in half while warm, place center of fold over rim of glass and gently press down ends to bend cookie in middle.

Favorite Island Cookery, Book IV, Honpa Hongwanji Hawaii Betsuin

GUAVA COOKIES

Makes approximately 2 dozen cookies

⅔ cup sugar
¼ cup butter
¼ cup shortening
6 teaspoons guava jelly
1 egg
1½ cups flour
½ teaspoon salt
1 teaspoon baking powder

Cream sugar, butter, and shortening together. Mix in guava jelly. Add slightly beaten egg. Sift flour, salt, baking powder together and add to batter. Blend thoroughly. Drop by spoonfuls onto greased cookie sheet and flatten out with floured finger. Sprinkle with sugar. Bake at 375°F for 8 to 10 minutes.

Cook 'Em Up Kaua'i, The Kaua'i Historical Society Cookbook

JIFFY ALMOND COOKIES

3 cups flour, sifted
1½ cups shortening Crisco
1 cup sugar
½ teaspoon baking soda
¼ teaspoon salt
1 egg, large, beaten
1 tablespoon almond extract
¼ teaspoon red food coloring

Put first seven ingredients in mixing bowl and mix well until mixture can be lifted clean from sides of bowl. Roll into balls the size of a large agate or about 1 inch in diameter. Place on ungreased pan or cookie sheet about 1½ inches apart. Press down on ball with thumb and dot center with red food coloring. Bake in oven at 350°F for 14 minutes until light tan around edges of cookies.

MABEL KOP WONG
Community Family Favorites, Community Church of Honolulu

HAWAIIAN DELIGHT COOKIES

Crust
2 blocks margarine
1 (8-ounce) package cream cheese
2½ cups flour
½ cup chopped macadamia nuts

Cream margarine and cream cheese, add flour gradually. Roll dough into 1-inch balls. Spread out dough like pie crust in greased muffin tins. Sprinkle nuts on top of dough.

Filling
3 eggs
1½ cups brown sugar
½ cup chopped macadamia nuts
2 tablespoons flour
½ cup shredded coconut
1 teaspoon baking powder

Beat eggs and add brown sugar and beat very well. Add remaining ingredients and mix again. Place mixture on crust.

Bake in preheated oven 350°F for 15 to 17 minutes; reduce heat to 250°F and bake for another 10 minutes.

LORNA BURGER
We, the Women of Hawaii Cookbook

KONA COFFEE COOKIES

Makes 4 dozen

1/3 cup shortening
1/2 cup brown sugar, packed
1/2 cup granulated sugar
1 egg
1 1/2 teaspoons vanilla
1 tablespoon milk
2 cups flour
1/2 teaspoon salt
1/4 teaspoon soda
1/4 teaspoon baking powder
2 tablespoons powdered instant coffee

Heat oven to 400°F. Beat shortening, sugars, egg, vanilla, and milk until fluffy.

Measure flour by sifting first, then mix with the other dry ingredients. Add to sugar mixture; mix thoroughly. Shape into 1-inch balls. If dough is too soft, chill until easy to handle.

Place balls 2 inches apart on ungreased baking sheet. Flatten to 1/8-inch thickness with greased fork dipped in sugar (press in only one direction) or greased bottom of a glass or mold dipped in sugar. Bake 8 to 10 minutes, or until lightly browned.

JOAN IMES
Cooking with Honolulu Gardeners,
Honolulu Community Recreational Garden Program

LEONA'S DISAPPEARING MOCHIKO CHOCOLATE CHIP COOKIES

Makes 50 cookies

1 cup margarine or butter
1 cup sugar
½ cup brown sugar
2 eggs
2 teaspoons vanilla extract
1¼ cups mochiko flour
1 cup all-purpose flour
1 teaspoon salt
1 teaspoon baking soda
1 (12-ounce) package semisweet chocolate chips
½ to 1 cup chopped macadamia nuts

Preheat oven to 350°F. In a large mixing bowl, cream butter and sugars until light and fluffy; add eggs and vanilla extract. Beat for 1 minute. Combine flours, salt, and baking soda. Add to creamed mixture and blend well. Stir in chocolate chips and nuts.

Drop dough by teaspoonful on ungreased cookie sheets. Bake at 350°F for 8 to 10 minutes. Remove to wire rack and cool. Store in airtight container. To prevent overly sweet cookies, you may cut white sugar to ¾ to ⅞ cup.

M&M COOKIES: Omit chocolate chips, stir in 1½ cups of M&M candies, or stir in 1 cup; reserve ½ cup to decorate tops of cookies.

VARIATION: We usually don't measure the amount of both flours because we mix by texture, but you may use 1 cup mochiko flour with 1¼ cups regular flour or use the measurements you desire. Cookies are light and crispy!

LEONA M. PAGAY
Lana'i Cooks, Lana'i High & Elementary School

OKINAWAN SUGAR COOKIES

3 eggs
1 cup sugar
½ teaspoon vanilla
2 tablespoons melted butter
½ teaspoon yellow coloring

Mix all ingredients together.

3½ cups flour
2 teaspoons baking powder

Mix and add to the first mixture.

Mix dough well. Roll dough into strips of 2½-inch wide and ½-inch thick; cut crosswise into ¾-inch. Fry in deep fat. Cookies keep for weeks in airtight container.

Favorite Island Cookery, Book II, Honpa Hongwanji Buddhist Temple

PEANUT BUTTER 'N CHOCOLATE CHIP COOKIES

Makes about 4 dozen cookies

¾ cup margarine or butter
1 cup granulated sugar
1 cup firmly packed brown sugar
½ cup peanut butter
2 eggs
2 teaspoons vanilla
2½ cups flour
1 teaspoon baking soda
½ teaspoon salt
1 (11.5-ounce) package Baker's Milk Chocolate

Heat oven to 350°F. Beat margarine, sugars, and peanut butter in large bowl with mixer on medium speed until light and fluffy. Blend in eggs and vanilla. Mix in flour, baking soda, and salt. Stir in chips. Drop by rounded tablespoon onto ungreased cookie sheet. Bake at 350°F 10 to 12 minutes or until lightly browned. Cool 2 minutes. Remove from cookies sheets onto wire racks.

SHARON HUGGINS
Haili Congregational Church, 175th Anniversary

PINK CLOUD COOKIES

Crust
1½ cups flour
¾ cup margarine
½ cup brown sugar

Mix ingredients together. Spread onto 8 x 12-inch pan. Bake at 325°F for 25 minutes.

Filling
2 cups sugar
½ cup water
2 packages unflavored gelatin
½ cup cold water
1 teaspoon vanilla
½ cup chopped nuts
2 to 3 drops pink food coloring (or any coloring desired)

Boil sugar and water for 2 minutes to make syrup. Dissolve gelatin in cold water; add to hot syrup. Remove from heat; beat for 10 minutes. Add vanilla, nuts, and food coloring. Pour over thoroughly cooled crust. Cut into squares.

The Hawaii National Guard Auxiliary Cookbook

POI COCONUT COOKIES

1 cup poi
¾ cup sugar
¾ cup margarine or butter, softened
1 egg
1 teaspoon vanilla
1½ cups flour or whole wheat flour
2¼ teaspoons baking powder
½ teaspoon salt
¾ cup shredded or flaked coconut

Heat oven. Mix first 5 ingredients. Combine dry ingredients; stir into poi mixture. Stir in coconut. Drop by teaspoonfuls onto lightly greased cookie sheet. Bake at 400°F for 15 minutes. Remove from cookie sheet immediately. Cool

Favorite Island Cookery, Book IV, Honpa Hongwanji Hawaii Betsuin

POTATO CHIP COOKIES

1 cup shortening
1 cup white sugar
1 cup brown sugar
2 eggs
2 cups sifted flour
1 teaspoon salt
1 teaspoon soda
2 cups crushed potato chips
1 cup chopped nuts

Cream shortening and sugars and add eggs; mix well. Mix flour, salt, and soda and add to batter. Add crushed potato chips and nuts. Shape into small balls. Press down on ungreased cookie sheets with a floured fork. Bake in a moderate oven, 325°F for 10 to 15 minutes.

North Kohala Favorites

SUNFLOWER SEED COOKIES

1 cup butter
1 cup packed brown sugar
1 cup granulated sugar
2 eggs
1 teaspoon vanilla
1½ cups unsifted flour
½ teaspoon salt
1 teaspoon baking soda
3 cups quick cooking oats
1 cup sunflower seeds (shelled and salted)

Thoroughly cream together butter, brown sugar, and granulated sugar. Add eggs and vanilla and beat to blend well. Add flour, salt, soda, and oats. Mix thoroughly. Gently blend in sunflower seeds.

Form in long rolls about 1½ inches in diameter. Wrap in clear plastic film and chill thoroughly. Slice ¼-inch thick. Arrange on ungreased cookie sheet and bake at 350°F for 10 minutes.

HANNELORE EMDE
The Hele Mai, Ai (Come Eat) Cookbook, Flavors of Upcountry Maui

LILIKO'I SHORTBREAD COOKIES

1 cup powdered sugar
1 cup butter
2½ tablespoons liliko'i (passion fruit) juice
2 cups flour
½ cup oat flour (rolled oats ground)
¼ teaspoon salt

Beat sugar and butter 2 to 3 minutes until creamy. Mix in liliko'i juice. Add flours and salt. Mix well. Cover and refrigerate 1 hour until firm.

Preheat oven to 325°F. Working with half the dough at a time, roll out on a lightly floured surface to ½-inch thickness. Cut with 2-inch cookie cutter. Place on ungreased cookie sheets and bake 12 to 14 minutes or until edges are lightly browned.

Wisteria Delights, A Collection of Recipes by Pearl City Hongwanji Mission

HAUPIA SQUARES

Crust

1 cup butter (2 blocks)
2 cups flour
½ cup chopped macadamia or walnuts
⅓ cup powdered sugar

Mix ingredients together and press into a 9 x 13 x 2-inch pan. Bake at 350°F for 15 minutes. Cool.

Filling

2 cans coconut milk
½ cup sugar
1½ cups water
½ cup cornstarch, mixed with ½ cup water
½ teaspoon vanilla extract

Heat coconut milk, sugar, and water. Bring to a boil; gradually add mixed cornstarch. Cool until thick; add vanilla. Cool thoroughly and pour over prepared crust. Chill until ready to serve. Top with Cool Whip or whipped cream. Sprinkle with grated coconut just before serving.

DELORES LEE
Community Family Favorites, Community Church of Honolulu

BAKED MOCHIKO SQUARES

Makes 12 servings

5 cups mochiko flour (rice flour)
3 cups brown sugar
1 teaspoon baking soda
1 (12-ounce) can coconut milk
2½ cups water
1 small package sesame seeds (1 cup)

Mix rice flour, sugar, and baking soda. Add coconut milk and water. Pour mixture into 9 x 13-inch greased pan. Top with sesame seeds.

Bake in a 350°F oven for 40 minutes. Reduce heat to 250°F and bake 20 minutes more. Remove from oven and cool on wire rack. Cut into 2-inch slices.

MARY PINHO
Hana Maui Recipes from Then to Now

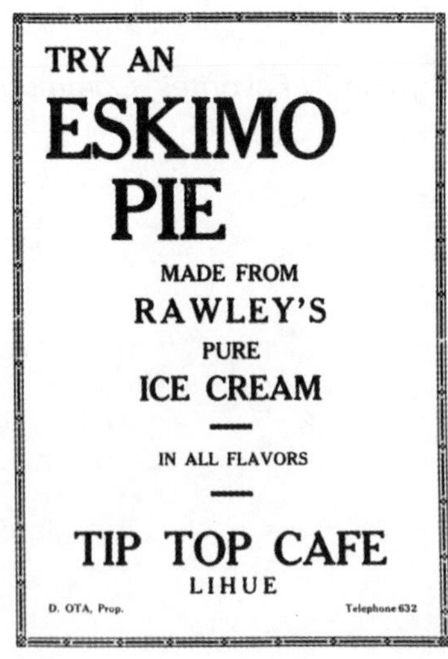

PORTUGUESE WALNUT SQUARES
Quadrados De Noz Portuguesa

Makes 16 squares

½ cup butter or margarine, softened
¾ cup light brown sugar
1 egg
½ teaspoon vanilla
2 tablespoons milk
6 tablespoons red port wine, divided use
1½ cups finely chopped walnuts, divided use
6 tablespoons flour
½ teaspoon baking powder
1 cup powdered sugar
Dash of salt
1 tablespoon butter or margarine

Preheat oven to 350°F. Grease and flour a 9-inch square pan. Cream butter and sugar. Add egg and beat well. Stir in vanilla, milk, 2 tablespoons of wine, and 1 cup of nuts.

Sift flour and baking powder and gradually add to creamed mixture. Pour into prepared pan and bake for 20 minutes. Remove cake from oven and brush top with three tablespoons of wine. Cool.

Cream powdered sugar, salt, butter, and remaining 1 tablespoon of wine. Spread evenly over cake. Sprinkle with remaining nuts and let stand until firm. Cut into squares.

NELLIE J. CARVALHO
Our Favorite Recipes from the Portuguese Heritage Club of Hamakua

ENERGY BARS

Makes 36 bars

2½ cups Rice Krispies
1 cup oats
¾ cup toasted sesame seeds
1 (10-ounce) package marshmallows
½ cup peanut butter
½ block margarine
¼ cup peanuts
½ cup raisins

Grease 9 x 13 x 2-inch Pyrex pan.

In saucepan combine rice cereal, oats, and sesame seeds; toast over medium heat for 3 minutes. In large saucepan, combine marshmallows, peanut butter, and margarine. Melt over low heat. Stir in cereal mixture, peanuts, and raisins. Press into buttered pan. Cool; cut into bars. Wrap in Saran wrap and chill.

TOMIE YASAK
Country Cookbook,
Compiled by the Wahiawa General Hospital Auxiliary

POI SPICE BARS

½ cup margarine, softened
1⅓ cups sugar
2 eggs
2 cups flour
1 cup poi
1 tablespoon cocoa
1 cup Rice Krispies
¼ teaspoon salt
1½ teaspoons baking soda
¾ teaspoon allspice
¾ teaspoon cinnamon
⅔ cup finely chopped nuts

Cream margarine and sugar. Add eggs. Combine other ingredients, except nuts; mix thoroughly. Spread in greased pan; sprinkle with nuts, press lightly. Bake. Cool; cut into bars.

Favorite Island Cookery, Book IV, Honpa Hongwanji Hawaii Betsuin

GINGER LEMON BARS

Makes 36 bars

¾ cup unsalted butter
⅓ cup powdered sugar
1 teaspoon lemon rind, grated, divided use
½ cup crystallized ginger, minced
¾ teaspoon ground ginger powder
1½ cups flour, divided use
3 large eggs
1⅓ cups sugar
6 tablespoons lemon juice
3 tablespoons flour
½ teaspoon baking powder
¼ teaspoon salt

Cream butter and powdered sugar. Add ½ teaspoon lemon rind, crystallized ginger, ground ginger, and ½ cup flour. Press into a 9 x 12 x 2-inch greased pan. Bake at 350°F for 12 minutes. Cool.

Blend eggs, sugar, remaining lemon rind, lemon juice, flour, baking powder, and salt together. Pour into baked crust. Bake at 350°F for 15 minutes. Cool and sprinkle top with powdered sugar. Cut into bars.

IRENE LEONG
Community Family Favorites, Community Church of Honolulu

HONEY GRANOLA BARS

Makes 24 bars

1 cup granola
1 cup quick-cooking rolled oats
½ cup all-purpose flour
½ cup flaked coconut
½ cup chopped almonds
½ cup raisins or semi-sweet chocolate pieces
¼ cup toasted wheat germ
¼ cup packed brown sugar
1 slightly beaten egg
½ cup honey
¼ cup butter or margarine, melted
1 teaspoon vanilla

In a large bowl, combine granola, oats, flour, coconut, almonds, raisins or chocolate pieces, wheat germ, and brown sugar. In a small bowl, combine the egg, honey, butter or margarine, and vanilla. Add wet mixture to the dry mixture, stirring till all are moistened. Spread evenly in a greased 12 x 7½ x 2-inch baking pan. Bake in a 325°F oven for 30 to 35 minutes or till light brown on edges. Cool completely in pan; to serve, cut into squares or bars.

ANGELA ORRIS
Haleiwa Elementary School 115th Birthday

MANGO SHORTBREAD

1½ cup margarine
1 cup sugar
4 cups flour
3 to 4 cups cubed mangoes
½ cup sugar
¼ cup flour
1½ teaspoons cinnamon

Cream margarine and sugar together. Slowly add flour and mix. Pour a little less than half the dough into a 9 x 13-inch pan.

Mix mango, sugar, flour, and cinnamon until well-combined. Pour over dough. Crumble remaining dough over top. (Optional: sprinkle with ⅛ cup chopped nuts.) Bake at 375°F for 45 minutes.

NOTE: Canned peaches or apple slices may be used in place of mangoes.

Hilo Missionary Cooks

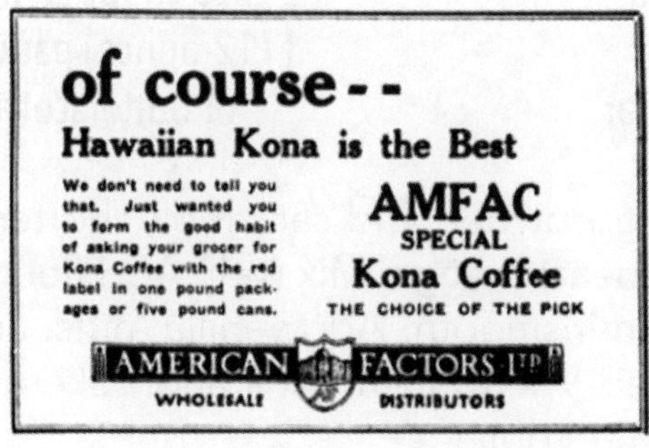

KAUA'I MAC NUT BRITTLE

1½ teaspoons baking soda
1 teaspoon vanilla
1 cup water, divided use
1¾ cups sugar
1 cup light corn syrup
2 cups chopped macadamia nuts
¼ cup butter

Mix baking soda, vanilla, and 1 teaspoon water. Set aside.

Combine water, sugar, and corn syrup and heat to 275°F. Add nuts and cook until 300°F, using a candy thermometer. Remove from heat; add butter and baking soda mixture. Stir then pour into greased cookie sheet to cool. When cooled, break into pieces. If peanuts are used, reduce first temperature to 225°F.

CAROL CUMMINGS
Hugs & Kisses of Aloha, Aloha Airlines Flight Attendant Cookbook

BLONDE BROWNIES

4 cups flour
1½ teaspoons baking powder
1½ teaspoons salt
1 cup shortening
4 cups brown sugar
4 to 5 eggs
1½ teaspoons vanilla
2 cups chopped nuts
1 (12-ounce) package chocolate or butterscotch chips

Sift flour, baking powder, and salt. Melt shortening; cool and add sugar and beaten eggs. Mix well. Add flour mixture gradually and mix until smooth. Add vanilla, nuts, and chips. Pour into two greased 9 x 13-inch pans and bake at 350°F for 30 minutes. Cut after cooling.

S. MUTSUO FROM E. SHIGETA
Kalaheo Missionary Church Cookin' Book!

FANTASTIC FUDGE BROWNIES

Makes 36 (2½-inch) squares

4 cups sugar
1½ cups flour
1 cup cocoa (do not use cocoa mix)
8 large eggs
1 pound butter, melted
4 teaspoons vanilla extract
2 cups chopped pecans or walnuts

Preheat oven to 300°F. Sift sugar, flour, and cocoa together.

Beat eggs well in a large mixing bowl. Add dry ingredients, butter, vanilla, and nuts and mix well.

Pour batter into a 3-quart lasagna pan. Set a larger, shallow pan containing hot water on the lowest oven shelf. Place the filled pan in the water bath and bake 1 hour. Do not overbake.

Cool on a rack in the baking pan. The brownies will firm up as they cool. The consistency should be like candy with a crusty top.

FATIMA CAMERON
The Kahikolu Country Cookbook

AZUKI PUDDING PIE

Makes 1 (9-inch) pie

Crust
1¼ cups graham cracker crumbs
¼ cup margarine, softened

Blend the above well with fork. Using back of large spoon, press crumb mixture firmly inside of greased pie plate to form a crust. Bake at 375°F for 8 minutes, and cool.

Filling
1 (18-ounce) can tsubushi-an
2 cups cold milk
1½ cups vanilla ice cream, softened
2 (3.75-ounce) packages vanilla instant pudding

Heat tsubushi-an in pot thoroughly; cool. Pour into pie shell and spread evenly. Thoroughly blend milk and ice cream in bowl. Add pudding mix. Beat slowly with rotary beater until blended, about 1 minute. Gradually pour pudding mixture over tsubushi-an enough to fill pie pan.

When mixture firms, about 5 minutes, pour remaining mixture in center of pie to mound. Chill 4 to 5 hours. Serve with whipped cream.

Favorite Island Cookery, Book IV, Honpa Hongwanji Hawaii Betsuin

BANANA PIE

6 cups sliced bananas
¾ cup pineapple juice
Pastry for 2 pie crusts
¾ cup sugar
1 tablespoon flour
1½ teaspoons cinnamon
1 tablespoon butter

Soak bananas in pineapple juice for 20 minutes. Preheat oven to 400°F. Line a 9-inch pie pan with pastry. Drain bananas, saving 3 tablespoons of juice. Place banana in pie shell. Combine sugar, flour, and cinnamon; sprinkle over bananas. Sprinkle with 3 tablespoons pineapple juice. Dot with butter; cover with top crust. Bake for 30 to 45 minutes or until crust is browned.

Ka'u Hospital Auxiliary, One More Time

CUSTARD PIE

Pie filling
4 slightly beaten eggs
½ cup sugar
¼ teaspoon salt
½ teaspoon vanilla
⅛ teaspoon almond extract
2½ cups scalded milk–coats top, not boiled
Nutmeg–sprinkle on custard just before baking

Bake in uncooked pie crust, 400°F for 25 to 30 minutes.

Pie crust
1½ cups flour
½ teaspoon salt
1½ teaspoons sugar
½ cup oil
2 tablespoons cold milk

Sift flour, salt, sugar, in ungreased pie pan. Mix oil and milk; whip with fork until cloudy. Pour over flour mixture and mix until flour is wet. Press with hand to shape into pie pan. Flute edge and prick. Bake at 400°F for 12 to 15 minutes.

PATTI YOSHIDA
Haleiwa Elementary School 115th Birthday

FRESH MANGO CREAM PIE

1 (3-ounce) package lite cream cheese
6 tablespoons powdered sugar
½ teaspoon vanilla
½ cup whipping cream, divided use
Macadamia Nut Crust
2 large firm ripe mangos, peeled and sliced
Fresh Orange Glaze

Whip cream cheese, sugar, vanilla, and 2 tablespoons whipping cream with electric mixer until smoothly blended. In another bowl, whip remaining whipping cream until it holds soft peaks, then fold gently into cream cheese mixture. Spoon filling into baked Macadamia Nut Crust. Slice mangos thinly in small pieces and lay evenly in overlapping circles on filling. Spoon Fresh Orange Glaze evenly over fruit. Chill until glaze is set.

Macadamia Nut Crust
1 cup flour
6 tablespoons butter or oleo
½ cup chopped salted macadamia nuts
1 large egg

With fingers, rub together the first 3 ingredients. Add egg and stir with fork until dough holds together. Press dough evenly over bottom and up sides of 9-inch pie pan. Bake crust at 325°F until golden, 25 to 30 minutes.

Fresh Orange Glaze
¼ cup granulated sugar
2 tablespoons tapioca
1 teaspoon grated orange peel
1 cup orange juice
1 tablespoon lemon juice

In a 1 or 2-quart pan, combine all the ingredients. Let stand 15 minutes to soften tapioca. Cook, stirring frequently, until mixture comes to a boil. Let cool and stir before using.

100 Years Sharing God's Love, United Community Church

HAUPIA PUMPKIN PIE

1 (1-pound) can pumpkin
2 eggs, slightly beaten
¾ cup sugar
½ teaspoon salt
1 teaspoon cinnamon
½ teaspoon ginger
¼ teaspoon cloves
1 (13-ounce) can evaporated milk
1½ cups grated coconut, divided use
1 unbaked 9-inch pie shell
1 (2-ounce) package haupia pudding mix
1 cup heavy cream
1 tablespoon sugar

Preheat oven to 435°F. Combine pumpkin and eggs. Stir in sugar, salt, and spices. Stir in milk and 1 cup of coconut. Pour in pie shell. Bake for 15 minutes. Lower heat to 350°F and bake 40 to 45 minutes longer until filling is set. Cool.

Prepare haupia mix as directed. Cool slightly and pour over pie. Chill until haupia is firm, before serving. Whip cream and stir in sugar. Spread on pie. Sprinkle with remaining coconut.

Ono-Licious, Na Poe Humukuiki O Hawaii, Hawaii Quilt Guild

IT'S A PLEASURE TO SHOP

In the handsomest store on Maui, where one finds a complete stock of Dry Goods, Furnishings, Notions, Groceries and general merchandise, where service and attention are the best

THE LAHAINA STORE

Phone 27-B, Lahaina. **Branch at Puukolii.**

HAWAIIAN CHESS PIE

Makes 1 (9-inch) pie

1 cup raisins
½ cup butter, melted
3 eggs, beaten
1 cup sugar
1 (8.25-ounce) can crushed pineapple, drained
½ cup macadamia nut bits
½ teaspoon vanilla
1 unbaked pie shell

Soak raisins in hot water until double in size. Drain well and pat dry. Combine butter, eggs, and sugar; beat well. Add raisins, pineapple, nuts, and vanilla. Pour into pie shell and bake in 400°F oven for 10 minutes. Lower heat to 350°F for 30 minutes. Bake until knife inserted comes out clean.

Hawaii's Aloha Recipes, The Japanese Women's Society of Honolulu

HELENE'S MANGO PIE

Makes 8 servings

Pastry for 2-crust pie
6 cups sliced mangoes, divided use
¾ cup sugar
1½ to 2 tablespoons flour
¼ teaspoon salt
½ teaspoon grated lemon rind
1½ teaspoons lemon juice
½ teaspoon cinnamon
¼ teaspoon nutmeg
1 tablespoon butter or margarine

Divide pie dough in half. Roll out each half to a 9-inch round. Line pie pan with 1 round. Put half of the mangoes into pie pan. Combine sugar, flour, salt, lemon rind, lemon juice, cinnamon, and nutmeg. Sprinkle half of sugar mixture over mangoes. Add remaining mangoes and sprinkle with the remaining sugar mixture. Dot with butter and cover with the remaining pastry. Bake at 350°F for 40 to 50 minutes.

Hana Maui Recipes from Then to Now

KAUA'I KEY LIME PIE

1¾ cups graham cracker crumbs
2 tablespoons sugar
6 tablespoons melted butter
3 eggs, separated
1 (14-ounce) can condensed milk
½ cup Key lime juice
1 tablespoon lemon juice
2 teaspoons lime rind
2 tablespoons sugar
1 cup whipping cream
1 tablespoon powdered sugar
½ teaspoon vanilla

Crust: Combine first 3 ingredients. Press onto bottom and 1 inch up the sides of a 9-inch springform pan. Chill 1 hour.

Filling: Whisk egg yolks. Add condensed milk and next 3 ingredients. Whisk until smooth. Beat egg whites at high speed. Gradually add 2 tablespoons sugar until soft peaks form. Fold into yolk mixture. Pour into crust. Bake at 325°F for 15 to 20 minutes until set and lightly browned. Cool on wire rack. Cover and chill 8 hours.

Topping: Whip cream at high speed until soft peaks form. Add powdered sugar and vanilla. Remove sides of springform part. Dollop whipped cream around top and if desired, garnish with lime slices.

GERALD JOERING
"No Ka Oi" The Best of Hawaii,
Favorite Recipes from Rotarians of District 5000

CHOCOLATE MOUSSE PIE

1 envelope unflavored gelatin
1½ cups milk
1 (5-ounce) package mint chocolate chips
1 teaspoon vanilla extract
1 (8-ounce) carton/tub frozen whipped topping, thawed
18-inch prepared graham cracker pie crust

In a saucepan, sprinkle the gelatin on the milk. Let this stand 1 minute, then stir over low heat until the gelatin is dissolved. Add chocolate chips and continue cooking. Stir constantly until the chocolate melts completely. Stir in the vanilla extract. Chill this mixture for about 1 hour. The mixture is ready when it is chilled enough to have jelled slightly. One approach to determine this is to stir it occasionally while it is in the refrigerator until the mixture mounds when dropped from a spoon. Or, simply tilt it and observe whether it moves or just sags a bit. At this point, the mixture may become quite stiff and lumpy with what appears to be a dark, hard surface skin. No worries!

Simply put the mixture in a mixer with an all-purpose blade and blend it till it is smoothly textured. Fold in the thawed whipped topping. Pour it out into either the pie shell, mold, or some other container, and chill 3 to 4 hours before serving.

Everyone will love you for this one!

NOTE: You need not use mint chocolate chips. You can use regular chocolate chips by themselves. If you like the mint taste but have a difficult time finding mint chocolate chips, you can use regular chocolate chips and a teaspoon of mint extract for every 5 ounces of chocolate.

MRS. HIROKO CHUN
"Pig Out" with Liholiho's Caring, Competent, Creative Cooks

LEMON MERINGUE PIE

½ cup cold water
7 tablespoons cornstarch
1½ cups hot water
1¼ cups sugar
3 egg yolks, slightly beaten
Juice of 2 lemons
Grated rind of 1 lemon
1 tablespoon butter

Mix cold water and cornstarch until smooth. Combine hot water and sugar in top of double boiler; bring to a boil over direct heart. Add cornstarch mixture; cook until it begins to thicken. Return to double boiler and cook until thick and smooth (15 minutes). Stir a small amount of mixture into beaten yolks; return to double boiler and cook a few minutes longer. Add lemon juice and rinds and butter and blend. Cool, stirring occasionally. Pour into baked pie shell, topped with meringue.

Our Favorite Recipes,
Maui Association for Family and Community Education

LILIKO'I PIE

1 package unflavored gelatin
¼ cup water
3 eggs
½ cup sugar
⅔ cup liliko'i juice
¼ cup sugar
½ cup whipped cream
9-inch baked pie shell

Sprinkle 1 tablespoon gelatin over ¼ cup water. Separate eggs and place whites in bowl. Put yolks in double boiler and beat in ½ cup sugar, stirring constantly until thick. Remove and stir in gelatin, stir until it dissolves. Cool 5 minutes. Gradually stir in liliko'i juice. Chill. Beat egg whites until stiff and gradually add ¼ cup sugar. As soon as yolk mixture begins to thicken, fold in egg whites and ½ cup whipped cream. Pour into baked shell and chill.

LOIS HUMPHREY
The Kahikolu Country Cookbook

MACADAMIA NUT CREAM PIE

Makes 8 servings

1 1/3 cups milk, divided use
¾ cup sugar, divided use
½ cup chopped macadamia nuts, divided use
Dash of salt
1 teaspoon vanilla
1 egg
5 teaspoons cornstarch
2 egg whites
1 (9-inch) baked pie shell
1 cup heavy cream, whipped

In a saucepan, combine 1 cup of the milk, ¼ cup of the sugar, ¼ cup of the nuts, the salt, and the vanilla; scald. Mix the remaining 1/3 cup milk with egg and cornstarch. Thoroughly stir some of the hot mixture into the egg mixture; return all to the saucepan. Cook 5 more minutes, stirring constantly, until mixture thickens. Cool 1 hour. Beat egg whites until soft peaks form. Gradually add the remaining ½ cup sugar, beating until stiff peaks form; fold carefully into cooled mixture. Pour into pie shell; chill. Before serving, top with sweetened whipped cream and remaining ¼ cup nuts.

North Kohala Favorites

MACADAMIA NUT PIE

2 eggs
½ cup sugar
1 cup Karo
1 tablespoon butter
½ to 2 tablespoons flour
1 cup chopped macadamia nuts
1 teaspoon vanilla

Beat eggs well with electric beater. Add remaining ingredients and beat well for about 2 minutes. Pour into unbaked pastry shell. Bake at 450°F for 10 minutes, then at 325°F for 35 minutes or a little longer till nicely browned and firm, but not solid.

NOTE: Most recipes for macadamia nut pies are for cream pies. This is like a pecan pie, and delicious.

KAY BOYUM
The Hele Mai, Ai (Come Eat) Cookbook, Flavors of Upcountry Maui

MOUNTAIN APPLE PIE

Pastry for 2-crust pie
6 cups sliced raw mountain apples or 4 cups cooked mountain apples
1 teaspoon lemon Juice
1 cup sugar, or to taste
¼ teaspoon salt
½ teaspoon cinnamon
2 tablespoons butter, to dot

Line pie plate with bottom crust. Mix all ingredients, except butter. Place in pie shell; then dot with butter. Put on top cover and slit it. Bake at 400°F for 35 to 40 minutes. If frozen, bake for 1 hour.

HARVEY CHONG, SR.
100 Years Sharing God's Love, United Community Church

ʻŌHELO BERRY PIE

If you have pals living at Volcano, you just might be able to persuade them to go ʻōhelo berry picking with you. Or if lucky like me, you know Ellen and Al Kai who keep milk cartons filled with the red and yellow berries down in their freezer. When I visit them at Volcano, they usually haul out one or two of the treasured cartons, wrap them well in newspaper, then I hop a plane for home and stick them in my freezer for a special event. One Thanksgiving, ʻōhelo berry pie went down in memory as really ʻono and won the vote over pumpkin and mince.

8 cups ʻōhelo berries (2 quarts)
2 cups sugar
6 tablespoons cornstarch
3 to 4 tablespoons butter

Place ʻōhelo berries in large colander and wash thoroughly, removing stems. Place berries in bowl and add above ingredients. Then add the following:

1 lemon rind, grated
¾ cup orange juice
1 teaspoon salt
Several dashes cloves

Be sure to taste it! Then adjust flavor accordingly. Have your favorite pie pastry ready to receive berries, using 2 (9-inch) pie pans. Add nuggets of butter here and there and cover with lattice work pie dough on top. Brush with milk and place in hot oven 450°F for 10 minutes, then turn down to 350°F for 35 minutes until golden brown. Serve warm with dollops of fresh cream.

DOROTHEA ELSIE WOODRUM
Dining with the Daughters, The Daughters of Hawaii

PASSION FRUIT CHIFFON PIE

4 eggs, separated
1 cup sugar, divided use
½ teaspoon salt
½ cup concentrated passion fruit juice
1 tablespoon unflavored gelatin
¼ cup water
1 teaspoon grated lemon rind
1 (9-inch) baked pie shell

Beat egg yolks until thick. Add ½ cup of the sugar, salt, and passion fruit concentrate. Cook over low heat in double boiler until thick, stirring constantly. Add gelatin which has been dissolved in ½ cup water. Add lemon rind and cool. Fold in stiffly beaten egg whites to which the remaining ½ cup sugar has been added. Pour into baked pie shell and chill until firm. Garnish with whipped cream (sweetened to taste) and slivered almonds.

MARY LU RICHARDSON
The Hele Mai, Ai (Come Eat) Cookbook, Flavors of Upcountry Maui

POHĀ PIE

Crust
1/3 cup oil
3 tablespoons (scant) water
1 cup flour

Filling
3 cups pohā berries
1 tablespoon lemon juice
½ cup water
1 cup sugar

To make Crust: Mix oil and water; add to flour, mixing just enough to get flour mixed in. Put into an 8-inch pie pan and pat evenly on all sides and bottom of pan. Prick well with fork and bake at 375°F until light brown.

To make Filling: Put all filling ingredients into a saucepan and bring to a boil. Let boil for 2 minutes, then stir in 1 heaping tablespoon cornstarch that has been dissolved in a little water. Stir constantly until mixture comes to a boil. Remove from stove to cool.

When filling mixture is cooled, pour into baked pie crust. Chill well and top with whipped cream or other cream topping.

EMMA I. KNIGHT
Grandma & Grandpa's Hawaiian Island Cookbook,
Honolulu Federal Savings and Loan Association

PRALINE BOTTOM PUMPKIN PIE

This recipe for fancy pumpkin pie comes from Kathleen Small. She served this delicious pie to a group of Lakesiders at her home and some have asked for the recipe. Thank you, Kathleen, for sharing!

4 tablespoons butter or margarine
½ cup chopped toasted pecans
⅓ cup packed brown sugar
1 (9-inch) baked pastry shell
1 (2.24 or 3-ounce) package no-baked custard mix
⅓ cup granulated sugar
2 teaspoons pumpkin pie spice
⅔ cup milk
⅔ cup evaporated milk
2 cups pumpkin
Toasted chopped pecans

In small saucepan, melt butter. Stir in the ½ cup pecans and brown sugar; cook and stir until mixture bubbles. Spread over bottom of baked pastry shell. Cool.

In 2-quart saucepan, combine custard mix, sugar, and spice. Stir in milk, evaporated milk, and pumpkin. Cook and stir until mixture bubbles. Cover and cool 10 minutes. Pour into pastry shell. Chill until firm. Garnish top with additional toasted pecans, if desired.

MRS. O.W. WILLARD
Cook 'Em Up Kaua'i, The Kaua'i Historical Society Cookbook

WAIOLI APPLE PIE

Makes 6 to 8 servings

4 cups fresh apple slices
1½ cups sugar
⅛ teaspoon salt
¼ teaspoon nutmeg
¼ teaspoon cinnamon
1 tablespoon lemon juice
½ teaspoon instant coffee
3 tablespoons flour
2 tablespoons butter

Pastry for 9-inch two crust pie

Combine all ingredients in a bowl; mix well and pour into pastry-lined pie pan; dot with butter. Cover with top crust that has slits cut in it; seal and flute. Cover edge with 2 to 3-inch strip of foil to prevent excessive browning. Remove foil during last 15 minutes of baking. Bake at 375°F for 45 to 60 minutes or until crust is brown and juice begins to bubble through slits in crust. Serve hot with slice of cheese or pour cinnamon sauce over.

THE ORIGINAL WAIOLI TEA ROOM RESTAURANT, 1974
The Tastes and Tales of Mō'ili'ili,
A Collection of Recipes & Stories by Mō'ili'ili Community Center

WILLOW'S SKY-HIGH COCONUT CREAM PIE

Makes 1 (9-inch) pie

3 cups milk, scalded
½ cup sugar
1 tablespoon butter
Pinch of salt
¼ cup grated fresh coconut
5 tablespoons cornstarch
4 egg yolks
½ teaspoon vanilla
1 (9-inch) pie shell, baked

Combine milk, sugar, butter, salt, and grated coconut in saucepan or double boiler. Let mixture come to near boil, stirring occasionally. Mix cornstarch with little water; add to hot milk mixture and continue cooking until thickened. Beat egg yolks. Add small amount of hot mixture to eggs; mix well. Add remaining hot mixture and vanilla. Cook over low heat for 3 minutes more, stirring constantly. Cool and fill pie shell. Top with meringue and place in 400°F oven for 10 minutes or until brown. Chill before serving.

Willow's Meringue

6 egg whites
¼ teaspoon salt
¼ cup sugar
½ teaspoon vanilla
Garnish
Grated fresh coconut

Beat egg whites and salt together until soft peaks form. Gradually beat in sugar until meringue is smooth and stands firm. Stir in vanilla.

NOTE: A little stabilizer may be used in meringue—such as ½ teaspoon cream of tartar—to help hold meringue.

WILLOWS RESTAURANT
Hawaii's Aloha Recipes, The Japanese Women's Society of Honolulu

FRESH COCONUT PIE

Filling
2 cups sugar
4 cups fresh grated coconut, well-packed
1 tablespoon cornstarch
1½ cups milk
1 teaspoon vanilla

Cook together sugar, coconut, and 1 cup milk. Mix cornstarch and remaining ½ cup milk. Add to mixture and boil until thick. Remove from heat. Add vanilla. Pour into unbaked pie shells and put on top crust. Slit top to let steam escape. Bake at 400°F for ten minutes. Reduce heat to 350°F and bake until done. Filling can be used also for turnovers, which should be baked for about 20 minutes. If pies are frozen before baking, bake pies at 400°F for 1 hour. Do not defrost.

Crust
1 cup shortening
3 cups flour
½ teaspoon baking powder
1 teaspoon salt
6 tablespoons water

Cut shortening into flour, baking powder, and salt. Add water gradually and adjust amount as necessary. Roll out as usual on lightly floured surface.

DOROTHEA MIRANDA
Our Favorite Recipes from the Portuguese Heritage Club of Hamakua

APPLE CRISP

1¼ cups sugar
1 pound margarine
5 cups oatmeal
1 large canned apples, or 5 large Fuji apples
2 limes, juiced
1¼ cups brown sugar
1 tablespoon cinnamon

Combine sugar and margarine. Add oatmeal and mix well. Set aside. Thinly slice apples and mix with lime juice, brown sugar, and cinnamon. Soak for 3 hours. If you use canned apples, adjust the amount of brown sugar and cinnamon. In a greased 9 x 13-inch pan, put a thin layer of the oatmeal mix. Spread the apple mix. Then spread the rest of the oatmeal mix over the apples. Bake at 350°F for 45 minutes to an hour. The topping should be nice and brown.

Wisteria Delights, A Collection of Recipes by Pearl City Hongwanji Mission

MANGO BROWN BETTY

2 cups breadcrumbs, divided use
¼ cup melted butter
4 cups sliced, nearly ripe, mangoes, divided use
½ cup sugar, divided use
¼ teaspoon nutmeg
¼ teaspoon cinnamon
Grated rind and juice of ½ lemon
¼ cup hot water

Cover bottom of buttered baking dish with ⅓ of crumbs mixed with melted butter. Spread half of the mangoes over them and sprinkle with half the sugar, nutmeg, cinnamon, lemon juice, and rind of ⅓ of crumbs. Add rest of mangoes and remaining ingredients, sprinkle with hot water and cover with crumbs. Bake in moderate oven, 350°F, for about 1 hour. Serve with cream.

MISS SHIZUE OKAMOTO
The Hilo Woman's Club Cookbook

PIE CRUSTS

Plain Pastry—Single Crust

1 cup enriched flour
¾ teaspoon salt
⅓ cup shortening
2 to 3 tablespoons cold water or cold milk

Rich Pastry—Double Crust

2 cups sifted flour
1 teaspoon salt
1 cup shortening
5 to 6 tablespoons ice cold water or milk

Sift flour and salt. Add shortening and cut it until the size of rice grain. Add enough water to moisten the flour mixture. Make 2 balls and roll 1 at a time on a floured board. While rolling the crust, fold in half twice. This will make the crust flaky. Roll out with rolling pin and shape into pie pan.

Crust—First Prize

1½ cups flour
¼ teaspoon salt
½ teaspoon baking powder
6 tablespoons Crisco
About 4 tablespoons water

Sift dry ingredients; cut in Crisco until crumbly in appearance. Add water, a tablespoon at a time, until mixture is moistened just enough to hold together. Chill 10 minutes before rolling out. Bake for 10 minutes at 450°F.

Pie Crust

1 cup sifted flour
1 teaspoon baking powder
1 tablespoon granulated sugar
⅛ teaspoon salt
½ cup shortening
1 tablespoon cold water

Bake at 450°F for 10 minutes.

50th Anniversary Best of Our Favorite Recipes,
Maui Association for Family and Community Education

MACADAMIA COCONUT TART

Makes 8 to 10 servings

The tart shell is pressed into the pan so rolling out the dough is unnecessary.

½ cup flaked unsweetened coconut
1¼ cups coarsely chopped macadamia nuts
6 tablespoons unsalted butter
3 tablespoons Hawaiian honey
3 egg yolks
½ cup light brown sugar
1 teaspoon vanilla extract to taste

Toast the coconut in a preheated 300°F oven until light golden brown, stirring occasionally to toast it evenly. Turn the oven up to 350°F and toast the nuts until lightly browned. Melt the butter with the honey, remove from heat, and combine with the egg yolks and sugar, whisking just until thoroughly mixed. Stir the nuts and coconut into the sugar mixture and add vanilla. Pour into the pre-baked Tart Shell and bake in a preheated 375°F oven about 20 minutes or until set and golden brown.

Tart Shell

1 cup flour
1 tablespoon sugar
¼ teaspoon salt
¼ teaspoon grated lime peel
½ cup unsalted butter
1 tablespoon water
½ teaspoon rum extract

Mix the flour, sugar, salt, and lime peel. If you use salted butter, omit the salt. Cut the butter into ½-inch slices and work it into the flour mixture with a pastry blender or a fork until the butter is in cornmeal size pieces and the mixture is beginning to hold together. Combine the water and the rum extract and work it into the flour-butter mixture just until blended and the mixture holds together. Gather the dough into a ball and wrap in plastic. Let it rest in the refrigerator for 30 minutes. The pastry may also be wrapped in foil and frozen for up to one month.

Press the pastry into a 9-inch tart pan, making sure that it is of even thickness on the bottom and sides, so it will bake evenly. Freeze before baking for 30 minutes. Bake in preheated 375°F oven for about 15 to 20 minutes or until light golden brown. Cool slightly before filling.

MICHAEL AND KATHALEEN LORENZ
Cook 'Em Up Kaua'i, The Kaua'i Historical Society Cookbook

HAUPIA GUAVA TARTS

Makes 6 servings

Haupia
3 cups frozen coconut milk, thawed
5 tablespoons cornstarch
¼ cup sugar
6 baked tart shells

Combine ¼ cup coconut milk with cornstarch and sugar to form a paste. Bring to a boil remaining coconut milk. Gradually add cornstarch paste to milk, stirring constantly. Cook until mixture thickens. Cool slightly and pour into tart shells. Chill in refrigerator and spoon on Guava Topping.

Guava Topping
2 tablespoons sugar
1 tablespoon cornstarch
⅔ cup guava nectar
1 drop red food coloring (optional)

Blend sugar and cornstarch. Slowly stir in guava nectar and food coloring. Cook until thick over low heat, stirring constantly. Pour over chilled Haupia. Chill and serve.

The Heritage of Hawaii Cookbook, Honolulu Gas Company, Ltd.

MANGO COBBLER

7 cups sliced ripe firm mangoes
¾ cup brown sugar
3 tablespoons cornstarch
¼ teaspoon salt
½ teaspoon cinnamon
½ teaspoon nutmeg
Pie crust
1 tablespoon lemon juice
1 tablespoon butter

Preheat oven to 400°F. Grease a 9-inch square pan. In large bowl, combine mangoes with sugar, cornstarch, spices, and salt. Prepare crust and roll into a square. Cut into ½-inch strips to make lattice top. Put mango mixture into pan, top with juice, and dot with butter. Put lattice work on, bake at 400°F for 45 to 50 minutes. Should be golden brown. Delicious served with ice cream.

JEAN KEYS
We, the Women of Hawaii Cookbook

MALASSADAS
(Overnight)

1 envelope yeast
¼ cup lukewarm water
2 tablespoons butter
¼ cup sugar
¾ teaspoon salt
½ cup boiling water
½ cup milk
4 large eggs, beaten well
3 cups sifted flour

Mix envelope yeast with ¼ cup lukewarm water. Set aside. Mix together butter, sugar, and salt in large bowl. Pour boiling water into mixture and mix well. Add milk and let stand until lukewarm. Add yeast then eggs. Add flour and mix. Chill in refrigerator. Cook in hot oil. Drop from teaspoon.

BETTY JOSE
Our Favorite Recipes from the Portuguese Heritage Club of Hamakua

OKINAWAN DOUGHNUT

3 cups flour
1 cup sugar
1 teaspoon salt
3 teaspoons baking powder
2 or 3 eggs
1½ cups milk
Handful sesame seeds (goma)

Sift dry ingredients together. Add eggs and milk; mix well. Heat oil to very hot. Drop teaspoonful in hot oil and cook few minutes until brown. Roll in sesame seeds.

BETTY OKOUCHI AND ANN CATANIA
Family Favorites, Oahu Extension Homemakers Council

CASCARON

1 (10-ounce) package mochiko
¾ cup brown sugar, packed
2 cups shredded coconut
1 cup coconut milk
1 quart oil for frying

Mix first three ingredients together thoroughly. Add coconut milk and stir only enough to moisten dry ingredients. Form dough into 1-inch balls or drop by teaspoonfuls into hot (375°F oil). Deep-fry 3 to 4 minutes or until golden brown.

Parks & Recreation Family Favorites

POI DOUGHNUTS

1 (14-ounce) bag poi (Taro brand)
2 pounds mochiko flour
1½ cups white sugar
½ cup brown sugar
2 cups coconut milk
½ cup water

Mix ingredients together. Form into balls about 1-inch diameter. Deep-fry.

CHARTA LEONG
Hugs & Kisses of Aloha, Aloha Airlines Flight Attendant Cookbook

BENANGKAL

8 cups flour
4 cups sugar
6 teaspoons baking powder
10 eggs
8 teaspoons vegetable oil
3 teaspoons vanilla extract
¼ cup fresh milk
1 teaspoon yellow food color (optional)
6 (1-ounce) packages sesame seeds
Vegetable oil for frying

In a large mixing bowl, mix flour, sugar, and baking powder together. In a separate mixing bowl, combine eggs, oil, vanilla, milk, and food coloring. Add to flour mixture all at once; stir just enough to moisten. Shape dough into balls about 1-inch in diameter. Coat balls with sesame seeds. Using a heavy skillet filled with approximately ½-inch of vegetable oil, deep-fry balls over medium heat until they are light brown. Benangkal usually crack as they cook. Remove from skillet and drain on absorbent paper.

DOLORES FABRAO
Lana'i Cooks, Lana'i High & Elementary School

BITSU-BITSU

Makes 6 servings

2 cups grated raw potatoes
¼ cup flour
¼ cup sugar
Oil for frying

Combine grated potatoes, flour, and sugar. Shape into 2 x ½-inch patties. Fry in hot oil until golden brown, turning once.

MRS. LEONARDA R. ESPLANADA
From the Hawaiian Kitchens of the Molokai Lions

BANDIAY BANDIAY
Filipino Banana Fritters

Makes 8 to 10 servings

1 cup all-purpose flour
2 teaspoons baking powder
3 to 4 tablespoons sugar
¾ cup milk
4 to 5 whole apple bananas
Oil to cover bottom of frying pan

Sift dry ingredients together; add milk and mix. Peel and slice bananas in half. Dip halves in batter. Heat oil in frying pan at medium heat and fry bananas until brown on both sides. Serve hot or cold (a part of main course).

Favorite Island Cookery, Book II, Honpa Hongwanji Buddhist Temple

BLACK SESAME SEED PUDDING
Gee Ma Koo

Taste so good, you gotta make this much.

2 cups black sesame seeds, washed, soaked overnight in enough water to cover
2 cups washed white rice, soaked overnight in enough water to cover
16 to 18 cups water (16 cups will make pudding thick, 18 cups make pudding more liquidy)
2 cups sugar (rock or brown sugar or combination)
⅓ teaspoon lemon extract

Drain sesame seeds and rice separately. Place sesame seeds and rice in a blender (set at purée) with 1 cup water. Blend until pulverized. Strain with some of the water. (May do purée-ing in smaller batches.) Add the sugar to remaining water and bring to a boil. Pour strained mixture gradually into the pot of boiling syrup, stirring constantly with a wooden spoon until mixture returns to a boil and thickens. Add lemon extract. Cool mixture a little before serving.

LILY, RANDY, AND LORNA CHOY
Community Family Favorites, Community Church of Honolulu

BREADFRUIT AND COCONUT PUDDING

Makes 6 servings

1 cup boiling water
1½ cups coconut milk from
    1 grated coconut
3 cups ripe breadfruit pulp
½ teaspoon salt
½ cup sugar

Pour boiling water over grated coconut and allow to stand for 15 minutes. Knead the coconut with hands and strain through 2 thicknesses of cheesecloth, squeezing out as much milk as possible.

Scrape out the pulp from a soft ripe breadfruit and add coconut milk, salt, and sugar. Pour into an oiled baking dish and bake 1 hour or more in a 350°F oven.

JULIA TOOMEY
The Friends of 'Iolani Palace Cook Book

GOOD MEALS IN HONOLULU

Await you at Child's

New, modern, high class restaurant, centrally located. Cool and comfortable. Intelligent, courteous service. European plan. Operated in connection with the

Blaisdell Hotel

J.F. CHILD, Proprietor.

ALMOND FLOAT

Makes 8 servings

2 tablespoons unflavored gelatin
1¼ cups water, divided use
¾ cup sugar
1 cup milk
1 tablespoon almond extract
1 (16-ounce) can peach slices
1 (15-ounce) can lychee
8 maraschino cherries, cut into halves

Soften gelatin in ¼ cup of the water. In a saucepan, bring remaining 1 cup water to a boil. Add softened gelatin and stir until gelatin is dissolved. Stir in sugar, milk, and almond extract. Pour into an 8-inch square pan and chill until firm. To serve, drain peaches, saving the liquid. Cut peaches into smaller pieces. Put back into liquid and add lychee and cherries. Cut almond gelatin into diamond shapes. Carefully put into fruit mixture.

North Kohala Favorites

GAU

Chinese New Year's Pudding

2 pounds mochi flour
3 cups water
3½ cups dark brown sugar
1 (12-ounce) can coconut milk
3 tablespoons oil
4 ti leaves, deveined
Sesame seeds
1 red date

Place mochi flour in a large mixing bowl.

In a heavy 3-quart saucepan, stir water and sugar together over low heat until sugar is dissolved. Increase heat to bring to a boil. Remove from heat and add coconut milk. Add mixture gradually to flour; add oil and mix well. Pour mixture into a pan or half-gallon aluminum can which has been lined with deveined ti leaves. Place pan or can in a steamer. Steam for 3 hours. When pudding is done, sprinkle with sesame seeds and place a red date in the center.

MARTHA EVANS
Lana'i Cooks, Lana'i High & Elementary School

HAUPIA
Coconut Pudding

1 quart coconut milk (3 to 4 coconuts)
4 tablespoons cornstarch
4 tablespoons sugar
1/8 teaspoon salt
1 teaspoon vanilla

Place milk in deep pan. When warm, add cornstarch, sugar, and salt. Stir until thickened. Add vanilla. Stir and pour into pan. Cool and cut into squares. Serve as dessert.

SAUCE: Combine coconut milk and cornstarch to desired thickness and add sugar to taste. A can of crushed pineapple or food coloring can be used for variety.

MONA KAHELE
The Kahikolu Country Cookbook

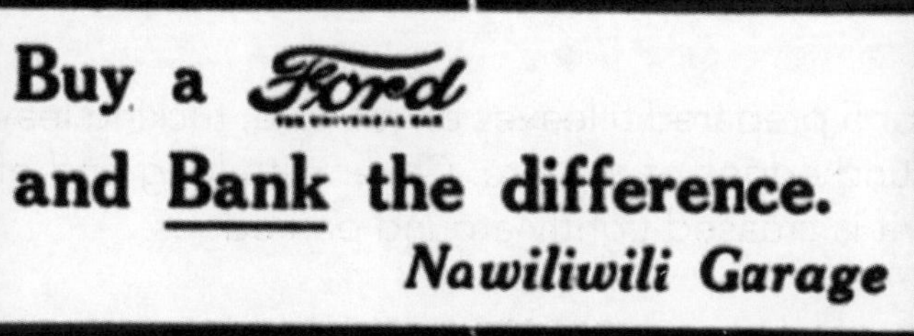

KŪLOLO

Makes 10 servings

- 2 medium-size Hawaiian taro (approximately 7 cups)
- 2 cups coconut milk (room temperature)
- 1 cup water (preferably coconut; tap water ok) at room temperature
- ⅔ cup honey
- 1½ cups dark brown cane sugar
- 10 medium ti leaves

Peel taro. Grate taro to fine or smooth texture. Mix grated taro, being sure no pieces of ungrated taro are present. Add coconut milk and water; mix well. Add honey; mix well. Add dark brown cane sugar and mix well. Taste. Add more honey and sugar if desired.

Grease pan very lightly; line with foil so that 1 end is long enough to use as cover and ends tuck tightly around lip of pan. Line foil with ti leaves on bottom of pan, being certain leaves overlap as well as rise up around pan edges about ½ inch. (Prepare leaves by removing center stem without tearing leaves.) Pour the entire mixture on ti leaves in pan and smooth out evenly.

Place 4 or 5 prepared ti leaves on mixture, tucking leaves carefully around edges of mixture. Cover with long end of foil being sure it is creased tightly around pan edges.

Bake in heated oven at 325°F for 4½ hours. After 3 hours, check to see that mixture is browning. After 4½ hours turn off oven and leave mixture in until oven cools. Kūlolo is ready to eat.

REVEREND WILLIAM KAINA, PASTOR
KAWAIAHA'O CHURCH AND MAMA KAHU SANDY
The Friends of 'Iolani Palace Cook Book

PUDDING TAHITIAN-STYLE

1 cup starch (corn or Chinese)
2 cups coconut milk
1 cup sugar
½ cup honey
½ cup papaya pulp
½ cup pineapple, crushed or tidbits
1 teaspoon vanilla

Mix starch and milk into paste, add other ingredients. Mix well. Pour into pan, cover top with ti leaves fitted tightly and bake in 350°F oven for 1 hour.

MONA KAHELE
The Kahikolu Country Cookbook

RICE PUDDING

¼ cup sugar
2 eggs (slightly beaten)
¼ teaspoon salt
2½ cups milk
½ cup raisins
1 teaspoon vanilla
¼ teaspoon cinnamon
1 teaspoon honey
1 cup cooked rice
2 tablespoons brown sugar

Pre heat oven to 350°F. Mix sugar, eggs, and salt. Heat milk over hot water but do not boil. Stir in the sugar and egg mixture. Add raisins, vanilla, cinnamon, and honey. Stir in rice and pour mixture into round casserole. Place casserole in a pan of hot water and bake for 1 hour at 350°F uncovered. Remove from oven, sprinkle with brown sugar and serve.

DANIELLE CUNHA
Hugs & Kisses of Aloha, Aloha Airlines Flight Attendant Cookbook

BREAD PUDDING

1 loaf Portuguese sweet bread
½ cup raisins
1 stick butter
1 cup sugar
2¼ cups milk
5 eggs, beaten
1 teaspoon vanilla
Sprinkle of cinnamon

Preheat oven to 350°F. Butter 13 x 9-inch baking dish.

Break bread into pieces and put in buttered dish. Sprinkle raisins on top.

Melt butter in saucepan and add sugar and milk. Heat until sugar dissolves. Add eggs to mixture (stir a small amount of hot milk into eggs, then whisk eggs into rest of milk) and stir in vanilla. Pour over bread and raisins. Sprinkle with cinnamon. Bake 20 to 25 minutes.

PATSY TAMEKAZU
Island Flavors, Favorite Recipes of the Historic Hawai'i Foundation

THAI TAPIOCA PUDDING

1 cup small Thai tapioca pearls (Cock Brand Bille de Tapioca)
8 cups water, divided use
3 cups coconut milk
1 cup sugar
½ teaspoon salt

Rinse tapioca in cool tap water. Drain. Place in a saucepan with 6 cups water. Bring to a boil over medium heat and cook 5 minutes, stirring constantly. Drain and rinse. Combine coconut milk and 2 cups water in a clean saucepan. Add tapioca mixture and bring to boil, stirring constantly. Add sugar, salt, and stir until sugar is dissolved. Remove from heat. Taste and adjust taste by adding more sugar or salt. Let mixture sit in saucepan for 30 minutes. Pour into dessert glasses and serve warm.

VARIATION: Serve chilled with ¼ cup honeydew melon added to each serving.

Wisteria Delights, A Collection of Recipes by Pearl City Hongwanji Mission

PAPAYA ICE CREAM

Makes 6 servings

2 cups soy milk (not light) or evaporated
1/3 cup sugar
1 teaspoon vanilla extract
1¼ cups ripe mashed papaya
Papaya slices for garnish

Combine ingredients except papaya slices in food processor or blender; process until smooth. If you have ice cream maker, follow manufacturer's instructions. If not, freeze blended papaya mixture in shallow pans or ice cube trays. Just before serving, chop frozen mixtures and process in blender or food processor until creamy.

Hilo Missionary Cooks

SOURSOP SHERBET

2 cups soursop juice
2 cups water
1 tablespoon lemon juice
1 egg white
7/8 cup sugar

Make a syrup of sugar and water by boiling for 5 minutes. Cool to lukewarm. Add soursop juice, unbeaten egg white, pour into freezing container. Use the same method of mixing as for other sherbets.

MOTOKO SHITABATA
Family Favorites, Oahu Extension Homemakers Council

BAKED MOCHI

Makes 32 servings

5 cups mochiko*
1 box light brown sugar**
1 teaspoon baking soda
2½ cups water
1 (12-ounce) can coconut milk
¼ cup sesame seeds

Mix mochiko, sugar, and baking soda well and add water. Add coconut milk and mix. Pour into a greased pan. Sprinkle with sesame seeds. Bake at 350°F for 45 minutes.

*2 pounds mochiko has 7½ cups flour, 2 (10-ounce) packages have 5 cups. ** 1 box has 3 cups, packed tight.

LISA OKINAGA
1988 4-H Local & Ethnic Food Show

BUTTER MOCHI

1 box mochiko flour
3 teaspoons baking powder
1¾ cups sugar
1 can coconut milk
1 cup milk
4 eggs
1 stick butter, melted
1 teaspoon vanilla

Preheat oven to 350°F. Mix dry ingredients together then add coconut milk, milk, eggs, butter, and vanilla. Pour into 13 x 9-inch pan. Bake for 1 hour. Let mochi cool for 30 minutes before cutting.

MONICA KALAHUI
Hugs & Kisses of Aloha, Aloha Airlines Flight Attendant Cookbook

BUTTER TARO MOCHI

Makes 24 or more bite-size pieces

½ cup butter
1 pound mochiko flour
1½ cups white sugar
1 cup brown sugar
1 teaspoon baking powder
3 cups coconut milk
5 eggs, beaten
1 teaspoon vanilla
1 cup taro, grated (Taro brand)

Preheat oven to 350°F. Melt butter, and then cool.

Combine mochiko, sugars, and baking powder. Add remaining ingredients. Stir into mochiko mixture. Mix well. Pour into 9 x 13-inch pan. Bake 1 hour. Cool.

CHARTA LEONG
Hugs & Kisses of Aloha, Aloha Airlines Flight Attendant Cookbook

COCOA MOCHI

2 cups mochiko
2 cups white sugar
1 teaspoon baking soda
¼ cup Hershey cocoa powder
2 eggs
¼ cup butter, melted
1 (12-ounce) can evaporated milk
1 (12-ounce) can coconut milk

Combine ingredients in a large bowl; mix well. Pour into greased 9 x 13-inch pan. Bake in preheated oven at 350°F for 45 minutes to 1 hour. Cool; cut into serving pieces.

RUTH YAMAUCHI
Kalaheo Missionary Church Cookin' Book!

CUSTARD MOCHI

½ cup butter
1½ cups sugar
4 eggs
4 cups milk
2 teaspoons vanilla
2 cups mochi rice flour
3 teaspoons baking powder
½ cup shredded coconut

Cream butter and sugar. Beat in 1 egg at a time. Add remaining ingredients and pour into a well-greased 9 x 13-inch pan. Bake at 350°F until done, about 1 hour.

"PINKIE" S.P. CRAUS
Cooking with Honolulu Gardeners, Honolulu Community Recreational Garden Program

EASY CHI CHI DANGO

1 (16-ounce) box mochiko
3 cups sugar
1 (14-ounce) can coconut milk
1 can water, using coconut milk can to measure
Food coloring (red color or other colors–3 drops)

Combine all ingredients. Blend well by hand till smooth. Pour into greased 9 x 13-inch pan. Cover securely with foil. Bake in 350°F oven for 1 hour.

After baking, remove foil and cool completely. Cut with plastic knife and roll in cornstarch.

Parks & Recreation Family Favorites

BLUEBERRY MOCHI

1 cup butter
2 cups sugar
1 large can evaporated milk
4 eggs
2 teaspoons vanilla extract
1 box mochiko
2 teaspoons baking powder
1 can blueberry pie filling

Melt butter; stir in sugar. Add milk and mix well. Add eggs and vanilla. Mix mochiko and baking powder. Add to milk mixture. Fold in blueberry pie filling. Bake in oiled 9 x 13-inch pan at 350°F for 1 hour or until toothpick test comes out clean.

KELLEY TACHIBANA
"Cooking with Lovely Hula Hands,"
Moana's Hula Halau, Kaunakakai

FILIPINO MOCHI

5 cups mochiko
3½ cups coconut milk
3 cups sugar
1 small can condensed cream (put aside a small amount for brushing the top)

Mix all ingredients together into a smooth paste. Add water to make up the 3½ cups coconut milk. Line a pan with foil and oil heavily. Bake. After an hour or so, brush the top with the cream that was set aside. Slice after it has cooled.

Favorite Island Cookery, Book II, Honpa Hongwanji Buddhist Temple

HAUPIA COCONUT MOCHI

8 tablespoons butter
4 tablespoons margarine
2½ cups sugar
2 boxes mochiko
2 packages haupia mix
½ cup dry milk
6 cups water
1 cup finely chopped macadamia nuts
½ cup shredded coconut (optional)

Mix softened butter and margarine with the sugar. Then add the mochiko, haupia mix, and dry milk. While mixing the powdered ingredients, slowly add the water until smooth. Add the macadamia nuts last.

Spray a large cake pan with Pam. Bake at 375°F for 1 hour. Completely cool before cutting. Roll mochi in kinako or potato starch.

Parks & Recreation Family Favorites

POI MOCHI

1 pound poi
1 cup sugar
1 box mochiko flour

Mix poi with a little water in the bag. Put in mixing bowl, add sugar and mix well. Slowly add mochiko flour. Add water a little at a time until dough is able to drop off spoon easily. Drop by teaspoonfuls in hot oil until golden brown. Drain on paper towel.

A Chorus of Recipes, Kamehameha School Children's Chorus

AN

Black Bean Paste

Makes enough to fill 24 mochi

1 (12-ounce) package azuki (black beans)
6 cups water
2 cups sugar
½ teaspoon salt

Soak the beans in water overnight and drain. Add fresh water to generously cover; cook, adding water as necessary. When very tender, add the sugar and salt. Bring to a boil, then simmer while you continue to stir until mixture is thick. Cool or chill. Shape into balls the size of walnuts.

Still More of Our Favorite Recipes,
Maui Association for Family and Community Education

BICO

Sweet Rice

5 cups mochi rice
1 box dark brown sugar
1 can coconut milk
1 block butter
1 tablespoon instant coffee (optional)

Wash rice in rice cooker and add water like ordinary rice. Mix ½ box brown sugar with the rice and water, then turn rice cooker on. While the rice is cooking, put the coconut milk pot with the butter and remaining brown sugar and till it boils. Then add coffee for darker coloring if you want. After rice is cooked, combine and mix it with brown sugar mixture. Place in a square aluminum and bake at 350°F for 20 minutes.

ROSE OLAYON
Country Cookbook,
Compiled by the Wahiawa General Hospital Auxiliary

CHINESE PRETZELS

1½ cups flour
¾ cup cornstarch
½ teaspoon salt
1 cup sugar
2 cups water
2 eggs

Sift flour, cornstarch, salt. Add sugar, water, beaten eggs. Mix well. Iron rosette should be hot. Deep-fry to golden brown.

DOROTHY PASSOS
Haleiwa Elementary School 115th Birthday

HALO HALO

1 (12-ounce) jar Halo Halo mix
1 (12-ounce) jar sweet sugar palm (Kaong)
1 prepared kanten, cubed
1½ cups shaved ice
6 tablespoons evaporated milk, sweetened as desired
Custard for garnish

Into a tall glass (16-ounces), arrange in layers 3 tablespoons Halo Halo mix, 1 tablespoon sweet sugar palm, 2 tablespoons kanten, and 1 cup shaved ice. Pour evaporated milk over the shaved ice and garnish with custard cut in 1 x 2-inch sized rectangular block. Mix well before eating.

BAYANIHAN RESTAURANT
Hawaii's Aloha Recipes, The Japanese Women's Society of Honolulu

STICKY RICE WITH BANANAS

Makes 6 to 8 servings

1 cup coconut milk
3 cups cooked sticky rice
¼ cup brown sugar
⅛ teaspoon salt (optional)
10 to 20 sheets of banana leaves, cut into 8-inch squares
6 ripe apple bananas, cut into 1-inch strips

In a saucepan, combine coconut milk, sticky rice, brown sugar, and salt. Cook on medium heat until thick. Place a layer, about 3 x 3 x ½-inch thick, of the rice mixture, then wrap it up by lifting up 2 opposite sides of the banana leaf at a time, so the rice goes up on top of the banana. Fold under the extra part of the leaf. Place in a steamer and steam for 25 minutes. Serve warm or cold.

JOYCE PAGARAGAN
1988 4-H Local & Ethnic Food Show

SESAME SEED CANDY

2 cups sugar
1 pound honey
½ cup water
Dash of salt
1 teaspoon ginger
3 cups (1 pound) sesame seeds
1 cup chopped peanuts

Cook sugar, honey, and water in a large saucepan over low heat for 5 minutes stirring constantly. Continue cooking over low heat but don't stir until a drop of syrup forms a very firm ball when dropped into cold water (260°F on candy thermometer). Remove from heat. Stir in remaining ingredients and quickly spread the mixture on a greased cookie sheet using a wet spatula. When still warm, cut into squares.

ALLYSON KANEKO
A Chorus of Recipes, Kamehameha School Children's Chorus

CONDIMENTS AND SAUCES

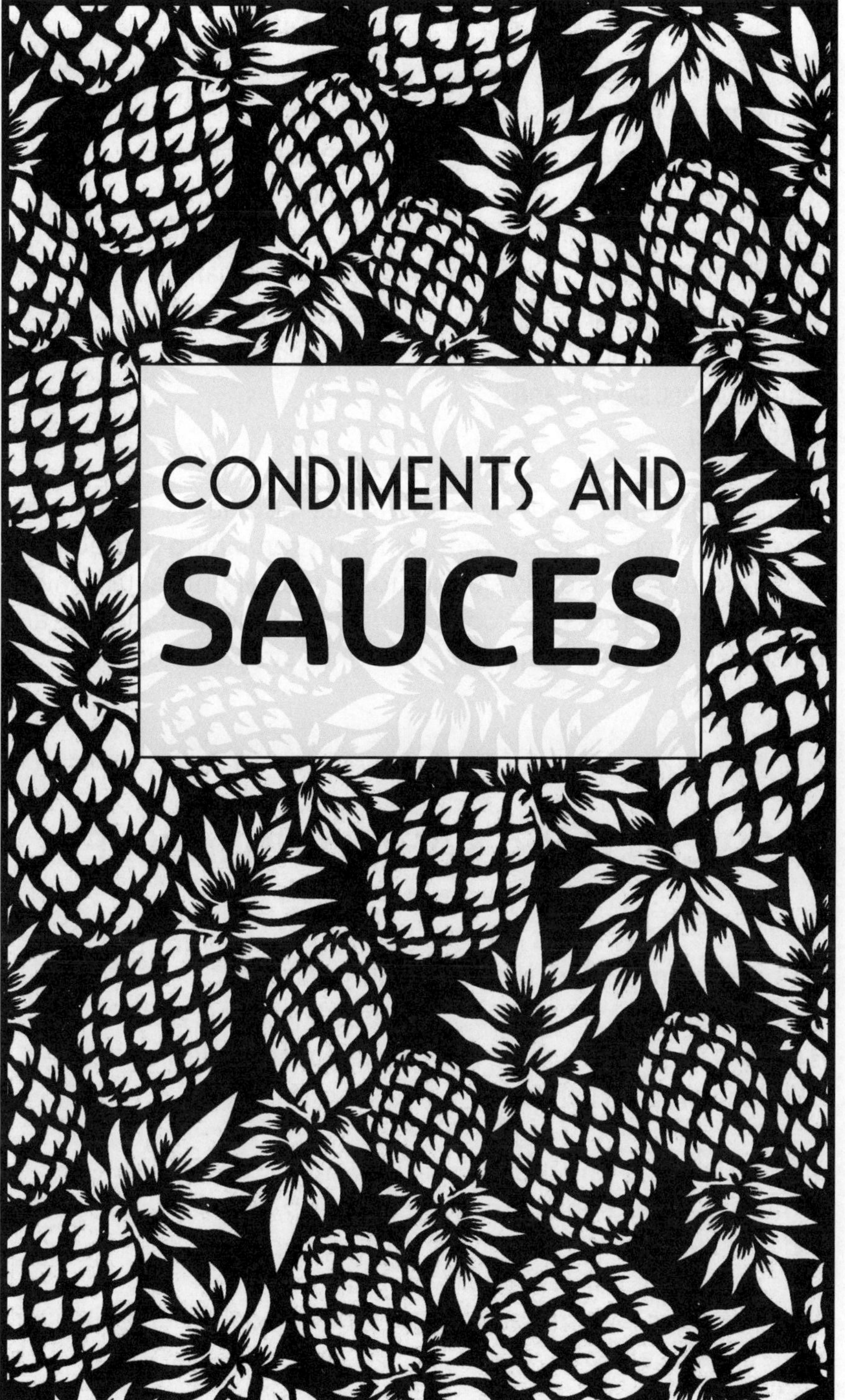

MANGO CHUTNEY

10 cups green mangoes, sliced
2 tablespoons Hawaiian salt
2 cups vinegar
4 cups granulated sugar
1½ cups brown sugar
½ cup chopped ginger
2 cloves garlic, minced
2 chili peppers, seeded and chopped
1 cup raisins
1 large onion, diced
½ orange, sliced thin
⅔ cup chopped macadamia nuts
1 teaspoon cinnamon
1 teaspoon cloves
1 teaspoon nutmeg

Sprinkle Hawaiian salt over mangoes and leave overnight. Rinse and drain. In large pot, combine remaining ingredients and bring to boil. Gently simmer for 1 hour or until sauce thickens. Add mangoes and cook for 2 hours until mangoes are translucent, stirring frequently. Pour into sterilized jars and seal with paraffin.

Hawaii's Aloha Recipes, The Japanese Women's Society of Honolulu

SPICED HALA KAHIKI (PINEAPPLE)

Makes 8 to 10 servings

1 (1-pound, 4-ounce) can Hawaiian pineapple
⅔ cup sugar
⅓ cup wine vinegar (white)
Dash of salt
1 teaspoon whole cloves
½ teaspoon whole allspice
2 sticks cinnamon

Drain pineapple and reserve ¾ cup syrup. Combine syrup with remaining ingredients in saucepan. Bring to boil. Reduce heat and boil gently for 10 minutes, stirring occasionally.

Pour hot syrup over pineapple; cover and cool. Then chill overnight in refrigerator.

Hana Maui Recipes from Then to Now

ʻŌHELO BERRY JAM

4½ cups ʻōhelo berries
⅓ cup water
3 cups sugar
Juice of 1 lemon

Boil ʻōhelo berries in water until berries begin to break, boil all at once (measure 4 cups). Add sugar and lemon juice, boil, stirring often, until it thickens. Pour into sterilized jars and seal with paraffin.

KAY TANABE
100 Years Sharing God's Love, United Community Church

MULBERRY-GUAVA JAM

Grand Prize Winner, 1985 Hawaiʻi State Farm Fair

6 cups mulberry-guava pulp
½ cup lemon juice
1 box Sure Jell
6½ cups sugar

Combine pulp, lemon juice, and Sure Jell; boil hard. Add sugar and boil hard. Skim. Pour into sterilized jars and seal with hot paraffin wax.

EMIKO ABE
Country Cookbook,
Compiled by the Wahiawa General Hospital Auxiliary

HOT PEPPER JELLY

'Ono and Hot!

¾ cup red bell peppers, remove seeds, veins, and chop or grind coarsely
¼ to ½ cup hot chili peppers, remove seeds and veins and chop or grind
6½ cups sugar
1½ cups cider vinegar
1 bottle Certo

After chopping, strain, but save juices. To measure, pack peppers tightly in cup and pour in juice to flood cup. Bring sugar, peppers, vinegar to hard boil in a large pan, stirring occasionally. Set aside for 15 to 20 minutes, stirring a couple of times and leaving uncovered. Bring to boil for 2 minutes. Remove from heat and stir in Certo. Pour into sterile jars and seal. Delicious on crackers, with meat, poultry, or pork.

HELEN WEEKS
The Kahikolu Country Cookbook

LILIKO'I JELLY

3 cups sugar
1 cup water
½ cup liliko'i juice
½ bottle or ½ cup Certo

Boil sugar and water together for 1 minute. Take off stove. Add Certo and stir well. Then add the liliko'i juice. Pour into sterilized jars and cover with paraffin.

DAISY ALEXANDER
We, the Women of Hawaii Cookbook

GUAVA JELLY

Makes 4 small jelly jars

4 cups guava juice
4 cups sugar

Bring guava juice to a rapid boil. Gradually add all the sugar and boil rapidly for 10 minutes. Pour into sterilized jars and vacuum seal.

NOTE: Watch pot as juice will boil over.

CURTIS M. ZEUG
1988 4-H Local & Ethnic Food Show

PAPAYA AND GINGER MARMALADE

Makes 2 quarts

2 lemons, thinly sliced
4 cups water
4 cups sugar, divided use
1 teaspoon grated fresh ginger root or 1 tablespoon chopped candied ginger
8 cups chopped firm ripe papaya

Cook lemons in 2 cups water until transparent. Boil the sugar, water (2 cups) and ginger to make a syrup. Add sugar and ginger syrup to lemon water along with papaya and boil on low heat for 30 minutes. Pour into sterilized jars and seal with paraffin.

L.P. IWANE
Hana Maui Recipes from Then to Now

MANGO STRIPS

Use 1 gallon green mango strips; partially dry in hot sun for 1 day, turning at intervals.

Syrup

1 box brown sugar
2 cups washed sugar
¼ cup lemon or lime juice (increase if mangoes are sweet)
½ cup water
1 tablespoon salt

Mix together and bring to a boil till sugar melts.

Add:

½ teaspoon Chinese Five Spice
½ teaspoon red food coloring
1 teaspoon sodium benzoate (preservative, optional if to keep long unrefrigerated)

Add mango strips into syrup and cook for about 15 minutes or until syrup is absorbed and thickened.

Still More of Favorite Recipes,
Maui Association for Family and Community Education

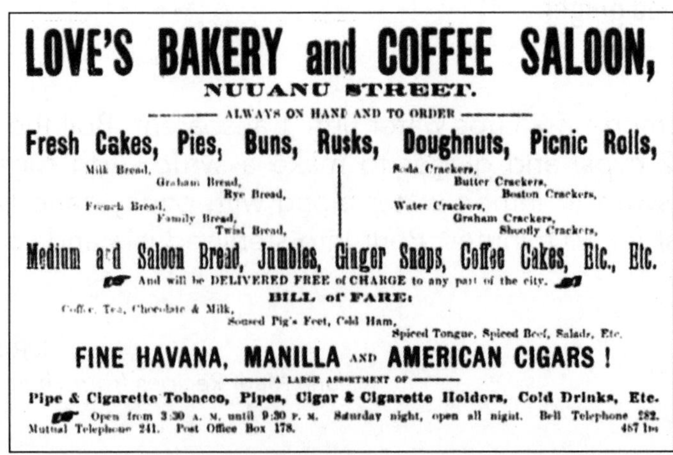

TŪTŪ'S PICKLED MANGO

3 cups white sugar
1 cup vinegar
3 tablespoons Hawaiian salt
10 to 12 medium size mango (preferably Chinese mango), peeled and cut into wedges
1 package li hing mui
Red food coloring (optional)

No cooking involved! Add sugar, vinegar, and salt to mangoes; mix well. Add li hing mui and food coloring; mix. Rotate jar by flipping over every so often. Soak overnight (or couple of days for tastier flavor). Enjoy!

NANI ROSA
"Pig Out" with Liholiho's Caring, Competent, Creative Cooks

PICKLED GREEN PAPAYA

1 large green papaya
Salt
Food coloring

Peel papaya, remove seeds, and slice into matchstick size. Sprinkle with salt.

Syrup
2 cups water
1 cup water
½ cup rice vinegar
¼ cup salt

Cook syrup ingredients until sugar dissolved. Add food coloring. Cool. Pour over salted papaya.

Favorite Island Cookery, Book IV, Honpa Hongwanji Hawaii Betsuin

PICKLED MAUI ONIONS

1 clove garlic, crushed
1 teaspoon sugar
1 tablespoon Hawaiian salt
2 chili peppers, seeded and crushed
Cider vinegar to fill jar to ⅔
Water to fill remaining ⅓ jar

Fill quart jar with small white onions, or Maui onions, cut in half or quarters depending on onion size. Add garlic, sugar, salt, peppers, vinegar, and water. Cover jar tightly and shake well. Let stand 3 days shaking jar at least once a day. Refrigerate.

EVE HENDERSON
Haili Congregational Church, 175th Anniversary

STAR FRUIT MUI

1 quart dried star fruit, sliced, dried in sun for 1½ days
3 lemons
1½ teaspoons salt
6 tablespoons sugar
⅛ teaspoon cloves, allspice, or Chinese Five Spice
2½ tablespoons vinegar

Rinse star fruit. Put all ingredients in pot and cook until transparent. Store in sterilized jars. After 2 to 3 days, turn jars upside down to mix fruits. Wipe covers with vinegar to keep indefinitely. Prunes (12 ounces) may be substituted.

Community Family Favorites, Community Church of Honolulu

PRUNE MUI

3 tablespoons Hawaiian salt
1 pound brown sugar
1 tablespoon Chinese Five Spice
3 tablespoons whiskey
10 whole cloves
1½ cups lemon juice
8 (12-ounce) packages pitted prunes
2 packages apricot
1 large package lemon peel
1 large package li hing mui

In a gallon jar, combine salt, sugar, Chinese Five Spice, whiskey, cloves, and lemon juice; mix well. Add prunes, apricots, lemon peel, and li hing mui. Toss mix to coat fruits. Let stand 3 to 4 days, tossing to mix several times a day.

Hawaii's Aloha Recipes, The Japanese Women's Society of Honolulu

MANGO BUTTER

12 cups peeled mango slices
3 cups water
6 cups sugar
½ teaspoon ground cloves
½ teaspoon allspice
1 teaspoon cinnamon
1 teaspoon nutmeg

Add water to mangoes and cook until soft enough to mash. Press through sieve if mangoes are stringy. Add sugar and spices and cook slowly for 45 minutes or until thick. Stir frequently to prevent burning. Pour into sterile jars and seal with wax.

MONA KAHELE
The Kahikolu Country Cookbook

MARINADE FOR WILD GAME

2 bottles red wine
9 ounces red wine vinegar
7 ounces olive oil
4 ounce sliced onions
1 ounce sliced celery
1 ounce sliced carrots
2 ounces sliced shallots
½ ounce minced ginger
2 cloves garlic, minced
1 bunch Italian parsley
1 sprig rosemary
1 bunch sage
10 basil leaves
6 thyme sprigs
2 bay leaves
3 whole cloves
1 teaspoon four spice
1 teaspoon whole black peppercorns
¼ teaspoon salt
½ teaspoon sugar

Combine all ingredients in a clean and sterilized container (stainless steel or ceramic crock is preferred). Add meat to marinade. Depending on size, marinate meat for 1 to 24 hours.

HENRY CLAY RICHARDSON
Lana'i Cooks, Lana'i High & Elementary School

MONA'S MARINADE

¼ cup vinegar or 1 cup pineapple juice
¾ cup water
6 tablespoons shoyu
4 tablespoons sugar or more
5 slivers of crushed garlic
2 fingers crushed ginger
½ tablespoon salt
1½ teaspoons dry mustard
Dash of black pepper

Blend all together. This may be refrigerated until used. Good on meat, fish, pork, chicken, or other fowl.

KAHELE COLLECTION
The Kahikolu Country Cookbook

HERBED LEMON PEPPER MARINADE

¼ cup chopped scallions
2 to 3 tablespoons fresh lemon juice
2 tablespoons vegetable oil
1 tablespoon honey
1 teaspoon dried tarragon leaves
1 teaspoon lemon pepper
1 teaspoon salt

Mix all ingredients in a small bowl. Good marinade for chicken.

Ono-Licious, Na Poe Humukuiki O Hawaii, Hawaii Quilt Guild

GUAVA KETCHUP

3 quarts guava pulp
5 medium onions, sliced thin
¼ cup water
2 large cloves garlic
1 tablespoon salt
2 tablespoons cloves
4 bell peppers, finely chopped
4 cups sugar
1 chili pepper
1½ cups vinegar
4 teaspoons allspice
3 teaspoons cinnamon
2 teaspoons nutmeg

Combine all ingredients and cook 30 to 40 minutes. Delicious served with meat, used as a base for barbecue sauce, or poured over cream cheese and put on crackers as a pūpū.

For pulp: Quarter guavas, boil with just enough water to bring to consistency where they can be pushed through a strainer to produce pulp.

EMMA FEE
The Hele Mai, Ai (Come Eat) Cookbook, Flavors of Upcountry Maui

HOT MUSTARD SAUCE

¼ cup melted butter
1 egg, well beaten
3 tablespoons white sugar (or less to taste)
1 tablespoon red wine vinegar
½ cup canned milk (undiluted)
5 tablespoons Coleman's dry mustard

Mix all together well and cook and stir in double boiler 10 min. Nice to serve with cold meats, ham, or with tiny wienies (hot) or meatballs for pūpū.

HAKU BALDWIN
The Hele Mai, Ai (Come Eat) Cookbook, Flavors of Upcountry Maui

QUICK LEMON CAPER SAUCE

¾ cup of chicken broth
2 tablespoons lemon juice
1 tablespoon cornstarch
2 tablespoons Dijon mustard
2 tablespoons capers
2 tablespoons nonfat yogurt

Combine all ingredients except capers and yogurt in saucepan. Cook, stirring until thickened. Stir in capers and yogurt. Pour over fish or chicken.

BECKY SWAN, BILL AND CODY GILLETTE
Hanalei School Collective Cook Book

TERIYAKI SAUCE

4 cups shoyu
8 cups water
4 cups brown sugar
2 cloves garlic, diced
¼ pound fresh ginger, diced
3 to 4 onions, chopped

In a large pan, stir together shoyu, water, and sugar over medium heat. Add garlic, ginger, and onions. Bring mixture to a boil and simmer for 30 minutes to 1 hour. Let the sauce cool, then store in the refrigerator.

Marinating tips:
chicken parts—2 to 3 days
beef and pork—1 to 2 days
fish and shrimp—1 to 3 hours

The longer you marinate, the stronger the flavor will be.

S. BENTO
Hanalei School Collective Cook Book

SUSIE'S SAUCE FOR BARBECUE

1 stick butter/margarine
1 large bottle ketchup
1 onion, diced
½ cup brown sugar
½ cup water
1 tablespoon mustard
1 tablespoon Worcestershire sauce
Dash of salt

Melt butter in a saucepan. Add ingredients; stir and simmer for 30 minutes. Apply generously to chicken, ribs, etc.

STOLEN BY RICK BUNDSCHUH
Kalaheo Missionary Church Cookin' Book!

CHILI PEPPER WATER

12 chili peppers
½ cup water
½ cup brown vinegar
½ teaspoon salt

Mix and use as seasoning.

JUNE TAKA
The Kahikolu Country Cookbook

KALBI SAUCE

1 cup shoyu
½ cup sugar
½ cup honey
6 cloves garlic, minced
1 teaspoon minced fresh ginger
1 tablespoon sesame oil
1 tablespoon sesame seeds
¼ teaspoon pepper
1 tablespoon chopped green onion
1 tablespoon chili sauce (optional)

Mix together and marinate kalbi overnight.

HILLORY KIM
Hugs & Kisses of Aloha, Aloha Airlines Flight Attendant Cookbook

WON TON DIPPING SAUCE

Makes approximately ½ cup

1 tablespoon vegetable oil
½ teaspoon sesame oil
1 tablespoon oyster sauce
2 tablespoons soy sauce
¼ teaspoon sugar
White pepper to taste

Place all ingredients in a container with a tight fitting lid. Shake until well-mixed. Use as a dipping sauce or to flavor chicken soup.

SHEILA BLACK
Lana'i Cooks, Lana'i High & Elementary School

TONKATSU SAUCE

½ cup ketchup
¼ teaspoon pepper
¼ teaspoon salt
3 tablespoons Worcestershire sauce
½ teaspoon sugar

Combine all ingredients and mix until thoroughly blended.

Hawaii's Aloha Recipes, The Japanese Women's Society of Honolulu

KOREAN SPICY SAUCE

3 stalks green onions
3 tablespoons toasted sesame
2 teaspoons sesame oil
2 crushed garlic
Korean red chili pepper (optional)
Generous amount of shoyu

Chop green onions and add all other ingredients in a quart size jar and store until ready to use. Stir before using. Good on tofu slices or meats.

KEIKO KIM
Our Daily Bread Centennial Cookbook, Iao Congregational Church

PORTUGUESE PICKLING SAUCE

1 cup vinegar
2 cups water
5 cloves garlic, crushed
1 teaspoon allspice
½ teaspoon cayenne pepper or 2 Hawaiian chili peppers, crushed

Combine all ingredients. Put into glass jar and store in refrigerator. Use as marinade for beef, pork, or poultry.

Hana Maui Recipes from Then to Now

WOW WOW SAUCE

Makes 1 pint

Sooo good and sooo hot.

2 tablespoons butter or margarine
2 tablespoons minced onion
2 tablespoons flour
1 cup beef broth (canned broth may be used)
1 tablespoon wine vinegar
1 tablespoon Worcestershire sauce
1 tablespoon dry mustard
½ teaspoon horseradish
Black pepper to taste

Melt butter in skillet. Sauté onions. Stir in flour and mix well. Add broth slowly while mixing until mixture is smooth. Add remaining ingredients and mix well. Serve over cooked meats or steamed vegetables. Also good over fried tofu.

Hana Maui Recipes from Then to Now

SUMISO SAUCE

Vinegared Miso Sauce

¼ cup miso
3 tablespoons sugar
3 tablespoons vinegar
1 or 2 tablespoons soup stock or juice of clam, abalone, etc.
1 or 2 tablespoons finely chopped green onion (optional)

Use sauce for boiled octopus, cuttlefish, or other dish.

A Lei of Recipes,
Kauai Association for Family and Community Education

AGGIE'S KO CHOO JUNG PASTE

Makes about 1 quart

4 cups cooked rice
¾ cup white miso
⅔ cup honey
½ cup ground red pepper
3 tablespoons salt
2 tablespoons paprika

Combine all ingredients; mix well. Pour into a 3 to 4 quart jar. (The jar should be twice the volume of the mixture to allow for rising.) Cover jar with aluminum foil or clear plastic wrap. Do not cover with jar lid. Let stand at room temperature for 1 month or until rice rises and becomes soft. (The mixture may keep longer on the shelf without any harm. It will not mold. Do not refrigerate.)

Put 1 cup of mixture into blender; cover and blend until a soft paste is formed. Repeat until all is blended.

Put paste into a Teflon pan to prevent scorching. Cook over low heat, stirring frequently, until paste becomes thick and heavy with a glossy look; cool. Store in jar, covered with lid. Ko Choo Jung does not need to be refrigerated.

Hawaii's Aloha Recipes, The Japanese Women's Society of Honolulu

TEMPURA BATTER

1 cup flour
1¼ cups cornstarch
¼ cup sugar
1 cup ice water
1 egg, beaten

Mix and store in refrigerator until ready to use. Vegetables that can be used are sweet potatoes, eggplant, string beans, carrots, round onion, and gobo. Slice, dip in batter, and deep-fry. Serve with following sauce.

Sauce
½ package dashinomoto
1 tablespoon sugar
¼ cup soy sauce
1 cup water

Boil ingredients together. Cool, refrigerate.

JUNE TAKA
The Kahikolu Country Cookbook

WAIKIKI, HONOLULU.

Fiist-Class Accommodation for Tourists and Island Guests.

SUPERIOR BATHING FACILITIES, Private Cottages for FamilieS.

T. A. SIMPSON,
cct9 Manager.

FRESH COCONUT MILK

With an ice pick or screwdriver, pierce eyes of a fresh coconut. Pour out the liquid. Reserve or discard. Place coconut on a 9-inch pie or cake pan. Bake in a 350°F oven for 15 to 30 minutes to help loosen meat from shell. Let cool briefly.

With a hammer, hit sharply along the middle until coconut breaks in pieces. With a rounded knife or screwdriver, pry white flesh free from shell. Peel brown portion, if desired. Coarsely chop meat. Measure chopped coconut. Place coconut in a food processor or blender, whirl gradually, adding an equal measure of hot water, until it is thick, pulpy mass. Pour in a fine sieve, let drain briefly in a deep bowl, then press firmly to extract all remaining liquid. Discard coconut flesh. Milk is ready to use. If made ahead, chill up to 3 days or freeze. One pound coconut yields 1½ to 2 cups coconut milk.

For artificial extract, mix ½ teaspoon each sugar and coconut extract with 1 cup whipping cream.

From dry coconut, prepare the same way. Two cups dry coconut yields about 1⅔ cups milk.

A Lei of Recipes,
Kauai Association for Family and Community Education

GLOSSARY

Abalone—A large ear-shaped marine gastropod mollusk with a single shell. The large muscle is most commonly consumed and generally requires tenderizing by pounding or long cooking time.

Aburage—Deep-fried soft tofu commonly sold in rectangular or triangular shapes with a light and airy internal structure. Used to make cone sushi, among other dishes. When preparing cone sushi, aburage is tricky.

Achiote oil—An oil flavored with the musky-flavored annatto seed. To prepare achiote oil, fry annatto seeds in oil to bring out their color and flavor. Achiote oil is essential in making Puerto Rican gandule rice.

Adobo—Spanish word for "marinade" or sauce. Locally, a very popular Filipino dish of meat, poultry, or seafood that's been simmered in vinegar, garlic, and soy sauce.

'Ahi—Hawaiian name for yellowfin or bigeye tuna. When the term 'ahi is used, it is assumed that it is fresh tuna, not canned. Served in the Islands as sashimi (Japanese-style raw fish) with a spicy mustard-soy sauce dip. Also the fish of choice in poke. Substitute fresh blackfin or bluefin tuna.

Ajinomoto—One of the many brand names for monosodium glutamate.

Aku—Hawaiian name for skipjack tuna. Deep red in color and stronger tasting than 'ahi. Good broiled, grilled, or used raw in poke. Substitute any tuna.

An—Japanese word for sweetened red bean paste made from red azuki beans.

Araimo—Japanese word for a starchy taro-like potato which becomes very slippery and slimy once it is peeled and comes into contact with water.

Arare—Japanese word for rice crackers made from sweet rice flour, often flavored with other ingredients such as dried seaweed and seasoned with soy sauce.

Arborio rice—Medium grain rice grown in Italy that is high in starch, providing a creamy texture to rice dishes.

Awase-zu—Japanese word for rice vinegar dressing.

Azuki—Japanese word for Asian red bean commonly sold dried. Cooked with rice or sweetened and mashed to make fillings for mochi and other Japanese desserts.

Bacalhau—Portuguese word for dried and salted cod used in Portuguese cooking.

Bamboo shoots—Cream-colored, cone-shaped young shoots of the bamboo plant. Canned shoots are fine to use.

Banana leaves—Used to wrap food cooked in an earth oven (see Imu). Substitute aluminum foil or parchment paper, corn husks, or ti leaves.

Bean sprouts—Sprouted mung beans usually consumed raw or lightly stir-fried. Available fresh or canned.

Bitsu-bitsu—Filipino fritters made from grated sweet potatoes.

Black beans (douchi)—Fermented Chinese black beans used for seasoning; dau see.

Breadfruit—A bland, starchy vegetable widely used in the Pacific Islands. Also known as ʻulu in Hawaiian. Substitute Irish or baking potatoes.

Bulgogi—Korean dish of grilled, marinated beef.

Butterfish—Salted butterfish, black cod, or sablefish. Used in many Hawaiian and local dishes such as laulau, lomi, stews, and soups.

Cajun spice—A mixture of spices that most commonly includes garlic, onions, chili peppers, black pepper, mustard, and celery.

Calamari—Italian name for squid. Substitute octopus.

Capers—Pickled, edible flower buds of the caper bush, native to the Mediterranean.

Char siu—Chinese word for Cantonese-style marinated pork that is barbecued or roasted.

Chili oil—Vegetable oil flavored with hot chili peppers.

Chili paste—Composition of pastes vary but generally include hot red chilies, vinegar, salt, and sometimes garlic.

Chinese Five Spice powder—A fragrant, spicy, and slightly sweet spice mixture made from ground star anise, Szechuan peppercorns, fennel seeds, cloves, and cinnamon.

Chinese parsley—The green leaves and stems of the coriander plant. A pungent flat-leaf herb. Also known as fresh coriander or cilantro.

Chinese taro—A land taro that is drier when cooked compared with Hawaiian varieties. White-gray on the inside, it has a mild flavor, but absorbs flavors of the sauce.

Chirimen iriko—Japanese word for small dried anchovies.

Chow fun—Chinese word for stir-fried, flat rice noodles.

Chow mein noodles—Chinese word for soft-fried wheat or egg noodles; sold dried or fresh.

Chung choy—Salted dried turnip, rutabaga, or kohlrabi used as a flavoring ingredient, but usually removed before serving.

Coconut milk—The rich, creamy liquid extracted by squeezing the grated meat of a coconut that has been mixed with liquid. Available fresh, canned, or frozen. Substitute 1 cup whole milk beaten with 1 teaspoon coconut flavoring for a thin use and 1 cup heavy cream with 1 teaspoon coconut flavoring for a thick use.

Coconut syrup—A syrup made from coconut milk and sugar.

Coriander seeds—The seeds of the coriander plant, which have a different taste than the leaves of the plant. Closely related to caraway, fennel, dill, and anise.

Crystallized ginger—Candied ginger root slices that are coated with coarse sugar crystals. Used as a confection or in desserts.

Cumin—The seeds of a flowering plant native to the Mediterranean and Asia. Used as whole seed or as powder. Abundant in Mexican cooking.

Curry powder—A mixture of spices including cardamom, chili, cinnamon, cloves, coriander, cumin, fennel seeds, fenugreek, mace, nutmeg, red and black pepper, saffron, sesame seeds, tamarind, and turmeric. Different curry powders use different spices in different proportions.

Cuttlefish—Similar to squid and octopus, it is more tender but still needs to be tenderized. In the dried form, it is usually soaked in water before cooking.

Daikon—Japanese word for a large Asian radish, usually white in color, used in Japan and Korea for soups and pickles or shredded raw for salads and garnishes. Substitute turnips or radishes. J

Dango—Japanese word for a dumpling made from mochiko; a sweet treat that can have a variety of flavors.

Dashi—Japanese word for clear, light, basic fish broth. It is the basis of all Japanese soups; used in cooking numerous dishes. Substitute chicken stock.

Dashinomoto—Japanese word for instant soup stock granules, similar to powdered bouillon.

Dijon mustard—A mild to hot prepared mustard originally from Dijon, France.

Ebi—Japanese word for shrimp and prawn. In Japanese cooking, often in dried form and added to dish mostly for flavor.

Egg roll wrapper—Square-shaped wrappers made with flour and egg used to wrap various fillings and then deep-fried. Most wrappers are 6 inches square.

Enoki mushrooms—A type of cooking mushroom often used in Asian cooking; has long, slender, white stems, with tiny caps and a mild, delicate flavor.

Fish sauce—A concentrated salty brown liquid typically made from anchovies fermented in brine. Used in Southeast Asian cooking. Substitute 1

part soy sauce plus 4 parts mashed anchovies.

Furikake—Japanese word for a condiment made from dried seaweed flakes, sesame seeds, bonito flakes, sugar, salt, and other seasonings. Substitute ground sesame seeds and finely chopped nori seaweed sheets.

Furikake nori—Japanese word for seasoned seaweed mix.

Gao (Gau)—Chinese steamed pudding made of glutinous rice flour.

Garbanzo beans—Tan-colored legumes, also called chickpeas. Cooked and puréed chickpeas are used to make hummus, a Middle Eastern dip that is eaten with pita chips.

Gau gee—Chinese word for dumplings filled with pork then deep-fried.

Ginger—Gnarled light brown root of the domestic ginger plant, indispensable to Asian cooking. It is used as a seasoning both in savory dishes (typically with garlic and soy sauce) and in sweets such as cookies, cakes, and candies.

Ginger juice—The liquid extracted when ginger is grated and squeezed; juice is strained of fibers.

Gobo—Japanese word for burdock root, a long slender root used in Japanese dishes like nishime or kinpira gobo.

Goma—Japanese word for sesame seeds that can be white or black.

Gon lo mein—Chinese word for stir-fried chow mein noodles flavored with soy sauce, oyster sauce, and sesame oil, then topped with char siu.

Green papaya—An unripe papaya. It has a starchy consistency unlike ripe papayas.

Guava—A round tropical fruit with a yellow skin and pink inner flesh and many seeds. Grown commercially in Hawai'i. Substitute liliko'i (passionfruit).

Guisantes—Filipino word for a pork, peas and pimentos dish.

Gyoza—Japanese word for dumpling or pot sticker, usually filled with ground beef and vegetables.

Hamachi—Japanese name for yellowtail tuna. Great for sashimi or cooked.

Haupia—Hawaiian word for a traditional coconut milk–cornstarch pudding often served at lū'au.

Hawaiian chili pepper—A very small (½- to 1-inch long) and extremely hot chili pepper grown in Hawai'i. It ranks about nine out of ten on the hotness scale. Substitute Thai bird chilies or any small hot chili pepper.

Hawaiian salt—A white, coarse sea salt gathered in tidal pools after a storm or high tide. Coarser than other natural salts (sea salt), these Hawaiian salts contain a lot of natural minerals. Substitute kosher salt or sea salt.

Hekka—Popular local Japanese dish that is a one-pot dish, called sukiyaki in Japan. Chicken is the common meat, with bamboo shoots, mushrooms, tofu, shirataki noodles. Each family has a favorite recipe for hekka. Made popular in the plantations days when families gathered and made this dish.

Hijiki—Japanese word for a brown sea vegetable rich in dietary fiber and essential minerals, eaten as a garnish or side or used as an ingredient.

Hō'i'o—Hawaiian word for edible fern shoots. Known on Maui as pohole or puhole.

Hoisin—Chinese word for a thick reddish-brown sauce made with fermented soybeans, garlic, rice, salt, and sugar. Used as a condiment or for flavoring.

Horenso—Japanese word for spinach grown and sold as whole heads. Cooked with leaves and stems attached.

Huli huli—Hawaiian term meaning "to turn repeatedly," as to turn a whole chicken on a spit.

Imitation crab—Crab-flavored fish product, most commonly used in California sushi rolls, but is used in other types of sushi and many other dishes such as salads, dips and spreads, chowders, and more.

Iriko—Japanese word for small, dried anchovies. Usually mixed with soy sauce and eaten with hot rice.

Japanese cucumber—Smaller and thinner skinned than most cucumbers; substitute with the youngest American cucumbers available, peeled and seeded.

Japanese vinegar—Rice vinegar, milder than white vinegar.

Jook—Chinese word for rice soup. Also known as congee.

Kaiware—Japanese word for daikon radish sprouts. Substitute clover sprouts.

Kaki mochi—Japanese word for rice crackers usually eaten as a type of Japanese snack.

Kalbi—Korean word for barbecued short ribs that have been marinated in soy sauce, ginger, and sugar.

Kālua pig—Pork that's been cooked in an imu until very tender and the meat shreds and falls apart easily.

Kamaboko—Japanese word for red or white fish cakes made of puréed white fish mixed with potato starch and salt, then steamed.

Kampyo, kanpyo—Japanese word for dried shavings or strips of a fruit in the *Cucurbitaceae* family known as calabash.

Kanten—Japanese word for gelatin; agar agar.

Karashi—Japanese word for dry mustard.

Katsu—Japanese word for breaded cutlet, usually pork or chicken, and served with dipping sauce.

Kimchi, kimchee—Korean word for a pickled vegetable dish usually made with Chinese cabbage (won bok), vinegar, salt, garlic, and chili peppers.

Kinako—Japanese word for soybean starch or flour produced by finely grinding roasted soybeans into powder. It is often used in traditional Japanese sweets.

Ko choo jung—Korean word for a hot sauce made from mochi rice and chili peppers.

Kombu, Konbu—Japanese word for dried kelp.

Kona coffee—Rich coffee made from beans grown in the Kona District on the Big Island of Hawai'i.

Kukui nut—Hawaiian word for the candlenut. See also 'inamona, a relish made with roasted kukui nuts. Substitute roasted cashew nuts.

Kūmū—Hawaiian name for goatfish. Substitute red snapper.

Laulau—Hawaiian word for packages of ti leaves or banana leaves containing pork, beef, salted fish, or taro tops.

Leek—Similar to onions and garlic, they have a mild onion taste.

Lemongrass—Citrus-scented grass with a distinctive lemon flavor and aroma. Substitute kaffir lime leaves.

Li hing mui—Chinese word for salty, dried plum. "Li hing" means "traveling" and "mui" means "plum."

Liliko'i—Hawaiian passion fruit. Passion fruit is the sweet-sour, yellow, lemon-sized variety, while the purple-skinned liliko'i is sweeter, growing wild in the mountains where its prolific vine bears fruit during summer and fall.

Lily buds—Dried buds of a certain day lily, available in Chinese groceries.

Limu—Hawaiian word for all types of plants living in the water or damp places. The word now refers to edible seaweeds. Substitute seaweeds with similar characteristics, such as kelp (kombu).

Limu kohu—Hawaiian word for a highly preferred, edible red seaweed that may range in color from tan through shades of pink to dark red. Substitute kelp. Often used to make 'ahi poke, to add a salty, ocean flavor.

Lomi—Hawaiian word meaning to rub, knead, crush, or massage.

Long bean—A green vegetable used widely in Asian cuisines. An ingredient in Filipino pinacbet.

Long rice—Translucent threadlike noodles made from mung bean flour.

Lotus root—Light brown root of the lotus plant, used in soups and stews; valued for its beautiful design when cut.

Lū'au leaves—The young green tops of the taro root. Substitute fresh spinach.

Lumpia—Filipino word for a spring roll filled with meat, vegetables, or fruit.

Lumpia wrappers—Sheets of rice-flour dough used to wrap lumpia.

Lup cheong (lop cheong or lop chong)—Chinese word for slender, aromatic, dried pork sausages. Substitute Portuguese sausage.

Lychee—A small (1 to 2 inches diameter) Chinese fruit with a bright red, rough outer shell and a translucent, juicy, sweet, and delicate flavored flesh surrounding a single inner seed.

Macadamia nuts—Rich, slightly sweet tree nuts with a creamy, slightly crunchy texture, harvested from trees grown on the Big Island of Hawai'i. Substitute walnuts, almonds, or pine nuts.

Mahimahi—Dolphin fish; has a firm, pink flesh. Substitute snapper, catfish, or halibut.

Makina—Japanese word for celery cabbage; won bok. Also known as Napa cabbage and Chinese cabbage.

Malasada (Malassada)—Portuguese doughnut; deep-fried dough, sometimes filled with jam, cream, or chocolate and dipped in sugar with a pinch of cinnamon.

Manapua—Local word for Chinese steamed buns filled with char siu bao or shredded barbecued pork.

Mandoo—Korean word for dumplings, similar to pot stickers, filled with meat and vegetables.

Mango—An oval tropical fruit with golden-orange flesh and an enticing, aromatic flavor; skin color ranges from yellow-orange to burgundy to green.

Mānoa lettuce—A tender-leaved, semi-headed (has loose leaves that form a semi-head in the middle unlike iceberg lettuce which has a round full head) lettuce similar to butter lettuce. Also known as green mignonette.

Maui onion—A large, mild, white onion known for its sweet flavor; originally grown in the Kula District of Maui. Substitute with other sweet onions such as Vidalia or 'Ewa onions.

Mirin—Japanese word for sweet rice wine.

Miso—Japanese word for fermented paste of soy mixed with koji and salt. .

Mizuna, mizoni, azoni—Japanese cabbage; a popular, leafy green vegetable; used in salads.

Mochi—Japanese word for a cake made from pounded, steamed sweet, glutinous rice, or a cake that is steamed or baked, made from glutinous rice flour.

Mochiko—Japanese word for a form of flour made from sweet rice and used in various recipes in Hawai'i, including mochiko chicken, butter mochi, chichi dango, and white sauce.

Mochi rice—Glutinous rice used for mochi.

Mochiko rice flour—Flour made from mochi rice.

Mountain apple—Small, pear-shaped fruit commonly found in Hawai'i, ranging from light pink to dark red. They are sweet and crunchy with a soft texture like a pear, their skins are very thin, and they have a single smooth pit.

MSG—Abbreviation for monosodium glutamate.

Musubi—Japanese word for rice ball, sometimes shaped into a triangle or block, wrapped with nori with other ingredients such as Spam® and eaten as a snack.

Namasu—Japanese word for a salad containing ingredients marinated in rice wine vinegar, sugar and salt.

Nam pla—Thai word for fish sauce, used instead of adding salt in Thai dishes.

Namul—Korean term for seasoned vegetables.

Napa cabbage—Pale green at the top to white at the stem with crinkly leaves. Also known as celery cabbage, Chinese cabbage, or won bok.

Nasu/nasubi—Japanese word for eggplant.

Nishime konbu—Japanese word for thin kelp strips usually used to wrap items (konbu maki), tied in knots and simmered (nishime) or to make a braising liquid (nishime) (Japanese).

Nishimi, nishime—Japanese word for a simmered stew that may contain beef, pork, or chicken and a variety of vegetables in a broth seasoned with soy sauce and sugar.

Nori—Japanese word for a deep purple or greenish-black seaweed generally sold dried, in tissue-thin 8-inch sheets.

Nori maki sushi—Japanese word for vinegar-flavored rice rolled in seaweed.

Ocean salad—Salad generally consisting of wakame seaweed ribs, sesame seeds, sesame oil, rice vinegar, sugar, and salt.

Ogo—Japanese name for Gracilaria, a reddish-brown seaweed.

'Ōhelo berry—Sacred to the Volcano Goddess Pele, growing wild on the Big Island of Hawai'i and east Maui. They range from bright red to yellow to orange and can taste tart or very sweet, depending on the plant and maturity of the fruit.

Okara—Japanese word for soybean curd residue.

Okinawan sweet potato—Purple sweet potato.

Ono—Hawaiian name for a large mackerel. Also known as wahoo.

'Ono—Hawaiian word for delicious or tasty.

'Ōpakapaka—Hawaiian name for pink snapper.

'Opihi—Hawaiian name for endemic limpets found on Hawai'i's rocky shores with strong wave action; dangerous to gather. Substitute any edible limpet.

Oyster sauce—A concentrated dark brown sauce made from oysters, brine, and shoyu. Substitute regular or vegetarian forms.

Ozoni—Japanese word for a mochi soup consisting of a broth with mochi, vegetables, and mizoni greens, made to bring in the New Year.

Pancit/pansit—Filipino word for noodles.

Panko—Japanese word for crispy, large-flaked breadcrumbs that add more texture than ordinary breadcrumbs. .

Papaya—Tropical fruit with usually orange flesh, shiny green or yellow skin, black seeds, and a perfumed scent..

Pāpio—Hawaiian name for young or small white ulua. Also known as giant jack trevally.

Passion fruit—The common variety found in Hawai'i is yellow with seeds and juicy pulp inside. Also called liliko'i in Hawaiian. Substitute orange juice concentrate.

Patis—Filipino word for a pungent fish sauce made from salted, fermented fish.

Pickled ginger—Young ginger root sliced thinly and pickled in sweet vinegar.

Pinakbet—Ilocano or Filipino word for a "wrinkled" vegetable dish made with mixed vegetables such as eggplant, bitter melon, okra, tomato, string beans and chili peppers all steamed in fish or shrimp sauce until the vegetables are wrinkled or shriveled.

Pipikaula—Hawaiian word for salted and spiced dried beef; "rope beef" is the literal Hawaiian translation. Paniolos carried pipikaula in their saddles for a snack.

Pohā berry—Hawaiian name for cape gooseberry. Also known as golden berry, ground cherry, or husk tomato.

Poi—Hawaiian staple; made from steamed taro that is pounded to a paste with the addition of water until it reaches a consistency that can be consumed by scooping with one, two, or three fingers.

Poke—Hawaiian word meaning to slice or to cut into small bite-sized pieces; now refers to a traditional Hawaiian dish made of sliced raw fish, Hawaiian salt, seaweed, and chilies.

Ponzu—Japanese word for a mixture of soy sauce and yuzu (a citrus fruit similar to limes) juice, usually served with sashimi.

Pork hash—A popular ground pork Chinese dish, now refers to dim sum made with pork hash or to raw ground pork. Also known as ji yuk beng in Chinese.

Portuguese sausage—Spicy pork sausage seasoned with onions, garlic, and pepper. Can be mild or hot. Substitute Italian sausage.

Potato starch—Purified starch from potatoes.

Pot stickers—Chinese dumplings filled with meat, seafood, and/or vegetables, steamed and fried.

Pūpū—Hawaiian word meaning appetizer or snack to enjoy with drinks.

Ramen—Japanese word for curly, thin, wheat-based noodles commonly served in a hot broth seasoned with salt, soy sauce, or miso; saimin noodles.

Red bean curd—Bean curd that has been fermented in a brine or mixture of rice wine, chili peppers, and red food coloring. It is then made into a paste by mixing it with some of its liquid.

Rice flour—Available as regular rice flour, made from regular white rice and used in baked goods or as sweet rice flour made from short-grain glutinous rice and used for confections, dumplings, or a thickener for sauces.

Rice vinegar—Japan's relatively mild rice vinegar is the type most often found in local supermarkets.

Rice wine—Typically made from steamed glutinous rice, this kind of wine is produced in different varieties in Japan, such as sake and mirin, and in China as chia fan and yen hung.

Saffron—Bright yellow-orange spice considered the world's most expensive spice, is used only in tiny amounts.

Saimin noodles—Japanese word for thin wheat or egg noodles; in Hawai'i, commonly served in hot broth or wok fried.

Sake—Japanese word for a clear, slightly sweet rice wine made with rice, koji, and water.

Sashimi—A Japanese dish of very thin slices of fresh, raw fish.

Satoimo (araimo)—Japanese word for Dasheen taro. This root vegetable is referred to as satoimo in Japan and araimo in Hawai'i.

Sea salt—A salt resulting from the evaporation of sea water, generally sold in its coarse form.

Sekihan—Traditional Japanese celebratory dish made with red azuki beans steamed with rice.

Sesame oil—A dense, flavorful oil pressed from sesame seeds.

Sesame paste—Made from unroasted, hulled sesame seeds that are ground into a smooth paste. Also known as tahini.

Sesame seeds—Seeds of a flowering plant found throughout Eurasia and Africa with a distinctive nutty flavor. Substitute finely chopped, toasted almonds.

Shallots—More like garlic than onions, with a head composed of one or two cloves and having a mild onion flavor. Substitute green onion bulb.

Shiitake mushroom—Second most widely cultivated mushroom in the world. It is a medium to large umbrella-shaped mushroom. It has floppy tan to dark brown caps with edges that tend to roll under. Also called black Chinese mushrooms and forest mushrooms.

Shingiku—Okinawan word for the leafy green of an herb in the chrysanthemum family.

Shirataki—Japanese word for gelatinous, noodle-like strips made from tuberous root flour.

Shiso—Japanese word for the leaves or seeds of the beefsteak plant, valued for its refreshing taste. Substitute mint or basil.

Shiu mai—Chinese word for steamed dumplings traditionally filled with pork or shrimp.

Shoyu—Japanese word for soy sauce. A salty liquid made from fermented boiled soybeans, roasted barley or wheat, monosodium glutamate (MSG), and salt.

Sinigang—Filipino word for sour fish soup.

Siu mai—Chinese word for steamed meat dumplings.

Snow peas—Young, edible, podded sugar peas consumed when the pods are thin and the seeds are still tiny.

Soba noodles—Japanese word for buckwheat noodles, thin and light brown in color, and eaten warm or cold. Substitute angel hair pasta.

Somen—Japanese word for very thin, white noodles made of wheat flour. Usually served cold with a light-flavored dipping broth. Substitute vermicelli.

Soy milk—In the course of tofu production, after soybeans are soaked in water, they are ground, boiled, and filtered. What passes through the filter is soy milk. What is left in the filtering sack is okara.

Spam®—Hormel's canned meat; popular in Hawai'i, especially in making musubi.

Star anise—A distinctive-looking, seedpod shaped like a star with eight points. Licorice-flavored and one of the components of Chinese five-spice mixtures.

Star fruit—This sweet-tart fruit has a five-pointed star shape when cut crosswise. Also known as carambola.

Straw mushrooms—Musty flavored, straw-colored mushrooms are most commonly found in canned form.

Sticky rice—Sweet rice or glutinous rice. The rice needs to soak in water for several hours before cooking.

Sudare—Japanese word for bamboo mat.

Sumiso—Japanese word for vinegar-miso sauce.

Suribachi—Japanese word for serrated bowl used for grinding; mortar and pestle.

Sushi—Japanese dish of vinegar-sugar mixture of rice served with raw or poached seafood, vegetables, sliced omelet, and other tasty morsels. Some sushi are wrapped in nori.

Sweet bread—Sweet egg bread. Also known as Hawaiian sweet bread or Portuguese sweet bread.

Sweet chili sauce—Thai hot sauce made of sugar, vinegar, garlic, and hot peppers and used as a dipping sauce or condiment.

Szechwan peppercorns—Dried red-brown berries with slightly lemon undertones. Commonly used in Asian cuisine; also used as an oil.

Taegu—Korean word for a popular appetizer made from shredded cuttlefish or codfish seasoned in a spicy sauce.

Takenoko—Japanese word for bamboo shoots.

Tako—Japanese name for octopus.

Takuan, takuwan—Japanese word for pickled radish, often dyed bright yellow.

Tamagoyaki—Japanese word for fried egg sheet.

Tamarind—A sweet-tart fruit from pods of the tamarind tree. Sold in pods, powder, and pulp. .

Taro—The starchy root of the taro, called kalo in Hawaiian, is pounded to make poi, the traditional Hawaiian staple.

Tatsoi—The flat, round leaves often mixed with mesclun in salads and garnishes. Also known as flat cabbage.

Tempura—Japanese word for battered and deep-fried seafood or vegetables.

Teriyaki sauce—A Japanese sauce or marinade with soy sauce, sugar, and fresh garlic and ginger—generally used for cooking meats, poultry, and fish.

Thai curry paste—Available in different colors with varying degrees of hotness, both of which may be determined by the type of chilies used.

Ti leaves—Leaves of the ti plant used to steam and bake fish and vegetables. Often called "Hawaiian aluminum foil." Substitute banana leaves, grape leaves, or corn husks.

Tinola—A Filipino dish consisting of chicken, green papaya, chili peppers, and a ginger, onion, fish sauce broth.

Tobiko—Japanese name for flying fish roe. Usually more expensive than masago roe.

Tofu—Japanese word for a bland-flavored soybean curd that can be custardlike in texture (soft tofu) or quite firm.

Togarashi—Japanese word for red chili pepper.

Tonkatsu—Japanese word for pork cutlet, traditionally served with shredded cabbage and a tonkatsu sauce which is similar to katsu sauce.

Tsubushian—Japanese word for coarsely mashed, unstrained red bean paste.

Tsukemono—Japanese word for pickled vegetables.

Udon—Japanese word for thick wheat flour noodle that can be eaten cold with tsuyu or hot in a broth.

Ukara (okara)—Okinawan word for cooked, ground soybeans; a by-product of the tofu-making process.

'Ulu—Hawaiian word for breadfruit.

Vinha d'alhos—Portuguese word for a dish of pork, chicken, or rabbit that has been marinated in vinegar, wine, garlic, and chili peppers.

Wakame—Japanese word for a type of seaweed that has been popular in Japan over the years. It is used as an ingredient for sunomono (vinegar dishes), salads, and soups.

Warabi—Fiddlehead fern shoots.

Wasabi—Japanese horseradish; a pungent root with an extremely strong, sharp flavor that comes in both powder and paste forms. Substitute hot dry mustard.

Water chestnut—A valuable ingredient in Chinese cooking and known for its crunchy texture.

Watercress—Member of the mustard family with crisp, dark green leaves that have a slightly bitter and peppery taste.

Won bok—Chinese or Napa cabbage. Substitute savoy or other green cabbage.

Won ton wrappers or pi—Flat, thin squares of wheat dough used to wrap various tasty fillings for frying or steaming.

Wun tun/won ton—Chinese word for meat dumplings.

Yaki dofu—Japanese word for tofu that has been fried and slightly hardened.

Yaki niku—Japanese term for grilled meat.

Yakisoba—Japanese word for wok-fried thick soba noodles.

Yakitori—Japanese term for grilled or broiled chicken, marinated in soy sauce, mirin and sugar before grilling.

Yuzu—Japanese word for a citrus fruit similar to the lime.

Zest—Colored portion of a citrus fruit rind, not including the bitter pith just below the colored portion.

BIBLIOGRAPHY

100 Years Sharing God's Love. United Community Church. Waverly: G&R Publishing Co., 1996.

175th Anniversary Haili Congregational Church. Kearney: Morris Press Cookbooks, 1999.

1988 4-H Local & Ethnic Food Show. Cooperative Extension Service. Waverly: G&R Publishing Co., 1988.

50th Anniversary Best of Our Favorite Recipes 1946-1996. Kahului: Maui Association for Family and Community Education, 1996.

A Book of Favorite Recipes Compiled by United Methodist Women of Wahiawa United Methodist Church. Kansas City: Circulation Service, Inc., 1968.

A Chorus of Recipes Presented by Kamehameha Schools Children's Chorus. Honolulu: Kamehameha Schools Children's Chorus, 1998.

A Lei of Recipes. Kauai Association for Family and Community Education. Waseca, MN: Walter's Publishing, 1997.

Community Family Favorites. Community Church of Honolulu. Honolulu: Community Church of Honolulu, 1990.

Cook 'Em Up Kaua'i: The Kaua'i Historical Society Cookbook. Lihu'e: Kaua'i Historical Society, 1993.

Cooking with Honolulu Gardeners. Honolulu Community Recreational Garden Program. Lenexa: Cookbook Publishers, Inc., 1995.

"Cooking with Lovely Hula Hands." Moana's Hula Halau. Lenexa: Cookbook Publishers, Inc., 2001.

Country Cookbook. Compiled by the Wahiawa General Hospital Auxiliary. Mililani: Wonder View Press, 1985.

Dining with the Daughters, A Collection of Recipes and Historical Anecdotes from The Daughters of Hawaii and the Support Group Calabash Cousins. Honolulu: The Daughters of Hawai'i, 1988.

Family Favorites, Recipes Compiled by The Women of East, South and West Oahu Extension Homemakers Councils. Honolulu: Oahu Extension Homemakers Council, 1987.

Favorite Island Cookery, Book I. Honolulu: Honpa Hongwanji Hawaii Betsuin, 1973.

Favorite Island Cookery, Book II. Honolulu: Honpa Hongwanji Buddhist Temple, 1975.

Favorite Island Cookery, Book IV. Honolulu: Honpa Hongwanji Hawaii Betsuin, 1985.

Food for the Body and Soul: A Collection of Recipes by West Kaua'i United Methodist Church. Kearney: Morris Press Cookbooks, 2001.

From the Hawaiian Kitchens of the Molokai Lions, A Book of Favorite Recipes Compiled by the Lionesses of the Molokai Lions Clubs. Shawnee Mission: Circulation Service, 1968.

Grandma & Grandpa's Hawaiian Island Cookbook. Honolulu: Honolulu Federal Savings and Loan Association, 1983.

Haleiwa Elementary School 1871-1986 115th Birthday. Haleiwa: Haleiwa Elementary School, n.d.

Hana Maui Recipes from Then to Now: A Book of Favorite Recipes. Compiled by Hana Heritage Society of Hana, Maui. Leawood: Circulation Service, Inc., 1968.

Hanalei School Collective Cook Book 1998-1999. Hanalei: Hanalei School, 1998.

Hawaii's Aloha Recipes. Honolulu: The Japanese Women's Society of Honolulu, 1982.

Hawaiian Hospitality: A Collection of Favorite Island Recipes. Honolulu: American Business Women's Association Eleu Chapter, 1980.

Hilo Missionary Cooks. Hilo: Hilo Missionary Women's Ministry, 1994.

Hugs & Kisses of Aloha, Aloha Airlines Flight Attendant Cookbook. Honolulu: n.p., 2006.

Island Flavors, Favorite Recipes of the Historic Hawai'i Foundation. Honolulu: Historic Hawai'i Foundation, 1996.

Kalaheo Missionary Church Cookin' Book! Kearney: Morris Press Cookbooks, 1990.

Ka'u Hospital Auxiliary, One More Time. Lenexa: Cookbook Publishers, Inc., 1999.

Lana'i Cooks. Lana'i City: Lana'i High & Elementary School, n.d.

"No Kai Oi" The Best of Hawaii, Favorite Recipes from Rotarians of District 5000. Kearney: Morris Press Cookbooks, 2004.

North Kohala Favorites. Compiled by the North Kohala Cookbook Committee. Olathe: Cookbook Publishers, 1991.

Ono-Licious Na Poe Humukuiki O Hawaii, Hawaii Quilt Guild. Compiled by Na Po'e Humukuiki O Hawaii Hawaiian Quilt Guild. Waseca: Walter's Cookbooks, 1993.

Our Daily Bread Centennial Cookbook. Compiled by Iao Congregational Church United Church of Christ. Olathe: Cookbook Publishers, 1994.

Our Favorite Recipes from the Portuguese Heritage Club of Hamakua. Lenexa: Cookbook Publishers, Inc., 2001.

Parks & Recreation Family Favorites. Honolulu: Department of Parks and Recreation, 1993.

"Pig Out" with Liholiho's Caring, Competent, Creative Cooks. Honolulu: Liholiho Elemenary School, 1994.

Puuloa Hawaiian Civic Club. Olathe: Cookbook Publishers, Inc., 1993.

The Friends of 'Iolani Palace Cook Book. Honolulu: Friends of 'Iolani Palace, 1987.

The Hawai'i Youth Opera Chorus Presents Nā Mea 'Ai Punahele: Favorite Foods. Waverly: G&R Publishing Copmany, 1000.

The Hawaii National Guard Auxiliary Cookbook. Honolulu: Na Kuhina Nui O Na Koa Hawaii, 1991.

The Hele Mai, Ai (Come Eat) Cookbook, Flavors of Upcountry Maui, History and Hospitality. Makawao: Seabury Hall Parents' Organization, 1977.

The Heritage of Hawaii Cookbook. Honolulu: Honolulu Gas Company, Ltd, n.d.

The Hilo Woman's Club Cookbook, Hawaiian Recipes. Hilo: Hilo Tribune-Herald, 1937.

The Kahikolu Country Cookbook. Napoopoo: Kahikolu Congregational Church, 1982.

The Kauai Museum Presents Early Kauai Hospitality, A Family Cookbook of Recipes 1820-1920. Lihue: Kauai Museum Association, Ltd., 1977.

The Tastes and Tales of Mō'ili'ili, A Collection of Recipes & Stories by Mō'ili'ili Community Center. Edited by Muriel Miura Kaminaka. Honolulu: Mutual Publishing, 1997.

We, the Women of Hawaii Cookbook, Favorite Recipes of Prominent Women of Hawaii. Kailua: Press Pacifica, 1986.

Wisteria Delights, A Collection of Recipes by Pearl City Hongwanji Mission. Kearny: Morris Press Cookbooks. 2005.

INDEX

APPETIZERS • PŪPŪ

BREADS

CONDIMENTS AND SAUCES

DESSERTS

Cakes

Cookies, Squares, and Bars

MAIN DISHES

Seafood

RICE AND NOODLES

SALAD DRESSINGS

SALADS

SOUPS

VEGETABLES AND SIDES